06/91

The Politics of Pollution

363
.73
56
0971
Macd

Macdonald, Doug.
  The politics of pollution / Doug Macdonald. --
Toronto : McClelland & Stewart, c1991.
  325 p.

Includes bibliographical references (p. 294-316) and
index.
04743229 ISBN:0771054009 (pb

1. Pollution - Government policy
Environmental policy - Canada.

D0968135

8096   91MAY23   75/   1-00554152

The Politics of Pollution

Doug Macdonald

M&S

Copyright © 1991 by Doug Macdonald

Canadian Cataloguing in Publication Data

Macdonald, Doug
  The politics of pollution

Includes bibliographical references and index.
ISBN 0-7710-5400-9

1. Pollution – Government policy – Canada.
2. Environmental policy – Canada.   I. Title.

HC120.E5M23   1991   363.73'56'0971   C91-093360-X

McClelland & Stewart Inc.
The Canadian Publishers
481 University Avenue
Toronto, Ontario
M5G 2E9

Printed and bound in Canada by John Deyell Company

CONTENTS

Dedicated to the memory of my parents,
Vivian Isabel Callan and Edwin Charles Macdonald

INTRODUCTION

Since the 1960s, and in some cases even earlier, Canada has had laws and policies in place to prevent or reduce pollution. In the thirty-odd years since then, the environment has moved from the fringe to the centre of Canadian political life. Why, then, do we continue to discharge millions of tonnes of toxic substances each year to the Canadian air, water, and land?[1]

The same question can be asked of every industrialized nation. Why, in the twenty-odd years since the industrialized nations first agreed on the need for concerted national action, at the Stockholm Conference of 1972, has the global environment become more, rather than less, imperiled?

All species have an effect on the environment in which they live. However, the power of our own species to disturb and modify the local and global environment has grown at an exponential pace over the past few centuries, and particularly in the period since 1945. Environmental stress caused by human activities is such that today homo sapiens and all other species on the planet face a threat to their continued existence more urgent than any since the time of the great extinctions, some sixty-five million years ago.

Perhaps the three most telling indicators of humanity's large and growing power to wreak environmental harm are species extinctions, toxic contamination, and atmospheric change.

(1) Through destruction and pollution of their habitats, plant and animal species are disappearing at a rate estimated to be in the thousands per year. The same forces, such as deforestation and desertification (the extension of desert regions due to climatic change and poor agricultural

7

practices), are bringing famine and death to large numbers of human communities, driving "environmental refugees" out of their homelands.

(2) The increasing toxic contamination of air, water, and land is endangering the health of many species, including our own. This contamination is caused by the growing manufacture and release to the environment of harmful products, such as pesticides and chemical weapons, and wastes, such as car exhaust, radioactivity from nuclear bomb tests, and the chlorine bleach that whitens our coffee filters.[3]

(3) The burning of fossil fuels and the release of other pollutants to the air are affecting the global atmosphere in ways we are only now beginning to comprehend. Climate patterns are thought to be undergoing change greater than any experienced since the last ice age, 10,000 years ago. The effects of this change, including inundation of coastal areas by rising seas and major changes in global food production, are likely to be compressed into a much shorter time span than any previous changes in the history of the planet, which means there is much less time available than ever before for our own and other species to adapt.[4]

This degradation of the global environment is caused by our ever-expanding consumption of the natural resources of the planet – fossil fuels, minerals, forests, arable land, and clean air and water. The problem has two primary roots. The first is the development of agriculture some 10,000 years ago, which by providing a secure food supply in one space allowed the transformation from hunting and gathering societies to ones dominated by complex, hierarchical, and, in relative terms, efficient social organizations. This greatly extended the power of tribes and villages to modify their surroundings. The second is the development of the empirical method in the latter part of the Middle Ages. Through technological development based on scientific discovery, humanity now has the power to alter or destroy its planetary environment.

The problem posed by science and technology has two components. The first is the way in which scientific advances in health care and food production have led to an exponentially increasing global population. The global population was 2.5 billion in 1950, 5 billion in 1987, and is projected to reach 6.3 billion in the year 2000 and 8.5 billion in the year 2025.[5] This means that global resource consumption is bound to increase dramatically over the next century. Although resources can be used much more efficiently and with less waste than at present, their total consumption over the next few decades is certain to increase, no matter what steps are taken to increase efficiency, simply due to this unprecedented increase in global population.

The problem of population growth is compounded by the ever-increasing productivity of industrial processes and the resulting per capita increases both in the production of goods and services and in the consumption of resources. As machines become more powerful and sophisticated, the quantity of goods and services one worker can produce in a day multiplies. Because of this increased productivity, those living in the industrialized nations today enjoy a living standard beyond the wildest dreams of even kings and emperors of previous ages – and the rest of the world's citizens, not surprisingly, want to join them in that happy state as soon as possible. But as they do so, and thereby increase that portion of the global population consuming at the level of today's industrialized nations, total consumption will grow accordingly.

These two factors, exponential population growth and increases in the amount each global citizen consumes, are placing stresses and demands on the resources of the planet that cannot be sustained indefinitely. Something will have to give.

Humanity's awareness of the damage it is causing to itself and others is very new. Not surprisingly, we are only now beginning seriously to search for solutions. For purposes of this discussion, three dates are used to mark advances in our awareness and initial attempts to grapple with the issue.

1962: With the publication of *Silent Spring* by Rachel Carson, the public in America and other countries first became aware of the harm associated with the deliberate release of such chemicals as DDT to our environment. The following decade was marked by a new awareness of the problem of chemical contamination of the natural environment, added to existing concerns over resource depletion caused by population growth and wasteful inefficiencies.

1972: At the United Nations-sponsored International Conference on the Human Environment, held in Stockholm, Sweden, a majority of nations of the world stated their willingness, in theory at least, to begin to reduce pollution and other forms of environmental stress. This was the first time that international environmental protection, to be achieved through collective action, was accepted as a common goal, although warning bells were rung when the Third World nations insisted that environment not be used as an excuse for delaying action on their fundamental problem of crippling poverty.

1985: Televised computer simulations of the hole in the ozone layer over Antarctica spurred action to reduce emissions of stratospheric ozone-destroying chlorofluorocarbons (CFCs) – a substance that, only fourteen years before, was thought by scientific authorities to be both useful and benign. Two years later, in 1987, forty-two nations signed the first international agreement to limit, on a global basis, annual emissions of a polluting substance.

Since 1962, the issue of environmental protection has moved from the far periphery to the centre of politics in most of the industrialized nations. The environmental threat, which until recently was dismissed as frivolous or was seen as something of concern only in faraway places or in the far distant future, has become something frightening and real. The environment now stands squarely beside the economy as one of the two top issues of public concern in opinion polls and election campaigns. But despite this change in public awareness and attitude, governments have not acted decisively. An international conference held in Ottawa in 1986 to measure global progress on environmental protection concluded that "there had been almost no discernible change in government attitudes.... In one country after another finance ministers and their economic advisors have remained oblivious to environmental thinking. Warnings given by scientific advisors and global thinkers have been ignored. Environment ministers have had low status and little influence in cabinets."[6]

Why is this so? What must be done to translate the new political support for environmental protection into meaningful and permanent action?

The subject of this book is one aspect of the larger problem of global environmental degradation and resource consumption – pollution of air, land, and water. "Pollution" is defined for these purposes as the deliberate or accidental introduction to the environment of contaminants, in the form of either wastes or products. The scope of the inquiry is limited to pollution within Canada and the Canadian contribution to pollution of the global environment.

Although scientific, technological, and other related aspects of the issue are addressed, the book focuses primarily on political decision-making related to pollution – how governments decide what they will or will not do – in Canada and on the Canadian contribution to international environmental politics. The term "politics," as used here, refers primarily to conflicts among the different actors, both in and outside government, who attempt to influence government decision-making. Government action is deemed to consist of two major types: allocation of its own financial resources, through the budgeting process, in accordance with what it sees as the priorities of the society it represents; and the use of law to set the rules for individual and organizational behaviour, again in accordance with perceived social priorities.

The problem of environmental degradation is a Gordian knot of interrelated causes and effects. The 1987 report of the World Commission on Environment and Development, the Brundtland report, did an excellent job of showing how any one aspect of the problem has implications for all the others. Brundtland demonstrated convincingly that all of the relevant policy fields – population, energy, food supply, industrial pollution, international trade and finance, Third World poverty, institutional and legal arrangements, and others – are interconnected, with action taken in one area having ramifications for all of the others. To date, however, neither Brundtland nor anyone else has been able to provide comprehensive and integrated solutions to these problems that are not only technologically but also politically feasible.

Pollution, on the other hand, taken as a sub-set of this larger problem, is an issue for which there are solutions, and ones, moreover, that can be implemented in the short-term – before the end of the century – taking full account of current political realities. This is particularly the case in the industrialized nations, which have in place the necessary financial resources, technological abilities, and political institutions. Although there would be a major price to be paid, Canadians could, if they wanted, stop polluting their environment almost immediately.

The premise of this book is that there is merit in concentrating on pollution as a first step in solving the larger problem of global resource consumption. This is both because pollution is a serious problem in and of itself and because developing and implementing the required political, legal, and administrative mechanisms in this one area will take us a considerable way toward addressing the larger problem.

The politics of pollution in Canada can be traced through the rise and fall on the political agenda of the various polluting substances of concern: infectious diseases, primarily carried by water, prior to World War Two; radioactive fallout in the 1950s; pesticides such as DDT in the early 1960s; phosphorous pollution and mercury in the later 1960s and early 1970s; spruce budworm spraying in New Brunswick and Nova Scotia through the remainder of the seventies; after the Love Canal alarm of 1978, hazardous wastes and the threat they pose to drinking water, symbolized by the term "dioxin"; acid rain in the early 1980s; CFCs and the ozone layer by the mid-1980s; and by the 1990s the enormous and truly global problem of atmospheric change caused largely by fossil fuel combustion.

The political conflicts surrounding each of these issues have gone through approximately the same stages: identification of the problem by scientists; communication to the general public; debate over the nature and extent of the threat between those pressing for action and those who would be forced to pay the cost if discharge to the environment of the substance in question were reduced; a search for alternative substances or technologies to allow such reduction; negotiation over who bears what portion of the cost; and, finally, some form of government-mandated action that is generally at least a step in the right direction even though the problem may still be far from solved.

This book explores the ramifications of that process as it has repeatedly unfolded in Canada over the past two decades. Several themes and questions are presented.

(1) Over the past half-century the physical nature of pollution has changed. What was a local problem, for instance, black smoke from the factory next door, has now become a global one, most particularly in terms

of global atmospheric change but also in other areas, such as transport of hazardous wastes. This in turn has meant that jurisdictional authority over pollution has begun to move toward the federal level, as the issue comes to be increasingly addressed in the context of international action, although no conscious decision to this effect has been made by Canadian governments. The provinces are still, however, the major players and are likely to resist increasingly such federal intrusion, but they in turn will continue to delegate major environmental responsibilities to the municipal level. Jurisdiction is a key issue and environmental politics in Canada will inevitably be influenced by, and contribute to, the new stresses in the post-Meech Canadian federation.

(2) Pollution has also changed from a visible to a largely invisible problem. Concern over black smoke has been replaced by fears of the effects caused by small concentrations of chemicals, detectable only with the most sophisticated equipment, which both act alone and in synergistic combinations with others. This means that scientific uncertainty is a major element in the political debate while fear of the unknown adds potency to the issue.

(3) Although the cost of pollution reduction will be high, measured in terms of such factors as government and industry spending, job dislocations, and availability of some consumer goods, cost alone is not a barrier to action. The real stumbling block is the still unresolved issue of allocation of that cost. Who pays for pollution prevention – governments, through spending, grants, and tax incentives? the polluting industry? the worker who loses his or her job? the province or country that sees economic growth transferred to its trade competitors because of its environmental regulation?

(4) In the 1970s the dialogue was framed by the phrase "jobs versus the environment." In the 1980s we attempted to reconcile what were no longer seen as such mutually exclusive goals by looking for ways to "integrate environmental and economic decision-making." Regardless of changing catch-phrases, the central issue remains the same – to what extent must environmental protection limit economic expansion and what will be the consequences of putting a permanent damper on growth?

(5) While there has been a tremendous increase in public support for environmental protection over the past two decades, environmentalists still do not walk in the corridors of power. Can environmentalism achieve true political power and bring about meaningful change? How?

(6) Finally, environmentalism is likely to be an important factor in shaping the new international order now emerging after the death of the Cold War polarity between the United States and the Soviet Union. International action on the global environment provides obligations and opportunities for Canada to put in place foreign policy objectives in keeping with new realities and values.

The book is divided into five parts. Part I, "Pollution Politics in the 1990s," provides an overview of current environmental politics in Canada. This includes an understanding of the price that polluters – ranging from the individual to the international corporation – would have to pay if they were to reduce pollution significantly; a survey of the different branches of the environmental movement fighting for governmental action and the resources, strategies, and tactics they bring to bear; a discussion of those aspects of Canadian political life of particular relevance to that battle; and a discussion of the social forces that provide political support for environmental action in this country.

Part II, after this review of the present state of environmental politics, further explores the subject through a narrative account of the evolution of environmental politics from its origins in the nineteenth century to the 1990s. Part III, "Regulating Pollution," offers an overview of the system used by governments in Canada to regulate pollution by setting standards, licensing polluting sources, and enforcing environmental regulations. The purpose here is to provide the lay reader with at least an initial understanding of this complex, technical, and somewhat daunting subject, particularly the key political issues and objectives for change in the regulatory system likely to be at the centre of environmental politics for the coming decade.

A narrative history of five pollution issues, ranging from garbage disposal in Ontario to international action on the ozone layer, is then provided in Part IV. These case studies are intended to illustrate, in concrete terms, both the workings of the political forces discussed in Parts I and II and the regulatory system that is the subject of Part III.

The book concludes with a presentation, in Part V, of the central argument. This can be summarized as follows:

• The political strength of the environmental and anti-pollution lobby in Canada has increased significantly over the past two decades but is still more potential than actual.

• The major impediments to action on pollution are, first, the cost (ranging through increased government spending, job dislocations, and a host of other impacts, to loss of the convenience of disposable diapers), and, even more important, political conflict over allocation of that cost – who will pay what portion of the price?

• Those impediments can only be overcome if we first strengthen environmental values, basing calls for action not on human health concerns alone but also on respect for the inherent value of the natural world, and second, if we develop an ideology of environmentalism that resolves the issue of allocation of cost. Such an ideology must make explicit the connections between environmental action and distribution of wealth and power, thus allowing environmentalism to make political alliances both with practitioners of traditional distributive left-wing politics and with other social movements, such as feminism, labour, animal protection, native and minority rights, which also have as their central goal fairness and equity.

• In addition to strengthening underlying values and ideology, it is argued, those fighting pollution should resist the siren calls of endless consultation over the means of implementing "sustainable development" and instead concentrate on the imposition and enforcement of pollution-reducing standards at the point at which pollution enters the environment – the end of the pipe.

• Finally, it is argued that we should take such action not only at home but also on the global stage by adopting a foreign policy devoted above all to global environmental protection.

"Zero discharge" of persistent toxic substances is the goal of the environmental movement. While such an objective would have been dismissed as impossible a few years ago, it is now seen by many Canadians as essential. Canada cannot transform itself into a non-polluting society, however, without paying a significant price. But it can and must be done, since the price for *not* doing so will be even higher. Perhaps the task will be made easier if we bear in mind that pollution in Canada is far from the largest environmental problem facing humanity today. Finding the political will and means to put an end to pollution in this country will allow Canadians to move forward, in concert with other peoples, to address the larger challenges that lie ahead.

During the past two decades Canadians have gained a vastly improved understanding of the various sources and types of pollutants, the ways in which they move through the environment, and the effects they have on humans and other species. Much less attention has been paid to the social, economic, and political forces that determine our collective ability to address the issue. It is hoped that this book will assist in redressing that balance.

PART I

Pollution Politics in the 1990s

A hint of the change that came over environmental politics in the late 1980s was given by the cover story of the November, 1989, *Globe and Mail Report on Business Magazine*, titled "The Great Forest Sell-Off: Behind closed doors, Alberta deals away timberlands almost the size of Great Britain. An economic windfall – or an environmental disgrace?"[1] When the *Report on Business* starts to worry about "an environmental disgrace," the times are, indeed, changing.

Another indicator of change is the prominence given to environmental issues during recent elections. Prior to 1985 the environment, if mentioned at all, came at the bottom of lists of election promises and opinion polls. The Kenora PCB spill, however, guaranteed that the environment was highlighted during the Ontario election in the spring of 1985, and it received prominence again in the Ontario election of 1987, the Nova Scotia election of 1988, and the Quebec election held two months after the disaster of the Montreal PCB fire of 1989.[2] While the proposed Canada-U.S. Free Trade Agreement was the dominant issue in the federal election of 1988, the environment was given greater prominence, both in party platforms and during the election debate, than ever before.[3] In the months leading up to the election the Tories announced a string of environmental spending goodies for different parts of the country, including establishment of a St. Lawrence River Centre in Montreal, a sustainable development centre in Winnipeg, and a clean-up of Halifax harbour, while the Liberal Party led off its election platform with the issue of environment. Many environmental organizations joined the coalition opposing free trade, and environmental implications of the deal became one of the major arguments against free trade.[4]

The politicians were not the only ones talking about the environment during the late 1980s. This electoral activity was played out against an ongoing marketing barrage in which a variety of industries, including supermarkets, bath and beauty stores, the fashion industry, and newspapers that use recycled paper, saw new opportunities to promote their products as being "environmentally friendly." Sinclair Stevens, the embodiment of Canadian business, turned to a new career as publisher of an environmental tabloid after being prevented from running in the 1988 federal election by the conflict-of-interest controversy of the previous year.[5] During the 1980s the demand for pollution control technologies as well as for environmental legal, management, and consulting services increased significantly. Environmental protection became, for the first time, a profitable business, symbolized more than anything else by Globe 90, the international trade fair held in Vancouver, March 19-23, 1990, which brought together environmentalists, politicians, and some 2,000 representatives of companies offering a variety of environmental wares.[6]

The final sign that environment had moved to the centre of Canadian politics was given in 1989, when its significance as an issue in federal-provincial relations sharply increased. On April 10, 1989, the Federal Court of Canada, ruling in a lawsuit brought by the Canadian Wildlife Federation (CWF), quashed the federal licence issued to approve construction by Saskatchewan of dams on the Souris River. The court ruled that the licence was invalid because federal environmental studies, required by a 1984 order-in-council setting out procedures for the Federal Environmental Assessment Review Process, had not been done – despite the fact that construction had already begun. In August another federal licence was issued, the CWF brought another suit, and in December, 1989, the court quashed the second licence.

In January, 1990, Saskatchewan agreed, in exchange for compensation of up to $10 million from the federal government, to halt work on the dams other than that required "for safety reasons" to allow time for the court-mandated federal assessment. A federal environmental assessment panel was appointed and began to review potential environmental impacts of the dams. In October of that year, however, members of the panel resigned, charging that Saskatchewan had continued to build the dams, in violation of its agreement with Ottawa.

Saskatchewan Premier Grant Devine, preparing the ground for a provincial election by the time-honoured method of attacking Ottawa, then traded blows in the media with federal Environment Minister Robert de Cotret, while the lawyers for each government did battle in court as the federal government sought an injunction to stop construction.

16

In the same manner the Federal Court ruled in March, 1990, that federal environmental assessment must be done for the Oldman River dam in Alberta, although it, too, was already under construction. In the summer of 1989, presumably because of fears of another court challenge, a joint federal-provincial environmental assessment, the first of its kind, was initiated for one of the new Alberta pulp mills. In 1990 the Alberta government acted on the recommendations of the federal-provincial panel, delaying approval of the plant until a new, less polluting process was substituted.

These decisions mark a major departure in environmental politics and decision-making in Canada. It is almost unprecedented for the courts to order government action on the environment in Canada. For the courts to do so in these cases, which revolve around the powers of the federal government to withhold approval of provincial projects, raises all the issues of federal-provincial powers at the heart of the Canadian federation. The court decisions were followed by long-promised federal environmental assessment legislation introduced in the House of Commons in June, 1990. Once approved, this legislation will replace the 1984 procedures. The implications this federal legislation will have for provincial powers of approval will not be clear until it is enacted and regulations prepared under its authority. The court decisions and legislation, however, have brought about a potentially significant change in the power of the federal government to approve either jointly funded federal-provincial projects or ones that require some form of federal environmental approval. (Federal approval of the Saskatchewan dams is required because the Souris River dips south across the Canada-U.S. border before returning to Manitoba and is thus an international water; the court ruled that federal assessment should have been done on the Oldman River dam by Transport Canada, because the river is a navigable water, and by Fisheries and Oceans, because of its potential impact upon a fishery.[7])

Not surprisingly, the provinces have strongly protested this latest threat of federal intrusion. On May 11, 1990, *The Globe and Mail* reported on a leaked memorandum prepared by a "senior Alberta government official" that described plans by Ontario, Quebec, Alberta, British Columbia, Manitoba, and Nova Scotia to "demand new legislation that would prevent Ottawa from making the final environmental decisions on major industrial projects unless a project is entirely within federal jurisdiction."[8]

This potential new federal power presented its greatest problems in terms of Quebec's authority to decide on environmental issues related to the latest stage in its James Bay hydroelectricity project. It was reported in the spring of 1990, in the days leading up to the Meech Lake failure, that because of the Rafferty and Oldman court decisions Ottawa "has no choice but to insist on extensive environmental hearings."[9] Quebec, not surprisingly, was not willing to accept any such expanded federal role. Lucien Bouchard, federal Environment Minister until his resignation in May, 1990, was in a difficult position because he wanted to defend Quebec's interests but was "under political pressure from Western Canada to stand up to Quebec because of the Federal Court of Canada decisions against completion of the Rafferty-Alameda dam in Saskatchewan and the Oldman River dam in Alberta."[10] Bouchard's successor, Robert de Cotret, spent the remainder of the year trying to negotiate with Quebec an agreement on the way environmental assessment should be carried out. At the same time, a split developed within the Quebec cabinet, with the Quebec Environment Minister publicly disagreeing with the Quebec Energy Minister over the same question.

Thus, by 1990 the environment had become a central factor in the issue most fundamental to Canadian political life – the regional power struggles that underlie all sharing of federal-provincial powers. Given all of these indications of the change that has come over environmental politics, is it safe to conclude that government action to protect the environment, and specifically to reduce pollution, has kept pace with the movement of the issue on the political agenda? Unfortunately, as the discussion in the following pages illustrates, the answer is no. While there have been some instances of success, such as the Canadian acid rain program and improvements in motor vehicle emissions and resulting urban air quality, the total quantity of pollution entering the Canadian environment each year has not been significantly reduced; in fact, it may well have increased, due to increases in population and economic activity, since the present regulatory system was established in the late 1960s.

Why is that so? Why has the steadily growing political support for environmental protection not yet resulted in meaningful action on pollution? Perhaps the best way to begin to answer this question is to review briefly the major sources of pollution in Canada today and to give at least an initial indication of what it would mean if these sources were to eliminate, or significantly reduce, the quantity of pollution they emit each year.

CHAPTER 1

Why Do We Keep on Polluting?

Traditionally, the "polluter" is thought of as the uncaring business corporation more interested in profits than the environment. Manufacturing industries are a major source of pollution, but to gain an understanding of the magnitude of the challenge that real pollution prevention presents we need to examine *all* sources of pollution, not just those most clearly visible.

The following discussion, therefore, is based on a classification of pollution sources into six major categories: individual citizens; energy producers, both public and private; agencies that dispose of waste, primarily municipalities but also private-sector firms and the Crown corporations established by some provinces to provide hazardous waste disposal services; resource extraction industries; manufacturing industries; and, finally, individuals and companies engaged in agriculture.

Canadian Citizens

Government action to eliminate or significantly reduce pollution will only be taken if those lobbying for environmental protection have sufficient political strength. That strength, in turn, depends on the changing attitudes of individual Canadians. Throughout the latter part of the 1980s opinion polls have consistently shown that attitudes are indeed changing and that there is steadily increasing concern over the effects of pollution and growing support for government action.[1] Furthermore, rising public concern over pollution is not limited to answers given in telephone interviews. Whenever provided the opportunity to match words with deeds, through such things as curbside recycling programs, household hazardous waste collections, or practising "green" consumerism, the Canadian public has convincingly demonstrated a willingness to take direct, personal action. It is ironic, therefore, that individual Canadians continue to remain a major source of pollution.

Canadians pollute both directly and indirectly. The two major sources of direct pollution are car exhaust and household waste. Privately owned and operated cars in Canada contribute a significant portion of the nation's total annual air pollution, contributing nitrogen oxides, which help form both acid rain and urban smog, benzene, polycyclic aromatic hydrocarbons (PAH), and other contaminants. Canadian cars also emit millions of tonnes of carbon dioxide a year, thus compounding the problem of global warming.[2] At the same time, Canadians generate, it is estimated, 1.7 kilograms of solid waste per capita per day, the bulk of which is disposed of in landfills, from which pollutants are leached into the surrounding groundwater, or incinerated, thereby adding to total annual air pollution loadings.[3]

Canadians contribute indirectly to the problem through their unquestioning acceptance of the lower cost and convenience of living in a polluting society. Agricultural productivity and the related cost of food are determined in part by the use of chemicals in fertilizers and pesticides; the price of products we buy does not include anything like the true environmental cost of disposal of the wastes associated with their manufacture; transportation, to either the corner store or the next continent, is readily available only because of our cheap and polluting consumption of fossil fuels.

Finally, Canadians contribute to pollution through their largely unquestioned acceptance of the premise that the quality of life in Canada is best measured by indicators of economic expansion and recession and that continual economic growth, coupled with full employment, is the primary national objective. That Canadians should accept these goals as givens is hardly surprising. The expanding economies of the Western nations throughout the past century have provided an improving standard of living for all, even for those at the bottom of the heap. This has been done through scientific and technological advances that have allowed a continually increasing per capita consumption of natural resources and production of waste. This increase in the quantity of material goods available for all classes has allowed Western governments to avoid the wracking social tensions and conflicts that would accompany the only other means of responding to the legitimate demands of the disadvantaged – redistribution of a finite and static economic pie. Never-ending economic expansion, with at least some benefits trickling down the class pyramid, has bought Canada and other nations a large measure of domestic political peace and is now fully accepted as the normal state of affairs. But this has been purchased at a price, the true extent of which we are only beginning to recognize – the disruption, depletion, and contamination of the natural environn. which we live.

What would it mean to individual Canadians if the amount of pollution produced by each of us were significantly reduced? The most obvious impact, in terms of the individual's own direct pollution, would be a loss, or reduction, of the convenience associated with travel by car and airplane and with unthinking disposal of waste. Beyond that, there would be a dollar cost through the increased price of products to account fully for environmental costs in their manufacture and distribution, lost wages caused by job dislocations, and tax increases required to pay for increased government action.

The larger issue of the stresses and difficulties – and, it is argued, opportunities and benefits – Canadians would experience in the transition from a continually expanding to a steady-state, sustainable, and non-polluting economy are discussed in Part V.

Energy Producers and Consumers

Any discussion of pollution inevitably centres on energy production and use. This is because access to relatively inexpensive energy – in the form of coal, oil, hydroelectricity, and nuclear power – has allowed industrialization to proceed at such a rapid pace over the past 200 years. A statement issued in 1989, at the conclusion of a symposium convened by UNESCO in Vancouver, set forth the connection between access to relatively cheap energy and the exponential change that has taken place in humanity's power to modify the global environment.

> Our planet is unstable – a constantly changing heat engine. Life appeared on its surface about four billion years ago, and developed in balance with an environment where sudden unpredictable change is the norm. The discovery, over 200 years ago, of free energy locked in fossil fuels has given humankind the power to dominate the whole planetary surface. In an unbelievably short span of time, unplanned and almost mindlessly, our species has become by far the largest factor for change on the planet.[4]

Production and distribution of fossil fuels have always been at the centre of the pollution debate in Canada. Tanker shipment of oil from Alaska or the Middle East, with inevitable spills on the coasts of North America, and proposed shipment by pipeline across relatively pristine and ecologically fragile areas of the Canadian North have played a large part in the emergence of pollution as a major political issue. Offshore oil drilling, in both the Arctic and the North Atlantic off Newfoundland, is a potential source of environmental damage. Leaking underground gasoline tanks are a major source of groundwater pollution.

The major pollutant associated with fossil fuel energy use is carbon dioxide emitted to the atmosphere. A change in the concentrations of carbon dioxide and other gases in the global atmosphere is responsible for the "greenhouse effect" – an increase in average global temperatures expected to bring with it adverse effects caused by changes in growing seasons, weather patterns, and sea levels. Fossil fuel combustion also carries with it other, more localized effects, such as acidification caused by sulphur dioxide released from the burning of coal. Twenty years ago we worried about running out of oil. Now we worry because we have, and burn, too much of it.

The two conventional alternatives to fossil fuel combustion are hydroelectricity and nuclear-powered generation. Energy in the form of hydroelectricity generated through the power of falling water is relatively benign, in terms of pollution, but, as in the case of the ongoing James Bay megaproject in Quebec, it carries with it the environmental and social impacts associated with damming rivers and constructing generator stations and transmission lines. The major pollution concerns associated with nuclear power are accidental releases of radioactive materials, the still unsolved issue of how to provide for long-term disposal of radioactive wastes, and the environmental threat posed by nuclear weapons.

It is possible, of course, to lower energy demand, through increased building insulation and appliance efficiency, and also to produce energy in a renewable, non-polluting manner, which neither contributes to atmospheric change nor imposes major waste disposal problems. Following the drastic rise in oil prices brought about by the 1973 OPEC oil embargo, considerable progress was made in this direction. It became clear that total energy consumption could decline, producing considerable savings for energy users, without a corresponding decline in economic activity.[5] In 1989, when interest in energy conservation was again stimulated, this time by global warming fears, the federal and provincial energy ministers appointed a task force, which concluded that achieving a full 20 per cent reduction in carbon dioxide emissions would cause "major changes to the ways in which Canadians produce and use energy," but that significant progress toward that goal could be made simply by increasing the efficiency of energy use. Such steps, it was pointed out, were "economically attractive to Canadian society in their own right," due to energy cost-savings regardless of their environmental benefits.[6]

Despite these potential benefits, annual global energy consumption continues to climb, with Canada and the United States leading all other nations in per capita consumption.[7] Although Prime Minister Mulroney has spoken strongly on the need to reduce carbon dioxide emissions, his government between 1984 and 1988, reduced spending on energy conservation and renewable energy research by 81 per cent.[8]

Given the economic and environmental benefits of increased efficiency and greater use of renewable, non-polluting energy sources, why has so little been done? Why have the provincial and federal governments largely dismantled the energy conservation programs they introduced after the OPEC embargo? It would seem that the answer is simply one of cost. Upgrading the energy efficiency of buildings and machines, whether by retrofitting or replacing with newer models, is expensive. This may result in long-term savings, but it also imposes immediate, short-term costs, and there is little incentive to undertake that cost as long as the price of energy, particularly in the form of oil, remains relatively low. In the 1970s it was thought that oil supplies in the ground would be depleted in the relatively near future; it is now apparent that yet untapped reserves are much larger than previously thought.[9] This means that the marketplace alone will not raise oil prices sufficiently to induce meaningful action – that action will have to be taken by government through either legislative means, setting energy efficiency standards to govern the design and manufacture of buildings, appliances, cars, and other machines, or fiscal means, by increasing the price of energy.

The concept of a "carbon tax," a tax imposed on fossil fuel consumption for the specific purpose of lessening demand and thereby reducing carbon dioxide emissions, combined with an end to federal financial support for major fossil fuel extraction programs such as the Newfoundland Hibernia and Alberta oil sands projects, has been recommended by the Canadian environmental community.[10] It is difficult to argue with the logic of the environmentalists' position, but it is hardly surprising that the Mulroney government has absolutely no interest in enacting either measure. Imposition of a new tax is one of the most politically unattractive measures any government can take, while taking away subsidies from projects that hold out the promise of jobs in western or eastern Canada is equally unpalatable. The environmental movement will have to gain considerably more political strength than it has at present before it can convince governments to implement any such measures to reduce the pollution impacts associated with energy production and consumption.

Waste Disposal

In one sense, all pollution is simply waste disposal since automobile exhaust, candy wrappers, and organochlorines in pulp mill effluent are all unwanted substances gotten rid of by discharge to air, land, or water. A distinction is usually made, however, between "pollution," which is the direct discharge of wastes, and "waste disposal," which implies that polluting substances are collected and packaged before being deposited in the natural environment.

A considerable portion of the total municipal solid and liquid industrial

23

waste produced in Canada each year is disposed of with very little attempt made to minimize environmental damage.[11] Even when done in such a way as to reduce environmental impacts, however, waste disposal inevitably causes pollution. This can take the form of leachate leaking from landfills, the residual contaminants released to the air after incineration of solid or hazardous wastes, or toxic substances discharged as industrial wastes to sewers, from whence the toxins pass directly through sewage treatment plants, untouched, and are discharged with the treated effluent to receiving waters. Thus, waste disposal agencies rank among the major polluters.

In Canada, although private-sector companies operate some landfill and incineration disposal facilities for solid waste under contract with local municipalities and also operate a few hazardous waste treatment and disposal facilities, waste disposal is done primarily by either municipal or provincial agencies. The one exception to this, and it is significant, is on-site industrial hazardous waste disposal. The bulk of the hazardous waste generated by Canadian industry each year is disposed of by the generating company on its own property, primarily by means of discharge to water or a sewer, but also through incineration or through some form of land disposal.[12]

As the level of government responsible for disposing of both solid wastes and the sewage and industrial liquid waste carried through sewer systems, municipalities are responsible for a considerable portion of the total annual pollution of the Canadian environment. As is discussed below, concern over pollution originated at the local government level when, during the latter part of the nineteenth century, it was realized that the high rate of death from such diseases as typhoid was caused by pollution of drinking water supplies by human and animal wastes. Sewage treatment and disposal and chlorination of drinking water were introduced in many of the larger Canadian cities prior to the First World War. However, the process is far from complete. Over one-quarter of the Canadian urban population lives in municipalities that continue to discharge sewage wastes directly to the environment with no form of prior treatment.[13]

Something like one-third of the industrial waste produced in Canada each year is discharged to municipal sewers and from there passed through sewage treatment plants to the environment, either directly with the plant wastewater or indirectly through disposal with the sewage sludge, which is often spread on fields as fertilizer.[14] This discharge is in theory regulated by municipal by-laws, but these by-laws are for the most part not intended to deal with the types of contaminants now regularly found in industrial wastes and their enforcement is sporadic or non-existent.

The other major waste management role of municipal government is disposal of household and commercial non-hazardous waste. This disposal is regulated by provincial governments, primarily in the form of design and operation standards intended to reduce groundwater contamination from sanitary landfills. As such standards are tightened and the difficulty of siting new landfills increases, municipalities find themselves facing a growing crisis of shortage of available landfill capacity. Incineration of solid waste, which originally was seen not only as a solution to the landfill problem but also as a source of low-cost energy, is running into public resistance. Environmental concerns centre on air pollution created when plastics and other substances are burned, as well as the argument that incineration, which requires an ongoing supply of fuel in the form of solid waste to cover capital and operating costs and meet contractual demands for energy production, inevitably takes away the incentive to reduce the quantity of waste initially generated.

Lessening the pollution associated with waste disposal can be achieved in two ways – by reducing the quantity of waste initially generated and by upgrading the design and operation of the disposal facility. Although considerable progress has been made in the latter area, for example, through tighter standards governing municipal landfills, there has been no regulatory action taken by any jurisdiction in Canada to reduce the quantities of either household or industrial hazardous waste generated each year.

Resource Industries

The forestry and mining industries have always been at the centre of environmental politics, both through wilderness preservation and through pollution prevention battles. Pollution from mining activities can include arsenic, cadmium, lead, and mercury, which leach from waste heaps to surrounding waters. Pesticide spraying by the forestry industry has been the subject of controversy in the Atlantic provinces, Ontario, and British Columbia on many occasions over the past two decades. Pulp and paper plants are responsible for a significant portion of total air and water pollution.

Because of their enormous importance to the Canadian economy and to the local economies of the towns in which they are situated, pollution regulation of the resource industries continues to be a highly sensitive and politically difficult task. Chapter 15 discusses in some detail the difficulties encountered by Canadian governments in their efforts to regulate the pulp and paper industry over the past twenty years.

Manufacturing Industries

Manufacturing industries contribute to total pollution quantities not only through waste and pollution emissions but also because of the toxic properties of many of the products they make. For instance, agricultural pesticides contaminate during their use, while mercury batteries contaminate only after they are disposed of as waste. In both cases, we continue to tolerate the environmental damage they cause because of our desire for the benefits these products bring.

The problem is compounded by the fact that in recent years a number of products originally thought to be both useful and environmentally benign have proven to be anything but that. Two of the best-known examples are PCBs and CFCs. Polychlorinated biphenyls (PCBs) were first synthesized in 1881 and were produced in the United States, beginning in 1929, for use as cooling and insulating fluid, primarily for electrical transformers. In 1968, 1,200 people in Yusho, Japan, suffered a variety of disorders after eating PCB-contaminated rice and their production in the U.S. was banned in 1977. In 1980 the Canadian government, under the authority of the Environmental Contaminants Act, limited their use to closed systems, such as transformers already in existence, and prohibited their manufacture or import. Although never manufactured in Canada, 40,000 tonnes had been brought into the country prior to the 1980 ban. Of that amount, 16,000 tonnes have escaped to the environment and the remainder still await destruction and disposal, representing one of the most publicized and intractable waste management problems to date.[15]

Chlorofluorinated carbons (CFCs) were first produced in the 1930s as a product that could provide refrigeration more safely than any of the existing alternatives. CFCs were found in 1974, however, to be responsible for depletion of the stratospheric ozone layer, thus increasing the quantity of harmful ultra-violet radiation that reaches the earth. Efforts to eliminate the production of CFCs in the past few years have primarily revolved around the economics of providing an environmentally acceptable alternative at a comparable cost. Although not the subject of the same public concern, disposal of CFCs already in existence poses the same type of problem as does disposal of PCBs. Many other products, such as asbestos, tires, and disposable diapers, have in the same way come to be viewed in recent years as threats to the environment.

Political controversy over polluting products tends to centre first on the issue of whether they actually do cause environmental damage, and if so, how much. Then, after some level of agreement is reached on that point, the focus shifts to the availability of non-polluting alternatives. Thus, political pressure to ban DDT was successful in large part because other chemical pesticides were available at a comparable cost. Those pressing for complete elimination of chemical pesticides point to non-chemical alternatives (the concept of "integrated pest management," which relies on manual pest removal, crop rotation, and other non-chemical means) as an alternative, but to date success has been limited. Presumably this is because the magnitude and cost of the change required are so great.

Industries pollute not only through the products they produce but also by generating wastes – unavoidable by-products – during the manufacturing process. Manufacturing industries in Canada generate something in the order of 8 million tonnes of hazardous waste, perhaps an equivalent amount of solid waste, and significant quantities of air pollution each year.[16] Until recently, the environment provided a convenient and inexpensive method of waste disposal. The dynamic of the issue is clear – cost is the determining factor. Canadian industries spend approximately one-third, on a pro rata basis, the amount spent by their American counterparts on environmental protection, and the difference is attributed completely to more stringent regulatory requirements in the United States.[17] Not surprisingly, industry resists attempts to introduce regulatory requirements that, by bringing Canada on a par with the United States, would triple its costs. Much stronger regulations than those in place in the U.S. would be required to bring about significant reductions in environmental damage, and they would, of course, bring with them even higher costs. A change in the classification of a waste from solid to hazardous, for instance, will increase the off-site disposal cost by a factor of ten or twenty.

Agriculture

A major source of environmental contamination is the application of chemicals to agricultural crops and farmland. These take the form of chemical pesticides and herbicides, used to kill insects and weeds that reduce crop productivity, and fertilizers. As they are applied to crops they enter the environment through both air transport and surface and groundwater movement. An example, albeit both limited and dated, is provided by the Environment Canada estimate that 6.3 tonnes of pesticides were used on field crops, fruits, vegetables, and roadsides in the Ontario portion of the Great Lakes drainage basin in 1978.[18] Undoubtedly that quantity is now much larger. It has been reported that pesticide sales more than doubled in the period 1978 to 1986.[19] Another recent study has stated that "Growth in the use of chemical pesticides and fertilizers has had profound impacts on environmental quality."[20]

Thus pollution is an essential part of the agricultural business since the use of chemicals to increase soil productivity and reduce crop loss has a direct impact on net financial return. In theory the unfettered marketplace could redress the situation if enough consumers were willing to pay the higher price charged for "organic" produce. In fact, however, as is the case for all forms of pollution, only government action will reduce the pollution caused by farming.

Pollution is built into almost every component of our modern, industrialized, affluent society. Indeed, *our affluence depends on pollution.* The energy to heat our homes and make us mobile, the food we eat, many of the products we make, and the wastes we generate each year all contribute both to our standard of living and to the worsening pollution of our environment. The advances in science and technology brought about by empiricism and the industrial revolution, combined with the availability of cheap fossil fuels and virtually free waste disposal, have allowed Canada to follow a rapid and environmentally destructive path of resource extraction, development, and industrialization during the past two centuries.

We keep on polluting because we would have to pay a high price to stop – a price measured in public and private spending, job dislocations, and the availability of many of the goods and services now deemed essential. The political strength needed by those lobbying to change practices so deeply entrenched in our way of life is enormous.

Other factors, such as our knowledge base, dissemination of information, and institutional inertia, to name just a few, also play an important part, but at the heart of pollution politics lies the issue of cost and, more importantly, conflict over who will pay that cost. When the "polluter" is asked to pay the price of pollution reduction – whether the commuter leaving the car at home and taking rapid transit, the farmer reducing the use of chemical pesticides and fertilizers, or the company paying the cost of pollution reduction – there is not only an initial reluctance to assume that cost but also, very understandably, a strong desire to see that the cost is applied in an equitable manner. Why should I take the subway when my neighbour drives to work? Will this same cost be applied to my business competitors, either here or in other countries? Why should I lose my job so that all Canadians can receive the benefit of a cleaner environment? Those who must pay the price of ending a particular type of pollution always form a powerful, because well-motivated, constituency to fight against the proposed government action. This is particularly so when they feel they have been singled out in an arbitrary manner and cannot see any fairness in the price they have been asked to pay.

Unfortunately, we are only beginning to develop principles and mechanisms for allocating that cost with fairness. In theory, governments in Canada are guided by the "polluter must pay" principle. The principle is sound, since without it the polluter has no incentive to stop polluting, but it must be further developed. If we were to ban all agricultural chemicals should the farmer alone pay the price of lost income due to reduced crop yield? If we were to shut down a polluting factory, something often threatened and seldom done in Canada, should we not help those thrown out of work? But why should workers who lose their jobs as part of our fight against pollution be more entitled to assistance than those who lose their jobs due to changing fashion or technology? And if we help the workers should we not also help the executive officers and shareholders? Where does it all end?

The political strength needed to win the war against pollution will only come when the values and perspectives of environmentalism are more deeply rooted than at present. And individual pollution battles will only be won when we have put in place principles for allocation of the cost that are accepted by all.

CHAPTER 2

The Environmental Lobby

The anti-pollution lobby is one part of the environmental movement and cannot be discussed in isolation from that larger movement. This chapter, therefore, provides an introductory summary of the three branches of environmentalism, the phases the movement has gone through during the past century, and the basic values and perspectives it holds today. The strategies pursued by different sections of the movement are reviewed and the chapter concludes with an evaluation of the political strength that the movement as a whole, and in particular the anti-pollution lobby, holds in Canada today.

Pollution and the Environmental Movement

The environmental movement is concerned with three issues – resource conservation, wilderness and wildlife preservation, and pollution. The objectives, values, and political strategies of the individuals and organizations working to influence government action on pollution reduction can only be understood by viewing them in the context of these three interconnected branches of the movement. This is because many individuals and organizations work in more than one area and because in any case the concerns overlap – those fighting to preserve wilderness areas in northern Ontario or Quebec, for instance, must guard against not only proposals for new roads and development but also pollution threats such as acid rain.

The three branches of the environmental movement, each of which has roots extending back into the previous century, are discussed in more detail in Part II. What follows, to provide a necessary context for the discussion of present-day pollution politics, is an overview of the evolution and current values and assumptions of the movement as a whole.

Resource management and conservation were initiated in the latter part of the nineteenth century when governments in Canada and elsewhere began to establish programs to survey geological resources, protect the headwaters of streams and rivers, and take first steps to ensure sustainable yields in such areas as the fishery and forestry. Wilderness preservation, which has as its aim the protection of wilderness areas in perpetuity, in distinction from the "conservation" or "management" of the wilderness resource, originated in the United States in the nineteenth century with the writings of Henry Thoreau and John Muir and was established after that date in Canada.

Conservation, defined as the wise management of natural resources to ensure sustainability, is distinguished from preservation by its underlying rationale – that resources are to be conserved for future *human* use, rather than for their own sake. The conservationist wants to limit the number of mountain goats killed each year by hunters not because of any ethical objection to sport-killing but because we must leave enough goats to breed and produce next year's sport. In terms of land use, areas are set aside and protected from development to achieve a number of *human* objectives, such as sustainable timber yield or wilderness recreation. The preservationist, on the other hand, works to preserve mountain goats and the range they live in because both have *inherent value in their own right*, regardless of any utility they may or may not have for human beings. It should be noted, however, that preservationists such as John Muir have also advanced a utilitarian argument in addition to that of inherent value: namely, that humanity receives moral benefit from knowing that some untouched wilderness remains, even if it is kept off limits, never visited, and does not offer wilderness recreation.

Awareness of the effects of pollution on human health stretches back many hundreds of years, but approximately a hundred years ago governments first began to establish local boards of health and to work to provide clean drinking water and sanitary waste disposal. Only in the post-war period has pollution concern extended to include the harm caused by pollution to the natural world.

The environmental movement can be said to have gone through four distinct phases during the past hundred years: origins, the post-war period, the politicization of the 1960s, and the contemporary era.

Origins

During the period from the late nineteenth century to 1945, government departments and programs were established in both the resource conservation and pollution fields. Those working in these fields were employed by government, industry, or universities and there were no public-interest organizations attempting to influence government policy. The public did join naturalist organizations such as, in the United States, the Audubon Society (1886) and Sierra Club (1892) and, in Canada, local naturalist organizations after the turn of the century that then came together to create such bodies as the Federation of Ontario Naturalists (1931). The primary objective of such organizations, however, was to serve the nature appreciation interests of their members, and their roles did not include lobbying government.

During this period the science of ecology, a branch of biology that attempts to gain understanding of the interconnected functionings of ecosystems, was established.

The Post-War Period

In the years following World War Two public interest in the natural environment, expressed through such things as camping trips and bird-watching, blossomed as a result of increased leisure time and mobility. The problem of global resource consumption caused by population growth was first brought to public attention in the late 1940s, and during the 1950s the first of the modern pollution concerns, radioactive materials disseminated by above-ground nuclear bomb tests, gained prominence.

Politicization during the 1960s

In the 1960s and early 1970s, toxic chemicals, primarily in the form of pesticides but with attention also paid to industrial wastes and air pollution, became an issue requiring government response in the form of both legislation and creation of new administrative agencies. The established naturalist organizations began lobbying government in a much more vigorous manner than previously, and at the same time many new organizations were created to fight for action on pollution and other aspects of environmental protection. Environmentalism became for the first time explicitly political, imbued with the social questioning and activism of the period.

The Modern Era

During the 1970s and 1980s environmental politics moved from the fringe to the centre of Canadian political life. Every few years concerns were raised over a new polluting substance, while scientific understanding of the effects of pollution steadily increased. Public attitudes changed and with them the rhetoric and, to a lesser degree, the actions of politicians.

Values and Assumptions

Although working in different areas and following different strategies, those in the modern environmental movement largely share a common set of values and assumptions. These can be summarized as follows:

- the understanding, which environmentalism gained from the science of ecology but which is in keeping with a number of religions and philosophies that have evolved over the past two millennia, that everything is connected to everything else and that the part can only be understood in the context of the whole;
- flowing from that understanding, a change in the imagery used to conceptualize the natural world: environmentalism has abandoned the eighteenth- and nineteenth-century concept of nature as a machine separate from humanity and has replaced it with that of a living organism, an image in which humans form an integral part of a universal whole that is in an ongoing process of growth and evolution;
- a changing view of the relationship between humanity and the natural world, moving away from the anthropocentric assumption that homo sapiens is at the top of an evolutionary pyramid, with all other creatures and objects having as their primary reason for existence the meeting of human needs, to a view of our species as one among many that have appeared, evolved, and disappeared over the long history of our planet: this new environmental ethic holds that other animals, species, and ecosystems, including inanimate objects, are imbued with inherent value;
- a questioning of the traditional social objective of never-ending economic growth, driven by ever-increasing demand for production of more consumer goods;
- a belief that small is better, expressed both in terms of size of social organizations and communities and in the use (or disuse) of large-scale, powerful technologies; coupled with this belief is the concept of "appropriate technology" on a scale suited to the task at hand and including the principles of durability and efficiency;
- a conviction that new technologies will inevitably bring new problems as well as benefits;
- a belief that decision-making, by both private and public agencies, that has implications for the larger society should be as accessible and accountable as possible.

As so defined, the environmental movement is concerned with far more than simply sulphur dioxide emitted from the Inco stack in Sudbury or creation of a new park on Baffin Island. Post-1960s environmentalism offers a new and inherently radical critique that underlies all aspects of

environmental politics. This radicalism, though seldom explicitly articulated, distinguishes today's environmentalism from the conservation and
other movements that preceded it. Robert Paehlke, in *Environmentalism
and the Future of Progressive Politics*, commenting on the writings of Barry
Commoner in the 1960s, describes the transformation in this way:

> At stake was not merely the 'wise use' of resources or the setting aside
> of ecological reserves. The new environmentalism claimed that prob-
> lems lie at the very heart of the modern political economy, even in our
> basic philosophical and cultural outlook. Everything fits together –
> the physical, chemical, biological, social, political, economic and
> philosophical worlds – and must be understood as a whole. The
> symptoms of environmental problems may be measured biologically,
> but the disease itself lies in our socioeconomic organizations, and the
> solutions are ultimately political.[1]

Different Strategies

The environmental lobby in Canada, as those in other countries, is divided
into two components. The first is made up of the single-issue citizen groups
that form around a particular issue and then dissolve when the issue reaches
a resolution of one sort or another. The impetus for their creation is usually
a proposed government initiative – siting a landfill or hazardous waste
treatment facility or construction of a dam – and the political pressure
applied by the group is focused solely on that particular decision. Examples
include Friends of the Oldman River, the group opposed to construction of
the Oldman dam, and Save the Rouge Valley System, a group in Metro
Toronto opposed to either development or siting of a landfill in the Rouge
area.

The other component of the lobby is made up of the permanent organizations, such as the B.C. Society Promoting Environmental Conservation
(SPEC), Ontario's Pollution Probe, and the New Brunswick Conservation
Council, which operate with a core of paid staff, supplemented by volun-
teer labour, out of offices equipped with computers, copiers, and fax
machines. These organizations move from issue to issue while maintaining
a permanent presence in the environmental dialogue. Citizen groups and
the permanent environmental organizations usually work in close alliance,
with the group supplying the political pressure by rallying its members and
supporters and the organization supplying the scientific, legal, and other
necessary expertise. Thus the Friends of the Oldman River had their financial and legal resources augmented by the Canadian Wildlife Federation,
which took the lead in bringing court action against the dam construction.

Such alliances either occur more or less spontaneously or are more systematically organized into a coalition that takes a united stand on the issue at hand, regardless of what their differences might be in other instances. One of the best-known and most successful coalitions is the Canadian Coalition on Acid Rain, which managed to bring together environmental activists, cottagers, tourist operators, and others with either an emotional or economic interest in the issue.

Many groups, initially established around a particular issue, have evolved into a permanent organization. Perhaps the best-known example is Greenpeace, formed in 1972 by a group of Vancouver activists who, looking for a way to protest the forthcoming U.S. nuclear bomb test in Amchitka, Alaska, seized on the idea of attracting media attention by chartering a boat and sailing into the blast zone. Greenpeace went on from there to establish an international, multimillion-dollar organization. The majority of Canadian organizations are indigenous but some, such as Friends of the Earth and the World Wildlife Fund, are Canadian branches of international organizations.

Although the permanent organizations and citizen groups usually differ in terms of size, expertise, and resources that can be brought to bear in a particular political battle, the major difference between them is the role they play in the ongoing process of environmental politics. By definition, the role of a citizens' group is limited to that of a veto power – slowing down and, if successful, stopping the particular initiative in question, be it siting a landfill, logging British Columbia or Temagami old-growth forest, or establishing the Ontario Waste Management Corporation hazardous waste treatment and disposal plant. The permanent organizations play a part in that process but their major function is to stimulate and directly participate in the ongoing development and implementation of government environmental policy.

The distinction between citizen group and established organization is less important for an understanding of the environmental lobby than are the three major strategic approaches that have evolved over the past twenty years. Although the labels are necessarily imprecise, these are reform environmentalism, deep ecology, and creation of green parties. Descriptions of each of the three follow. Less attention is paid here to reform environmentalism, but it should not be assumed that this reflects its relative importance or political strength. Quite the opposite is the case. Both deep ecology and the Canadian green parties are very much on the fringes of the environmental movement, although it will be argued that both offer perspectives and approaches that must be adopted for environmentalism to gain anything like real political strength.

Reform Environmentalism

This is the approach used by the vast majority of environmental organizations, whether they are in the pollution, conservation, or wilderness preservation field. Reform environmentalism refers to a reliance on traditional methods of public education, lobbying, and litigation intended to achieve very specific goals, such as creation of a new park or reduction in sulphur dioxide emissions, without making explicit reference to underlying social or economic issues. Nor does reform environmentalism rely to a great extent on protest actions, in the form of either rallies and demonstrations or illegal actions such as tree-spiking.

Almost all of the major Canadian environmental organizations concerned with pollution, such as SPEC, the Alberta Environmental Law Centre, the Canadian Environmental Law Association (CELA), the Canadian Arctic Resources Committee (CARC), Pollution Probe, the Canadian Coalition on Acid Rain, and the Société pour Vaincre la Pollution (SVP), fall within this mode. Greenpeace, although it still relies on confrontational tactics intended to generate maximum media attention more than preparation of detailed briefs and reports, is now an established, and in fact the largest, environmental lobby organization and as such falls at least partially within this classification.

One of the most successful examples of reform environmentalist lobbying has been provided by the Canadian Coalition on Acid Rain. The Coalition initiated direct-mail fund-raising and lobbying in the early 1980s, when the technique was just being established in Canada; as mentioned, brought together a diverse and therefore powerful coalition of interests; continually achieved media exposure for its issue; and made skilful use of high-level business and government contacts.

Reform environmentalism is criticized on the basis that while it tinkers with the system, it fails to come to grips with the enormity of the environmental crisis. Its critics argue that because the environmental organizations have opted to become mainstream players, they must compromise their objectives to the point that even if they win all of their small-scale battles, the larger war will have been lost. Barry Commoner, describing the U.S. experience, argues that the established organizations are far too willing to compromise: "The older national environmental organizations, in their Washington offices, have taken the soft path of negotiation, compromising with the corporations about how much pollution is acceptable, and sometimes helping to market their products, even when they are ecologically unsound."[2]

Another criticism, developed in more detail in the following pages, is that because reform environmentalism is for the most part human-centred, appealing to rational self-interest in its arguments for increased environmental protection, it leaves itself open to the counter-argument that adaptation is a cheaper and more effective means of achieving the goal of human well-being. Furthermore, by basing its position on logic and self-interest instead of any moral imperative, reform environmentalism badly weakens its political appeal.

Deep Ecology

The phrases "deep ecology" and "shallow ecology" were coined by a Norwegian philosopher, Arne Naess, in the early 1970s. Naess distinguishes between the anthropocentric approach of reform environmentalism, which, while working toward preservation of the natural environment, still takes human well-being to be the primary objective, and what he refers to as the "biocentric" approach of deep ecology, which is motivated by a concern for the natural world in its own right. Deep ecology differs from reform environmentalism because it relegates humanity to the status of simply one species among many and also because it emphasizes individual change in addition to societal change. While both deep ecology and reform environmentalism seek to change the actions of governments and business corporations, deep ecology is as much concerned with the spiritual growth a new relationship with the natural world offers to its adherents.[3]

Deep ecology holds forth two cardinal principles. The first is the concept of "biocentric equality," defined as the "intuition . . . that all things in the biosphere have an equal right to live and blossom and to reach their own individual forms of unfolding and self-realization within the larger Self-realization."[4] The second principle, as referred to above, is that of "self-realization," which is the process of "spiritual growth, or unfolding, . . . [when we] begin to identify with other humans . . . [and then proceed to] an identification which goes beyond humanity to include the nonhuman world. . . . The process of the full unfolding of the self can also be summarized by the phrase, 'No one is saved until we are all saved,' where the phrase 'one' includes not only me, an individual human, but all humans, whales, grizzly bears, whole rain forest ecosystems, mountains and rivers, the tiniest microbes in the soil, and so on."[5]

Its most visible practitioners are members of Earth First!, an organization established in the early 1980s that now has approximately 100 branches in the U.S. and three in Canada – two in B.C. and one in Ontario. Earth First! members practise what is known as "monkey-wrenching," a phrase taken from the Edward Abbey novel *The Monkey Wrench Gang*, which refers to such forms of sabotage as disabling bulldozers by putting sand in the gas tank and pulling up surveyors' stakes. Paul Watson of the Sea Shepherd Society, who achieved notoriety by sinking two whaling ships in Reykjavik harbour and then left Canada, disgusted by the meekness of this country's environmental movement, works in association with Earth First![6] Although the moral arguments offered by deep ecology are as applicable to pollution as to any other area of environmental concern, groups such as

Earth First! tend to focus almost exclusively on wilderness preservation issues.

Deep ecology, and more particularly Earth First!, can be criticized for a failure to offer anything in the way of either policy analysis or positive suggestions for change. After a condemnation of the moral turpitude of humanity, the major policy proposal the organization is able to advance is that of wilderness preservation, "So that there is something to come back after human beings, through whatever means, destroy their civilization."[7] The movement is also criticized, in particular by Murray Bookchin and the adherents of "social ecology," for its failure to move beyond consideration of the inequitable relationship between the human and non-human world to address the inequitable relationships among classes, races, and occupational sectors *within* the human world.[8]

It is argued in Part V, below, that the central message of deep ecology – the need for a personal affirmation of oneness with the natural world and a grounding of political action in an ethical regard for the inherent value of the natural world – must not be dismissed by the rest of the environmental movement. If it is, those fighting battles for pollution reduction deprive themselves of one of their most powerful weapons – the simplicity, eloquence, and power of a moral imperative. It is suggested, however, that Bookchin is right – environmentalism must develop an ideology that links natural justice with social justice, since neither can be achieved without the other.

Green Parties

Green parties trace their origins to the 1972 manifesto titled "Blueprint for Survival," published in the British magazine *The Ecologist*, which argued that establishment of a new political party was the best strategy for environmentalists. Shortly afterward, the Value Party was established in New Zealand and the Ecology Party in Great Britain.[9] It was not until the establishment of the German Green Party, Die Grunen, in 1979, however, that green parties achieved any electoral success. Die Grunen ran on a platform of the "four pillars" – ecology, social change, grassroots democracy, and nonviolence – advocating "a radical reorganization of our short-sighted economic rationality," an "active partnership with nature and human beings," and abolition of the "concentration of economic power in state and private-capitalist monopolies."[10]

The first major issue advanced by the Greens in Germany was uncompromising opposition in 1983 to the placement by NATO of additional nuclear weapons in that country. Assisted since then by the Chernobyl incident of 1986 and the German electoral system of proportional representation, the party has come to hold seats at the local, state, and federal levels.

In 1986 the British Ecology Party changed its name to the Green Party.

In 1989 the British Greens achieved 15 per cent of the popular vote for elections to the European Parliament and later that year placed third in opinion polls, behind Labour and the Tories but ahead of Social Democrats. This movement in the party's popularity may have influenced former Prime Minister Thatcher's new-found interest in the environment. (After ignoring the issue consistently since it was first elected in 1979, Thatcher's government did an about-face when it hosted an international conference on global warming in March, 1989.) The British Greens have provoked cries of alarm in the Tory party – Kenneth Baker, chairman of the party, warned in late 1989 that "We should all be wary of Green politicians, because, just like tomatoes, they start green and end up red."[11]

Greens were elected to the Swedish parliament in September, 1989, and have won seats in the Dutch parliament in the last two elections. France, Germany, Italy, the Netherlands, Spain, and Portugal have all elected Greens to the European Parliament.[12]

The Green Party of Canada was established in June, 1983, and held its founding convention in Ottawa in November of that year. Provincial green parties had been established earlier that year in British Columbia and Ontario.[13] In the federal election of 1984 the Green Party fielded sixty candidates and gained 29,000 votes. In 1988 the party fielded sixty-eight candidates and won 47,228 votes – less than the 52,173 won by the Rhinoceros Party but considerably more than the 7,168 votes for the Communist Party.[14] In Ontario provincial elections eleven Green candidates ran in 1985, nine in 1987, and fifty in 1990. Candidates also ran in the British Columbia election of 1986 and the Quebec and Newfoundland elections of 1989. In all of these elections the Greens captured something like 0.1 or 0.2 per cent of the vote – except in Quebec, where in 1989 forty-six candidates received 2 per cent of the vote.[15] The Ontario Green Party received 0.75 per cent of the vote in the September 6, 1990, Ontario election.[16]

By 1990 green parties, in addition to the national party, had been established in British Columbia, Alberta, Ontario, Quebec, and Newfoundland, and parties are in the process of being established in Saskatchewan and Manitoba. True to its philosophy of decentralization, the party has no central office, national leader, or set of policies to which all provincial parties subscribe.[17]

The Canadian electoral system, which denies representation in the House of Commons unless a party can win a plurality in one or more ridings, makes it very difficult for any new party without a regional base of support to establish itself. The one new party to have become firmly established at the federal level in this century is the Co-operative Commonwealth Federation (CCF), now the New Democratic Party, and it was able to do so largely because it became the vehicle for expression of western alienation during the Depression. Other parties that gained federal visibility and representation, such as Social Credit, have come and gone. The two new parties that, in 1990, appear to be gaining strength, the separatist Bloc Québécois and the western Reform Party, draw their strength from regional sensitivities. Environmentalism, while a stronger political force in some provinces than in others, simply does not have that regional basis, which may prove to be a fatal hindrance. Not surprisingly, Canadian Greens, like their British counterparts, advocate a move to proportional representation, in which the number of seats held by a party in the legislature is based on vote percentage and not on winning ridings outright. This system has proven successful in Europe, especially because a vote for a "fringe" party is not necessarily lost, and consequently voters are more inclined to support such a party at the ballot box.

The 1988 platform of the Ontario Greens illustrates the way green parties explicitly make the links between environment and a variety of social issues:

- eventual transformation to total dependence on sustainable energy;
- an abandonment of nuclear power;
- universal access to publicly funded child care and increased financial support to single parents;
- access to abortion;
- alternative approaches to paid labour, such as job-sharing, environmental protection, job creation, and increased financial support for the unemployed;
- sustainable, organic agriculture;
- transportation policies aimed at reducing automobile use;
- education reform to promote democratic participation in decision-making and to "promote the philosophy that we are part of nature and must live in harmony with it";
- achievement of "zero discharge" of pollution by giving citizens the right both to take legal action against polluters and to institute judicial review of failures of government action;
- increased taxes on tobacco, with a ban on cigarette advertising, imports, and exports;
- preventative health care;
- recognition that "All species have the intrinsic right to exist. Their existence need not be justified by their usefulness to humankind. All animals, whether wild or domesticated, have the right to fair and ethical treatment by human beings."[18]

Critics of the Green strategy make several points. It is suggested that establishment of a political party in 1983 was premature and that it has diverted time and energy from the task of establishing a grassroots movement needed to support a party.[19] Another criticism is that because of the

Canadian electoral system the party is doomed to irrelevance and will only succeed in splitting the left-wing vote, since if it attracts voters from any of the three major parties it will be from the NDP.[20] If the Canadian green parties achieve any electoral success at all, environmentalists across the political spectrum will be faced with the dilemma familiar to all social movements – should they work within an existing party to reform its policies, join the Green Party, or stay aloof from all parties, voting on the basis of candidate and policy, regardless of party?

Political Effectiveness

In the final analysis it is impossible to make a definitive judgement on the political effectiveness of any lobby movement, since government actions are decided by a complex mix of factors, with political pressure brought to bear by one set of lobbyists being only one of them. However, some indication of the political strength of the environmental movement in Canada, and especially the pollution lobby, can be gained by looking at three things – the financial resources it can bring to bear, its access to expertise in such areas as science and law, and its credibility in the eyes of the public.

Resources

Environmental non-profit organizations have three sources of revenue: the sale of goods and services in the marketplace, primarily through holding conferences and selling copies of the reports they produce; charitable donations, primarily from individuals but also, to a much smaller extent, from foundations and business corporations; and grants given by governments.

Business activities generate only a small amount of total net revenue – probably no more than 5 to 10 per cent for most organizations. Charitable donations from foundations and corporations might provide another 10 to 20 per cent, while grants from governments bring in a further 10 to 20 per cent. Small-scale donations from individual Canadians, thus, make up the greatest portion of total revenues, probably in excess of 50 per cent of the total. This individual support is provided through memberships or in response to direct mail and other forms of solicitation.[21]

The most recent, and perhaps notorious, method used to generate donations has been the Green Products campaign of Loblaws Supermarkets, in which organizations like Friends of the Earth and Pollution Probe endorsed products that were then marketed as being "environmentally friendly" on the basis of that endorsement. Through a contractual relationship with Loblaws, the organizations then received a portion of total revenues generated by sale of the products. The practice has encountered stiff criticism on the grounds that the only weapon environmental organizations have in the battle for public opinion, their credibility, is jeopardized as soon as their publicly stated opinion is tied in some way to pecuniary gain. A similar charge has been laid at the door of the environmental organizations for years, however, since their opponents have always accused them of deliberately exaggerating environmental and health threats in order to get headlines, which in turn stimulate public donations.

Environment Canada provides $150,000 each year, which is divided among approximately 350 organizations, and a further $225,000 to support the Canadian Environmental Network (CEN).[22] The Network has provided a co-ordinating and liaison function for the Canadian organizations since it was established, with a total membership of eighty groups, in 1978 by the Canadian Environmental Advisory Council, a federally funded secretariat. Administrative expenses of the Network have been paid by Environment Canada since 1986. The provincial governments also provide some funding to organizations within their jurisdictions. In comparison, the federal government provided $600,000 annually, before funding was cut in half in 1989, to the National Action Committee on the Status of Women, and it provides $800,000 annually to the Consumers' Association of Canada.[23]

Until the late 1980s environmental non-profits, particularly those concerned with pollution, operated on relatively limited budgets, ranging from almost nothing to half a million dollars a year in a few instances. As the environment moved up on the political agenda, however, their financial resources have been augmented. Foundation, government, and corporate support has not significantly increased but individual donations very definitely have – donations to the Greenpeace organizations in Vancouver and Toronto tripled in the period 1987 to 1990, bringing that organization to an annual budget level of $7.4 million, none of which is received from government or corporations.[24]

No other pollution lobby (distinguished from such organizations as the avowedly apolitical Nature Conservancy of Canada, which preserves natural areas by buying them and has always had access to substantial financial support) has annual revenues in that league. The next largest in Canada would be Pollution Probe, with revenues in 1988-89 of slightly over $1.6 million, followed by the Canadian Arctic Resources Committee with revenues of $700,000. Another fourteen pollution-oriented organizations operate with annual budgets in the $100,000 to $500,000 range.[25] The remainder of the approximately 1,800 environmental organizations now registered with the Canadian Environmental Network operate with annual budgets of less than $100,000.

How does this compare with the spending by trade associations to lobby on behalf of the industries they represent? Since industry will not or cannot divulge its spending in this area no precise answer can be given.[26] The spending of the environmentalists is probably not significantly less, however, and might even be more, than the annual spending on environmental policy of the trade associations – most notably the Canadian Chemical Producers, the Canadian Manufacturers' Association, the Canadian Pulp and Paper Association, and the Canadian Petroleum Association – all of which write briefs and speeches and make submissions to government, the same things their counterparts in the environmental movement do. What must be borne in mind, however, is that the bulk of industry spending on environmental policy issues (distinct from capital and operating costs of pollution prevention and waste management operations) goes to individual regulatory actions. This is the money each polluting company pays for scientists, engineers, lawyers, public affairs officials, and other company staff who participate in the ongoing negotiations with government over pollution standards and their enforcement. No estimate is available of the amount spent by Canadian industries in attempting to influence the regulatory requirements imposed on them. Given the costs of pollution reduction, and resulting incentives each company has to spend in this area, the amount is undoubtedly many times larger than the combined expenditures of both industry trade associations and the environmental organizations on more general policy discussion.

Expertise

Environmental organizations simply do not have the financial resources to hire in the marketplace expertise comparable to that mustered by either government or industry. This does not mean it cannot be obtained, however. When a group of University of Toronto students created Pollution Probe in 1969, their first step was to enlist the active support and assistance of Dr. Don Chant, then head of the Zoology Department and an entomologist with a background in biological pest management who had the expertise and credentials the group needed. Environmental organizations have continued in that tradition ever since, attempting as best they can to recruit scientists, lawyers, and other professionals to boards and honorary directorates. Obviously, however, only so much can be done through voluntarily donated expertise.

In the absence of money to hire expert staff and consultants, environmental organizations have had to develop expertise themselves, relying on the published work of others. The track record of the Canadian environmental movement in developing this type of expertise has been mixed. Some areas, such as the physical sciences, are simply beyond the realm of possibility, given the high capital and operating costs of labs and equipment. Although Greenpeace has brought *Beluga*, its boat equipped to monitor water quality, into the Great Lakes and Pollution Probe has done some work in such areas as quality of Toronto drinking water and pollution effects associated with solid waste incineration, the contributions of the non-profits to the environmental scientific literature have been almost nil.

Their purpose, of course, is not to practise academic science but to use science to influence the policy process. Perhaps the most successful example of this, discussed in Chapter 15, is the 1988 discovery by Greenpeace of dioxin contamination in pulp mill effluent in Harmac, Vancouver Island, which played a large part in pressuring new regulatory activity by the B.C., Ontario, and federal governments.

In other areas, most notably environmental law, the public-interest organizations have led the way. Five environmental law organizations – the West Coast Environmental Law Association (WCELA), the Alberta Environmental Law Centre, CELA, the Canadian Institute for Environmental Law and Policy, and the Canadian Institute for Resource Law in Calgary (CIRL) – employ a combined total of about twenty lawyers and provide a venue for work done by at least that many more. Only a handful of academics offer environmental law courses throughout the country, and while recent trends in enforcement have meant that established law firms are hiring environmental lawyers for the first time, those individuals tend to concentrate on litigation rather than policy. As a result, during the past two decades, almost all of the environmental law publications, which provide detailed analyses of different regulatory regimes and make recommendations for change, have emanated from the public-interest sector.

The record in other policy areas is less impressive. Environmental organizations have provided little analysis of government spending or administration and have presented few policy alternatives. In 1989 a Canada-wide coalition of native and environmental organizations published an excellent work, *Greenprint for Canada: A Federal Agenda for the Environment*. Unfortunately, it is the first time such an initiative has been taken at the national level in Canada. The greatest failing is in the field of economics, although the non-profit sector is not alone here. With a few exceptions, little work has been done on the economic implications of environmental protection and pollution control by *anyone* in Canada – public-interest organizations, academics, or governments. The Economic Council of Canada, for instance, sponsored an excellent series of studies that were summarized in the 1980 publication, *Environmental Regulation in Canada*, edited by Andrew Thompson.[27] Since then, the Council has done nothing in the area, other than sponsoring a 1985 colloquium on resource management that, for whatever reason, did not focus on economics at all.[28] More recently, the C.D. Howe Institute and the Fraser Institute have, for the first time, entered the policy discussion with publications suggesting (not surprisingly, given their political agenda) that "market approaches" be used to ensure environmental protection.[29]

Other work in the environmental policy area has been done by the Canadian Environmental Advisory Council and, more recently, by the Institute for Public Policy Research. The most significant work, by far, has been done by the Science Council of Canada, which published *It Is Not Too Late - Yet* (1972), *Canada as a Conserver Society* (1978), and *Regulating the Regulators: Science, Values and Decisions* (1982). The Science Council has also done work in such areas as biotechnology policy and water demand management. The Law Reform Commission of Canada has also published a number of useful works, the most significant policy analysis being Ted Schrecker's *Political Economy of Environmental Hazards.*

Credibility

Environmental organizations have more credibility in the eyes of the public than does government or industry, presumably because they are seen to be working in the public interest. This discrepancy was acknowledged in 1986 by then federal Environment Minister Tom McMillan, who told an audience of chemical industry professionals that neither he nor they had credibility in the eyes of the Canadian public. Referring to several recently released opinion polls, he stated:

> If your own polls can be believed, Canadians do not think highly of the chemical industry. . . . not even 1 in 4 persons accepts the word of government on environmental, health or safety issues. By contrast, nearly 7 out of every 10 Canadians credit information from environmental and consumer groups. Put crudely, with all the resources at our disposal, neither your sector of society nor my own has been able to convince our fellow citizens that we speak honestly and reliably about one of the most important matters [pollution and health effects] affecting them and their children.[30]

In their public pronouncements environmental organizations must walk a very careful line. They need to make their points forcefully to capture attention, but at the same time they must do everything possible - by using neutral, non-emotive language - to avoid charges of hysteria and extremism. Since environmental protection moved into the political mainstream in the 1980s, the charges of scare-mongering have lessened, although some, like Adam Zimmerman of Noranda, still complain of "environmental attacks on the [forest] industry that go far beyond what might be described as fair or reasonable or even necessary" and make references to "environmental terrorists."[31] Perhaps the most delightful pronouncement along these lines has been made by Terence Corcoran, business columnist for *The Globe and Mail.* Corcoran, in March, 1990, pronounced then Ontario Environment Minister Jim Bradley to be the "emerging Caligula of regulatory environmentalism" and then went on to shed tears over a recent television debate and "the mauling the cement industry received at the hands of an environmentalist, a lioness trained to pounce on innocent businessmen."[32]

* * *

The environmental movement in Canada, unlike its American counterpart, is forced, presumably by a lack of financial resources, to operate largely in a reactive mode, commenting on proposed government and industry initiatives but rarely developing policy alternatives for public debate. To give one example, the environmental movement has been noticeably absent throughout all of the constitutional discussions of the 1980s. When women and native peoples have presented their cases for constitutional protection so strongly, why has the environmental movement been unable to mount any pressure for a constitutionally guaranteed right to a clean environment? The Canadian organizations do not have available to them, because of rules governing legal action against governments, the weapon of litigation that has been used so effectively in the United States. By continually taking governments to court, something almost unheard of here before the Oldman and Souris River initiatives, the American environmentalists accomplish two ends – they force government action, if successful, and generate considerable public attention and support for their specific issues.

This does not mean the Canadian environmental movement has been totally without effect. The Canadian Environmental Law Association in 1975 played an important part in both developing and lobbying for adoption of the Ontario Environmental Assessment Act. The study released by Pollution Probe in 1980, *Profits from Pollution Prevention*, was a forerunner of the interest on the part of both government and industry in the financial benefits accruing from improved waste management. The problem of inadequate enforcement of environmental legislation in Alberta was brought to light primarily through the work of the Alberta Environmental Law Centre. The Canadian Coalition on Acid Rain successfully forced government action during the period 1980-85, and, as mentioned, lobbying by Greenpeace in the late 1980s forced the federal government to take new regulatory action on pulp mill pollution. Most importantly, the organizations and *ad hoc* citizen groups have maintained, particularly during the difficult years of the late 1970s, a watching brief, constantly reminding governments and the public that environmental damage will not go unmarked.

CHAPTER 3

Pollution and Canadian Politics

What is the stage, or to use a perhaps more apt metaphor, the battlefield, upon which contests between the polluters and the environmental lobby take place? The following chapter describes the major social forces and institutions that shape the form of pollution politics.

Geography

Canadian geography – both the country's location on the face of the globe and its physical make-up – has had an effect on our national culture and political evolution that carries over to environmental politics.

Location on the Globe

Canada's global location has two major implications for environmental politics. First, as a northern nation, no matter how much we may insulate ourselves by living in cities, huddled close to the southern border, we Canadians think of ourselves as living in a northern land – looking instinctively to the north, just as Americans look to the west – which means, by definition, living in what is often a hostile and cold environment. Thus, the simple fact of geography has contributed to the "garrison mentality" described by Northrop Frye and others, in which the human and natural worlds are viewed, at least by the non-aboriginal population, with fear and suspicion from behind the stockade walls. The harsh rigour of a northern environment historically reinforced the Canadian perception, brought over from Europe, of this northern environment as something to be feared and, therefore, to be dominated and exploited.

But a northern environment does not lead only to alienation from the land. It also offers the purity of ice and snow and the stillness and quiet beauty of rock and trees encircling a northern lake. Above all, our North American environment offers a sense of being new, fresh, and unsullied. Like the Americans, although to a lesser degree because we did not sever our ties to Europe by means of revolution, we have traditionally seen ourselves as a people who by crossing the ocean left the decadence of the old world and came to live in a new one. For the Americans this fostered a conviction of moral superiority; in Canada it produced something very different – a perception of innocence. Canadians see themselves as venturing forth from their new land to do nothing but good in the world, perhaps naive but certainly well-meaning and unburdened by the guilt and corruption of world power.

Innocent people, living in a pure, northern land, will instinctively abhor the pollution that threatens this purity and, by extension, the national consciousness of self. One of the most potent representations of pollution is the picture that appears occasionally in the media of fish caught in the Great Lakes with grotesque, cancerous tumours bulging from their sides or stomachs. The emotional response such images evoke comes only in part from a fear that we might ourselves get cancer from pollution. Far more, it comes from being forced to confront such damning evidence of the way we have soiled the purity we found in this new world.

The second factor arising from Canada's physical location is proximity to the United States. This has meant that environmental politics has often focused on pollution originating from south of the border. Examples include west coast oil tanker traffic, the concerns over phosphorous and other forms of pollution of the Great Lakes, and acid rain. Since transboundary pollution requires Canadian-American negotiation, such pollution, due to the central importance of the American relationship in almost every aspect of Canadian life, automatically becomes a major political issue in this country.

Physiography

The predominant aspects of Canada's physical make-up are, first, the size of the country and, second, the fact that the bulk of the population lives in a relatively narrow corridor, stretching from east to west. These factors have reinforced the tendency, arising from our history, toward a federated rather than centralized state. Federation has meant that environmental politics, like every other aspect of Canadian life, is continually dominated by the issue of federal and provincial jurisdictional authority.

The other dominant factor of our geography is the central importance, throughout Canadian history, of resource development. The country was founded, at least in terms of the European arrival, first on the fishery and the fur trade, and then on forestry and mining. This has had the effect of ensuring that environmental politics will be central to Canadian political life, since the concern for pollution and environmental degradation associated with resource development quickly clashes with some of the most powerful economic and political interests in the country.

Political Traditions
Native North American Traditions

Native North Americans first came to Canada some 10,000 years ago, or perhaps earlier, crossing from Asia by a land bridge dividing the Bering Sea and then moving south along a corridor running through present-day British Columbia into the centre of North America. From there, over the next few thousand years, they moved back north, both up the western coast and into the central regions of present-day Ontario and Quebec. Subsequent migrations established native people throughout Canada, the Inuit in the North and a large number of linguistic and cultural groupings spread across the remainder of the country.

These various peoples, some of whom lived by hunting alone and others by a combination of hunting and agriculture, evolved a number of political and cultural traditions that are of direct relevance to environmental politics today. Their pantheistic view of the natural world, which led them to a continuing communication and interaction with the spirits animating the rocks, trees, and animals of the world around them, in which these beings were granted the respect due to an equal, is completely in keeping with the emerging consciousness of the environmental movement. Some of their technological achievements, such as the canoe and snowshoe, are perfect embodiments of the "appropriate technology" touted today by environmentalists, while their collective decision-making and societal life – decentralized, communal, and based on discussion and consensus – are again representative of the ideals of environmentalism. Finally, their art is rooted in their sense of place and their relationship to the land.

If environmentalism actually does begin to transform the Canadian political ethos it will do so, at least in part, by drawing on these traditions. As the environmental ethic becomes more firmly established it will inevitably look for inspiration to people like the Kunghit Haida, who lived for thousands upon thousands of years in the village of Ninstints, looking out on the Pacific, drawing in with each breath the solemn and changing beauty of the ocean, the rain forest, and the mountains, and then pouring that beauty back out in the symmetry and wholeness of their art.

The challenge, as the aboriginal minority and the European-descended majority redefine their relationship, is to find ways for the majority culture to gain sustenance from, without violating or encroaching on, native traditions and culture. That there is as much potential for conflict as there is for harmony has already been demonstrated by the development of environmental politics in Canada to date. During the 1970s animal rights organizations such as the International Fund for Animal Welfare and Greenpeace (one of the few organizations that has worked in both the environmental and animal protection movements) waged a successful campaign against the east coast seal hunt. In the early 1980s these groups moved on to campaign against trapping, bringing considerable economic pressure to bear through campaigns aimed at European fur buyers. Those on the receiving end of this latter campaign were, primarily, the Inuit and other aboriginal trappers, who make up over half of the 100,000 registered trappers in Canada.[1] Not surprisingly, considerable hostility between native peoples' organizations and animal rights organizations has been generated. On the other hand, wilderness preservation campaigns, such as at South Moresby in B.C. and Temagami in northern Ontario, have drawn strength from alliances between environmentalists and native peoples and have also shown a convergence of interest between the environmentalist goal of wilderness protection and the native goal of securing land title.

European Traditions

The political traditions brought to Canada in the seventeenth and eighteenth centuries from France and England were based on the new-found concerns for property rights, individual liberties, and representative government. Unlike the United States, the evolution of the Canadian political tradition has provided for electoral representation of each of the three dominant ideologies of the twentieth century – liberalism, conservatism, and socialism. A 1983 study of Canadian political traditions states:

> We have identified three distinct ideological approaches to politics which Canada has inherited from Europe: liberalism, organized around the two concepts of individuality and liberty; toryism, built upon collectivism, and hierarchy or privilege; and socialism, sharing the tory's collectivism, but seeking to replace privilege by equality . . . this ideological diversity – the existence of tory and socialist elements in a dominant liberalism – sharply distinguishes Canada from the United States.[2]

It is generally held that the existence of this socialist tradition allows governments in Canada to play a larger role than in the United States. As noted above, however, pollution regulation in this country has imposed costs on industry that are only one-third of those imposed by American governments. Despite their much more vocal commitment to the virtues of free enterprise, Americans have been much more willing to see governments intervene to protect the environment than have Canadians.

Perhaps of more significance is the fact that this socialist tradition led to creation of the CCF in 1932 and the New Democratic Party in 1961. Environmentalism has always been seen as part of the progressive agenda and therefore it might be assumed that environmentalists form a natural constituency for the NDP.

In fact, however, the NDP has been no more successful than either of the other two parties in articulating environmental policy and NDP governments have not been particularly noted for action on the issue. It would be difficult to argue that British Columbia, Saskatchewan, and Manitoba, in which NDP governments have held power, have introduced more stringent pollution control measures than Ontario, where, until 1990, the NDP had not formed a government. A 1985 review of the record of the NDP government in Manitoba since it assumed power in 1982 reached this conclusion: "Changes in [environmental] legal arrangements and institutions have also been minimal; not one change seems to strike environmentalists as having great significance."[3]

The question is not whether the socialist foundations of the NDP will lead that party automatically to environmentalism, since they will not, but whether environmentalists can draw on that party's concern for fairness and social justice as they work to put in place policies based on fairness and justice for the natural world.

Constitutional and Political Jurisdiction

Constitutional authority over environmental protection is shared by the federal and provincial governments. At the same time, municipal governments, which have no constitutional authority, play a role in pollution prevention as significant as that of their federal and provincial counterparts.

Although there is no explicit reference to environmental protection in the British North America Act of 1867 (now the Constitution Act), there is general agreement today that the constitution provides authority for federal environmental action through the "peace, order, and good government clause," interprovincial and international trade, navigation and shipping, fisheries, jurisdiction over native peoples, criminal law, and ownership of federal land. As discussed in Part III, when Environment Canada was established in 1971 the federal government looked particularly to its constitutional authority over fisheries, which was explicitly assigned by the British North America Act in 1867. The Canadian Environmental Protection Act of 1988, the only new federal environmental statute to be enacted in the 1980s, is based in part on the peace, order, and good government clause,

51

making reference in the preamble to national concern over toxic substances in the environment.[4] The Supreme Court of Canada has upheld the constitutional validity of the Ocean Dumping Control Act, based on this authority.[5] Use of the federal powers enshrined in the Criminal Code has often been suggested as a means of approaching pollution regulation, but no such action has been taken in this regard.

Primary provincial authority comes from ownership of the public lands and natural resources located within each province, particularly minerals and forests, which are specifically referred to in the BNA Act.[6] Provincial authority over "local works and undertakings" and "property and civil rights" gives the provinces "a very wide ambit to deal with matters relating to the environment and to delegate responsibility to municipalities."[7] An example of the forthright claim of the provinces to primary jurisdiction over air and water pollution was given in April, 1987, by Rod McLeod, who at the time was deputy minister of environment for Ontario: "Who has the primary responsibility for the protection and enhancement of the quality of air, land and water? I think the answer is very clear. It is the provinces."[8] At the same time, the federal authority to regulate air emissions under the Clean Air Act, now consolidated with other legislation in the Canadian Environmental Protection Act, has been upheld by the courts on the basis that such emissions may cross provincial boundaries.[9]

Although municipalities have no constitutional authority, being created by provincial governments to carry out duties established by provincial legislation, they are still primarily responsible for preventing pollution in the areas of drinking water, sewage treatment, hazardous waste discharged to sewers, and solid waste disposal. An indication of the significance of the municipal role is given by the following comparison[10] of total expenditures on environmental protection by the three levels of government in 1981-82:

federal:	$1,510,472,000
provincial:	$2,254,600,000
municipal:	$2,533,807,000

The constitutionally ordained division of federal and provincial authority in this area has clearly been of less significance to date than the politically determined division. This may change in future as environmental protection becomes more central to governmental decision-making, as in the case of the Quebec James Bay development, and as authority comes to be challenged more than it has been in the courts. To date, the division of federal and provincial powers has been decided by negotiation rather than court action.

Alistair Lucas has suggested that provincial legislation was enacted in the early 1970s, following passage of the federal Canada Water Act, Clean Air Act, and other legislation, more to prevent federal encroachment in this new area than for any other reason and that in the years following "federal-provincial disputes over natural resources and energy and negotiations leading up to the patriation of the Constitution in 1982 had the effect of augmenting *de facto* provincial powers."[11] This concern over expanding federal powers was expressed in 1988 when, during enactment of the federal Canadian Environmental Protection Act, a series of federal-provincial negotiations were initiated to establish the extent to which this new legislation would complement or supplant existing provincial powers. The negotiations, none of which had been completed by the fall of 1990, are centred on the concept of "equivalency," which provides that when provincial regulations are considered "equivalent" to those proposed by the Canadian government under CEPA, they would take precedence. This concept was immediately put to the test in the fall of 1988, following the fire in the PCB warehouse at St.-Basil-le-Grande near Montreal. The Mulroney government, determined to appear capable of decisive action during a federal election, immediately announced that it would use its new-found powers under CEPA to regulate PCB storage directly throughout the country, upon which all of the provinces except Prince Edward Island, equally determined to resist any expansion of federal power, applied for exemption from such federal regulation on the basis of equivalency.[12]

It is fair to say that no final resolution has yet been made of either *de facto* or *de juris* authority and that as the structure of Canadian federalism is inevitably reshaped after the demise of the Meech Lake Accord, environmental politics will both contribute to and be affected by that process.

Institutions of Governance

The system of representative government based on seats in the House of Commons or a provincial legislature has particular relevance for environmental politics since, as discussed, it makes it extremely difficult for green parties to gain a seat at either level of government. In many ways, however, bureaucracies, not legislatures, are the focus of pollution battles. Pollution regulation is an administrative function in which the relevant departments – environment, agriculture, health, natural resources, and others – wield considerable power relative to the legislatures and ministers to which they report. This is done through the setting of standards, in regulations that implement legislation enacted by elected bodies, and even more importantly through the licensing of polluting industries and subsequent enforcement, or lack thereof, of the conditions of such licences.

Environmental civil servants also play a major role in initiating and guiding through to adoption new policies or legislative amendments. When a newly appointed environment minister, traditionally a rookie with no interest or experience in a portfolio that is seen primarily as a stepping-stone to bigger things, looks around for policy advice he or she is likely to end up relying heavily on the environment department bureaucrats. This is because, as discussed, the environmental lobby operates primarily in a reactive mode and there are few academics working in the area. Thus one of the most significant environmental policy steps taken in Ontario in the 1980s – establishment of a separate Investigations and Enforcement Branch, staffed not by waterworks engineers but by ex-cops – was an initiative of the bureaucracy, taken without prompting from either environmental organizations or politicians.

Governments in Canada have always delegated considerable regulatory and administrative powers to appointed boards and commissions. Examples include such agencies as the Canadian Broadcasting Corporation and Canadian Radio-television and Telecommunications Commission. This pattern has been followed in the environmental sphere. Water pollution regulation was delegated to appointed commissions by most provinces during the 1960s and regulatory authority has also been exercised by such bodies as the National Energy Board and environmental assessment boards in a number of provinces. Two such agencies, the Canadian Council of Ministers of the Environment and the International Joint Commission, are of particular relevance.

The Canadian Council of Resource Ministers (CCRM), as it was then known, was established in 1961, following the Resources for Tomorrow Conference, which had been convened by the federal and provincial resource management departments. As a body consisting of all of the provincial and federal natural resource ministers, the CCRM had no direct program delivery or regulatory authority but instead provided a permanent forum for co-ordination and information-sharing. In 1971, reflecting the changing emphasis from resource management to environmental protection and after several jurisdictions had moved to establish departments of the environment, environment ministers joined the group and the name was changed to the Canadian Council of Resource and Environment Ministers. In the mid-1970s, perhaps because it was working in what had by then become a highly sensitive area and presented a potential political challenge to governments, the size of the Council was drastically scaled back and its role changed from an advisory to a purely liaison function.[13] In 1989, resource ministers withdrew and the name was changed yet again, to the Canadian Council of Ministers of the Environment (CCME).

As presently constituted, the Council consists of all federal and provincial ministers, meeting once a year with a rotating chairmanship. Reporting to the Council is a Committee of Deputy Ministers, which in turn appoints committees in different areas, such as the Water Advisory Committee and Air Advisory Committee. These subcommittees consist of staff from federal and provincial environment departments. Thus the work of the Council is done by provincial and federal staff not on a seconded basis but in addition to their regular duties. Co-ordination is provided by a secretariat, originally located in Toronto and since moved to Winnipeg, headed by an executive director. The secretariat has a total staff of four and an annual budget in the area of $350,000.[14]

The International Joint Commission (IJC) was established by Canada and the United States in 1909 with the signing of the Boundary Waters Treaty. The Commission consists of six members, three appointed by each country, and has offices in Washington, Ottawa, and Windsor. The Commission has limited approval powers over the diversion of waters flowing across the international border, but its primary function and importance lie in investigating and reporting on matters referred to it by the two governments. The Commission was asked to investigate Great Lakes pollution in 1912, 1946, and again in 1964, and it has been instrumental in implementing the 1972 Great Lakes Water Quality Agreement. When the Agreement was renewed, in 1978, the focus of concern had shifted from phosphorous pollution to toxic chemicals, including not only those discharged directly to water but also those arriving at the Great Lakes through urban and rural run-off and airborne transport. The Commission is of significance to environmental politics in Canada both because it is one of the best sources of information on pollution and because it provides Canada with a forum, in which representation is equal, for discussion with the Americans of transboundary pollution issues.[15]

Parties and Elections

None of the three major Canadian political parties has played a major role in either mounting political pressure or developing specific environmental policies. This is hardly surprising, given the brokerage role of political parties, which reflect, but do not determine, social consensus. All three have declared themselves on the side of clean air and water since pollution became an electoral issue in the 1970s, but each party has also been constrained in the extent to which it is willing to place environmental protection ahead of the more traditional goals of economic expansion and employment. In the case of the Liberals and Conservatives this constraint has come from reliance on financial support from the business community, while the NDP faces a similar problem – financial support from labour places constraints on environmental policies thought to threaten jobs.

Through the 1970s and early 1980s, when the environmental debate was governed by the perception that there was no middle ground between "jobs or the environment," this was a particularly difficult task for the NDP. Although by 1990 that perception was changing, with growing acceptance of the notion that environmental protection might create more jobs than it eliminated, the NDP was still faced with internal struggles. Examples include the protests from the local NDP riding association when Bob Rae, the Ontario provincial leader, went to Temagami to join the anti-logging protests in 1989, and the difficulties Michael Harcourt, B.C. NDP leader, has had in preventing open warfare between the loggers and environmentalists within his party.[16] The traditional approach of the NDP to the corporate community, dating back to the "corporate welfare bum" days of David Lewis, is one of refusing corporate donations and not hesitating to advocate increased regulation. This perhaps gives that party more credibility than the others when it talks about getting tough with industrial polluters. (Certainly more than Larry Grossman had in 1987 when, as leader of the Ontario Tories, he ran on a plank of putting corporate polluters in jail.) Whether or not the NDP can capitalize on that credibility, as elections increasingly come to be affected by environmental issues, and avoid having its environmental vote siphoned off by the Greens, remains to be seen.

It would seem that the personal commitment a cabinet minister brings to the environmental issue may be more important than party policy. John Fraser, an environmental lawyer from British Columbia with a personal commitment to the issue, was Environment Minister in the short-lived Joe Clark government of 1979-80 and then Fisheries Minister, under Brian Mulroney, until he was driven from office by the tainted tuna scandal of 1985. Both in and out of office, Fraser has worked to advance the environmentalist cause. Another example is Liberal Charles Caccia, Environment Minister under Pierre Trudeau and John Turner from 1983 until the election of September, 1984. Caccia, more than any other elected official, was responsible for development of the Canadian acid rain program – "he was like a terrier with a bone," as one of his officials described his determination to force the issue with the provinces.[17] Caccia has continued to work on environmental issues since leaving office. Another example is Jim Bradley, Ontario Environment Minister in the Peterson government from 1985 to 1990, whose clashes with other ministers in cabinet as he pursued his environmental agenda were widely reported.[18]

As noted earlier, the Ontario election of 1985 was the first in Canada in which pollution was a significant issue and it has remained so in almost all provincial and federal elections since. It cannot be said, however, that it has been a determining issue in any election. The major relevance of elections for environmental politics, in addition to providing an opportunity for raising awareness of issues, has been the actions that have followed the election of minority governments. These include the appointment of the Berger Inquiry by the minority Trudeau government in 1974, passage of the Ontario Environmental Assessment Act by the minority Davis government in 1975, and actions taken under the aegis of the Liberal-NDP accord in Ontario after the minority Peterson government assumed power in June, 1985.

International Environmental Protection

Prior to the nineteenth century, air pollution and water pollution were seen as local problems. To the extent they were dealt with at all, this was done by the town, village, or city council. By the turn of the century pollution of international waters, such as the Great Lakes, emerged as a problem. In the 1920s and 1930s air pollution from Trail, British Columbia, caused damage in Washington state. Arbitration of the dispute between Canada and the United States clearly established the responsibility, under international law, to guard against transboundary pollution. The range of this responsibility was extended, in the 1970s, with the discovery that air pollution such as acid rain could be carried hundreds and even thousands of miles. Then in the mid-1980s air pollution became truly global, with the discovery of stratospheric ozone depletion and global atmospheric change.

It had become obvious that a single nation, acting alone, could not protect the environment within its borders. Collective action was needed, not only to protect the global commons but also to protect the domestic environment of each nation-state.

International environmental protection encounters a number of obstacles not present when a nation acts to protect its own environment. The world, after all, is made up of sovereign states, which will accept any externally imposed limitations on their freedom of action only with the greatest reluctance. Our experience in creating and operating international organizations, which provide the necessary framework for concerted action among nations, is still very limited.

Sovereignty has been the major point of contention since the first major attempts to co-ordinate international action on the environment were made in 1972. The tension between the desire for autonomy and recognition of the fact of interdependence is set out in Principle 21 of the Stockholm Declaration:

> States have in accordance with the Charter of the United Nations and the principles of international law, the sovereign right to exploit their own resources pursuant to their own environmental policies, and the responsibility to ensure that activities within their jurisdiction or control do not cause damage to the environment of other States or of areas beyond the limits of national jurisdiction.

Sovereignty poses several problems in attempts to solve international environmental issues, all of which stem directly from the fact that global environmental problems, unlike those contained within the borders of any one country, cannot be addressed by a single governing body that has been accorded by its constituents the powers to make and enforce laws.

The Tragedy of the Commons

Sovereignty impedes international environmental protection in the first instance because of the well-known "tragedy of the commons," the phrase made popular by the American author Garrett Hardin in the late 1960s and paraphrased by Robert Paehlke as follows:

> the commons is a shared land on which each herder has the right to graze as many animals as he or she wishes. But the limited carrying capacity of the commons is ultimately exceeded as each individual herder adds additional animals without considering the long-term results. If individual, short-term decisions dominate, the commons will be destroyed, since the individual gain from an additional animal always seems greater than the loss that is shared by all.[19]

In a world of sovereign states, users of the commonly owned and shared resources, such as the oceans and the atmosphere, have absolutely no incentive to curtail their consumption or pollution of that resource, no matter how clearly its imminent depletion can be seen, when they have no assurance that all other users will cut back their consumption or pollution by the same amount.

The Absence of Law

The government of a nation can use law and its monopoly on the use of force to allocate and then enforce such reductions, but on the global stage, in which each nation will allow only the slightest infringement of its sovereignty and then only when it is clearly in its own self-interest, no such mechanism exists. International law is a codification of the ideals of inter-actions among nations, defined by one observer as follows: "International law is the body of binding rules of conduct among nations, expressed in treaties, in consistent and established behaviour by nations, in the writings of distinguished scholars and the rulings of judicial bodies."[20]

The problem, of course, is that compliance with international law is a purely voluntary matter. Although creation of such institutions as the United Nations and World Court is a step in that direction, there is no agency with the moral, political, or military power to enforce international law.

International Agreements

No nation will assume the cost of working to protect the global environment unless it is sure that at least some other nations, particularly its trade competitors, will do the same thing. In the absence of enforceable law, that assurance can only come in one of two ways – through collective agreements, arrived at by the slow and cumbersome processes of diplomacy, or by granting some powers to international institutions, no matter how marginal, to allocate such costs.

Historically, the primary purpose of agreements among nations has been for security through military alliances. NATO and the now defunct Warsaw Pact are only recent examples in a long string of agreements that see nations trade some element of freedom of action in return for assurances that they will not be left alone in time of need. In this century, agreements have been extended from the military to other spheres, including trade (e.g., Canada-U.S. Free Trade Agreement; General Agreement on Tariffs and Trade), fisheries management, and the environment. Bilateral and multilateral agreements in the environmental area have existed for some time, although their number has proliferated in the last two decades. The 1909 Boundary Waters Treaty between the U.S. and Canada is an early example, followed by such undertakings as the Migratory Birds Convention, signed by the two nations in 1917, the international convention on whaling of the 1940s, and the Nordic Convention of the 1960s that provides for common action by the Scandinavian countries to protect their shared environment. Since the Stockholm Conference, nations have signed the Convention on the Protection of the World Cultural and Natural Heritage (1972); the Convention on the Prevention of Marine Pollution by Dumping of Wastes and Other Matter (1972); the Convention on International Trade in Endangered Species of World Fauna and Flora (1973); the Economic Commission for Europe Convention on Long-Range Transboundary Air Pollution (1979); and the Global Convention on the Control of Transboundary Movements of Hazardous Wastes (1989).

The development of agreements for collective action usually consists of several stages. First, as in the case of domestic pollution, is identification of the problem by the scientific community, followed by alerting others: other scientists through the learned journals, then the public and elected representatives through the popular press. By the time the magnitude of the problem and some potential steps for addressing it have become clear, the process enters the next phase – negotiation of a plan for collective action. This may extend over several years and, since it ultimately depends on the willingness of governments to act, must be accompanied by political pressure within each nation, urging governments to reach some form of agreement. Usually, agreement is first reached only on the preliminaries – the means of co-ordinating research and sharing information. Negotiation then continues, spurred on by additional data that generate additional publicity for the problem, and culminates in agreement on emission reductions and time frames. Such an agreement is signed by the diplomatic representatives of the nations involved but must then be ratified by the governing body of each nation. Domestic laws then have to be drafted to reach the reduction limit for the particular nation stipulated by the agreement. In a federated state such as Canada, in which the laws involved will almost certainly be provincial as well as federal, this process requires another set of negotiations. In practice, these intranational discussions will have been instituted well before the international agreement was signed – no nation will commit itself to a plan of international action in the absence of at least some assurance of agreement on the part of its sub-federal partners. Such federal-provincial negotiations may be almost as complex and time-consuming as the original international negotiations. The final stage in the process is implementation of the domestic laws, which raises all of the difficulties, discussed in Part III, inherent in enforcement of environmental legislation.

International Institutions

While the formal instrument for international collective action is the agreement, the engines that drive the process, in terms of both coaxing and coercing governments to sign the agreement in the first place and then monitoring to ensure they live up to its terms, are international institutions. Such institutions are made up of members from many different nations and therefore have at least some degree of autonomy and are not the instrument of any one state. Examples include the United Nations and its agencies, such as the United Nations Environment Program and the World Meteorological Organization; multinational business corporations doing business in, and therefore subject to the laws of, many nations; professional organizations in each of the various sciences, which provide a means for both transmitting information on new discoveries throughout the world and bringing together its members for regular face-to-face discussion; and international environmental pressure groups, such as Greenpeace and Friends of the Earth, which can work in a co-ordinated way to bring simultaneous pressure on governments in different parts of the world. As well as such formal networks for co-ordinated sharing of information and discussion of collective action there are other, perhaps just as important, informal networks, including the thousands of annual conferences that attract international audiences for discussion of common problems.

International organizations, other than religious bodies, are quite new, dating only from the nineteenth century. Such organizations devoted to international environmental protection, like their domestic counterparts, are even newer. The seminal event was the establishment, in 1945, of the United Nations, which then led to creation of new organizations in a large number of spheres, including the environmental. In 1948 the International Union for the Conservation of Nature and Natural Resources (IUCN) was established, with a mandate for collaborative scientific research. This led to the founding in 1961 of the World Wildlife Fund. The WWF and the IUCN, working with the United Nations Environment Program (UNEP), in 1980 developed the World Conservation Strategy, a set of principles to be used by nations of the world in developing plans for resource conservation. The United Nations Environment Program, with administrative headquarters in Nairobi, Kenya, was the major outcome of the 1972 Stockholm Conference.

In addition to such international organizations established with a specific environmental mandate, others, such as the OECD and the Commonwealth, have begun to add environmental protection to their areas of concern.

The Canadian Internationalist Tradition

The Canadian foreign policy tradition has been shaped by its origins as a colony of Great Britain and its continuing struggle to maintain political and cultural independence from America. Participation in the two world wars brought Canada an opportunity to play a part, however minor, in each of the post-war international configurations – the League of Nations established at Versailles in 1919, and the United Nations and North Atlantic Treaty Organization established after World War Two. Canadian post-war military activity, other than the Korean War, has been largely limited to UN peacekeeping missions, and Canadians have come to see themselves as peacekeepers and honest brokers in the community of nations, heirs to the "linchpin" theory that saw Canada in the early years of the century playing, in her own eyes if nobody else's, a critical role of mediation between Great Britain and America.

Canada has always been aware of events in the outside world, simply because external events have such an influence on our own affairs, given our status as a colonial and quasi-colonial country. Although the tone may be excessively self-laudatory, the following passage from a Canadian Institute of International Affairs publication accurately sums up Canada's ongoing involvement with foreign affairs:

> As an international player, Canada is unusual, if not unique. Few nations rival its membership in international bodies, its commitment to peacekeeping, its generosity in development assistance and its interest in free trade. . . . Its seat on the Security Council places it at the fulcrum of power at the United Nations, and its participation in the North Atlantic Treaty Organization (NATO), the Commonwealth, la francophonie, the International Monetary Fund, the World Bank and as one of the summit seven economic powers confer *locus standi*.[21]

This internationalist tradition has been carried over to the global environmental field during the past twenty years. Canada provided support for the 1972 Stockholm Conference, which was chaired by a Canadian, Maurice Strong. Canada played similar roles in the two major UNEP initiatives of the 1980s, development of the World Conservation Strategy and the work of the World Commission on Environment and Development. As described in Chapter 16, Canada has played an important role, working closely with the Scandinavian nations, New Zealand, and other middle powers on international approaches to the global problems of ozone layer depletion and atmospheric change and is heavily involved with preparations for the 1992 Brazil conference on sustainable development.

It will be argued in Chapter 17 that global environmental protection is very much in the Canadian tradition and offers an opportunity for a realignment of foreign policy objectives, something badly needed as we move from the Cold War into a rapidly changing international order.

CHAPTER 4

What Drives the Issue?

The previous three chapters have examined the polluters, the anti-pollution lobby, and the ground upon which they meet. To complete this introductory overview of current pollution politics, this chapter examines the intellectual and moral arguments that give credence and legitimacy, in the eyes of the Canadian public, to calls for action on pollution. Are they sufficient to carry the day? If not, what others are needed?

Public support for environmental action originates from the three streams of environmental concern that developed in the latter part of the nineteenth century. Conservation and "wise use" of natural resources are still central to the environmentalist argument, although added to traditional concerns such as fishery and forestry depletion are such new issues as the need for energy conservation to prevent global atmospheric change. Appreciation of wilderness and the natural world for its own sake has been maintained in its original form – birdwatching is more popular than ever – and has given rise to new and distinct political drives such as the animal rights movement, deep ecology, and the more spiritualized and personalized aspects of bioregionalism, ecofeminism, and other approaches. A concern for pollution effects on the public health of city-dwellers, now focused more on carcinogenic chemicals than infectious diseases, is still today probably the major source of political support for action on pollution.

To these have been added a new source of support, which only began to appear during the 1970s and 1980s. This is the growing realization, emerging from the politicization of environmental protection in the 1960s, of the way in which environmentalism is inherently linked to a variety of other social issues.

This chapter briefly reviews the current status of each of those sources of support. We then return to the subject in Part V with a more detailed discussion of the values of a new environmental ethic and of an ideology of environmentalism that might foster alliances with other movements.

Resource Conservation

The conservationist approach to environmental protection is based on the logical and powerful argument that we should make less wasteful and more efficient use of natural resources so that they will last longer and provide maximum benefit to humanity. Conservation has always been the mainstay of the political pressure for environmental protection. There is a direct link between Sir Wilfrid Laurier's 1909 Commission on Conservation, the 1961 Resources for Tomorrow Conference, the conserver society of the 1970s, and the late 1980s rhetoric of sustainable development.

Resource conservation has been the argument advanced in favour of action on soil erosion, soft-drink bottle recycling, energy efficiency, land-use policies to protect agricultural land from development, and many other issues. In a sense it directly underlies the pollution debate since clean air and water are often envisaged as "resources" that must be protected.

As noted, adherents of deep ecology argue that there are limits to the political effectiveness of the conservationist approach and that these limits ultimately constrain its potential power. They argue that because the approach is based on logic and rational discussion, it leads inevitably to "cost-benefit" analysis, a weighing of the costs of environmental protection against the benefits it brings. Costs are measured primarily in dollars and the major criteria applied are human costs and benefits – effects on other species, although taken into account, are given less weight. The argument made against this approach is not only that the inherent value of the natural world is discounted but that, for the environmentalist, it is a fool's game because the benefits, whether the aesthetics of a spruce bog or even a reduced cancer rate, are almost impossible to quantify, while the costs can easily be identified and added up. When a specific dollar cost is compared to a vague and unsubstantiated benefit, the environmental case almost always loses.

Further, because the political appeal is based on logic instead of emotion, it can never generate widespread political support – no political movement has ever been able to call on its supporters for the sacrifice and effort needed by appealing only to the intellect. At the same time, the conservation argument cannot be ignored. As environmental concerns increasingly come to compete with other issues for public and private spending, the environmental lobby must be able to present its case in the language of the realm – dollars and cents and human self-interest.

Human Health Concerns
Perception of Risk

An argument often advanced by one voice in the environmental dialogue is that the actual danger to the health of the average citizen posed by such things as PCBs or dioxins is much less than that of driving cars, smoking cigarettes, or jogging on some city streets after sunset. Since the public accepts those risks, although working to reduce them, and is not lobbying for a complete ban on those activities, the argument is made that the public should also be willing to accept the much lesser dangers of toxic chemical pollution in exchange for the benefits of modern industrialization.[1] But time and again individual citizens, regardless of the fact that just moments ago they stepped outside for a smoke, will rise in a public forum to state their opposition to *any* risk posed by chemical pollution. How can we explain this apparent double standard?

The environmentalist response to the argument that some level of risk should be accepted is that the risk level is simply too high to be tolerated. The dangers to health posed by the chemicals and wastes released by the millions of tonnes to the environment each year are very real, and because of such factors as the latency period associated with their health effects we are only now realizing the true extent of the risk to which we continue to expose ourselves. We simply do not know whether, in the long run, the annual generation of millions of tonnes of toxic substances will prove to have been more dangerous than, for instance, driving automobiles.

A more important aspect of the debate, however, is the fact that the *actuality* of the risk is less important, in terms of the political strength of pollution-related health fears, than is the public *perception* of that risk. The public perception of danger from environmental pollution is influenced by three things: the current state of knowledge of the toxicologists and other authorities dealing with the issue; the manner in which their statements are filtered through the various learned and popular media; and the credibility those authorities, or other sources of information, have in the eyes of the public.

During the past twenty years, the body of knowledge on health effects associated with various toxic substances, ranging from asbestos to cigarette smoke to PCBs, has increased substantially. Many substances are seen as dangerous today that until recently were thought to be benign. In addition, the technological ability to detect substances at low concentrations has increased substantially in recent years. Although there may be no indication that a particular substance poses a health threat at very low concentrations, such as one part per billion or quadrillion, the simple fact of its detection is seen as a cause for alarm. Thus, public health concerns are fuelled by the ever-increasing quantity of available data.

Another parallel and reinforcing trend is the fact that the dangers of pollution are news now in a way that twenty years ago they were not. Because public attention is focused on the issue, a newly released report on health effects associated with such problems as air and water pollution, no matter how speculative or preliminary the analysis, will receive far more media attention than in the past. New information or theories travel from the scientific to the popular media far more quickly than ever before.

Finally, for a variety of reasons, it seems that the credibility of scientific and other authorities is less today than in the past. This may be because these same authorities, when the new chemical and nuclear technologies were introduced in the middle part of the century, took pains to assure the public of their safety. Events such as the accident in the Three Mile Island nuclear plant in Pennsylvania, the escape of toxic gas at the pesticide plant in Bhopal, India, and the PCB fire at St.-Basil-Le-Grande, Quebec, have served to undermine the credibility of those statements. These events, with their powerful visual images of disaster and havoc, reinforce public suspicion and mistrust of claims for safety.

Thus, regardless of whether the risk to health posed by environmental pollution is greater or less than it was twenty years ago, the *perception* of risk has undoubtedly increased.

Acceptance of Risk

The political strength of health concerns is further compounded by changing public attitudes toward the extent of risk deemed acceptable. Public willingness to accept risk, from whatever source, is declining rapidly. Although people still accept the inherent risk of travel by car or airplane, they are fast approaching the point, in the case of chemical contamination, of accepting nothing less than the complete absence of risk.

Formal risk assessment and standard-setting procedures are premised on the notion that all parties involved can agree on an "acceptable" level of risk – usually expressed in terms of the number of anticipated additional deaths from cancer that will be caused by exposure to a particular toxic substance in the predicted dosages and time frames. But in the informal arena of public opinion this premise is absurd. Why should the public, or any one individual, accept *any* risk due to the introduction of a substance to their environment from which they will receive no immediate or tangible benefit?

It seems that the willingness to accept risk is in inverse relationship to the extent of risk present. As we continually strive to make our world a safer place our expectations of safety increase, perhaps faster than our ability to fulfil those expectations, and what used to be a fatalistic acceptance of the ever-present fact of death from illness or accident has been replaced by a demand, given tangible expression through liability litigation, that the authorities keep us safe from harm. Thus, the political support given to the environmental movement by public health concerns is likely to increase in future, even if the actual risk lessens.

Connections to Progressive Politics
Environmentalism and the Left-Right Spectrum

Since the 1960s the environmental movement in Canada has drawn at least some portion of its strength from the fact that wilderness preservation and pollution reduction are seen, by some at least, as left-wing issues that those politically active in other left movements will automatically support, even if they have no particular interest in the environmental issue at hand. The sword cuts both ways, of course. From the 1960s to the present day, environmentalism has been tagged by its enemies with all the pejoratives – subversive, woolly-minded, and impracticable – laid at the door of socialism and the left.

It will be argued in Part V that environmentalism can only achieve its potential political strength through explicit development of the underlying values and ideology that will allow it to build on the support it receives from the left connection and to give new sustenance to the basic left-wing objectives of redistribution of wealth and power. The discussion here, however, is limited to (1) an examination of the position of environmentalism on the traditional left-right spectrum and (2) a review of the successes and failures the movement has had to date in making strategic alliances with other progressive movements.

A majority of those in the Canadian environmental movement, if asked, would likely place themselves left of centre on the political spectrum.[2] This does not mean, however, that the values and objectives of the movement can automatically be so categorized, since environmentalism encompasses a number of perceptions and values traditionally associated with a conservative viewpoint. For instance, the "small is beautiful" mistrust of large administrative structures, whether government or private, is a view from the conservative end of the spectrum. In the same way, the environmentalist call for a return to more traditional ways of relating to the natural world, drawing its inspiration from a remembered, pre-technology pastoralism and looking to such sources as the Romance poets, is not very different from the Golden Age argument of the right wing when it calls for a reestablishment of the moral values that held sway in a rose-coloured, small-town past.

Thus environmentalism has affinities with some conservative positions and is in opposition on others – attitudes toward military spending, corporate concentration and power, and economic growth being only a few. In the same way environmentalism, while instinctively allied to leftist thought through common opposition to corporate and government power, also finds itself in opposition to a number of traditional socialist positions. These differences stem largely from the fact that socialism, as it evolved from its nineteenth-century origins, fully accepted the notions of industrialization and economic expansion. The quarrel between socialism and capitalism has always been over distribution of the financial benefits of such activity, not the activity itself. Environmentalism, on the other hand, maintains that industrialization *itself* is a major part of the problem.[3]

This antagonism has been expressed, in Canadian politics, in opposition by some members of labour and the NDP to a number of environmental positions, primarily concerned with forestry but also with such issues as pulp mill pollution. In these instances, environmentalism is seen to be threatening jobs.

The Green slogan "Neither Right nor Left, but in front!" is intended to convey the message that environmentalism is not only stronger than the traditional camps of socialism or conservatism but is also somehow *different*, not easily placed on the traditional right-left ideological spectrum. Robert Paehlke agrees, saying "environmentalism is inherently neither left nor right. Some of its dimensions fall on the left side of the spectrum, others seem more conservative. Some noted environmentalists identify with the political left; others are just as clearly more comfortable with the right."[4] Paehlke goes on to argue that the traditional ideological spectrum of left and right must be redrawn, as follows:[5]

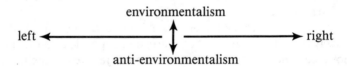

Paehlke proposes that environmentalism must eventually establish itself as an ideology in its own right, separate from the traditional ideologies of conservatism, liberalism, and socialism. Roderick Nash, on the other hand, argues that the extension of ethical regard and inherent value from the human to the non-human world is nothing more than a logical extension of classical liberalism. Thus Nash places environmentalism on the traditional spectrum, suggesting only that one end of the spectrum has been extended to the left. This allows Nash, an American author, to portray environmentalism as a direct heir to the glorious traditions of the Revolution and the fight against slavery.

But he does not deal with some of the arguments that might be made against a classification of environmentalism as nothing more than the next stage in the evolution of liberalism. There are two such arguments. First, liberalism takes as its greatest good the freedom of the individual to reach his or her full potential. In contrast, the ecology movement has always been concerned not with the individual so much as the collective. Second, liberalism, like socialism and conservatism, fully accepts the goal of economic expansion achieved by means of technological development, which allows increased per capita resource consumption. This commitment to high living standards and to economic "progress" as inherently good would have to undergo a substantial modification of goals and assumptions before it could continue its triumphant march, this time behind the banner of environment. Environmentalism cannot be classified as simply the latest manifestation of liberalism.

Two aspects of environmentalism suggest it is more likely to find its home, in terms of both ideology and day-to-day politics, on the left than either on the right or on a new north-south axis. These are (1) the establishment of environmental assessment, based on public hearings before an independent tribunal, as a component of decision-making and (2) the recognition by all parties that global environmental protection can only be achieved through a transfer of wealth from the industrialized to the developing world. Both of these aspects of environmental politics directly reinforce traditional left-wing concerns for increased access to decision-making and a redistribution of wealth.

As discussed in Part III, the concept of environmental assessment encompasses far more than a review of potential impacts of a proposed road or dam on the immediate environment. Increased application of environmental assessment to both government and corporate decision-making is a primary objective of the environmental movement in Canada, but it is also a new and powerful expression of a traditional progressive objective – increased public access to decision-making. In the same manner, a change in the distribution of wealth, which of course lies at the very heart of traditional distributive politics, today finds its most powerful expression in the issue of global environmental protection. The threat to the global rain forests, the loss of agricultural lands to spreading deserts, and the problem of atmospheric change have brought about agreement, at least on the level of rhetoric if not action, on the need to slow the rate of global growth to make it "sustainable" and to transfer wealth from the developed to the developing nations to assist them in paying the cost of environmental protection. As environmental pressures increasingly place constraints on domestic economic expansion, political pressure for redistribution of wealth within Canada, which is now almost completely dormant, will be given new impetus by environmentalism, simply because the safety valve of a continually expanding economy will no longer be as readily available.

Progressive Alliances

Undoubtedly environmentalism has received some of its political support in Canada (as well as engendering some of its opposition) from the fact that it has been seen as part of the progressive agenda. The instances in which those links have been made explicit, however, and political alliances made based on those links, have been few.

The Canadian labour movement has struggled with its environmental position over the years, caught between its desire to enter into alliance against the common enemy and the hard fact that, in at least some instances, environmental protection will result in job losses. The Canadian Labour Congress sponsored a conference in 1978 on the issue of jobs and the environment and a similar event was held in 1986 by the Ontario Environment Network.[6] The OEN was specifically looking for ways to fight "job blackmail," whereby corporate interests, particularly in single-industry towns, have successfully managed to make political alliances with labour in their fights against increased environmental regulation. As discussed below, although movement has been made in redefining the problem as something more than a black or white choice between jobs or the environment, much more needs to be done.

Environmentalists and native peoples, as noted earlier, have fought as allies in a number of battles, but they have also found themselves in opposition on other issues. Feminism and environmentalism have explored their theoretical connections, in various writings and conferences, but have seldom joined forces in specific political battles. In the same manner environmentalism and the peace movement have much in common on a theoretical basis. Both share an opposition to nuclear power, regardless of its use as a weapon or an energy source, and both are very much aware that global spending on arms and defence gobbles up time, money, and energy that could be spent on bettering the lot of the global population and saving the planet. The European green parties have successfully linked feminism, peace, and environment in political campaigns, but despite the efforts of their Canadian counterparts, no such linkages have yet been accomplished in this country to produce real political strength.

The three most successful examples of broad-ranging alliances in Canadian political battles, all discussed at length in the pages that follow, are the Canadian Coalition on Acid Rain, which brought together environmentalists, business people who own cottages in Muskoka, and the tourist industry; the west coast alliance against pulp mill pollution, co-ordinated by the West Coast Environmental Law Association (WCELA), which combines environmental, native, and labour interests; and the environmentalists (not all – some organizations, such as Pollution Probe, were conspicuous by their absence) who joined with labour, the cultural community, and a variety of social-justice interests in the Pro-Canada Network to work against the 1988 free trade deal.

The Emerging Environmental Ethic

The Judeo-Christian view of human beings as the last and crowning achievement of a god who created all the other creatures in order that humanity may have dominion over them is central to the Western understanding of the world and, as such, has been accepted without question throughout Canadian history. Modern environmentalism offers a direct challenge to this perception, but it is a challenge only made possible by the gradual changes over the past few centuries in the Western view of ourselves and our place in the universe. There are two reasons for this change. The first is a new perception, provided by science, of the space and time around us. The second is an initial, tentative extension of the ethical regard humans accord one another to the non-human world.

New Perceptions of Time, Space, and Matter

During the past three centuries three changes in scientific knowledge have weakened the anthropocentric view of humanity as the species at the apex of Creation. These are increased awareness of the magnitude of time and space, establishment of the theory of evolution, and the discovery, coming from such disciplines as physics and biology, of the interdependence of all parts of the animate and inanimate world.

Kepler's discovery in the early 1600s that the earth was not at the centre of the universe but instead revolved around the sun was followed in the eighteenth and nineteenth centuries by an understanding for the first time of the vast distances that separate our star from even its closest neighbours. This was followed, in this century, by the realization that our Milky Way galaxy did not comprise the entire universe – a theory confirmed by physical observation in the 1920s when Edward Hubbell used the new 100-inch Mount Palomar telescope to resolve individual stars in what until then had been, even in the best instruments, the smokey-gray haze of our neighbour, the Andromeda galaxy, 2.2 million light years away. We now know that ours is only one among countless galaxies in a universe that has been inexorably expanding for some fifteen or twenty billion years.

This tremendous increase in the perceived size of the universe has been accompanied by a similar expansion of our time-horizons. The great scientific achievement of the past century, the theory of evolution, was only made possible by the discoveries of nineteenth-century geologists that the planet had been in existence for much more than the 4,000-odd years allowed for by the Bible. We now view our planet's past as encompassing more than four billion years, during which time continents have moved, mountain chains have repeatedly been thrust up and worn down, and countless species have emerged, evolved, and disappeared forever – all of this on a planet and in a solar system that did not come into existence until some ten or fifteen billion years after the creation of the universe.

The humbling effect of our changed perception of our place in the universe – a species preceded by many before it, on a relatively new planet circling one star among countless many – has been reinforced by the way popular acceptance of Darwinian evolution has confirmed the connections between ourselves and other species, particularly the other primates and the dolphins and whales. Other branches of science have underscored our connections not only to particular species but to *all* elements in the universe. The Heisenberg uncertainty principle, which demonstrated the impossibility of separating the observer from the observed, was a step in that direction, as is the present search of physicists for the Grand Unified Theory, the very name of which suggests integration and connection. Perhaps the most vivid awareness of this interconnectedness comes from the discovery that all of the chemical elements constituting our planet were created long before the solar system condensed and formed from masses of swirling gases. The knowledge that every element in the earth, the biosphere, and the bodies of every one of us was forged in the blast of a supernova explosion, millions or billions of years before our planet came into existence, connects us to realities that stretch across vast reaches of time and space.

Extension of Ethical Regard to the Non-Human World

With this change in our perception of humanity's importance in the scheme of things has come an increased appreciation of the inherent value of the natural world. Roderick Nash, in *The Rights of Nature: A History of Environmental Ethics*, suggests that human history has been characterized by a steady broadening of the group to which the individual is willing to ascribe some form of ethical rights, what he calls membership in the "moral community." Nash argues that in pre-historic times the boundaries of this community were expanded from the individual to the family and from there to the tribe and beyond to other larger groupings based on geography, language, and race. During the past century, according to Nash, there have been two significant advances in this process. The first was a broadening of the classes of human beings deemed to possess inalienable rights, for instance, by abolishing slavery in the past century, by granting the vote to women, and by the other advances in minority rights. The second advance, Nash argues, has been the extension of the moral community to include at least some elements of the non-human world.[7]

This process of extending ethical rights from the human to the non-human world has in this century followed two very different paths. One is the emergence of the values of the ecology movement, the other the animal rights movement. Expressed by Aldo Leopold's concept of the "land ethic," the ecology movement is based on the conviction that species or collections of species within a given ecosystem have some still undefined right to remain undisturbed by human activities. The animal rights movement, on the other hand, is concerned with the *individual* animal – usually a farm animal or one used in scientific experimentation and not one living in the wild – and the ethical duty humans have to avoid causing it undue pain and suffering.

The animal rights movement had its origins in England in 1824 with the creation of the Royal Society for the Prevention of Cruelty to Animals. This was followed by the establishment of comparable organizations in the United States and Canada and the adoption of legislation throughout the English-speaking world that accorded domestic animals some degree of ethical rights by making certain abuses illegal. During the past few decades the movement has not attracted the same political attention and support as environmentalism, but it has become strongly established nevertheless. The philosophical basis for animal rights is presented in Peter Singer's *Animal Liberation* (1975) and Tom Regan's *The Case for Animal Rights* (1983).

The major issues of concern to the animal rights movement in Canada during the past twenty years have been the Atlantic coast seal hunt, trapping, the use of animals in research labs, and the well-being of livestock. Those campaigning against the Newfoundland seal hunt included both animal rights organizations, such as the International Fund for Animal Welfare, the Animal Fund, and the Animal Protection Institute, and environmental organizations, such as Greenpeace and Paul Watson's Sea Shepherd. The original rationale for Greenpeace's involvement was that the harp seal was an endangered species. By 1978, however, it was clear that quotas on the seal hunt imposed in 1971 had resulted in an expansion of the seal population. Greenpeace continued its campaign, however, centring it not on an ecological concern for the species as a whole but on an animal rights concern for the pain and death suffered by the individual seal.[8] Similarly, Greenpeace in England worked with the Royal Society for the Prevention of Cruelty to Animals to organize an advertising campaign intended to convince consumers not to buy fur. In 1985, in response to protests from Canadian native peoples, it withdrew from the campaign.

The animal rights movement in Canada is riven with internal political differences and its organizational structure is still heavily influenced by its origins, approximately a hundred years ago, in the establishment of humane societies in most of the major Canadian cities. There are approximately 300 animal protection groups operating in Canada, with primary strength in Ontario, British Columbia, and Quebec. Although established in the other Atlantic provinces, no groups operate, not surprisingly, in Newfoundland.

Like the environmental movement, there are both Canadian branches of international organizations – most notably the International Wildlife Coalition and the World Society for Protection of Animals – and domestic organizations. The latter include the Canadian Federation of Humane Societies, Lifeforce in Vancouver, the Animal Defence League in Ottawa, and the Animal Alliance of Canada in Toronto. Although precise information is not available, financial support from public donations is much less than that which Canadians provide to the environmental movement.[9]

Since the early 1980s the most radical arm of the animal rights movement has been the Animal Liberation Front, which undertakes direct action campaigns by breaking into research labs, taking the animals, and filming the methods used to contain and care for them. Such films, by exposing the suffering to which animals used for scientific research are necessarily exposed, have generated publicity and support for their cause.[10]

Some of the groups are now explicitly making the connections between animal protection and environmentalism. Animal Alliance, for instance, in its promotional material makes the connection this way: "Animals are used in every conceivable manner – the overt cruelty. And as people continue to pollute the world and destroy the environment, the animals die – the hidden cruelty."[11] Interestingly enough, their opponents make the same connection between their activities and environmental protection. The fur industry presents fur-trapping as an environmentally friendly activity, drawing on a renewable, non-polluting resource in a sustainable manner.[12]

One obvious area in which the concerns of environmentalists and animal protectionists overlap is the captivity of wild animals in zoos and ocean aquaria. An example is the attempt in 1990 by the animal rights group Lifeforce to prevent the capture of three Beluga whales in the Churchill River by crews working for the Vancouver Aquarium.[13]

Despite such examples of congruence of interest, environmentalism and the animal rights movement have very different backgrounds and operate in almost total isolation from one another. Greenpeace is almost the only organization in Canada to have worked in both camps. There are two major differences between them. The first is the point at which they draw the line marking the extension of ethical rights from the human to the non-human. Singer and his colleagues, whose ethical criteria are centred on the pain suffered by the individual animal, extend the line to sentient beings, capable of experiencing pain, but no farther. Environmentalism, on the other hand, extends the line to include not only animals but also rocks, trees, rivers, and entire ecosystems, a notion that strikes the animal protectionist as absurd. The other difference between the two camps is the concern of the animal protectionist for the individual animal, in contrast to the concern of the environmentalist for the collective – the species or the ecosystem. To the environmentalist, the infliction of pain and death, for instance, the predator catching and eating its prey, is a part of the normal order of things and does not violate any ethical norms. For the animal rights movement, on the other hand, the infliction of pain is the major evil to be fought against.

One environmentalist, Mark Safaft, has suggested that if the suffering of the individual animal is the only criterion of concern, then precisely that predator-prey relationship, and not domestic or lab animals, should be the primary focus of animal rights activities: "Environmentalists cannot be animal liberationists. Animal liberationists cannot be environmentalists. The environmentalists would sacrifice the lives of individual creatures to preserve the authenticity, integrity and complexity of ecological systems. The liberationist – if the reduction of animal misery is taken seriously as a goal – must be willing, in principle, to sacrifice the authenticity, integrity and complexity of ecosystems to protect the rights, or guard the lives, of animals."[14] Pursuing this argument to a *reductio ad absurdum*, Safaft proposes that the liberationists, in theory, should seek to domesticate wilderness, putting animals into cages and caring for them to achieve the goal of protection of each individual from the pain inherent in the natural world.

While it is true that the two movements have different starting points and objectives, they do share a concern for non-human species – Greenpeace campaigns to save dolphins from death at the hands of tuna fishermen; animal liberationists campaign to release them from the captivity of amusement parks – that may at some future date provide a basis for co-ordinated political action. The differences dividing them are no broader than those separating environmentalism from either labour or native peoples, two other movements environmentalists in the past have both worked with and been in conflict with.

Environmentalism expands Nash's moral community to its farthest extreme when it moves beyond animals to include trees, rivers, rocks, and stars. The first major step taken by the environmental movement in this direction was publication in 1972 of Christopher Stone's "Should Trees Have Standing?" in the *Southern California Law Review*. Written in connection with a lawsuit the Sierra Club had brought to protect a valley in the California Sierras from development as a ski resort, Stone's article argued that the American legal system should "give legal rights to forests, oceans, rivers . . . indeed, to the natural environment as a whole."[15] The Sierra Club had lost the first round of litigation through a court ruling that it had no standing in court, that is, no legal right to take action to protect the valley. Stone thereupon argued that the valley itself should have that right, a right that would be exercised on its behalf by its human defenders, just as the rights of children or the mentally deficient are represented by others who act for them in the legal system.

The Law Reform Commission of Canada, discussing the issue of environmental rights as a basis for Criminal Code action on pollution, necessarily dealt with the same subject, since it had to decide whether such rights were *human* rights (the right of an individual to live in a clean environment that did not pose a threat to the individual's health) or the rights *of the environment itself* (the right of a fish, or a river, or a mountain to live in a clean environment that does not pose a threat to its well-being). Although ultimately opting only for a human right to a clean environment, the Commission acknowledged the argument for extending ethical and legal rights to the non-human world.

> Some environmentalists also argue that, pushed to its logical conclusion, a policy of environmental protection based only on *human* goals and rights could progressively weaken claims for the protection of endangered aspects of the environment, the pollution or destruction of which would not constitute economic or aesthetic loss, or danger to human health. Some fear that as our capacity increases to supply by artificial means those human needs and desires now supplied by the natural environment, the checklist of those forms of life and inanimate entities in nature which we deem worthy of protecting would progressively shrink.[16]

Thus we see that during the past few decades recognition of the inherent value of nature has been expressed in a number of different forms. Ultimately it rests on awareness of the way in which each of us is part of the larger whole, connected not only to the other animals but to the physical elements of the planet as well. One of the most eloquent statements of this, which is often included in deep ecology writings, is Robinson Jeffers's "Oh, Lovely Rock" (1938). It is worth reproducing in full.

> We stayed the night in the pathless gorge of Ventana
>   Creek, up the east fork.
> The rock walls and the mountain ridges hung forest
>   on forest above our heads, maple and redwood,
> Laurel, oak, madrone, up to the high and slender
>   Santa Lucian firs that stare up the cataracts
> Of slide-rock to the star-color precipices.
> We lay on gravel and kept a little campfire for warmth.
> Past midnight only two or three coals glowed red in
>   the cooling darkness; I laid a clutch of dead bay leaves
> On the ember ends and felted dry sticks across them
>   and lay down again. The revived flame
> Lighted my sleeping son's face and his companion's, and the vertical
>   face of the great gorge-wall

Across the stream. Light leaves overhead danced in the fire's breath,
    tree-trunks were seen; it was the rock wall
That fascinated my eyes and mind. Nothing strange: light gray
    diorite with two or three slanting seams in it,
Smooth-polished by the endless attrition of slides and
    floods; no fern or lichen, pure naked rock . . . as
    if I were
Seeing rock for the first time. As if I were seeing
    through the flame-lit surface into the real and bodily
And living rock. Nothing strange . . . I cannot
Tell you how strange: the silent passion, the deep
    nobility and childlike loveliness: this fate going on
Outside our fates. It is here in the mountain like a
    grave smiling child. I shall die and my boys
Will live and die, our world will go on through its
    rapid agonies of change and discovery, this age will die,
And wolves have howled in the snow around a new
    Bethlehem: this rock will be here, grave, earnest,
    not passive: the energies
That are its atoms will still be bearing the whole
    mountain above: and I, many packed centuries ago
Felt its intense reality with love and wonder, this
    lonely rock.[17]

PART II

The Evolution of Pollution Politics in Canada

Does the environmental movement have the power to achieve its potential? The answer depends on whether today's environmentalism is solidly rooted in Canadian political traditions, growing naturally from our understanding of ourselves and our relationship to the land we live in, or is, instead, a recent import, given prominence by the health fads and other fashions of the past decade. If environmentalism can never move beyond the fringes of political life, without staying power when it competes for public spending with more traditional Canadian political concerns, its long-term impact on the Canadian polity will be slight. If it does achieve significant power, however, the radicalism inherent in the movement guarantees that its impact will be large.

The purpose of Part II is to review the evolution of the politics of pollution in Canada and thereby afford a better understanding of the forces that first politicized and then moved the issue to the centre of our political life.

CHAPTER 5

Origins of the
Environmental Movement

Resource Conservation and Management

Brian Woodrow, writing in 1980, made very clear the relative influence in
Canada of the conservation and preservation movements:

> "Wise use" conservationists, who were primarily interested in pro-
> moting the efficient utilization of natural resources and the environ-
> ment, tended to emphasize new resource management principles like
> sustained-yield forestry or extensive resource development activities,
> which were not fundamentally incompatible with good business prac-
> tices and soon came to be accepted by government and industry alike.
> The smaller group of "preservationists" who were more concerned
> about protecting natural resources and the environment from exploi-
> tation and retaining them in a relatively untouched state, could not be
> so easily accommodated and consequently continued over the years
> to be little more than voices crying in the wilderness.[1]

Resource management in Canada has been undertaken by governments
in five major areas: geological surveys, to provide the information needed
for mining and fossil fuel extraction; water management, through damming and diverting rivers for lumber movement and hydroelectrical power,
plus, in the urban context, use of water for sewage and waste disposal and
provision of safe drinking water; forest management; agricultural soil conservation; and fish and game management.

One early step in resource management was the creation of federal and provincial parks, such as Banff in 1887 and Algonquin Park in 1893. These and other parks were created for purely utilitarian reasons – to promote the tourist industry, to provide for the protection of headwaters of major rivers, and to protect forestry resources. Janet Foster, in *Working for Wildlife*, has described the 1887 adoption of the Rocky Mountains Park Act in the following terms:

> creation of a wildlife reserve in the Rocky Mountains was not the intention of John A. Macdonald's government. Parks were to be "commercial assets," sources of revenue to a government foundering in economic depression and burdened by debt from building the Canadian Pacific Railway. From the outset, the parks' chief function was to popularize and help promote the CPR; the railway, in return, was to bring in a steady stream of passengers with their tourist dollars. . . . far from the park being preserved in a "virgin state", the working of mines and development of mining interests within the park were allowed to continue, as was the pasturing of cattle and leasing of hay lands. Even timbering was not ruled out under the park regulations.[2]

The Canadian Geological Survey had been established more than a decade earlier, in 1873, and in 1892 Ontario, responding to fears that the resource was being depleted too quickly, established a Royal Commission on Fish and Game.

By the turn of the century a number of Canadian governments had established departments responsible for protecting the forest resource, both through establishment of fire-fighting measures and in the first steps to regulate the lumber industry. The Canadian Forestry Association was established in 1900 with a membership of 8,000.[3] Schools of forestry, to teach the new forms of management, were established at the University of Toronto in 1907 and University of New Brunswick in 1909. Water management was also actively being addressed by governments of the day through such bodies as the IJC.

In 1909 the government of Sir Wilfrid Laurier, following the lead of U.S. President Teddy Roosevelt, an ardent conservationist, created the Conservation Commission, a body with both federal and provincial representation and chaired by Clifford Sifton, a former Minister of the Interior. During the next eight years the Commission undertook a series of studies in such areas as forestry, lands, fish and wildlife, water, minerals, and public health. Sifton resigned in November, 1918, and the Commission was dissolved two years later, probably because of opposition from established departments such as the Department of the Interior, whose turf it was treading on.[4] Another major conservation initiative was taken in 1917 with the signing by Canada and the United States of the Migratory Birds Convention, which was intended to limit kills of birds that summered in Canada and wintered south of the border.

During the interwar period federal and provincial departments continued to work in such areas as forestry, soil, water, and wildlife management. The August, 1945, Dominion-Provincial Conference on Reconstruction provided the venue for, among other things, the most comprehensive discussion of resource management since the demise of the Sifton Commission.[5] Ontario passed the Conservation Authorities Act in 1946, which encouraged municipalities within a particular watershed to create an administrative agency that would work toward conservation of the resource. This was simply the latest in a series of steps taken by the provinces, particularly those in the West, to conserve and manage water. In 1960 the federal and provincial resource departments jointly staged the Resources for Tomorrow Conference. As was explained in a background paper for the Conference, the motivation was purely anthropocentric and bore no relation to what the author referred to as the "emotional" and "sentimental" approach of the "preservationists": "The growing interest in resource development in Canada is attributable to many factors not the least of which is the need to meet increasing competition throughout the world. How well we meet this competition depends in no small measure on how well we manage our resources."[6]

Conservation and resource management remain central and powerful political issues to the present day, whether the subject is oil-drilling in the Beaufort Sea or the Hibernia field off Newfoundland, lumbering in British Columbia, or the economic return from the west and east coast fisheries. The major conservation concern of the environmental movement is the need for increased energy efficiency and reduction in fossil fuel consumption because of the contribution of carbon dioxide emissions to changes in the global atmosphere.

The ongoing political dialogue surrounding any of these issues is today influenced by a number of voices, including native peoples and environmental organizations, not directly connected with either government or industry. This was not the case, however, during the first half of the century. During that time, the dialogue was conducted exclusively by the professional resource managers, trained in universities in Canada or abroad and then taking up their positions in the public or private sectors. During the course of this century the conservation issue has received much of its political strength from the support given by the professional resource management sector. Since their professional standing and self-esteem are determined by the prominence given to the issue, they formed an articulate and powerful constituency for promotion of resource management on the political agenda.[7]

Nature Appreciation and Wilderness Preservation

Roderick Nash, in *Wilderness and the American Mind*, has outlined the way North American and European cultures over the past few centuries have developed two equally strong and yet contradictory views of wilderness. The first is a perception of wilderness as a benign place of shelter, a refuge from the fast-paced stress and clamour of urban life that allows the wilderness traveller to move into closer contact with the self and the wonders of the universe – a source of the moral and the sublime. The other perception is the dark side – wilderness as a place of fear and loathing, of chaos and disorder, inhabited by fierce and dangerous creatures, whether animal, man, or demon. Until the mid-nineteenth century, the latter view prevailed and it was assumed without question that human destiny was to tame and domesticate wilderness, turning it into farm or city so that it might better serve human needs.

Thus the first Europeans to arrive in North America saw their duty as one of imposing order on chaos – cutting the trees, dividing the land into planted fields and villages, and turning the native inhabitants of the continent into Christian farmers and artisans like themselves.

This view of wilderness first began to change in the late eighteenth and early nineteenth centuries with the writings, in Europe, first of Rousseau and then of the Romance poets, such as Byron, who proclaimed the virtues of the natural and unsullied countryside over the artifice, noise, and dirt of the city. This romantic view, which was a largely urban phenomenon, with its origins, as Nash points out, in the classical salons of Europe and not the log cabins of the frontier, then spread in the mid-1800s to the American cities of the eastern seaboard. The travelogue genre long popular in England and Europe, whereby the gentleman traveller became an amateur ethnologist/biologist/geologist reporting back to civilization and empire his fabulous observations, was given a particularly American twist in numerous books recounting travels through the then unsettled South and West and depicting the beauties and wonders of the American wilderness – wilderness being the one thing America had and Europe did not. Such works, according to Nash, allowed at least some relief from the sense of inferiority that plagued the American psyche at that time.[8]

The next stage in the development of wilderness appreciation in America came with the work of such philosophers as Henry Thoreau and John Muir. As the century advanced and the population expanded west, the benign view of wilderness was increasingly accepted, and the belief that "in Wildness is the preservation of the World" was translated into the political objective of setting aside wilderness areas, not to conserve resources but to add to the spiritual good and national glory of the nation. In America, the wilderness preservation movement achieved its first notable success with the creation of Yellowstone National Park in 1872, and was reflected in the establishment of the Sierra Club in 1892, continuing through to creation of Earth First! in the 1980s.

George Woodcock has provided an example of these contrasting views of nature in nineteenth-century Canada. Woodcock cites an 1842 poem by Standish O'Grady, "The Emigrant," as an example of the earlier view of nature:

> Thou barren waste: unprofitable strand,
> Where hemlocks brood on unproductive land,
> Whose frozen air on one bleak winter's night
> Can metamorphose dark brown hares to white.

This is contrasted with Charles Sangster's "The St. Lawrence and the Saguenay," written in 1856:

> A wilderness of Beauty, stern and rude,
> In undulating swells of wavy green;
> Soft, airy slopes, bold, massive and serene;
> Rich in wild beauty and sublimity, . . .
>
> Is there a soul so dead to Nature's charms
> That thrills not here in this divine retreat?[9]

A movement to preserve wilderness for its own sake did not evolve in Canada during the nineteenth century, however. Although Canada in the latter part of the century was beginning to put in place means of conserving and managing natural resources, these actions were not taken in response to the kind of public pressure being exerted in the United States. The closest analogy in this country to the American political drive for wilderness preservation was the naturalist's appreciation of nature, but even this did not receive significant public support until after the turn of the century.

In the early years of the twentieth century, however, a number of "field naturalist" clubs were established in Canada. This interest in the natural world was stimulated by the nature writings of Ernest Thompson Seton, who in 1898 published *Wild Animals I Have Known*, and Charles G.D. Roberts, who published, among many such works, *The Kindred of the Wild* in 1902. Woodcock suggests that the Canadian enthusiasm for nature writing was an expression of a new regard for the natural world: "both Roberts and Seton go to considerable lengths to emphasize the nobility of their animal heroes. They are shown as reasoning beings within the limitations of their special intelligences, and the writers stress the need to accept them as fellow participants in the scheme of nature."[10]

Canadian interest in the North was stimulated during this period by accounts of Arctic exploration, most notably the books published by Vilhjalmur Stefansson describing his expeditions of 1906-07, 1908-12, and 1913-18.[11] During the 1930s nature writing was given new impetus by the writings of Grey Owl, a displaced Briton who successfully portrayed himself as a native Canadian.

Nature appreciation was stimulated by painting as well as writing when Canadian landscape artists began to interpret the Canadian environment in the late nineteeth century. This received its most powerful impetus around the time of the First World War when Tom Thomson and the members of the Group of Seven began to take their inspiration directly from the tangled disorder of black spruce, swamp, and wind-chopped northern lakes. The paintings of Lawren Harris and others, by the time of the Second World War, had turned Canadian minds to the North, giving them, despite the fact that the majority lived in southern cities like Vancouver, Toronto, and Montreal, a sense of identity with the land of the Canadian Shield.

Identification with the Canadian land was strengthened by the cottage, canoe-tripping, and youth camp experiences that have been a part of so many urban Canadian lives throughout the century. By the 1920s growing numbers of cottagers started making annual migrations to Muskoka, Haliburton, and the Laurentians; many other eastern Canadians continued the tradition, established with the building of the railway, of travelling west to the Rockies and the Pacific during the summer months.

In addition to such factors as these, Woodcock has argued that the changing technology of travel and transmission of information – the transition from canoe to York boat, to Red River wagon, to train and telegraph – made the land accessible and thereby changed attitudes:

> parallel with the opening of the land by transportation systems, with the telescoping of its distance by a series of inventions like the electric telegraph and that innovation associated with Canada, the telephone, there had come about a changing attitude to the environment and the beginning of a process by which fear of the land, a desire to subdue and conquer, was replaced by a mystique of the land, a desire to cherish and to understand what had once seemed entirely impenetrable.[12]

By 1963, with the establishment of the National and Provincial Parks Association, followed a few years later, in Ontario, by creation of the Algonquin Wildlands League, political support for wilderness preservation in Canada had become firmly established. Battles such as Temagami and South Moresby have clearly demonstrated that the preservationist movement is now an established political force in Canada.

Urban Public Health

Pollution as a threat to health is a theme that runs throughout human history, at least since the development of agriculture and a settled existence in villages and towns meant that steps had to be taken to cope with the problem of waste disposal. Evidence of action taken during the past thousand years to reduce the health threats of pollution includes the first rudimentary air pollution legislation, passed in England in the thirteenth century, and subsequent movements, particularly after such plagues as the fourteenth-century Black Death, to provide some form of urban sewage disposal. Concern over pollution by substances other than human and animal wastes was restricted to the health of workers exposed to a variety of toxic wastes and products, although little was understood about the dangers and less done to guard against them.

By the nineteenth century, growing population pressures, coupled with increased scientific and popular knowledge, led to the first modern public health legislation in England, such as the British Public Health Act, enacted in 1875, followed by the Rivers Pollution Act of 1876, intended to guard against sewage pollution; in Canada, the Ontario Public Health Act of 1876 provided for the establishment of local boards of health. In 1882, Ontario's Provincial Health Board was formed to provide guidance and leadership to local boards.

The major health threat associated with pollution at that time was typhoid. European cities had demonstrated convincingly that the death rate could be significantly lowered by the installation of sewage treatment systems. The larger Canadian municipalities had constructed underground sewer systems but the effluent was discharged, untreated, into bodies of water that often were also the source of drinking water. Various means of treatment, prior to discharge, were then available and public debates ensued over expenditure of the relatively large capital amounts required to build treatment plants (harbingers of the debates over pollution control expenditure in which we now find ourselves engaged). A referendum in Toronto in 1908 approved expenditure of $3.1 million for sewers and a sewage treatment plant, and similar expenditures were subsequently approved in other Canadian cities.

Ninety-five municipal sewage systems were operating in Ontario by 1929. These systems served nearly 1.8 million people, and forty-six of the systems included treatment plants. At the same time, health authorities were moving toward chlorination of drinking water to guarantee safety. In 1956 Ontario established the Ontario Water Resources Commission, with a primary mandate to assist municipalities with the capital funding and operation of sewage disposal and water treatment plants. The OWRC also acted as the first pollution regulation agency in the province, paying attention not only to health threats from sewage plant effluent but also, for the first time, to the problem of industrial wastes discharged to water.

During the 1950s health authorities became concerned about another threat to urban health – air pollution. As is usually the case, large-scale events focused attention on the issue. Air pollution in Donora, Pennsylvania, on one occasion, affected the health of 6,000 people, while the London smog of December, 1952, killed 4,000 people.[13] These events prompted the first regulatory actions to control air pollution, primarily in the form of black smoke, first by local boards of health and then, in Ontario in 1967, by the provincial government.

Thus by the 1950s and 1960s, when attention was first drawn to other pollution health threats, such as radioactive fallout and pesticide spraying, awareness of the issue already existed and the first legislative and administrative steps had been taken. The fact that pollution was originally an urban public health issue still has a significant influence on pollution politics today. As an urban issue, jurisdiction originally rested exclusively in the hands of municipal governments. As concern over pollution has moved from immediate, local, and short-term effects to more subtle, longer-term health threats based on regional and global air and water pollution, jurisdictional authority in Canada and all other countries has necessarily moved. However, significant aspects of the regulatory structure in Canada remain at the municipal level, and this has a number of implications for pollution regulation and political decision-making. As well, the division of government authority in the area between waterworks engineers and public health officials has continued. The Canadian Environmental Protection Act, for instance, is jointly administered by Environment Canada and Health and Welfare. Finally, the propensity of some to see pollution as basically an engineering problem, which can be solved without regard to any larger political, social, or economic questions, is an unfortunate legacy of the issue's origins in municipal works departments.

The Science of Ecology

Ecology, that branch of biology concerned not with individual organisms or species but with an understanding of the relationships among organisms and their environment, is one of the few scientific disciplines to have lent its name to a social movement. The term "ecology" was in use as early as 1869, coined apparently by a German biologist, Ernst Haeckel.[14] One of the founding fathers of the discipline was the American scientist George Perkins Marsh, author of *Man and Nature: Physical Geography as Modified by Human Action* (1864). In the first part of the twentieth century, biologists, zoologists, and other scientists became aware of the implications of interconnectedness, with the realization that an organism cannot be understood in isolation from its environment. The phrase "web of life" was introduced by a Scottish biologist, J. Arthur Thompson, in 1914, to describe the mutual dependencies among plants and animals in a given area.[15] During the 1930s the concept of the "food chain" became established – a method of conceptualizing the natural world that reverses the anthropocentric image of nature as a pyramid with the animals at the top ruling and commanding those below. Studies of food chains immediately turned the pyramid upside down, since they demonstrated the complete dependence of the large animals at the end of the chain on all the links, including "the bacteria which sustained the grass which fed the cattle which became steaks."[16]

In 1935 an English scientist coined the term "ecosystem" to describe a given environment, which was coming to be understood primarily in terms of the energy transfers among the organisms it contained. Practitioners of the new branch of biology termed "ecology" did not set out to make value judgements or to apply their new perspective to social and political questions. Questions of values and ethics naturally arose, however, as soon as the scientific perspective shifted from the organism in isolation to its relationship with, and dependency on, other organisms. If plants and animals have worth because they sustain one another and each plays a part in the make-up of the whole, they inevitably become candidates for at least some portion of the ethical regard that humans, until then, had reserved largely for themselves.

The writings most influential in transforming a new scientific discipline into a social movement were those of Aldo Leopold, a 1909 graduate of the Yale School of Forestry. At the beginning of his career, Leopold fully subscribed to the utilitarian conservation perspective then coming into vogue, in which trained professionals like himself would manage natural resources with the sole objective of bettering the lot of humanity. But, as Roderick Nash has pointed out, the study of ecology brought Leopold to include a new ethical concern in his understanding of the natural world. By 1933, when he was appointed professor of wildlife management at the University of Wisconsin, Leopold had "come to believe that 'the complexity of the land organism' was the 'outstanding scientific discovery of the twentieth century.'"[17] That the "land organism" might have some inherent ethical rights was the subject of a paper Leopold wrote that same year in which he examined the relationship between humans and the land by drawing analogies with slavery. Leopold suggested that, just as an expansion of ethical rights to those humans held in slavery had eventually resulted in the abolition of slavery, so, too, an extension of ethical rights to the natural world would bring about changes in such things as land ownership. Leopold's most famous work, *A Sand County Almanac*, published posthumously in 1949, set forth his notion of "the land ethic": "We abuse land because we regard it as a commodity belonging to us. When we see land as a community to which we belong, we may begin to use it with love and respect." His statement of the principles that should govern human interaction with the natural world rested on the holistic value of "integrity." Leopold held that a decision "is right when it tends to preserve the integrity, stability, and beauty of the biotic community. It is wrong when it tends otherwise."[18]

This notion of the inherent value and worth of any given ecosystem was a cornerstone of what became known as the "ecology movement" in the 1960s – a blending of wilderness appreciation with new concerns over pollution, which, in accordance with the changing values represented by Leopold's "land ethic," included not only the effects pollution had on the health of humans but also on that of fish, trees, and entire ecosystems.

The science of ecology added greatly to the political strength of the environmental movement for two reasons. First, because it was one of the empirical sciences, it gave an automatic credibility to environmental concerns. As ecologists provided more information about the disruptive effects of human activity on natural ecosystems, the political pressures to reduce those impacts were correspondingly strengthened. At the same time that ecology allowed environmentalists to take a stand on what was claimed to be the firm rock of science, it also, because of its holistic perspective, opened the door to the spiritual and aesthetic impulses that had always been the basis of wilderness appreciation. Thus, by the 1960s, the ecology movement had brought together greying professors of zoology with flower-child devotees of expanded consciousness, Zen, and organic food – a potent political mix.

CHAPTER 6

Creation of the Modern
Environmental Movement

Post-War Affluence, Radiation, and Pesticides

The social questioning and protest of the 1960s can be explained, in part, by the fact that the generation reaching young adulthood during that decade was the first since the pre-1914 years to have grown up without the experience of either world war or depression. Theirs was the first generation in a half-century that could afford the luxury of disinterested social involvement. Several authors have suggested that the environmental movement, which came of age in the 1960s, was the direct product of the economic prosperity and security enjoyed since 1945. The American author Samuel Hays has argued that environmental concern was one manifestation of the new interest in "quality of life," which was made possible by rising individual incomes. The same impulse that drove the middle class in the 1950s to leave the noise and grit of the inner cities in exchange for the green lawns, quiet, and safety of the suburbs also manifested itself in a new concern about the health effects of pollution and the aesthetics of wilderness and countryside.[1]

As environmental concerns were tied to affluence, so were they directly related to class and education: "Evolving environmental values were closely associated with rising standards of living and levels of education. . . . With each level of age from younger to older, environmental interest fell; and with each level of education from elementary school to college degree, it rose."[2] Hays also documents the way in which the first stirrings of environmental concern in the United States varied greatly by region, with, for instance, the relatively affluent Northeast spawning many more new

90

public-interest organizations than did the South. Although no comparable studies have been done in Canada, a similar trend can be recognized. By the early 1970s many more environmental organizations had been established in British Columbia and Ontario, for example, than in other parts of the country. One of the criticisms levelled at the modern environmental movement is that it is a solely middle-class affair, motivated more by the protection of property values than anything else.

Hays points out that the first issue to link pollution directly with health, beyond the traditional issues of smog and sewage, was radioactive fallout: "The initial public concern about the toxic environment was shaped by knowledge about the radioactive fallout from atomic testing after World War II."[3] Fears of the dangers posed by atomic testing were given a credible voice in 1958 when a group of scientists, including Barry Commoner, established the Greater St. Louis Committee for Nuclear Information, an organization that regularly distributed information on testing being done by the United States and other countries. The Committee did not limit its investigations to radioactivity, however. It also began to investigate the potential dangers associated with the new pesticides, many developed for potential use in chemical warfare during World War II, which by the late 1950s were coming into widespread use. "The newer pesticides were synthetic chemicals, chlorinated hydrocarbons, which were long-lived. Previous pesticides, such as arsenic and mercury, had been acutely toxic to the applicator, while newer organics were far less so." But concern arose over effects on wildlife with the result that preliminary investigations were undertaken. "In 1957 scientists persuaded Congress to provide funds for research, which was then conducted at the Fish and Wildlife Service research station at Patuxent, Maryland. In 1962 the situation received wide public attention when Rachel Carson, a researcher at Patuxent, published *Silent Spring.*"[4]

Carson wrote with the intent of shocking the American public into an awareness of the dangers posed by DDT and the other newly developed pesticides, and she did not use understatement to make her case. Because *Silent Spring* had such a powerful impact and because the approach used by Carson did so much to set the stage for the polarized and often vicious debate of the next two decades, her introductory sentences are worth quoting at some length.

There was once a town in the heart of America where all life seemed to live in harmony with its surroundings. The town lay in the midst of a checkerboard of prosperous farms, with fields of grain and hillsides of orchards where, in spring, white clouds of bloom drifted above the green fields. In autumn, oak and maple and birch set up a blaze of color that flamed and flickered across a backdrop of pines. . . .

Along the roads, laurel, viburnum, and alder, great ferns and wildflowers delighted the traveller's eye through much of the year. . . . Then a strange blight crept over the area and everything began to change. Some evil spell had settled on the community: mysterious maladies swept the flocks of chickens; the cattle and sheep sickened and died. Everywhere was a shadow of death. The farmers spoke of much illness among their families. In the town the doctors had become more and more puzzled by new kinds of sickness appearing among their patients. There had been several sudden and unexplained deaths, not only among adults but even among children, who would be stricken suddenly while at play and die within a few hours. . . . No witchcraft, no enemy action had silenced the rebirth of new life in this stricken world. The people had done it themselves. . . . This town does not actually exist, but it might easily have a thousand counterparts in America or elsewhere in the world. I know of no community that has experienced all the misfortunes I describe. Yet every one of these disasters has actually happened somewhere, and many real communities have already suffered a substantial number of them. A grim spectre has crept upon us almost unnoticed, and this imagined tragedy may easily become a stark reality we all shall know. What has already silenced the voices of spring in countless towns in America? This book is an attempt to explain.[5]

For modern-day environmentalists, made chary of *any* reference to the health implications of pollution by the many charges of alarmist scaremongering levelled at them over the years, this talk of children dropping dead while they play is strong stuff indeed. Not surprisingly, a number of people thought so in 1962 as well. *Time* magazine, in a review of *Silent Spring* (the book was published shortly after being serialized in *The New Yorker*), had this to say:

the book has already raised a swirl of controversy about the danger to man and wildlife of those modern chemical compounds that have vastly increased agricultural production, banished some diseases, and kept at bay the most bothersome and harmful of insects and rodents. . . . Scientists, physicians and other technically informed people . . . consider [*Silent Spring* to be] . . . unfair, one-sided and hysterically overemphatic. Many of the scary generalizations – and there are lots of them – are patently unsound.[6]

Time went on to argue that chemicals used as pesticides for the most part "break down quickly into harmless substances and so leave no poisonous residue on fruits or vegetables or in the soil." DDT in particular was not a health threat: "A mere trace of DDT kills insects, but humans and other mammals can absorb large doses without damage." The review concluded on this note: "Many scientists sympathize with Miss Carson's love of wildlife, and even with her mystical attachment to the balance of nature. But they fear that her emotional and inaccurate outburst in *Silent Spring* may do harm by alarming the nontechnical public, while doing no good for the things that she loves."[7]

Oil Spills and Phosphorous

In 1967, the tanker *Torrey Canyon* ran aground on the southwest coast of England, releasing 118,000 tons of oil into the English Channel. This was followed by a blow-out of an oil rig off Santa Barbara, California, on January 28, 1969, which polluted "beaches along twenty miles of the California shore, and the story occupied front pages of newspapers across the nation for two or three weeks."[8] In that same year Ohio's Cuyahuga River caught fire, largely because of spilled oil. A spill occurred in Canadian waters the next year, on February 4, 1970, when the tanker *Arrow* struck a rock in Chedabucto Bay and spilled 16,000 tons of fuel oil into Nova Scotia's waters.[9]

Oil spills, from the 1967 *Torrey Canyon* to the December, 1988, pollution of beaches on Vancouver Island, the January, 1989, *Exxon Valdez* spill in Alaskan waters, and the January 1991, wartime spill in the Persian Gulf have always been a powerful force working to foster a new pollution awareness, since they are large, visually striking events that serve to focus attention on the issue – oil-fouled ducks and polluted beaches make for gripping television visuals. In particular, they have stimulated environmental lobbying on both the east and west coasts and have been an ongoing point of contention in the context of offshore drilling. During the late 1960s oil spills contributed significantly to the new awareness of pollution without, interestingly enough, being seen as a threat to human health.

Concern was also rising during that time over another pollutant with no direct links to human health. This was the excessive discharge of nutrients, primarily phosphorous, to lakes and rivers, a process known as eutrophication that causes algae to grow, depriving fish of oxygen, causing bad smells, and detracting from the appearance of sparkling waters. Phosphates used in laundry and industrial detergents, which after 1945 had largely replaced soap as a cleaning agent, were thought to contribute a significant measure of the total phosphorous loading.[10]

At this time, too, the metaphor of a "dead" Lake Erie became popular. The language of the contemporary pollution dialogue is exemplified by a *Toronto Star* article of August 19, 1972, on Great Lakes pollution. A few sentences illustrate the tone of the article.

> Lake Erie has been choked by rotting algae, its fish gasping for oxygen, its surface black from oil slick, its waters poisoned by pesti-

cides and chemicals, and heavy with bacteria from human waste. . . . Lake Erie takes the brunt of the Detroit-Windsor pollution, adding to that the sewage from Cleveland and Erie and Buffalo. . . . Two years ago 2,000 square miles of its shallow lake bottom was without oxygen, while on the surface the algae thrived. Lake Erie was said to be "dead" – though in fact it was too much alive – and it became the classic example of how a modern civilization could ruin a great and vital natural resource.[11]

Stimulated by publicity such as this and by the independent research undertaken by the IJC, governments in Canada and the United States by the late 1960s, virtually for the first time ever, attempted to use environmental regulation to reduce total loadings to the environment of a particular polluting substance. What is of most significance today is the way the phosphorous debate went through all the stages of a pollution issue, which have been repeated many times since – initial detection of a problem by scientists; denial by those who must bear the cost of prevention that a problem exists or, if it does exist, that they are responsible; provision of more data by scientists, which occasions public protest; a search for alternative substances; followed, finally, by regulations requiring a reduction of the pollutant at issue.

The problem of phosphates pollution had first been identified by IJC scientists in the 1950s:

A number of key scientific studies on the Great Lakes during the late 1950's and early 1960's demonstrated the historical trend toward serious pollution levels. The key role of phosphates, although a matter of some dispute until approximately the mid-1950's, was generally accepted by scientists in the mid-1960's, at least those not in the employ of the soap and detergent industry.[12]

In 1964 a reference to the IJC was made by Canada and the U.S. for another Great Lakes pollution study further to those of 1912 and 1946. In the fall of 1965 the Commission presented the two governments with an interim report, setting forth possible action to control phosphorous. No action ensued, however. Further studies were done and the IJC released its next report in 1969, calling eutrophication "the most significant water pollution problem in the lower Great Lakes"[13] and pointing out that the majority of phosphorous, not surprisingly given the relative populations on the Canadian and American sides of the Great Lakes, came from the American side.

The IJC then held public hearings in January and February of 1970. By that time environment and pollution had become a matter of great public interest in both countries. President Nixon had signed the National Environmental Policy Act on New Year's Day, 1970, and stressed environmental issues in his State of the Union address that same month. A few months later, millions of Americans celebrated the first Earth Day. On the other side of the border, the government of Canada had just passed the Canada Water Act, was preparing the Clean Air Act, and was taking initial steps toward the establishment of Environment Canada, which began operations in 1971. The IJC hearings did not pass unnoticed.

Governments had two means of reducing phosphorous entering the Great Lakes. One was to regulate quantities used in detergents, the other was to upgrade the ability of sewage treatment plants to remove phosphorous. In a break from normal patterns, the Canadian government placed greater reliance on regulation than did the U.S. The detergent industry responded to the threat of regulation by arguing that a causal connection between its product and eutrophication had not yet been established and that, in any case, "no safe and adequate substitute for phosphates in detergents was then available."[14] In the U.S., after intense industry lobbying, this argument was accepted and the federal government decided in 1971 that the alternative to phosphates, a substance named NTA, should not be used in detergents because of uncertainties regarding long-term environmental effects.[15]

In Canada, however, the federal government announced in April, 1970, that, in addition to more research and assistance for upgrading of sewage treatment plants, it would require a reduction of phosphates in detergents to 20 per cent by weight with more stringent measures to be put in place by the end of 1972. Woodrow and Munton have described the means of establishing this regulatory requirement as follows: "The 20% figure itself, however, could not be arrived at on scientific grounds alone but was based upon a 'guesstimate' as to what level would be sufficient to bring about a significant short-term reduction in phosphorous input to Canadian waters while at the same time being attainable on short notice by the detergent industry and also prompting the industry to search more vigorously for substitutes."[16] A further target of 8.7 per cent was then set, followed, in May, 1972, by a government announcement that regulations would limit phosphates in detergents to 5 per cent by weight by the end of the year. The latter figure was, again, based more on an estimate of what the industry could achieve than on comprehensive study of the needs of the receiving environment.[17]

Following the signing of the Great Lakes Water Quality Agreement of 1972, sewage treatment plants were upgraded on both sides of the border and regulations put in place, in some jurisdictions, limiting the quantities of phosphorous in detergents. Annual phosphorous loadings in Lake Erie were estimated at 28,000 tonnes in 1968 and by 1985 had been reduced to less than half that amount – 11,180 tonnes.[18] During the 1980s, when pollution concerns in the Great Lakes shifted to toxic chemicals, the fight against eutrophication was cited as a success story to be emulated. Whether that can be done or not remains to be seen. Like sulphur dioxide, phosphates in detergent are an easily identified, single-substance form of pollution, and this factor is likely primarily responsible for the degree of success in reduction of total loadings.

Establishment of the Environmental Organizations

During the 1960s government and university scientists were working to draw attention to the dangers of pollution, but an independent, public-interest voice had not yet been established. In 1966, the Canadian Council of Resource Ministers convened the Pollution and Our Environment conference, a follow-up to the 1960 Resources for Tomorrow conference. Held in Montreal, the conference provided a comprehensive overview of the current state of knowledge of sources and effects of pollution and legislative and technical means available for its control. It was attended by some 800 representatives of government, academe, and industry, but not, in contrast to participation in any such event held today, by any representatives of public-interest organizations.[19]

In September, 1969, the Canadian Society of Zoologists, headquartered at McGill University, published *The Rape of the Environment: A Statement on Environmental Pollution and Destruction in Canada*. This report opened by saying that "The year 1969 may well become known as 'Pollution Year'. . . . There has been a surge of public and governmental awareness of pollution, numerous articles in newspapers and magazines, radio and television broadcasts."[20] Because of this concern, at its January, 1969, meeting the Society had decided to issue a statement, drawing attention to two principles: (1) the need for an "ecological" approach, since, it was pointed out, environmental damage may often be long-term and indirect; (2) the need to include consideration of "biological impacts" in the planning of new projects.[21] The report concluded by making reference to chemical companies, which were producing new products "without any knowledge of the way it [the chemical substance] works biochemically." In keeping with the rhetoric of the day, the Society suggested that "In a well-organized civilization, such behaviour would be classified as criminal."[22]

By the time these remarks were published Canadians, often university students working in association with academics, had begun to establish the first non-profit organizations to press for government action on pollution and the environment. As is often the case, Canadians were following the American lead. In that country, the League of Women Voters had adopted protection of water resources as a major lobbying objective as early as 1956. The League continued its work through the 1960s, launching in 1969 a "Citizen's Crusade for Clean Water" intended to convince Congress to provide $1 billion for water and sewage treatment works.[23] Established conservation groups such as the National Wildlife Federation and the Izaak Walton League began work on the new pollution issue by the mid-sixties, and at the same time new organizations were created with a specific mandate to fight pollution. An example is the Environmental Defense Fund, established in 1967 with a primary objective of pressing the U.S. Department of Agriculture to restrict use of DDT.

One of the first such organizations in Canada was the Canadian Scientific Pollution and Environmental Control Society (SPEC), established in Vancouver in January, 1969, by "a group of seven concerned persons" who felt there was a need for an organization that would give voice to "the concern British Columbians feel toward their environment." A few years later SPEC, as it was known, had 5,000 members and thirty-eight branches throughout British Columbia and was concerned with a wide range of issues, including: a ban on offshore oil-drilling and tanker traffic in the Strait of Georgia; pulp mill pollution; the B.C. forestry; testimony at a B.C. inquiry into pesticide use; and a campaign for secondary treatment at the Annacis Island sewage plant in Greater Vancouver.[24]

Another mainstay of the Canadian environmental movement came into being in Ontario in 1969. The CBC had broadcast a television documentary, "Air of Death," on fluoride air pollution in the Cornwall-St. Regis area of Ontario. The program was immediately the centre of controversy, with sufficiently serious charges of bias being laid by the concerned industries that the Canadian Radio Television Commission launched an investigation. This stimulated a group of students at the University of Toronto to prepare a brief in the program's defence. For assistance they turned to Dr. Donald Chant, an entomologist who was chairman of the Department of Zoology and a well-known friend of the environment. The group went on from preparation of the CRTC brief to a range of other issues, among them a mock-funeral for Toronto's polluted Don River, and with space donated by the university Pollution Probe came into existence.[25] The next year a group of Toronto law students formed the Canadian Environmental Law Association (CELA), an organization that would assist Probe and other environmental organizations by providing legal advice, lobbying for law reform, and, it was rather optimistically hoped, undertaking on their behalf "private prosecutions and suits."[26]

A few years later Greenpeace, the most famous of the Canadian environmental organizations, came into being. Greenpeace originated with a small group of peace activists and environmentalists in Vancouver who, in the fall of 1971, were searching for ways to draw media attention to their planned protest of a U.S. underground nuclear test explosion on Amchitka Island, a small island situated toward the end of the Aleutian Islands chain that runs out from Alaska toward the Bering Sea. A previous test on Amchitka, in

1969, had generated significant concern in Canada and the United States, both in the peace movement and among those worried about the environmental effects of the blast. Several members of the peace movement, who also belonged to a Canadian branch of the Sierra Club, hit upon the idea of protesting the 1971 test by taking a small boat into the immediate vicinity of the blast. When the Sierra Club objected to having its name associated with such radical politics, those involved searched for a new name to symbolize their combined objectives of an end to nuclear proliferation and environmental protection. They found it by joining "Green," then as now the colour used to denote environmental concern, and "peace."

Funds were raised, a boat chartered (her name changed for the duration of the voyage from *Phyllis Cormack* to *Greenpeace*), and on September 15, 1971, the protest vessel and her crew pulled out of Vancouver harbour, heading north for the first of many Greenpeace protest events, all carefully designed to provide gripping media images. The connection between environmentalism, native North American values, and political action was symbolized by a collection of North American Indian stories, *Warriors of the Rainbow*, brought along for the voyage by one member of the newly formed Greenpeace crew and read by many others over the days at sea. One of the stories told of the time when "the earth would be ravaged of its resources, the sea blackened, the streams poisoned, the deer dropping dead in their tracks. Just before it was too late, the Indian would regain his spirit and teach the white man reverence for the earth, banding together with him to become Warriors of the Rainbow."[27]

For the next few years Greenpeace volunteers continued to focus on nuclear testing, shifting their operations to the South Pacific where, operating out of New Zealand and Australia, they repeated the successful tactic of generating media publicity by sailing small ships into the blast zone. They then turned their attention to wildlife protection – protesting the whale hunt in rubber dinghies and going on to the Labrador ice floes in a protest that eventually, as a result of European boycotts, ended the Newfoundland seal hunt. It was not until the late 1970s that Greenpeace first took an interest in pollution, concentrating initially on European dumping of hazardous wastes at sea.

In the years since it was founded, Greenpeace has become a multi-million-dollar international organization, one of the most powerful voices calling for both wilderness protection and pollution reduction.[28]

A snapshot of the environmental movement as it existed in Canada at the start of the modern environmental era is provided by a 1973 Environment Canada publication, *Index to Canadian Citizens' Environmental Organizations*, which lists 344 organizations and includes all types of "environmentally interested citizens' groups" – naturalist, fish and game, alpine, youth hostel, conservation, wilderness preservation, and pollution organizations.

Table 1 lists by province and territory the total number of environment organizations in each jurisdiction and an estimate of the number that may have had a specific interest in pollution – as indicated by such words as "environment," "ecology," or "pollution" in the title.

Table 1

Environment Organizations in Canada, 1973

Province/Terr.	Number of Groups	Number of "Pollution" Groups
Yukon	3	1
Northwest Territories	4	1
British Columbia*	77	53
Alberta	44	7
Saskatchewan	15	3
Manitoba	10	2
Ontario	120	29**
Quebec	31	5
New Brunswick	19	7***
Nova Scotia	11	3
Prince Edward Island	2	–
Newfoundland	4	2

*Forty-two of the British Columbia "pollution" groups were SPEC branches.
**Ten of the Ontario "pollution" groups were Pollution Probe branches; Probe also had some branches in other provinces, which are reflected in the totals.
***Four of the New Brunswick "pollution" groups were Conservation Council branches.
SOURCE: Environment Canada, *Index to Canadian Citizens' Environmental Organizations* (Ottawa, January, 1973).

Thus, in the decade following publication of *Silent Spring*, pollution had not only moved to the front pages but had also generated a strong public response, as indicated by the number of Canadians willing to give time and money to non-profit organizations. The fight against pollution had begun in earnest.

CHAPTER 7

The Lunatic Fringe

Canada and the Stockholm Conference

The United Nations Conference on the Human Environment, held in Stockholm, Sweden, had its origins in a United Nations resolution co-sponsored by Canada and Sweden in 1968. Maurice Strong, a Canadian businessman, was appointed secretary-general of the Conference in 1970. Strong was born in Manitoba and during the 1950s and early 1960s established himself as a prominent force in the Canadian mining and energy fields. He moved to the international arena in 1966 when he became head of the Canadian International Development Agency, a position he held until his appointment to the Stockholm Conference in 1970. He later acted as executive director of the UN Environmental Program for the first years of its existence, 1973 to 1975, and then returned to Canada and the business world, where he assumed the position of head of Petro-Canada. Strong has since held a variety of international positions and will serve as secretary-general of the Brazil conference on sustainable development in 1992.

The secretariat for the Stockholm Conference was established in Geneva, with a branch in New York, in 1970. A twenty-seven nation preparatory committee then held four meetings between March, 1970, and March, 1972. During this period various other international initiatives – including scientific conferences, diplomatic discussions, negotiation of agreements on such things as pollution caused by marine shipping, trade in endangered species, and preparations for the Law of the Sea conferences – were undertaken. Third World nations were initially extremely sceptical of Stockholm.

Their position was described a few weeks before the Conference in the following terms:

Probably the major hurdle to be over-come [at Stockholm] is the widely-held theory among "emerging" nations that the whole environment issue is something dreamed up by the "have" countries to maintain their position of industrial leadership in the world, by restraining future development.[1]

Canadian preparations were carried out by three bodies, a federal inter-departmental committee, a federal-provincial preparatory committee, and a national preparatory committee. Robert Shaw, Environment Canada deputy minister, devoted full-time to prepare for the Conference as of March 1, 1972. Canadian environmentalists, according to Don Chant, were "openly dismayed" at the "semi-secret" process that produced drafts of the Canadian position to be presented at Stockholm. According to Chant, these were "trivial, over-written, self-congratulatory overviews of the Canadian environment and the progress being made by our government and industry to clean up pollution."[2]

Perhaps in response to this criticism, the federal government held a series of public consultation sessions, one in each provincial capital, at which members of the public were invited to express their opinions to members of the Canadian delegation to Stockholm. Some 1,200 Canadians participated, with approximately 400 oral and written briefs being presented.[3] A glimpse of the polarized politics of the day is given by the following description of those sessions from Don Chant:

Tokenism and condescension were so obvious as to be almost visible, hanging like a fog in the meeting halls across the country. The atmosphere was not improved by a number of obvious and sarcastic remarks about "academic ecologists" who made up a large part of the audience at most of the sessions. The word "ecologists" slipped from some tongues with what can only be described as venom, almost as though we were Communists and these were the 1950s, or socialists to B.C. Premier W.A.C. Bennett's followers.[4]

The Conference, held in Stockholm, June 5-16, 1972, was attended by some 2,000 delegates and advisers from 113 nations, although it was boycotted by the U.S.S.R. because East Germany was not invited. The Canadian delegation was led by Jack Davis, the first federal Minister of the Environment, and included environment ministers from Quebec and Alberta.[5] Delegates to the Conference adopted the Declaration on the Human Environment, which recognized the need to address both the problems of the global environment and the poverty-ridden state of the Third World. In the fall of 1972 the UN General Assembly received the report of the Conference and adopted its major recommendation, creation of the United Nations Environment Program.

At the conclusion of the Conference Maurice Strong said, "We have taken the first step on a new journey of hope for the future of mankind."[6] Two decades later, it is fair to say that the hopes and plans of those attending have been far from realized, yet his words remain true. Stockholm established the necessary administrative structure, in UNEP, to allow co-ordinated international efforts. It further strengthened the impetus for environmental action in Canada and all other participating nations. Finally, it provided recognition and legitimacy for the principle that action on Third World poverty is an essential component of global action on the environment. This connecting of environmentalism with the central concern of traditional progressive politics – distribution of wealth – may eventually prove to have been the most influential legacy of Stockholm.

Limits to Growth

In 1968 Dr. Aurelio Peccei, an Italian businessman with an interest in public policy, brought together a group of some thirty individuals from different countries, representing a mix of academic and professional backgrounds, to discuss "the present and future predicament of man."[7] The group, known as the Club of Rome, went on to publish *The Limits to Growth* (1972), which advanced the argument that population growth, combined with increasing consumption of resources and pollution on the part of the affluent West, meant that very soon the industrialized nations would run into a series of economic shocks and accompanying social dislocations. The report called for replacement of the objective of economic expansion with the goal of "a society in a steady state of economic and ecological equilibrium."[8] Ever since, "growth" has been the most emotional and divisive term in the environmental lexicon.

The book used strong language to make its case. The introduction, written in 1969 by United Nations Secretary-General U Thant, said that "the Members of the United Nations have perhaps ten years left ... [before] the problems I have mentioned [war, environmental degradation, population growth, and the need for Third World development] will have reached such staggering proportions that they will be beyond our capacity to control."[9]

Limits was very much in the resource conservation school and sounded the same warnings regarding global population growth as had a number of earlier publications. It achieved its effect in part, however, because of the way it combined resource depletion with pollution concerns.

Upon its publication *Limits* struck a chord in the public consciousness that Brown, Osborn, and Ordway [earlier writers on world population growth] were unable to reach. By the 1970s the runaway character of global population growth was difficult to deny, and pollution was rapidly gathering the attention of the media and the public. *Limits* brought these issues together in a chilling way.[10]

Dr. Chant, a participant in the dialogue at the time, has described the report as a "shooting star" that immediately attracted both public attention and bitter opposition.[11] Coming at a time of polarization and heightened rhetoric, with self-described radicals condemning virtually every facet of the existing social and economic order as racist, immoral, hypocritical, and unjust, the effect of *Limits* was to pour gasoline on an already raging fire, as it weighed in with the voice of environmentalism to add yet another attack on growth, the central tenet of capitalism.

Publication of *The Limits to Growth* further polarized the environmental debate, seeming to force participants into either a posture of doom-saying prophecy or a defence of the existing order, warts and all, that left no room for compromise. The study was based on the use of computer analysis to predict various possible future scenarios. This basis in "science" – computer modelling still being something of a novelty in the public mind – gave it the same cachet that naturalists had received from the science of ecology some thirty years before. And like most environmental disputes, the science itself became the battleground. Those unsympathetic to its message went to great lengths to demonstrate, fairly successfully, that the study was based on flawed assumptions and logic.[12] The dispute became more heated, however, with the OPEC oil embargo of the next year, which brought home to Canadians in a very personal way, through price increases at the gasoline pump, the message that resource depletion was a real, and compelling, political issue.

The Conserver Society

During the remainder of the decade this focus on resource consumption and depletion led the policy debate in two related directions – efforts to improve energy efficiency and thus reduce demand and an emphasis on such things as pop-bottle and newspaper recycling to conserve resources. Energy policy discussions led to development of a comprehensive energy policy, the "soft path" in which controlling demand through more efficient energy use was as important as developing new sources of supply in the form of underground oil reserves. This policy development process was carried forward primarily by the work of Amory Lovens in the United States and, in Canada, by such works as David Brooks's *Zero Energy Growth for Canada* (1981).[13]

For a brief period in the late 1970s and early 1980s, before the sense of urgency disappeared with declining oil prices, energy conservation became very much a mainstream issue, with considerable government and private financial resources made available not only for specific conservation programs but also for research and policy analysis. The result is a body of literature in Canada and other countries that, in terms of a clear definition of the problem, review of policy options, and development of practicable recommendations for action, far exceeds the quality and depth of comparable work done either before or since in the pollution field. Unfortunately, the quality of this work alone, in the absence of compelling economic or political pressure, has not been sufficient to induce government action.

During this time active protests were mounted against construction of nuclear-powered electricity generating plants in southern Ontario and New Brunswick, centred on the safety of building such plants in proximity to urban centres and the yet unsolved problem of radioactive waste disposal. Proponents of nuclear power argued, of course, that it represented a solution to the problem of oil scarcity, just as it was argued a few years later that nuclear power could help solve the problem of acid rain and global warming. The fight against nuclear energy in Canada was led by Energy Probe, an organization that separated from its parent, Pollution Probe, in the late 1970s. Unlike the United States, where public opposition, stimulated by the Three Mile Island accident of 1979, managed by the 1980s to halt completely the construction of new plants, Canadian jurisdictions such as Ontario continue to rely on nuclear power for a considerable portion of their total energy generation.

The concept of the "conserver society" brought together pollution, waste, resource depletion, energy, and other related issues, such as urban planning and transportation, into one comprehensive policy package. *Canada as a Conserver Society*, the Science Council of Canada report of 1977 prepared under the direction of Dr. Ursula Franklin, is an excellent example of the work done in this area.[14] The recommendations form a comprehensive and integrated package of proposed actions, which could be implemented in stages through incremental, manageable steps using the tools of taxation, regulation, and financial incentives to reduce resource and energy consumption. Measures recommended included federal standards to improve automobile fuel efficiency, combined with greater municipal spending on public transit and federal spending on the railways; building standards to improve the heating efficiency of buildings, combined with energy pricing to encourage conservation; a variety of steps to improve waste recycling and further efforts in areas such as job retraining and upgrading to assist in the transition to a "conserver society."

Unlike *Limits to Growth*, work such as this in the area of resource conservation and that being done at the same time on energy policy did not provoke sharp opposition. Like the Brundtland report ten years later, the

Conserver Society report did not directly challenge the value of economic growth; instead, in the reform environmentalist tradition, it used temperate language to recommend a series of incremental steps, which guaranteed the proposals would be viewed as part of the mainstream dialogue. *Conserver Society* quickly slid beneath the waves and was forgotten, as Canada moved into recession and oil prices declined; the Brundtland report, on the other hand, has been hailed since 1987 with fulsome praise. The impact of both, however, is likely to have been the same – governments will have praised the vision and depth of analysis and carefully avoided acting on a single recommendation.

Mercury Pollution

During the early 1970s a new substance, mercury, was added to the roster of water pollution concerns. Although mercury had been known for some time as a toxic substance that posed occupational health threats, concern for its transmission through water was new. As is so often the case with controversies over newly discovered polluting substances, the issue blew up quickly, moving from a state of no scientific knowledge or concern to the front pages of newspapers in less than five years. The process has been described this way:

> In the mid-1960's, some Canadian scientists asked federal authorities to undertake a survey of mercury in fish but such action was not taken, presumably because there were no organic mercury discharges from chemical plants in Canada. In 1967, however, Swedish scientists showed inorganic mercury can be converted by bacteria in sediments into toxic methylmercury which can bioaccumulate. In 1969, a university biologist produced first public evidence of mercury-contaminated fish in Canada, from Lake St. Clair, downstream from a chloralkali plant. The federal government then started an extensive survey of mercury levels in Canadian waters.
>
> Commercial fishing was banned by Environment Canada in 1969 in the South Saskatchewan River, and in April, 1970, newspaper headlines across Canada read "Fish poisoning stops $4 million-a-year Lake Erie fish catch."[15]

Public attention centred on two Ontario cases – the Dow pollution of Lake St. Clair and the Reed Paper Company pollution of the English-Waubigoon River system. Unlike the usual process of lengthy public dialogue and equally lengthy private negotiations between the polluting industry and government, in this instance action was taken almost immediately – presumably because of the direct human health implications. Both companies were ordered by the Ontario government on March

26, 1970, to put an end to their mercury emissions. Although expeditious action was taken and the ongoing mercury contamination was largely stopped, subsequent events in both cases did nothing to instil in observers any faith in the willingness of the Ontario Conservative government, led by Bill Davis, to act in good faith on environmental protection and did much to inspire the cynicism and mistrust that pervaded relations between governments and the environmental community by the early 1980s.

In the Dow case, mercury contamination of fish in Lake St. Clair, caused by the company discharges of approximately thirty pounds of mercury per day over a period of twenty years, was sufficiently severe that the commercial fishery was closed, thus ending the business activities of approximately forty family-run fisheries. This led the provincial government in 1971 to initiate a $35 million lawsuit against Dow, intended to pay for both compensation to the fisheries and the cost of dredging an estimated 40,000 pounds of mercury from the sediments at the bottom of the St. Clair River. After winning the 1972 provincial election, during which the Davis government pointed to the lawsuit as evidence of its tough stand on corporate polluters, the case was allowed to drag on until, in 1978, it was settled out of court with a $250,000 payment by Dow as compensation to the affected fisheries and a further $100,000 "contribution" to the Ontario government to pay for water quality research. No action was ever taken to remove the mercury from the river.[16]

In the case of Reed Paper, mercury contamination as one of a number of pollutants emitted by the pulp and paper plant at Dryden, Ontario, had begun in 1962, with emissions of mercury totalling some ten tons by 1970.[17] As in the Dow case, the provincial government banned commercial fishing at the time it ordered an end to the emissions, again with a direct financial impact on local fishermen, in this case the Ojibway Indians living in the area. Health tests taken at the time revealed blood levels as high as fifty parts per billion (ppb), more than double the upper maximum of twenty ppb, beyond which mercury was considered to represent a threat to human health. Controversy continued over whether Reed had in fact fully complied with the 1970 order to stop all mercury emissions until, in October, 1975, the company switched to a new production process that did not involve mercury.

The Ontario and Canadian governments then entered into a series of discussions of the steps that might be taken to redress both the health and economic problems of the Ojibway caused by the pollution, and an order was issued to Reed to reduce its other types of pollution. The timetable for compliance with the abatement order was extended several times until, in 1976, prosecution was finally initiated. In that same year a secret agreement between Reed and the Ontario government, giving the company exclusive timbering rights over a 19,000-square-mile-area, was made public and blew up into a major political issue, leading the Davis government to the tried and true expedient of tossing the hot potato to a royal commission in the hopes that by the time it finally reported the original controversy would have faded from the public mind.

In July, 1976, Reed was fined $5,000 but did nothing to abate its water pollution. In 1978 Reed said it could not afford pollution abatement and threatened to close operations, with the loss of 1,700 jobs in a town of 7,000 population, if pollution orders were enforced. Faced with such a stark choice between pollution reduction and jobs, the Ontario government, with the concurrence of both the Liberals and NDP, bowed to the political realities of the day and extended the date of compliance with the abatement order.[18] In 1984, Ontario, Canada, Ontario Hydro, and Reed Paper established two trust funds of $8 million each for the two Indian bands affected by the mercury pollution. As of 1990, twenty people were receiving compensation from those funds for disabilities attributed to mercury poisoning.[19] In 1986, some ten years after it was appointed, the Royal Commission on the Northern Environment submitted its long overdue report to the Ontario legislature, where it was completely ignored, thus proving the success of the Davis strategy.

The Berger Inquiry

The other issue that did more than anything else to foster environmental awareness in Canada during this period was not related to a particular polluting substance but instead centred on public access to the environmental decision-making process. This was the heated debate, which ran from 1971 to 1978, over plans to build a pipeline through the Mackenzie River Valley to transport oil and gas from Alaska to the southern United States. Large pipeline projects, like large dams, seem inevitably to engender political controversy. This may be because they involve large capital expenditures and thus often require not only government approval but also financing, which guarantees political in-fighting among the corporate interests involved as they carry out their complex negotiations among one another and with the various government agencies. But controversy also arises from the fact that such projects are inevitably a powerful visual manifestation of the Western, capitalist approach to the natural world. Their magnitude makes it impossible to ignore the fact that a technological solution, which relies on millions of tons of concrete in preference to any more subtle approach, has been found for the issue at hand, thus guaranteeing opposition from those who do not share that particular vision. Hence the proposed northern pipeline of the 1970s was a direct descendant of the Trans-Canada Pipeline, which in 1956-57 allowed John Diefenbaker to defeat C.D. Howe and his colleagues in the St. Laurent Liberal government, and was a forerunner of the court actions surrounding the Oldman and Souris River dams twenty years later.

Planning for the pipeline was initiated in 1969 by a grouping of corporate interests, predominantly American oil companies such as Sohio and Humble. Not long afterwards rival plans were being developed by a Canadian company, the Alberta Gas Trunk Line of Calgary, and for the next few years the issue gained increasing prominence.

Opposition to any such construction came from native North Americans, who by the early 1970s had taken their claims for land ownership to the courts. The three major cases were the Nishga claim to an area of the Nass River Valley in British Columbia, argued before the Supreme Court in 1972 by their counsel, Thomas Berger; the claim of the Dene of the Northwest Territories; and, third, the injunction sought by the Cree and Inuit of Quebec, who were fighting to halt construction of the first James Bay power project and thereby save their homes and hunting territories from flooding. By 1973, all three cases had lost in the courts but a sufficiently strong legal case had been made to give considerable impetus to the fight by natives and their allies for compensation in some form for the land lost when Europeans came to dominate the northern part of the continent.

Opposition to the pipeline on environmental grounds came from a number of sources, most notably the newly formed Canadian Arctic Resources Committee, but also from Pollution Probe and others. A further source of opposition was the Canadian nationalist opposition to an American-owned project of this magnitude, serving primarily American interests and symbolizing yet again Canada's subservient role on the continent.[20] As was the case a decade later with opposition to various proposals to divert waters from the Great Lakes or Hudson Bay to the American southwest, and again in the free trade election of 1988, environmental and nationalist interests, combined with an enduring mistrust of large-scale technology and the self-interest of the corporate community, merged to mobilize a co-ordinated opposition.

By early 1974 the pipeline issue had reached sufficient political proportions that the Trudeau government, influenced perhaps by the fact that it held only a minority of seats in the House, felt it expedient to appoint a commission of inquiry and on March 22, 1974, creation of the Berger Inquiry was announced to the House of Commons. As Robert Page has pointed out, the commission of inquiry is a device often used in Canada. Governments appoint commissions because they provide a convenient method of both delaying action and shifting the focus of public attention. Once appointed, however, they may assume a life of their own and a few, among the approximately 2,000 appointed by the federal government since Confederation, have had an impact on Canadian history.[21]

The Berger Inquiry was one of these. The public hearings conducted by Mr. Justice Berger – an NDPer, B.C. Supreme Court judge, and former counsel to the Nishga – established the concept of public funding to ensure intervenors a voice in the regulatory hearing process. But perhaps even more important was the way the hearings throughout the North (with only a brief foray to southern cities) provided a forum for native peoples to talk to Canadians about their homeland and for Canadians of the south to express their emerging views of themselves and the land in which they lived. The Berger report (which became a bestseller) offered a powerful alternative vision to the accepted view of the northern environment as something of value only in terms of resource exploitation and development. Berger gave urban Canadians a view of the North as homeland, connected both to each individual and to the cultures of the peoples who lived there. The inquiry gave Canadians a glimpse of the "land ethic" of Canada's native peoples, and by doing so helped further develop their own.[22]

The conclusion of the inquiry, set forth in its 1977 report, was that a ten-year moratorium should be placed on any pipeline development to allow time to prepare for and mitigate the social and environmental effects. This recommendation was quickly made irrelevant by the changing economies of oil production, which transformed the economically attractive project of 1969 into a fiscal impossibility not long after Berger submitted his report. The influence of the inquiry, however, extended far beyond the fate of the pipeline that had given it birth.

Decline and Revival of the Pollution Issue
Decline

By the late 1970s pollution concerns began to lessen, in part because pollution as an issue was eclipsed by other environmental concerns, most notably the save-the-whales campaigns of Greenpeace and others and the protests against the Newfoundland seal hunt. Also, however, there was a relative decline in public concern about the environment. Brian Woodrow, writing in 1980, talked about the "rapid rise and subsequent decline of the pollution issue in Canada," explaining that "During the early 1970's, public awareness and concern reached its peak and has since dropped off, although by no means back to its earlier low level."[23]

The economic good times of the 1960s, which did so much to fuel the sunny optimism of the counter-culture, giving it the luxury of a disdain for seeking personal security through employment, were sharply buffeted through the decade of the seventies, first by the inflation following the OPEC oil embargo and then by the slide toward recession, which by the time it reached rock bottom in 1981-82 was on a scale comparable to that of the 1930s. Worries about fish killed by pollution from a pulp and paper plant seemed an irrelevant luxury when a company like Reed claimed that 1,700 jobs were on the line.

Other events also served to turn public attention away from pollution. The 1976 election of the Parti Québécois, the first time in Canadian history that Quebec had elected a government with an explicit intent to withdraw from Confederation, threw the country into a state of shock. The fear that the fragile bonds holding Canada together in a thin line, 4,000 miles long, might someday be snapped has meant that separatism has always been *the* primary Canadian political issue, whether the threat has been from Nova Scotia in 1869, Quebec in 1917, or the western provinces in the 1980s. From 1976 through the defeat of the sovereignty-association proposal in the May, 1980, Quebec referendum and the patriation of the constitution in 1982, the environment, like other issues, was eclipsed by constitutional concerns. It seems likely that in the early 1990s constitutional issues, combined with economic recession, will again threaten to draw attention away from the environment. Whether these other issues will again completely stall environmental action will be a test of the political strength the movement gained during the 1980s.

Events outside the country also distracted attention from environmental issues. In the United States the New Conservatism, speaking through such oracles as the American Heritage Foundation, had been working since the defeat of Barry Goldwater in 1964 to put new life into the conservative policy platform, pointing to what was claimed as the failure of liberalism in the 1960s, the need to restore America's Vietnam-damaged pride in the international arena, and, at home, a need to bring prosperity by freeing business from the fetters and constraints of government regulation. This renewed credibility of right-wing thought was translated in 1980 into electoral success with the defeat of President Carter by Ronald Reagan and the assumption of power by an administration explicitly hostile to environmental protection. This trend had been foreshadowed across the Atlantic when Margaret Thatcher was elected Prime Minister of Great Britain in 1979, and it was to find further expression with the 1984 election, in this country, of Brian Mulroney.

Thus Canada went through the elections of 1979 and 1980, marking the beginning and end of the brief Joe Clark interregnum, with little attention paid to environment as a political issue. The one controversy of the time was the issue of aerial herbicide spraying in Nova Scotia and New Brunswick by the forestry companies. The issue came to a head in the early 1980s when residents of Cape Breton, led by Elizabeth May, went to court to seek an injunction to stop the spray program on the grounds of threats to health. A temporary injunction prohibiting spraying by the Swedish-owned pulp and paper company Nova Scotia Forest Industries Ltd. was granted in August, 1982. The case for a permanent injunction was then heard in the spring of 1983, with a group of sixteen landowners attempting to prove that the spray – a mixture of 2,4-D and 2,4,5-T, similar to the defoliant Agent

Orange used in the Vietnam War, which was the subject of extensive litigation in the U.S. over health effects suffered by the soldiers handling it – posed a threat to their health.

The case generated considerable publicity throughout Canada, with more than $180,000 raised at the grassroots level to defray expenses. The final decision went against the citizens, however, which reinforced the conviction in the Canadian environmental community that the Canadian legal system, unlike the American, did not lend itself to the use of litigation as a political tactic.[24]

Revival: Acid Rain, Hazardous Waste, and Drinking Water

Two other issues – acid rain and hazardous waste – did more than the Cape Breton legal proceedings to reverse the decline of pollution as a public policy issue.

Although acid rain had no direct implications for human health, it twitched a Canadian political nerve as soon as the issue was portrayed in terms of American pollution blown across the border to contaminate Canadian lakes. Furthermore, the symbolism of the issue, dying lakes and forests, struck at the heart of the Canadian identification with our northern land. Powerful voices in Canada, such as the Ontario government, were all too happy to portray the issue as one primarily involving a threat from south of the international border, thus diverting attention from their own failure to reduce emissions from Canadian sources. Acid rain awoke all the quiescent Canadian fears that if their country was not pulled apart by internal dissension it would succumb to invasion by the Yankees. Furthermore, acid rain was the first pollution issue the federal government – instead of trying to downplay – actively *drew* to public attention, presumably because there was political benefit to be gained by appearing to take a strong stand against the traditional Canadian enemy.[25] Thus reverberating with the emotional overtones of Canadian nationalism and propelled by the sophisticated lobbying of the Canadian Coalition on Acid Rain, established in 1980 with far more financial assistance from the governments of Ontario and Canada than had ever before been given to an environmental organization, acid rain quickly became the first environmental issue ever to rise to the top of the Canadian political agenda.

If acid rain played on Canadian nationalism, the other new issue of the time, hazardous waste, drew its strength directly from the perception of toxic contamination as a threat to health. Love Canal, which came to symbolize the issue, is one of several sites in the vicinity of Niagara Falls, New York, that had been used by the Occidental Petroleum Company, then known as Hooker Chemical Company, for the dumping of hazardous wastes in the 1950s. The dumpsites were closed and sold to municipal authorities and no attention was paid to the contamination until the 1970s, when residents living in the vicinity became aware of what seemed to them an abnormally high incidence of a variety of illnesses. The result of the ensuing controversy was a declaration, by President Carter and the Governor of New York state, in the spring of 1978, that the site was a disaster area. A number of residents were evacuated from their contaminated homes.

Love Canal became a large-scale, dramatic event that, virtually by itself, ushered in the present age of toxic contamination concern, burning the toxics issue into the public consciousness with images of ordinary people, residents of a quiet suburban town, threatened by sickness and death coming from their basements, their backyards, or the kitchen faucet. Rachel Carson's hyperbole of 1962 had become the daily news of 1978.

Love Canal quickly found its Canadian counterparts in landfills throughout the country suspected of leaking toxic wastes into underground drinking water supplies, and became itself a Canadian issue when concerns arose over the safety of drinking water in Ontario towns and cities drawing their supply from Lake Ontario, which was threatened by Love Canal and the other New York state hazardous waste dumpsites in the vicinity of the Niagara River.

Maclean's magazine, in June of 1981, carried a cover story titled "Don't Drink the Water," which chronicled various drinking water threats such as pollution from landfill leachate, pulp and paper plant discharges, and traditional sewage pollution concerns in British Columbia, Saskatchewan, Ontario, Quebec, and Nova Scotia. Two themes were presented in the story: (1) that health and environment officials were usually unable to state categorically that no health threat existed, given the inherent uncertainties of the data and their analysis; (2) that local citizens, in the absence of unambiguous statements from experts, very understandably tended to think the worst and expressed their suspicions and mistrust in an increasingly politically active manner.[26]

The debate over drinking water quality was also carried forward by the established environmental organizations. In 1981 Pollution Probe published *Toxics on Tap: A Report on the Quality of Drinking Water in Toronto*, the first of two reports claiming that Toronto drinking water was threatened by contaminants that the traditional water purification method of chlorination was not designed to remove:

There are many toxic chemicals that penetrate the defenses of our water treatment plants. The water treatment system, as it is presently constituted, was not designed to remove those chemicals that contaminate Lake Ontario, such as benzene, mirex, DDT, acetone, toluene or dioxin. Scientific studies generated over the last decade, mainly in the United States, show an increasing concern that infiltration of these chemicals into our water supplies does, indeed, pose a threat to public health.[27]

Not surprisingly, public officials were quick to react to this criticism. In a written commentary dated November 4, 1981, the Metropolitan Toronto Works Department referred to the Pollution Probe report as "largely a rehash of reports published in the past several years," which was likely to "induce a state of panic" because it contained "inaccurate and distorted" statements. The Department concluded by stating that "Toronto's drinking water is not only safe, but is among the very best of North American supplies."[28] In 1983 Pollution Probe returned to the fray. This time, in a report titled *Drinking Water: Make it Safe!*, Probe claimed that not only did chlorination not solve the problem of chemical contamination, it actually made the contamination worse:

> Chlorination of drinking water significantly increases mutagenicity and can result in the formation of more than 40 new hazardous compounds in treated water. Chlorination of Toronto water has resulted in chloroform and bromodichloromethane levels that are predicted to result in an additional 72 to 156 cancers in Metro Toronto based on lifetime ingestion of 2 liters of water per day.[29]

The Works Department again fought back. The commissioner, Frank Horgan, charged that "Pollution Probe deliberately sensationalizes the indicated presence of minute quantities of contaminants in the water. . . . They like to draw attention to themselves [because] . . . publicity is needed to generate funds."[30] At the heart of the debate was the estimated $100 million cost of building new water treatment systems designed to cope with the variety of contaminants found in Lake Ontario water. To officials such as Horgan, as well as Metro Chairman Paul Godfrey and then Ontario Minister of Environment Andy Brandt, spending in that order of magnitude to cope with a health threat surrounded by so much uncertainty simply could not be justified. Pollution Probe did not directly oppose such a position but did call for significantly increased spending on research into alternative treatment systems, at the same time pointing out that the only real solution was to reduce drastically the quantity of toxic pollutants entering Lake Ontario waters.

The Metro Toronto dispute ultimately revolved around the issue of Great Lakes pollution. Aside from localized controversies related to particular sources of pollution, such as the landfills and pulp mills cited in the 1981 *Maclean's* article, water quality discussions chiefly centred on pollution of the Great Lakes. As was repeatedly pointed out, some 36 million people on both sides of the border relied on the lakes for drinking water supplies and the quality of the water was threatened by direct discharge of industrial wastes, discharges through municipal sewage systems, pesticide and fertil-izer run-off from land in the drainage basin, and airborne pollutants car-ried hundreds of miles from their original sources. It is likely, though, that the Great Lakes received such attention not because their waters were so much more polluted than any others, but simply because information concerning water quality in the Great Lakes was more available than for virtually any other water bodies in Canada or the United States. This was because the International Joint Commission, after renewal of the Great Lakes Water Quality Agreement in 1978, prepared a series of three biennial reports, as required by the Agreement, and these reports brought together the best information on threats to water quality that the relevant Canadian and American environmental agencies could supply. Every two years the IJC reports provided new grist for the environmentalist mill, thus amply demonstrating the political importance of neutral, credible sources of data and analysis.

Thus, by September 4, 1984, when the Progressive Conservative Party of Brian Mulroney won 211 seats in the House of Commons, pollution – now perceived as an insidious, often invisible threat that sometimes originated hundreds of miles away – was again established as a Canadian political issue.

CHAPTER 8

We're All Environmentalists Now

"We're all environmentalists here," Alberta Minister of Forestry LeRoy Fjordbotten was quoted as saying in November, 1989; "I am, Premier Getty is. We want to do what's right so our kids and your kids can enjoy the environment in future generations."[1] Fjordbotten was talking about his government's position on regulation of effluent discharges from the new pulp mills proposed for northern Alberta. Some Albertans doubted his claim, but one thing is certain – the tone of Alberta politics had changed considerably. Just two years earlier Alberta Environment Minister Ken Kowalski had said that those opposed to construction of the Oldman River dam were "social anarchists."[2]

During the period 1985-90 more changed than just the throwaway rhetoric of politicians. Starting with the acid rain agreement announced by Prime Minister Brian Mulroney in March, 1985, committing Canada to reduction from the 1980 allowable annual sulphur dioxide loading of 4.5 million tonnes to an annual allowable loading in 1994 of 2.3 million tonnes, and running through a series of commitments to pollution reduction in such areas as solid wastes, ozone-destroying CFCs, pesticides, and industrial wastes, governments in Canada have made commitments to future action on pollution that, if kept, will represent unprecedented progress in the fight to protect the Canadian environment. Although action has not yet caught up with rhetoric, the fact remains that the response of elected officials to pollution changed dramatically during the last half of the 1980s. What happened?

One reason for the change is that there simply was more information available on pollution and its effects, information forcefully presented to the Canadian public by increasingly skilful environmental lobbyists. Another is the periodic cymbal clash of explosive events – in 1984 a pesticide gas leak from a Union Carbide plant in Bhopal, India, killed some 2,000 people and permanently injured thousands of others; in 1985, in Auckland, New Zealand, the French secret service blew a hole in the Greenpeace ship *Rainbow Warrior*, killing one environmentalist; in 1986, in Chernobyl, U.S.S.R., a nuclear power plant caught fire, killing thirty-one people and releasing a cloud of radioactive gas that reached Canada seven days later, drifting in from the Pacific over British Columbia and across the Rocky Mountains heading east, reminding us of the tiny size and vulnerability of the planet we live on. In 1988, closer to home, a Montreal warehouse filled with PCB-contaminated wastes caught fire, forcing the evacuation of several thousand nearby residents, while in 1990 piles of discarded tires caught fire in both Ontario and Quebec, burning for days and releasing pollutants to both air and land.

Not surprisingly, the increased flow of information, repeatedly punctuated with dramatic spills, explosions, and toxic fires, has changed public attitudes, which in turn have stimulated a change in the way politicians deal with the issue. During the late 1980s, politicians, for the first time, realized that taking action on pollution was good politics. Whether or not, in the final analysis, they will be able to deliver fully on their promises, governments in Canada have now started to make commitments to specific objectives, to be achieved in accordance with specified timetables and deadlines. The beginning of this new political response was the Ontario election of 1985.

Ontario Preaches the New Environmental Politics

For a period of forty-one years, from the election of 1944 to 1985, the Progressive Conservative Party of Ontario successfully ruled Canada's most industrialized, and presumably therefore most polluted, province. The Conservatives had stayed in power this long by a process of shedding their skin every five to ten years when the party, by electing a new leader – passing the baton from George Drew to Lesley Frost to John Robarts to Bill Davis – both met the voters' desire for change, the major threat to any long-established government, while placating the voters' contradictory but equally powerful impulse, a fear of the unknown. The Tory Big Blue Machine managed the impressive trick of including "new and exciting" in the same package as "old, reliable, and comforting," and this, combined with the good fortune of facing two opposition parties who were forced to divide the anti-government vote between them, allowed the party to win elections over and over again.

By the mid-1980s Bill Davis, first chosen by the party in 1972 and a veteran of minority government and various scandals during the 1970s, had a permanent lock on power in the province – bland, avuncular, comfortably answering any question with a gentle patter of circumlocution that left the listener vaguely confused but somehow also vaguely reassured, Bill Davis was as comfortable as an old pair of slippers. Attempting to repeat the patterns that had worked in the past, Davis announced his retirement on October 8, 1984. Frank Miller, a former Minister of Health and Natural Resources during the 1970s and a veteran of the mercury pollution issue of those days, was chosen as his successor at the Tory convention on January 24, 1985. Miller then made the mistake of trying to ride the popularity generated by the convention spotlight directly into an election, instead of giving himself and his government time to consolidate their hold on power by demonstrating their ability to govern, announcing enough new policies and programs to dissociate themselves from the Davis regime, and then presenting the electorate, yet again, with a confident new mask painted on the old familiar Tory face. As a result, on May 2, 1985, Frank Miller managed to win the provincial election, but was left with a minority government – holding fifty-two seats against twenty-five for the NDP and forty-eight for the Liberals. The NDP held the balance of power and after much soul-searching threw in their lot with the Liberals, striking a deal whereby, in exchange for a guaranteed two years' support in the legislature, the Liberals promised to act on a specified list of policies spelled out in the Liberal-NDP accord of May 28, 1985. A number of policies were in the environmental area. Some were very specific, such as a commitment to proclamation of the "Spills Bill" – an amendment to the Environmental Protection Act, passed by the legislature in 1980 but never proclaimed, that imposed increased liabilities on owners of toxic substances accidentally released to the environment. Some were so vague as to be almost meaningless, such as the call for "new enforceable mechanisms for the control of pollution to enable Ontario to deal effectively with acid rain and to establish the principle that the polluter pays." The accord also committed the new Liberal government to "wind up the Royal Commission on the Northern Environment and obtain release of all working papers and reports."[3]

The election was decided more by voter dissatisfaction with the Tory government, and Frank Miller's failure to establish a new, separate image, than anything specifically related to environment. However, for the first time in a Canadian election the environment was a significant issue – the new Liberal minister, Jim Bradley, speaking a year later, said: "There is good reason ... to treat environmental issues seriously. Last year pollution played a major role for the first time in a provincial election."[4]

This was in part because the Ontario environmental community played a more active role in the 1985 election than it had previously, with lobbying done by such groups as the Canadian Coalition on Acid Rain and a newly formed amalgam of organizations, spanning interests from wildlife conservation to nuclear energy to pollution, titled the Project for Environmental Priorities. More important than environmentalist electioneering, however, was the Kenora PCB spill. In late April, during the early days of the campaign, a truck on the Trans-Canada highway near Kenora, carrying PCB-tainted wastes from Ontario to Alberta for storage and ultimate disposal at the Swan Hills facility, began leaking fluid that sprayed a following car. The driver of the car informed the truck driver of the leak when both vehicles pulled into the next gas station, found out what had sprayed his car, called the police, and immediately found himself, with his pregnant wife and young child, at the centre of a national news storm, complete with pictures of workers in moon-suits ripping up miles of the PCB-contaminated highway. The spill became a major issue in the Ontario election, with environmentalists and the opposition parties accusing the Tory government of failure to act decisively and effectively in protecting the environment and health of Ontario citizens. There is now general agreement that the dangers of PCBs have been exaggerated by the popular media, both in this instance and others, but that is less significant, in terms of the politics of the issue, than the error made by the Tories in responding to the spill. The newly appointed Environment Minister, Morley Kells, repeated the old Tory line that dangers had been exaggerated by irresponsible fringe groups and the opposition, saying that "only a rat eating PCBs on the Trans-Canada highway" was in danger from the spill. This, of course, was believed by no one, regardless of what the real dangers might have been, and was seen as yet more evidence of the Tory propensity not only to downplay the seriousness of the environmental threat but also, a far more serious charge, to lie to the public.[5]

The Tories never had learned that bland assurances of safety were simply not believed, and for that reason were almost always a political error. In 1983, when dioxin was first discovered in Lake Ontario, the source of drinking water for millions of Ontario citizens, then Tory Minister Keith Norton immediately responded in the same vein as Kells two years later, saying there was no need to worry since the dioxin did not represent any threat to human health. The minister's statement may well have been true, but it showed a complete misreading of the public mood on health and pollution.

The Peterson Liberal government, which took office on June 16, 1985, did not make the same mistake. Jim Bradley, the Liberal Environment Minister, received considerable public credit for acting on one of the NDP requirements, proclamation of the Spills Bill, in his first months in office and then for moving quickly to bring in the acid rain program agreed to by his predecessors. When confronted with his first environmental crisis in the following year, the "toxic blob" caused by a hazardous waste spill from the Dow Plant in Sarnia, Bradley wasted no time with public reassurances but immediately dropped everything and rushed to the site, there to be filmed by the television cameras wearing a hardhat and peering earnestly into the waters of the St. Clair River.

Jim Bradley, with his personal commitment to environmental protection, had taken the hitherto unheard of step of appointing members of the environmental community, albeit ones with strong Liberal backgrounds, to his office staff. What is more significant, however, is that the Premier and his cabinet gave the minister room to manoeuvre, at least in the early days of the Peterson government, on pollution issues. When he first took office, Bradley underlined the differences between his ministry and that of his Tory predecessors by releasing for public scrutiny a series of reports that until then had been kept secret. After the Spills Bill and acid rain program, Bradley brought in new pop can regulations (although, as discussed in Part IV, environmentalists are still not sure this was a step in the right direction), accompanied by the blue box recycling program, and went on in 1986, spurred by the toxic blob, to announce plans for a new set of regulations governing industrial wastes discharged to rivers and lakes – the Municipal Industrial Strategy for Abatement (MISA). In 1987 legislation was introduced to increase significantly fine levels set in environmental legislation.

As a result of these initiatives pollution did not figure as prominently in the 1987 election as it had in 1985. An article in the *Toronto Star* of September 4, 1987, noted that "many pollution issues have been defused by the activism of Bradley and his staff on pollution issues" and quoted Jeffrey Shearer, president of the Canadian Coalition on Acid Rain, as saying, "This government has kept its promise on acid rain."[6] The one environmental issue hurting the Liberals in 1987 was the Temagami logging dispute, another in the string of what have now become classic Canadian confrontations, particularly on the west coast, in which the issue is not pollution but land use, with governments, environmentalists, loggers, and native peoples locked in a many-sided battle.

The environment returned as an issue in the 1990 Ontario election, however. By the time the election was called, in August of that year, the Peterson government had not yet implemented its long-promised programs, such as MISA and new air pollution regulations, while almost every Ontario municipality was agonizing over the controversies and hostilities surrounding the siting of new landfills. A perception of inaction on environment was one more factor that led to the defeat of the Peterson government and the first-ever election of an Ontario NDP government.

Environmental Policies of the Mulroney Government

In November, 1984, some two months after the Mulroney government was first elected, the Minister of Environment, Suzanne Blais-Grenier, announced that as part of the new government's restraint program her department's spending would be significantly reduced. One branch of the department, the Canadian Wildlife Service, suffered a 22 per cent staff reduction, which affected, among other programs, toxic contaminant monitoring in the Great Lakes, a review of agricultural chemical use in the western provinces, and the monitoring of the effects on songbirds of herbicide spraying in New Brunswick.[7] Bitter protests from the environmental organizations and general public greeted the cutbacks, but no one was surprised that the Tories had taken the same approach to environmental protection as had their ideological mentor, the Reagan administration, four years previously in the United States.

Not long afterward, however, the Mulroney government, whatever its true preferences might have been, was dragged into a posture of at least appearing to act on environmental issues. There were two reasons for this. First, acid rain by 1985 had become the premier environmental issue, and one firmly established in the public mind, due to the federal and provincial posturing of the past years, as primarily an issue in Canadian-American relations. This meant the Prime Minister was unable to discuss publicly his own plans for moving Canada into a closer trade relationship with the United States without at the same time discussing acid rain. The politics of acid rain by the mid-eighties were such that the Canadian government had no choice but to bill it as the top bilateral issue, even coming ahead of trade and jobs, at the annual meetings between Prime Minister Mulroney and President Reagan from 1985 to 1988. The two leaders went through some bizarre contortions over the years as they danced around the issue, twisting and turning in their efforts to hide the simple fact that the Reagan administration never had the slightest intention of acting, no matter what protestations were heard from north of the border, or, for that matter, from the New England states. The second force pushing the Mulroney government in the direction of environmental action was the increased prominence of international issues such as the ozone layer and global atmospheric change. These issues, due to their global nature, *had* to be dealt with at the federal level and could not be sloughed off to the provinces.

Thus the Prime Minister and his new Environment Minister, Tom McMillan, who on August 20, 1985, replaced the disastrous Suzanne Blais-Grenier,[8] found themselves increasingly drawn into the environmental policy area both by the rising prominence of the issue and by international events. The major environmental action taken by the Mulroney government at home in its first term, aside from the acid rain program it had inherited from the Trudeau Liberals and a reduction in environment spending, was not the development of any new regulatory requirements for pollution reduction but instead a consolidation of existing federal environmental legislation. Enactment of new legislation – to give the Canadian government clear power to regulate toxic pollution directly – had been considered by Environment Canada in the early 1980s but never went beyond discussion.[9] Rather, the department had developed, through a consultation/bargaining process including representatives of government, industry, and the environmental lobby, a series of amendments to the 1975 Environmental Contaminants Act. Instead of introducing these amendments, however, the new minister combined them with a consolidation of the ECA and parts of other federal legislation. That process was completed with adoption by the House of Commons in the summer of 1988 of the new Canadian Environmental Protection Act. McMillan had alienated large parts of the environmental community by calling what was nothing more than a consolidation of existing and proposed legislation, with no new requirements to reduce pollution, the toughest environmental legislation in the world and boasting of its million-dollar-a-day fines.

During the spring and summer of 1988 the Mulroney government fired the first shots in the as yet to be called election campaign by throwing out a string of promises that offered something for every region. Environment figured high on the list, with the emphasis, whenever possible, placed on the job creation potential of the new initiative. Thus Winnipeg was promised a new $5 million centre for the promotion of sustainable development; Metro Toronto residents, fighting a landfill proposed for the Rouge River in Scarborough, were offered $10 million toward the cost of establishing the site as a park; Quebec was given a $110 million centre for the clean-up of the St. Lawrence; and Halifax was promised $75 million toward the cost of cleaning up the harbour. All of this was in addition to the most highly publicized initiative, taken the year before – establishment of the South Moresby Park, in the Queen Charlotte Islands, at a cost of $106 million.[10]

By 1988 the Environment Canada budget had barely returned to its pre-November, 1984, level, yet the government got through the election campaign largely unscathed by its environmental record, doubtless because of the campaign focus on the free trade issue. Environmentalists joined the opposition to free trade, pointing to the way it would promote increased resource depletion, through sale to the U.S. of Canadian natural resources, and put in jeopardy industrial subsidies intended to assist with pollution control in conjunction with plant modernizations. The government responded to one aspect of environmentalist lobbying – opposition to damming or canal construction that would divert freshwater across the border to the U.S. – by introducing legislation in the House, although it was never enacted, specifically ruling out such large-scale water diversions.

After the November 21 election, in which Tom McMillan lost his P.E.I. seat in the House of Commons, the Prime Minister took steps to demonstrate a new-found commitment to the issue both by creating a new Cabinet Committee on the Environment and by appointing a powerful voice within the Conservative Party, Lucien Bouchard, to the portfolio. Throughout his tenure as minister, however, which ended with his resignation from the cabinet in May, 1990, Bouchard remained preoccupied with Quebec-Canada relations and Meech Lake. Nevertheless, under Bouchard the federal government moved to establish the first new regulations governing pollution – new standards for pulp and paper mill discharges – to have been introduced since the late 1970s. Bouchard's major environmental initiative, however, was a "secret plan" for action on the environment, which apparently included taxes on gas and oil consumption – the "carbon tax" recommended by Canadian environmentalists in their 1989 *Greenprint for Canada*. Bouchard's plan was met by internal opposition from other departments and ministers, however, and since it had been developed without consultation with the environmental organizations, it was without advocates or support outside the government. By December, 1989, the plan was clearly a non-starter.[11]

Shortly before he resigned, Bouchard moved from secrecy to public consultation, releasing a document titled *The Green Plan* that was said to provide the basis for extensive public discussion of steps the federal government might take on environmental protection. *The Green Plan* was immediately denounced by environmentalists as being so simplistic that it "gave an impression of naiveté which one can only hope is false" and for ignoring the fact that over the past twenty years "considerable progress has been made in defining the key issues and in reaching consensus on priorities."[12] As well as moving the policy debate backward by raising as questions issues that had already been thoroughly debated and settled as government policy,[13] *The Green Plan* also left the impression that responsibility for environmental protection rested, in the final analysis, not with government but with individual citizens. The statement that "environmental problems are the result of the failure of Canadians at all levels of society – as individuals, in their business lives, and through our political institutions – to make decisions that fully take the environment into account"[14] suggests that all Canadians, including the Prime Minister, the CEO of a polluting corporation, and every one of the 4,000 citizens who attended consultation sessions on *The Green Plan*, have equal powers to protect the environment. Such a suggestion is not only ridiculous but an abdication of responsibility by the government of Canada.

By August, 1990, Environment Canada had completed its public discussions and was again working in secret to prepare a new cabinet submission for action on the environment. On December 11, 1990, Robert de Cotret announced the Green Plan, which after eighteen months had finally received cabinet approval. It envisaged spending $3 billion over five years, $850 million of which would be on pollution and the remainder on such things as new parks, science and education, and energy conservation. The plan set out general objectives with little detail and made no provision for either legislative action, such as new pollution reduction regulations, or fiscal measures, such as the proposed "carbon tax." Environmentalists generally denounced the plan, while business gave it "cautious kudos."[15]

The Brundtland Commission and Sustainable Development

By far the most important initiative taken during the 1980s, in terms of its impact both in the global arena and on environmental politics within Canada, was the work of the United Nations World Commission on Environment and Development, known after its chairman, Mrs. Gro Brundtland, then Prime Minister of Norway, as the Brundtland Commission. A central contention at the 1972 Stockholm Conference and in other discussions of international environmental protection was that the industrialized nations, having achieved power and prosperity without concern for the damage caused to their own and the planetary environment, could not, in fairness, expect the Third World to play by a different set of rules, assuming in connection with their own industrialization the added cost of environmental protection. The central importance of Third World economic development as essential for coping with overwhelming poverty, albeit in as environmentally sound a manner as possible, has been accepted by the industrialized nations as a starting point for discussion of international environmental action since 1972.

By the early 1980s, however, it had become obvious that many of the non-industrialized nations were becoming poorer, in both absolute and relative terms, and that for them environmental stresses, such as desertification, shortages of wood for heating and cooking, and contamination or reductions in water supplies, were very literally life-and-death issues. There was a recognition that poverty and environment must both be addressed on a global scale, and also that poverty in many cases *causes* environmental damage, which in turn causes greater poverty, in an ongoing cycle of cause and effect.

The Brundtland Commission report provided this illustration:

> Debts that they cannot pay force African nations relying on commodity sales to overuse their fragile soils, thus turning good land to desert. Trade barriers in the wealthy nations – and in many developing ones – make it hard for Africans to sell their goods for reasonable returns, putting yet more pressure on ecological systems.[16]

The report went on to state that "Environmental degradation, first seen as mainly a problem of the rich nations and a side effect of industrial wealth, has become a survival issue for developing nations."[17] In an eloquent and oft-quoted sentence, Brundtland went on to explain why the mandate of the Commission was structured to give equal emphasis to environment and development. "But the 'environment' is where we all live; and 'development' is what we all do in attempting to improve our lot within that abode. The two are inseparable."[18] She went on to point out that population growth and poverty were causing unbearable environmental stress in many parts of the world, saying "The downward spiral of poverty and environmental degradation is a waste of opportunities and of resources. In particular, it is a waste of human resources."[19] She then set forth the basic premise of her Commission: "These links between poverty, inequality and environmental degradation formed a major theme in our analysis and recommendations. What is needed now is a new era of economic growth – growth that is forceful and at the same time socially and environmentally sustainable."[20] Thus the Brundtland Commission placed itself squarely on one side of what, from the days of *Limits to Growth*, has been the major dividing line in environmental politics – growth or no growth.

Canada, true to its tradition of support for international environmental protection, made a strong contribution to the work of the Brundtland Commission. Maurice Strong was a member, while another Canadian, Jim McNeill, acted as secretary. Canada provided significant financial support and hosted one of the Commission sessions, and Canadian environmental organizations, Environment Canada, and a number of provincial ministries made submissions. Environment Minister Tom McMillan was one of the first to address the UN General Assembly, on October 19, 1987, when the Brundtland report was formally submitted to the Assembly.

The Brundtland report, titled *Our Common Future*, is a masterful document. It pulls together, in true ecological fashion, all of the interconnected themes that together comprise the global crisis we face: population growth; the growing poverty of much of the Third World; desertification and other threats to food supply; species extinction; energy consumption and its implications for the global atmosphere; industrial pollution; resource depletion and urbanization; the channelling of badly needed resources into arms manufacture. The Commission convincingly demonstrated how action on any one of these issues had implications for all of the others and sent forth a call for action to integrate economic and environmental decision-making: easing the burden of Third World debt to allow those nations to spend more on environmental protection; a co-ordinated approach to protection of the global commons; strengthening national and international environment laws; making the central government agencies with mandates for trade and economic development more accountable for the environmental implications of their actions. Most importantly, the Brundtland Commission demonstrated, in a way that had not been done before, the inevitable connection between environmental protection and distribution of wealth.

The response in Canada, when the report was released in 1987, was one of genuine enthusiasm across the spectrum of government, industry, and the environmental organizations. This may have been because the report seemed to offer something for everyone – giving the environmental community a renewed and credible call for action on long-sought principles such as access to decision-making, while giving business and government the assurance that economic expansion *has* to be the first priority. That the Commission had called on the industrialized nations to "adopt life-styles within the planet's ecological means," said that growth must be concentrated in the Third World and not the first, and called for an international redistribution of wealth in order that "the poor get their fair share of the resources required to sustain that growth"[21] did not seem to dampen the enthusiasm of such organizations as the Canadian Chamber of Commerce for the Brundtland message.[22]

"Limits to growth," the rallying cry of the early 1970s, had placed the environmental movement very clearly on the other side of the growth/no-growth divide, and the business community had attacked it head-on, suggesting that the notion of questioning growth was subversive and portraying those who did so as doomsayers, somehow responsible for the oil embargo, the recession that followed, and the doubting, unhappy mood of the late 1970s.

U.S. President Jimmy Carter had fallen headlong into that trap when he commissioned the Global 2000 report, a further attempt, building on the Club of Rome work, to look at the implications that future resource shortages might have for present policy. He attempted to put in place new energy policies and also sought, in a televised address, to speak honestly to the American people about the malaise in which they were caught. For his pains, he lost the 1980 election and the Americans gladly turned from a Cassandra to a genial and optimistic (if somewhat absent-minded) Ronald Reagan, who restored their pride by launching the U.S. on the greatest peacetime arms build-up the world has yet seen, which was also perhaps the largest government handout and transfer of wealth from one class to another in American history. The American defence contractors got rich, America for the first time became a debtor nation, and President Reagan, smiling all the while, did everything he could to forestall action on both American and international environmental protection.

The Brundtland Commission avoided that trap, since the logic of its starting point inevitably led it to an endorsement of continued economic expansion. Thus two warring camps were brought together in a single phrase, and for better or worse "sustainable development" has become the touchstone of environmental politics.

Given its previous commitment to the work of the Commission and the ready acceptance of the message, it is hardly surprising that Canada launched a major effort to consider ways of implementing the Brundtland report in this country. The National Task Force on Environment and Economy, convened by the Canadian Council of Resource and Environment Ministers in October of 1986, before the Commission had completed its report, was chaired by Gerard Lecuyer, Minister of Environment for Manitoba, and co-chaired by Roy Aitken, executive vice-president of Inco, and was composed of a number of environment ministers, heads of the Chamber of Commerce and Canadian Petroleum Association, and CEOs of a number of polluting companies such as Dow and Noranda. The environmental lobby was represented by Susan Holtz of the Ecology Action Centre, Halifax, and Charles Mallory of STOP in Montreal. The Task Force issued its report in September, 1987, less than a year after it was convened and at approximately the same time that the Brundtland report was presented to the United Nations. The Task Force report calls for a "dialogue on environment-economy integration," "good will, leadership and new processes for decision-making and planning," and making the "ideals" of sustainable development the "foundation for our institutions," but it gives no specific suggestions for how these changes should be accomplished. No mention is made of possible changes to environmental legislation or enforcement, of use of tax or pricing policies to increase costs of energy or waste disposal, or of specific targets for either pollution reduction or conservation objectives. Instead, the major Task Force recommendation is that each province and the federal government create a Round Table on Environment and Economy, multi-sector bodies with a purely advisory role. Other recommendations include development of conservation strategies (a process already, in theory, initiated in Canada in the early 1980s through adoption of the UNEP-sponsored World Conservation Strategy), increased use of environmental assessment, calls for increased accountability of ministers, and annual awards for "outstanding work on environment-economy integration."[23]

In June of 1988 the Conservation Council of Ontario sponsored a conference on sustainable development, followed by a similar event in October of that year sponsored by the Air Pollution Control Association. A report on the two sets of discussions states that "Conference participants were generally reluctant or unable to define precisely the term 'sustainable development.' This made it impossible to determine what we need to achieve sustainable development, how far we are from this goal and at what point we may have succeeded." Although perhaps not completely clear on the goal, participants apparently were clear on another point – the way to get there is not through legislative action.

The official Canadian response to the Brundtland Report, the creation of tripartite roundtables at which government, industry and nongovernmental environmental organizations cooperate to find means to achieve sustainable development, shows that cooperation, rather than greater regulation, is viewed as the best road. Industry participants were particularly strong proponents of this approach.[24]

In late 1989 the Mulroney government announced that it intended to save money by reducing Via train service. Given the fact that rail transport is far more energy-efficient and less polluting, on a person/mile basis, than the major alternative, the private automobile, it is hardly surprising that the Prime Minister was asked in the House of Commons if his government, proud defender at the United Nations of the concept of integrating economic and environmental decision-making, had considered the environmental implications of the cancellation of a number of train routes. Mulroney replied with a clear and emphatic "no."[25]

By the summer of 1990 all of the provinces had established the round tables recommended by the Task Force on Environment and Economy. Whether these round tables will achieve any concrete results is very much an open question. The Ontario Round Table held its first meeting in December, 1988, and then spent the next year and a half drafting and redrafting a "Challenge Paper," which, like Lucien Bouchard's Green Plan, was intended to provide the basis for yet more public discussion. It took eighteen months to produce the document because the Ontario government, worried about its environmental image and commitments to future action that might be made on its behalf, kept sending it back for revisions. When the document was finally released, immediately before the August, 1990, Ontario election, it contained many self-congratulatory "examples of what is being done," a recycling of "suggestions" for action advanced by the environmental lobby over the past few years, and exactly two recommendations for action – first, that "all Ontario organizations . . . adopt 'Codes of Practice' for sustainable development," and, second, that "universities, research institutes, governments and industry associations should develop more and better indicators of progress."[26]

The National Round Table held its inaugural meeting in June, 1989, and one year later released a report saying it had "moved ahead much more slowly than most of its members or contributors would have liked" but that, to date, it had established subcommittees, begun studies of "successful changes to decision-making practices . . . programs decreasing residential and commercial waste . . . economic incentives and disincentives . . . [and] 'measurement indicators' . . . to assess progresss towards sustainable development." The Round Table had also "articulated a series of objectives for sustainable development as a means of sparking dialogue" and had established a "$2,500 annual award for the Youth Science Fair participant whose entry best exemplifies sustainable development precepts."[27]

Is the Change More than Cosmetic?

Ontario was not the only province to take new environmental initiatives during the late 1980s. British Columbia, in tandem with the federal government, placed new regulatory restrictions on pulp mill discharges and in the spring of 1990 introduced an "environmental sin tax" on disposable diapers.[28] Both Quebec and Alberta in 1989 began to follow the Ontario lead, taken in 1985, to add to enforcement staff and enact legislation increasing fine levels. The Alberta government in 1990 introduced the Environmental Protection and Enhancement Legislation, a consolidation of existing legislation that also provided for increased public access to the environmental approvals process. New Brunswick and Nova Scotia both moved to enact legislation increasing fine levels for air and water pollution.[29]

All of the provinces and the federal government, working through the Canadian Council of Environment Ministers, have given collective commitments to solid waste reduction, new motor vehicle exhaust regulations, and a program for clean-up of abandoned waste sites.

This flurry of activity and commitments to future action is a logical outcome of the movement of the pollution issue over the past twenty years from the fringes to the centre of Canadian political life. Environmentalists and the business community no longer exchange invective across an abyss of misunderstanding and diametrically opposed values and perceptions. This is in part because of a maturing and toning-down of environmental rhetoric, but also, perhaps in larger part, because majority opinion has come to accept the arguments of environmentalists as something more than hysteria or utopian dreaming. The environmental threat is now accepted as something real, carrying with it direct economic and social consequences, and thus requiring serious attention and action.

What we have not yet seen is whether governments will be able to carry through on these new commitments. A simple indicator – federal spending on Environment Canada – does not suggest a major new emphasis on environment, regardless of what the opinion polls might say. In 1972-73 Environment Canada accounted for 1.22 per cent of total federal expenditures. That figure had dropped by 1985-87 to 0.82 per cent and to 0.84 per cent in 1987-88.[30]

Canadians have only begun to grapple with the two major stumbling blocks to action – the extremely high cost of pollution reduction and the political conflicts that will inevitably accompany the process of deciding how that cost will be allocated, particularly in the area of job dislocations. Resolution of these problems depends on whether or not the change in pollution politics is more than skin-deep. When the crunch comes, will Canadians be willing to pay the necessary price, in terms of taxes, consumer prices, jobs, or lifestyle changes? That will depend on what has motivated change to date. If it has been nothing more that a new perception that toxic chemicals pose a threat to health, coupled with a general increase in health awareness and a reduced willingness to accept risk, then it is unlikely that sufficient political momentum exists to navigate the rough seas ahead. If, on the other hand, the changing politics is based on more fundamental changes in values and perceptions of the world, and in particular if such changes are grounded at least in some measure in the Canadian past, giving new voice to enduring Canadian themes, then perhaps the new environmental politics will have the required staying power.

What was it, then, that caused the growth in public support for action on pollution over the two previous decades? A number of factors can be pointed to: much more information was available on pollution and its effects than ever before; drinking water contamination sparked new health fears; the environmental lobby received more financial support from the Canadian public and used these resources in an increasingly sophisticated manner. Perhaps just as important, the affluence that contributed to the rise of modern environmentalism after World War Two returned after the recession of the early 1980s and again allowed the luxury of environmental concern.

Of particular importance to the thesis advanced here – that political strength in the long term depends on acceptance of a new ethic, not the rational self-interest of resource conservation – is how much the environmental concern of the past two decades was motivated by a disinterested concern for the natural world. The answer is not clear. Acid rain appears to be an issue with no direct health implications, while mercury and Love Canal-type wastes clearly are health-related. Perhaps most significant is the new identification with the planet as a whole – given expression by the now common views of Earth seen from space. "If you love this planet, vote for it," said the Ontario Greens in 1990. If the environmental lobby can achieve its potential political strength during the coming decade, many more Canadians will do precisely that.

PART III

Regulating Pollution

Elected legislatures and parliaments enact legislation but administrative bodies, acting under the authority given them by such laws, develop and implement regulations. While a law will necessarily describe only in relatively general terms the activity that is and is not allowed, regulations are made as exact and specific as possible. The Ontario Environmental Protection Act, for instance, states that "No person shall deposit in, add to, emit or discharge into the natural environment any contaminant ... in an amount, concentration or level in excess of that prescribed by the regulations," but it is Regulation 308, under that Act, which states that, for instance, concentrations of acetic acid emitted from a given source shall not exceed 2,500 micrograms per cubic metre of air, on average, over any thirty-minute period.[1]

Environmental regulation can best be understood by comparing it to a more common type of government regulation – the system governing ownership and operation of a motor vehicle. No one is allowed to drive a car on a public road without a valid licence, which can only be obtained by meeting certain conditions – being of a certain age, having passed a test on the rules of the road, and so on. Those in possession of a licence must then act in compliance with a number of regulatory requirements – for instance, not exceeding the speed limit. Governments work to maximize compliance by appointing agents with special powers, the police, to detect illegal action. When violations are detected governments prosecute in the courts in order to impose sanctions, such as fines or imprisonment, which are intended to deter future illegal action on the part of both the individual involved and others.

In general terms, pollution regulation works in the same way. An individual or company cannot operate a polluting source, such as an ore smelter, without a licence (called exactly that in some provinces, and a Certificate of Approval in Ontario). To obtain a licence certain things must be done, such as installation of pollution control equipment to ensure emission standards are met. The operation must then comply with the conditions of the licence. Unlike motor vehicle regulation, in which the same rules apply to everyone, pollution rules are generally specific to the particular source and are stated as part of the licence, having been based on general policies and then modified to meet the circumstances of the particular operation. If the operation does not comply governments have the option of going to court to seek a penalty, although, as we shall see below, that option is exercised less frequently by environment departments than it is by traffic police.

The system described above refers to new pollution sources. When environmental regulation was introduced, of course, it applied primarily to existing sources. Various methods, ranging from requests for voluntary action to imposition of legally binding orders, are used to reduce pollution from sources already in operation.

In general terms, pollution regulation consists of the following steps:

- establishing desired objectives for environmental quality of air, water, and land;
- limiting pollution emissions from existing sources to achieve those objectives;
- imposing pollution control requirements on new sources, again with a view to achieving the objectives;
- monitoring pollution sources and, where necessary, taking action to enforce environmental regulations.

The following discussion of pollution regulation rests on a distinction between the following three activities:

- *cleaning up existing pollution* – termed, for these purposes, "remediation"; an example is the program presently being undertaken by the Ministry of Environment in Smithville, Ontario, to remove PCB-contaminated wastes from the storage lagoons and soil of a former waste disposal site and to destroy them by high-temperature incineration;
- *preventing new pollution* – setting legal limits on the amount of pollution that industries, municipalities, or other sources can discharge to air, water, or land;
- *waste management* – as set out above, all pollution is nothing more than waste disposal, since air and water emissions are used as a means of getting

rid of unwanted wastes; however, the term is used here to refer to "contained wastes" – substances not directly discharged to the environment but which are first contained, possibly treated to reduce toxicity, and then either discharged or transported to some type of disposal site. It is this treatment, transportation, and disposal activity, plus any steps taken to reduce, re-use, or recycle wastes, that is referred to as "waste management."

Pollution regulation, like the regulation of a number of other business activities, is made difficult by the fact that governments are attempting simultaneously to achieve two somewhat contradictory ends – to safeguard the health of humans and the natural environment while not interfering with business activity to the point that efficiency and productivity suffer, with resulting economic costs for the larger society. In the case of pollution regulation, the latter objective, until very recently, has been given clear priority by environment departments and their elected masters. Now that greater priority is being given to the first objective, the quality of environmental regulation needs to be improved so that both objectives can be achieved.

Like regulation in any other field, the ability of pollution regulation to meet its objectives depends on two things: the financial and staffing resources available to the regulatory agency and the sophistication of the instruments used by regulators – for instance, the data available, the systems used for evaluating and deciding on acceptable pollution impacts, the means of detecting illegal behaviour. Most of the discussion here will be concerned with regulatory instruments and their effectiveness, but this does not detract from the simple fact that pollution regulation, from the time the system was established in the different provinces in the 1960s, has been chronically underfunded. The Ontario Ministry of the Environment, for instance, which has undergone substantial expansion since the Liberal government was elected in 1985, had a total budget in fiscal year 1989-90 of $528.5 million, representing just over 1 per cent of the Ontario budget, and total staffing of 2,956. This can be compared, to continue the analogy of traffic regulation, with the Ontario Ministry of Transportation, which in that same year had a budget of $2.3 billion and a staff complement of approximately 9,300. Unlike Environment budget and staffing, this figure does not include the transportation enforcement arm – that portion of provincial and municipal police forces devoted to traffic policing.[2] Put in its simplest terms, Ontario gives a priority, expressed in public spending, to transportation over four times greater than that given to environmental protection. Pollution regulation will simply not be able to achieve its stated objectives until government spending is brought closer into line with what the public and their governments now agree is the priority that must be given to environmental protection.

Pollution regulation is still evolving. Many of its instruments, such as environmental assessment, are new and largely untested. The sciences it is based on, such as ecology and toxicology, are also new and are plagued with uncertainties. Environmental law has undergone very little testing and refinement through court challenges and resulting case law. Finally, the technology used to achieve the objectives of the regulatory system is changing every year as it responds to changing regulatory requirements.

Because the system is still in its infancy, having been in existence for less than thirty years, it is bound to go through significant further evolution in the years ahead, the shape of which will be decided by the political dialogue surrounding pollution regulation. The fundamentals, however, are sound.

The argument presented here is that the system for regulating pollution provides all the tools needed to eliminate pollution from the Canadian environment. All that need be done is to fund adequately and then actually use the system we have spent thirty years putting in place.

CHAPTER 9

The Regulatory System

Establishment of a System: 1945-1972

Prior to the 1940s, the limited existing environmental regulation in Canada was administered primarily by health authorities and was intended not to protect the natural environment but to limit the spread of infectious disease. The province of Quebec in 1908 assumed regulatory authority over municipal drinking water supplies and sewage disposal, followed by Ontario in 1912. Regulatory authority was exercised, in each case, by the Provincial Board of Health. The other provinces took similar action in the years between the two world wars.[1] Air pollution, to the extent that it was regulated at all, was also addressed by local boards of health, relying on municipal by-laws to limit emissions of black smoke.

During the 1950s and 1960s, the federal and provincial governments began to establish legislative and administrative mechanisms for pollution regulation, giving themselves more far-reaching powers than those vested in health authorities. It seems likely that this action was stimulated by the same combination of forces that has determined the pace of government action on pollution ever since – increased availability of scientific data on pollution combined with large-scale, dramatic events that have forcibly brought the problem to the attention of the public and their elected representatives.

The drama was provided by such catastrophes as the London smog of 1952. The increase in data was provided, after 1945, both by the growing number of government and academic scientists working in such fields as biology, zoology, and ecology and by specific studies, such as the IJC examination of Great Lakes water pollution undertaken between 1946 and 1949. The IJC study was of particular importance because it was one of the first to draw attention to the previously ignored issue of industrial waste disposal.

Enacting legislation

Models for Canadian pollution regulation were taken largely from the United States. In that country, the post-war concern over environmental quality and pollution had led quickly to passage of legislation. The Water Pollution Control Act was adopted in 1948, amended in 1956, and in 1965 revised to allow for federal and state standard-setting, with increased enforcement capacities. The U.S. federal government assumed responsibility for control of interstate air pollution with passage of the 1963 Clean Air Act, and in 1965 motor vehicle emissions were regulated for the first time.[2] President Johnson, in his State of the Union addresses for 1964 and 1965, drew attention to the need for action to protect the American environment.[3] The Wilderness Act of 1964 set aside federal lands to be held safe from development, while the Endangered Species Act in the same year provided increased legislative protection for wildlife.

The first step was taken in this country in 1955, when the Ontario legislature established a Select Committee on Air Pollution with a mandate to investigate and recommend steps for the protection of Ontario air quality. The Committee reported to the Ontario legislature in 1957, pointing to the problems caused by municipal waste incineration and motor vehicle exhaust and calling for the creation of an Air Pollution Control Commission with regulatory powers.[4] Although a full commission was not created, an Air Pollution Control section was established in the provincial Department of Public Health in 1957, and in 1959 the Ontario Air Pollution Control Act was enacted, giving municipalities legislative authority to pass by-laws regulating air pollution. In 1963 the province assumed control over approval of new industrial air pollution sources, and in 1967 the Act was amended to transfer all regulatory power from the municipal to the provincial level. The Act was administered by the Air Pollution Control Division of the Department of Health until 1969, when administration was transferred to the Department of Energy and Resources Management. Administration was transferred again in April, 1971, when the Act was incorporated into the new Environmental Protection Act, administered by the newly created Department of the Environment.[5] The development of air pollution standards and their establishment in regulations under the 1967 Act are described in Chapter 11.

Although air pollution regulation in Ontario remained in the hands of health authorities (first municipal, and then provincial), responsibility for water quality protection was vested in an independent body, the Ontario Water Resources Commission (OWRC), created in 1956 with a primary mandate to assist municipalities with capital financing of sewage and water treatment facilities. The Commission consisted of five members, appointed by the Ontario government. Its first general manager was Dr. Albert Edward Berry, formerly chief engineer with the Department of Health and one of the leading world authorities on sanitary engineering.[6]

The OWRC had authority not only to provide funding but also to regulate both liquid industrial and municipal sewage discharges to water.[7] This authority was shared with municipalities, since the OWRC regulated only those industries discharging wastes directly to water, while all those connected to municipal sewer systems or disposing of liquids in a municipal landfill were regulated by the relevant municipal by-law.

By 1966 most provinces had followed the Ontario lead in regulating water quality through an independent commission, although some still vested control in the hands of their health department. Listed below are the agencies that were primarily responsible for water quality in that year.[8]

British Columbia	Pollution Control Board
Alberta	Department of Public Health, Sanitary Engineering Commission
Saskatchewan	Water Resources Commission
Manitoba	Sanitary Control Commission
Ontario	Water Resources Commission
Quebec	Water Board
New Brunswick	Water Authority
Nova Scotia	Water Authority
Prince Edward Island	Water Authority
Newfoundland	Department of Health

By the end of the 1960s, the OWRC came to hold all of the regulatory powers now vested in provincial environment departments – setting water quality objectives; working to meet those objectives through the licensing of polluting industries; using administrative orders to force pollution abatement and prosecuting infractions of regulatory requirements in the courts. What follows is a cursory examination of each.

The first Ontario water quality objectives, used as the basis for establishing discharge standards, were set by the OWRC. This was the forerunner to the "Blue Book," the water quality objectives set by the Ontario ministry in the 1970s.[9] These objectives, in theory, allowed the Commission to set emission limits for individual polluting sources.

In the same manner the Alberta Department of Health, in 1967, set water quality objectives for the North Saskatchewan and Saskatchewan rivers. A total of ten objectives was established, setting concentration and other objectives for such things as Biological Oxygen Demand (BOD), coliforms, odour, oil and grease, and "heavy metals and other deleterious substances." Concentration limits for the latter were based on U.S. standards.[10]

The permitting system for allowable pollution concentrations, done through issuance of a Certificate of Approval governing new pollution sources, was also initiated by the OWRC. By December, 1971, there were 497 industries discharging wastes directly to Ontario waters under the authority of either an OWRC certificate or administrative order, of which "approximately 60 per cent ... generally meet current OWRC effluent requirements."[11] From July, 1965, when the permitting system began, and December, 1971, the OWRC issued 593 certificates of approval for industrial waste treatment facilities.[12]

The use of administrative orders to require reductions in pollution from existing sources was also initiated by the OWRC. During the period 1965-71 the Commission issued thirty-two orders for pollution abatement, twelve of which went to the pulp and paper industry.[13] The OWRC approach to regulatory compliance was one of negotiated abatement rather than enforcement. An undated OWRC pamphlet from the sixties, *The Story of Water*, illustrates the prevailing philosophy:

> Many industries are self-sufficient enough to treat their own wastes. However, there are some types of industrial wastes which present persistent problems. The continual development of new products also compounds this problem in that little or nothing is known concerning their wastes.
>
> This, naturally, constitutes a challenge to the research facilities of the industries concerned and, in Ontario, the Ontario Water Resources Commission. The OWRC, through its Division of Research and the Division of Industrial Wastes co-operates with these industries to solve stubborn waste disposal and treatment problems.[14]

Charges that were laid were usually withdrawn if they were successful in inducing action.[15] Some prosecutions, however, were carried through to conviction. During the seven-year period 1965-71, ninety-five charges were laid, seventy-three convictions were obtained, and fines totalling $27,405 were levied by the courts, resulting in an average fine for the period of $375.41.[16]

The federal government in Canada did not play a large role in pollution regulation during the 1950s and 1960s. Since there was little political pressure surrounding the issue, the governments of John Diefenbaker and Lester Pearson were happy to leave regulation in the hands of provincial and municipal governments. As in the 1980s, international pollution, such as the phosphorous pollution of the international waters of the Great Lakes, led the federal government in the 1960s, because of its jurisdictional mandate, to play the limited role it did. By 1970, however, in response to growing public pressure, the Trudeau government was moving into the pollution regulation field, its first major initiative the regulation of phosphorous discharges and the development of pulp and paper discharge standards, which, it was said, would be directly implemented by federal officials.

Creation of Environment Departments

When the provincial and federal governments began establishing new departments of the environment at the beginning of the 1970s they were faced with two basic options. Should they amalgamate all existing "environmental" functions, including resource management, pollution prevention, parks services, and wilderness preservation, into an existing or a new department? (At the time it was assumed that such a distinction between environmental and other government functions could easily be made, since "environmental protection" and "resource management" were considered to be more or less synonymous – it was not until the late 1980s that the crucial environmental implications of such government functions as taxation, trade, foreign aid, and industrial development came to be widely recognized.) Or should they leave such functions, plus others with direct environmental implications such as public health and agriculture, in the existing departments and provide the new environment department with co-ordinating powers? In the latter case, how extensive should those powers be – should the new department be given the power to regulate not only municipalities and industry but also other government departments? Or should each department be expected to play a self-regulatory role?

Although no jurisdiction opted for a full amalgamation, presumably because the established departments and their ministers were strong enough to fend off any such challenge, the federal government, at least initially, went further in that direction than did the provinces. Plans for the new Department of Environment were announced by Prime Minister Trudeau on October 9, 1970, and the department came into being on June 11, 1971, through proclamation of the Government Organization Act, 1970. The new department was based on the existing Fisheries and Forestry Department and for a time the first minister, Jack Davis, was referred to as Minister of Environment and Fisheries. Because of the constitutional authority given to the federal government over fisheries, this was one of the largest and most significant of the resource departments. With a new pollution prevention function added, it became the new environment department, Environment Canada.[17] This amalgamation of resource and pollution prevention functions did not last long, however, and in 1978, fisheries was taken from the Environment ministry with creation of the new Department of Fisheries and Oceans.

The new federal department in 1971 was divided into seven branches, as follows:

- Atmospheric Environment Service
- Environmental Protection Service
- Fisheries Service
- Lands, Forests and Wildlife Service
- Water Management Service
- Policy, Planning and Research Service
- Finance and Administration Service.

A review of Environment Canada functions undertaken in 1986 provides this description of the way the federal government originally divided environmental protection functions among departments:

> The government of the time finally settled for a partial integration. Building around the renewable resource/research responsibilities of the then Department of Fisheries and Forestry, it was finally decided to incorporate in the newly-formed department other environmental quality functions such as the Water Sector – freshwater and oceans from EMR, the Atmospheric Environment Service from MOT, Air Pollution Control and Public Health Engineering from NHW, the Canada Land Inventory from DREE and the Canadian Wildlife Service from DIAND.[18]

Desfossés provides the following list of other environmental functions maintained by existing departments:

> The Department of Agriculture retained relevant responsibilities for agricultural soil quality and for pesticide research and control; EMR kept its responsibility for the use of water resources for hydro-electricity generation; External Affairs maintained broad responsibility for the International Joint Commission (IJC), including its dealings on water pollution; Indian and Northern Affairs remained responsible for water pollution in the North and for National Parks; National Health and Welfare was to continue to deal with the effects of pollution on human beings, including air, water and radiation; the Department of Transport continued to look after water pollution from ships, air and noise pollution from aircraft and motor vehicles, and historic and recreational canals; the National Research Council was authorized, as a continuing responsibility, and in concert with other scientific organizations, to prepare and publish Scientific Criteria for Environmental Quality and to operate a Scientific and Technical Information Service on Pollution.... DOE was therefore not created as a super-ministry, responsible for all things environmental.[19]

Thus, even in the federal government, which went further in amalgamating environmental functions in the new department than did the provinces, substantial powers were still left in the hands of the established departments. This inherent weakness has continued to the present day to be a major factor working against effective environmental protection in Canada, since the only department with a clear mandate for environmental protection has little influence on government decisions or the actions of other departments.

The House of Commons adopted the first of the new pieces of federal environmental legislation, the Canada Water Act, in 1970, and almost immediately the government undertook a direct regulatory role with enactment of the Phosphorous Concentration Control Regulations, effective August 1, 1970. The new Clean Air Act, and amendments to the existing Fisheries Act to give increased powers for pulp mill regulation, followed in 1971. The next major piece of legislation was the Environmental Contaminants Act of 1975.

The Alberta Department of Environment was created a few months before the federal department, on April 1, 1971. The Water Resources and Pollution Control divisions were transferred to the new department from, respectively, Agriculture and Health. The department had two major functions – air and water pollution control and water resource management.[20]

The Ontario Ministry of the Environment (MOE) was created April 1, 1972, by the Government Reorganization Act, replacing the Department of the Environment, created the previous year, and amalgamating the department with the Ontario Water Resources Commission. The OWRC was dissolved and all of its functions, both regulatory and financial (the funding, building, and operating of water treatment and sewage disposal plants), were transferred to the new ministry. The two major pieces of legislation administered by the new ministry were the Environmental Protection Act, dealing primarily with air pollution and waste management, and the Ontario Water Resources Act, which provided the legislative authority over water quality previously administered by the OWRC.

An MOE organization chart dated March 31, 1973, shows the ministry with three main branches: water resources and pollution control; air and land pollution control, which included both air pollution and waste management; and laboratory and research division. By 1972, Quebec had also established an environment department to carry out pollution regulation activities. Unlike the federal department, the new provincial departments did not include resource management functions. The remaining seven provinces divided the function among special commissions and health and natural resource departments.[21]

British Columbia	Department of Lands, Forests and Water Resources
Saskatchewan	Natural Resources Department and Saskatchewan Water Resources Commission
Manitoba	Department of Mines, Resources and Environmental Management
New Brunswick	Department of Health and Welfare and New Brunswick Water Authority
Nova Scotia	Nova Scotia Water Resources Commission
P.E.I.	Environmental Control Commission
Newfoundland	Clean Air, Water and Soil Authority

Thus, by 1972, four jurisdictions had established environment departments and environmental regulation was provided in different ways by all of the others. The fundamentals of the regulatory system were in place.

Subsequent Modifications: 1972-1990

During the next two decades all of the provinces put in place the legislative and administrative components of a system for regulating pollution emissions comparable to that which had been established in Ontario, Quebec, and Alberta. The major modifications made to pollution regulation as the system has evolved since 1972 include the following:

- a significant increase in the information available on pollution sources and environmental effects, although a truly adequate information base for pollution regulation has not yet been achieved;
- a continuation of the confusion over jurisdictional responsibility both among the three government levels and, within any one level, between departments;
- initial steps toward opening the regulatory process to at least some measure of public scrutiny and involvement in decision-making;
- a move from almost complete reliance on negotiation and moral suasion to achieve regulatory compliance to an increased use of court prosecutions.

The Information Base

Changes in the available information on pollution, more than anything else, have influenced the course of pollution politics. Perhaps the two most significant changes in scientific understanding have been the ability to detect toxic substances at increasingly lower concentration levels and to monitor airborne movement of pollutants over hundreds and thousands of miles. This changing science has provided the basis for the major pollution concerns of the 1980s – pervasive, low-level toxic contamination that poses subtle, long-term threats to health and the environment, and the regional and global air pollution concerns of acid rain and CFC destruction of the stratospheric ozone layer. The science supporting concerns about global atmospheric change is primarily computer modelling of effects associated with various scenarios of changing concentrations of substances such as carbon dioxide. Given the inherent complexities and uncertainties of such work, the debate over global warming in 1991 is plagued with all of the confusion that characterized the acid rain debate ten years earlier.

Jurisdiction

When it was first created, Environment Canada set out to play, in at least a limited fashion, a direct regulatory role. During the 1970s regulations were promulgated under the Fisheries Act governing pollution discharges from six industrial sectors; motor vehicle emission standards were established in 1972 under the Motor Vehicle Safety Act, administered by Transport Canada, and amended in 1975 and 1979; lead in gas was regulated under the Clean Air Act in 1973 and 1974; and ocean dumping of waste was regulated in 1975. A major new piece of legislation, the Environmental Contaminants Act, was enacted in 1975, giving the federal government powers to control the introduction of new toxic substances in either pollution or products.

Environment Canada has never been able to fulfil this ambition of direct regulation, however. In most cases administration of such standards set forth in federal legislation has been left to the provinces. The federal role has been limited almost entirely to scientific research, establishment of policies and guidelines that could then be incorporated into provincial legislation or regulations, and co-ordination of provincial approaches. Co-ordination has been attempted both through the Canadian Council of Resource and Environment Ministers (now CCME) and through federal-provincial agreements outlining in general terms the way federal and provincial environmental protection activities would be co-ordinated. During the 1970s the federal government concluded agreements with all provinces except Newfoundland, Quebec, and British Columbia setting out the division of environmental responsibilities. Although these agreements have lapsed, the working relationships established under them still continue.[22] Since 1987 the federal and provincial governments have been bogged down in negotiation of a new series of agreements for implementation of the 1988 Canadian Environmental Protection Act. The other instrument for co-ordination used extensively in the 1970s was standard-setting by joint federal-provincial committees, with actual implementation left to provincial legislation administered by the provincial environment departments.

This limited federal role has been dictated in part by provincial objections to what was seen as encroachment on their constitutionally protected field of resource ownership and management. The Desfossés report states that provincial resistance to federal action was based not only on constitutional grounds:

> They [the provinces] began to express increasing concerns over what they considered to be undue federal intrusion into provincial jurisdiction, over the consequent financial impacts federal decisions could have upon their treasuries and over the impact federal regulations could have on the short-term profitability of firms providing employment, often in single-industry towns.[23]

Desfossés argues that as the provinces gained a stronger presence in the field, through establishment of environment departments and enactment of their own environmental legislation, they grew more confident in their objections to federal activity.[24] During the past decade, provincial objections to federal activity have received a sympathetic hearing in Ottawa, since neither the Trudeau nor Mulroney governments have demonstrated – as measured by spending on Environment Canada and willingness to leave regulation to the provinces, for example – anything beyond a superficial commitment to environmental protection.

Public Access

The major effort to increase public access to the system of pollution regulation is the concept of an "environmental bill of rights," a major goal of the Canadian environmental movement since the early 1970s. The phrase refers to proposed legislation that, if enacted, would grant the public a right to a healthy environment and introduce a series of reforms to increase the powers of private citizens to protect themselves, and their environment, from the effects of pollution. Such legislation would grant increased powers to sue in civil court for damages caused by pollution and to initiate private prosecutions of pollution offences in cases where government had refused to act. It would also provide increased access to information on pollution and rights to participate in standard-setting and other processes.

Opposition parties introduced such bills in the Alberta and Ontario legislatures in 1979, in Saskatchewan in 1982, in Ontario, again, in 1982 and 1987. To date, however, no such legislation has been enacted, despite the fact that in Ontario the Liberal Party, which introduced the 1979 and 1982 bills, assumed power in 1985. When the NDP brought in a 1987 bill very similar to the Liberals' own 1982 proposal, the Liberal government began a series of procedural moves to ensure it died a quiet death without ever requiring an explicit avowal of the government's change of heart when it moved across the floor of the legislature.[25] Ruth Grier, Ontario NDP

Environment Minister, announced on December 13, 1990, her intention to introduce an environmental bill of rights.

The one area in which the fight for increased public access to decision-making has achieved at least a limited measure of success has been the increased use of environmental assessment as part of the approvals process. The concept of environmental assessment, introduced by the federal government as a policy in 1973, and through legislation by Ontario in 1975, and Saskatchewan and Newfoundland in 1980, is based more on the principles and instruments of land-use planning than on pollution regulation. It is an attempt to implement the "preventative" approach to environmental protection (which all agree is preferable to "react and cure") by predicting environmental impacts of proposed projects while they are still in the planning stages and then requiring that steps be taken to "mitigate" or reduce them. A central principle of environmental assessment is guaranteed public access to decision-making through the requirement that the assessment be considered in a public hearing before an administrative board. The provincial and federal governments, not surprisingly, have made very limited use of this inherently radical departure in environmental regulation.

Movement in the area of access to information has been similarly slow. The most notable legislative development has been in the occupational health field. The system known as WHMIS (Workplace Hazardous Materials Information System) was negotiated by unions, industry, and federal and provincial labour departments during the mid-1980s and now requires employers to provide their employees with more information than previously on toxic substances used in the workplace. In the United States more far-reaching legislation was enacted in 1986 to ensure the "community right to know." Industrial plants in the U.S. are now required to provide information not only to workers but to local citizens and municipalities concerning the types and quantities of pollution they emit. Although some pressure along these lines has been brought to bear in Canada, the community right to know has not been a major political issue.

Enforcement

In the area of enforcement and compliance, the major change has been the first steps taken toward a move from the "abatement" to the "enforcement" approach. During the 1970s the same environment officials, usually referred to as abatement officers, were responsible for all phases of the compliance process – from provision of technical information and advice on the best means of reducing pollution to meet requirements, through negotiation of abatement programs, to the decision to prosecute. Prosecutions were few.

The key change came in 1985 when Ontario, the first jurisdiction to do so, established a separate Investigations and Enforcement Branch, headed by an official whose technical expertise was not in the field of pollution engineering but in police enforcement. The establishment of a department whose only relationship with the regulated industry is one of investigation and enforcement, and which has adequate staffing and financial resources, has significantly changed the approach to enforcement and compliance in Ontario. In the nine-year period from 1972 to 1980 there were sixty-nine convictions for environmental offences in that province.[26] Between April 1, 1988, and March 31, 1989, by contrast, there were 164 Ontario convictions.[27]

CHAPTER 10

Cleaning Up Existing Pollution

The Nature of the Problem

The bulk of the organic and inorganic chemicals, metals, and other toxic contaminants emitted to the environment each year are dispersed and carried by water or air to such destinations as riverbeds, fields, and the fatty tissues of animals living toward the higher end of the food chain. For the most part, concentration levels are relatively low. The pollution poses problems of bio-magnification and build-up, but it is not such an immediate threat to health that steps must be taken to remove it from the environment – something that in any event would be virtually impossible. In other cases, however, contaminants have accumulated in concentrations and quantities that pose an immediate threat to human health and the natural environment. In those cases they must be removed from the environment, if possible destroyed or treated to reduce toxicity, and then transported to another resting place that is, hopefully, safer.

This process of clean-up or remediation is used not only for pollutants in the open environment but also for contained wastes – for example, asbestos that must be removed from buildings, and PCB-contaminated wastes that have been kept in storage, awaiting final treatment and disposal.

Pollutants in the open environment that require remediation are found primarily in two locations – sediments at the bottom of rivers or harbours that have been increasingly contaminated over the years as toxic substances are carried downstream and settle out of the water above, and in soil exposed to pollution over a period of years. Examples of the latter include municipal landfills that have received industrial as well as household wastes and the sites of former factories that disposed of toxic wastes, in all likelihood, by throwing them out the back door.

Canada is only now coming to grips with the problem of cleaning up past pollution. In the 1970s plans were developed for cleaning up the mercury pollution in Lake St. Clair and the English-Waubigoon River system, but no action was ever taken. During the 1980s, however, several clean-ups were initiated, the largest being the PCB-polluted soils at a former waste disposal site in Smithville, Ontario, and destruction by incineration of coal tars built up over the years at the steel works in Sydney, Cape Breton Island. The cost of each program is expected to be in the neighbourhood of $50 million.

Clean-up of existing pollution, either of contained wastes or of contaminated soils or sediments, is largely an urban issue. In recent years it has become a particularly pressing issue in the context of urban redevelopment. As cities move to rehabilitate and redevelop areas that, because of previous use by polluting industries, are heavily contaminated, they are faced with the need to restore environmental quality to the lands in question. The reason for this focus on urban clean-up is simply one of visibility – a contaminated site in the natural environment, such as a former landfill, that does not pose an immediate threat to human health and offers no great development value is likely to be ignored by governments and the public. Urban land, on the other hand, offers a major return on investment and will not receive zoning, building, and other approvals until it is declared safe by health, environment, and planning officials, and it will not therefore be ignored. The unforeseen cost assumed by the unwary buyer of polluted land – termed "toxic real estate" – has become an issue of urgent concern for land developers over the past few years.

One of the most prevalent urban problems is coal-tar pollution left by former coal gasification plants:

> As early as the 1820's, much of the gas used for lighting, heating and some industrial processes was produced in coal gasification plants. . . . Most of the larger cities, and some smaller towns across Canada had such plants until the introduction of natural gas and pipeline transmission drastically reduced their commercial viability. By the 1950's, most gasification plants were abandoned, demolished or converted into other industries.[1]

Toronto faces such a situation with land slated for redevelopment in the industrial area just east of the downtown core and close to Lake Ontario. Known as the Ataratiri site, the joint city-provincial project takes its name from the Huron word meaning "supported by clay" and is intended to assist the Toronto housing crisis by providing 12,000 new housing units. During the past hundred years the site has been used by a variety of industries, including a coal gasification plant established in 1848, tanneries, scrapyards, a battery company, and others, with the result that the clay is now contaminated with metals, PCBs, PAHs, oil, grease, and other substances. Between 70,000 and 700,000 cubic metres of soil, depending on the standards that will eventually govern the clean-up, will have to be removed for disposal, some portion of which will require hazardous waste disposal.[2] The cost of the clean-up has been estimated at between $80 and $100 million.[3]

Vancouver and British Columbia face an estimated cost of $60 million to clean up the land used for Expo 86, which has been sold to a private developer and is slated for redevelopment. This cost will be borne by the taxpayer since the conditions of the sale stipulated that the land "be suitable for development."[4]

An indication of the potential costs of clean-up in Canada is given by the American Superfund program. After Love Canal had brought the issue forcefully to public attention, the U.S. government, in 1980, established a program to clean up former waste disposal sites that posed similar threats to surrounding communities. Between 1980 and 1988, allocations of $4.5 billion were approved by Congress, of which $2.6 billion have been spent to clean up thirty-four of the 1,175 sites on the Environmental Protection Agency's National Priority List. At that rate, something in excess of $800 billion would be required to clean up all of the 1,175 sites. Some indication of the absolutely staggering costs involved is given by the estimate that before the program is completed some 30,000 sites will require remediation.[5]

Although the Canadian Council of Ministers of the Environment has made an estimate of the potential cost of the clean-up in Canada, the figure and the study on which it is based have not been made public.[6] The CCME announced in 1989 that $200 million of federal and provincial funds had been designated for clean-up of fifty "abandoned" sites, and a further $50 million was committed for "decontamination technology development and demonstration."[7] Those fifty sites were said by the Council to represent 5 per cent of the estimated 1,000 sites in Canada "where contamination poses an existing or imminent threat to human health or the environment."[8] If the estimate of $200 million to clean up 5 per cent of the contaminated sites is correct, the total cost estimate might be twenty times that figure, or $4 billion.

The $200 million estimate is far from reliable, however, because clean-up cost depends on the pollution standards governing the operation. Costs will vary depending on the amount of material to be remediated and the total portion that then requires expensive disposal as hazardous waste. Since those decisions have not yet been made for the estimated 1,000 sites requiring remediation, the CCME cost estimate has no real validity.

An example of the relationship between standards and the cost of clean-up is given by the 1976 and 1989 programs to remove lead-contaminated soil in Toronto in the vicinity of the Toronto Refiners and Smelters plant on Niagara Street and the Canada Metal plant in the Riverdale neighbour-hood. Before any work could begin on either program a decision had to be made on the contamination level considered unacceptable and therefore how much soil would be removed and replaced. In 1976 the process used to determine this figure was a public hearing conducted by the Ontario Environmental Hearing Board (forerunner of the present Environmental Assessment Board). This resulted in a decision by the Board that soil contaminated beyond 2,600 parts per million (ppm) would be removed.[9] The cost of the 1976 program was $83,000.[10]

By 1989, when a comparable program was again initiated in Toronto, the standard had been tightened from 2,600 to 500 ppm.[11] This had the effect of increasing the number of properties requiring remediation from approximately fifty, which would have been the case if the earlier standard had been used, to 1,000.[12] The 1989 cost of removing and replacing 25,000 tonnes of lead-contaminated soil in the Riverdale neighbourhood, plus associated costs such as cleaning of houses, was approximately $12 million.[13]

Thus the standard for lead clean-up in Toronto was made more stringent by a factor of five over little more than a ten-year period. This same process is almost certain to happen in future clean-up programs, making attempts to predict future clean-up costs almost impossible. The problem is well illustrated by the issue of remediating contaminated sediments in harbours and rivers surrounding the Great Lakes. A 1990 study commissioned by the Ministry of the Environment estimates that the cost of dredging such sediments and transporting them to a municipal landfill will be $50 to $70 per cubic metre, which in turn leads to an estimate that it would cost slightly more than $2 million to clean up the sediments in Hamilton harbour. But this estimate rests on the assumption that the sediments will not be so toxic as to be classified as hazardous waste and therefore will be accepted in a solid-waste landfill. If they are classified as a hazardous waste, the study points out, the cost will be five to ten times higher: "Costs for sediment removal if the sediments are too contaminated for conventional removal could rise to between 10-20 million dollars."[14] But even that figure may be low since the cost of hazardous waste treatment and disposal depends entirely on the methods used. It has been estimated that treatment by means of incineration of contaminated sediments might cost as much as $1,800 (U.S.) per cubic yard – a figure approximately twenty-five times higher than the Ontario estimate, which would mean the cost estimate of cleaning up sediments in Hamilton harbour could rise from $2 to $50 million.[15]

With cost estimates in that range, the issue of who will pay for clean-up programs becomes particularly compelling. The polluter-must-pay principle often cannot be applied to remediation costs because the party responsible for the contamination either cannot be identified or no longer exists. It is simply impossible, for instance, to list all the parties who contributed, over the past hundred years, to the contamination of the sediments in Hamilton harbour. In a similar vein, the PCB disposal companies that operated at Smithville, Ontario, and St.-Basile-Le-Grande, Quebec, have both gone bankrupt and left the public to pay their clean-up bills. The problem is compounded by the fact that much of the pollution that now must be cleaned up was discharged legally to the environment. When the polluter operated in compliance with all regulatory requirements the argument can be made, with justice, that government cannot change the rules and then apply them retroactively to impose liability for past pollution that at the time was legal. For this reason, the lead smelters paid only one-third of the $83,000 cost of the 1976 lead clean-up. The $12 million cost of the Riverdale clean-up has, to date, been paid entirely by government.[16] The taxpayer will likely pay a substantial portion of the total cost of clean-up in Canada, even though much of the pollution originated with private-sector operations.

The subject of remediation poses another issue, in addition to those of cost and liability: how to dispose of the polluting materials, such as lead in Riverdale soil or PCB-wastes in drums in a Montreal warehouse. Canada does not have sufficient disposal capacity – measured in terms of space in landfills licensed to accept hazardous waste or volume of material that can be handled by the few existing hazardous waste incinerators – to accommodate all of the hazardous waste newly generated in the country each year, let alone past waste. As remediation efforts increase, the quantities of waste requiring disposal will increase, compounding an already difficult problem. Contaminated soil, which occupies a high volume of landfill space in relationship to the total quantities of toxic substances it contains, will especially aggravate this problem.

Identifying Contaminated Sites

In Canada, as in the United States, publicity surrounding Love Canal first spurred government action to identify previously used waste disposal sites that might present threats to human health and the environment. In the early 1980s joint federal-provincial programs were conducted in all of the Atlantic provinces, Manitoba, Saskatchewan, Alberta, British Columbia, and the two territories. Ontario and Quebec conducted their own surveys. Preliminary lists of contaminated sites were developed through review of government files, examination of topographical maps and aerial surveys, and questionnaires and interviews with municipal officials.

Federal involvement in this joint program was cancelled by the Mulroney government as part of Environment Canada cutbacks in November, 1984.[17] The provincial governments, however, have continued the program. By 1990 nearly 10,000 former waste sites had been identified in Canada and had received at least a preliminary assessment of the risk they posed to the surrounding environment.[18] An Environment Canada report dated October 30, 1987, identifies 719 of those sites as Priority 1, defined as "sites which could present a high risk potential to health and the environment and which should be immediately assessed."[19] As noted above, the CCME in 1989 put the number of such sites at 1,000.

By 1990 the Ontario program had identified a total of 2,455 closed waste sites and 1,395 still active ones, of which 170 had been given priority for further investigation.[20] During the course of these investigations, Ontario had identified coal-tar contamination as a major problem. Forty-six sites had been identified in thirty-six Ontario cities and six of those, located in Ottawa, Sudbury, Thunder Bay, Sioux Lookout, Cornwall, and South River, had been given priority for further investigation.

Identification of contaminated sediment sites requiring remediation has been done almost exclusively under the Remedial Action Plan (RAP) program co-ordinated by the IJC. The IJC has developed a listing of what it refers to as "Areas of Concern" – forty-two sites around the Great Lakes, seventeen on the Canadian side, that pose particularly difficult pollution problems. The Commission developed the RAP program as a process by which local, state/provincial, and federal authorities, working in consultation with polluting industries, public-interest groups, and others, would develop plans and programs for restoration of environmental health in each area of concern. The plans include both pollution prevention, such as separating combined sanitary and storm sewers to reduce the flow of untreated sewage to the lakes and reductions in industrial wastes, and clean-up of existing pollution, primarily contaminated sediments at the bottom of harbours and rivers but also including leaking hazardous waste landfills.

Although planning has commenced in each of the forty-two areas, actual work, as of 1990, has not yet begun. Total cost of the RAP program has been estimated at between $100 and $500 billion, in U.S. funds, a large portion of which will go toward such needs as upgrading sewage treatment plants and reducing ongoing industrial pollution.[21] The conservative cost of contaminated sediment clean-up at nine U.S. sites is $184 million (U.S.). The high-end cost at those same sites is "into the billions of dollars."[22]

Establishing a Clean-Up Program

Although initial steps have been taken, the provincial and federal governments by 1990 had not yet established clean-up programs with clearly identified sources of revenue, criteria for deciding clean-up priorities and objectives, and standards governing the extent of remediation required. The Ontario Environment Minister announced on November 1, 1986, that his government would provide $10 million annually toward the cost of clean-up in Ontario, a program that was referred to as an Environmental Security Fund.[23] The amount was increased the next year to $20 million. In fact, however, Ontario has simply provided funds as required, either through this budget or, in the case of the Smithville clean-up, from general revenues, and has not established a fund with clearly identified sources of revenue and criteria for use. Nor has any other province established a fund.

In 1986, the year that Ontario first budgeted funds for this purpose, Premier Peterson called on the Prime Minister and other premiers to establish a national fund. Presumably in response to this proposal, the Canadian Council of Ministers of the Environment initiated a study of clean-up needs and in the fall of 1989 announced the joint federal-provincial funding of $200 million, referred to above, for clean-up costs "which cannot be recovered from the polluter."[24] At the same time the CCME released the first set of recommended guidelines for clean-up programs to be developed in Canada. The guidelines are intended to be used by the provinces in regulating or undertaking PAH clean-up from coal-tar pollution.[25] Although the CCME has not yet established criteria for clean-up priorities, objectives, and standards, other than those for PAH, the program began in the fall of 1990. At a press conference on November 30, 1990, B.C. and the federal government announced signing of the first federal-provincial agreement under the CCME clean-up program, with $29 million allocated to clean up "orphaned" sites in the province. The location of only one site, at Cariboo Mountain, was revealed and the list of other B.C. sites to be cleaned up under the program was kept secret.

Ontario, in 1989, became the first jurisdiction to establish guidelines for decommissioning and cleaning up former industrial sites.[26] The guidelines are based in part on experience gained with two private-sector clean-ups – restoration of refineries owned by Shell in Oakville and Texaco in Port Credit to an environmentally acceptable condition. Shell closed its refinery in 1983 and applied to the Ontario ministry for approval of a clean-up program that would allow the 512-acre site to be converted to future residential and industrial uses. Initial investigations revealed a total of forty-three toxic substances in the soil, but at the time the MOE did not have guidelines setting forth acceptable soil concentration levels. These were developed on the basis of research conducted jointly over several years by Shell and Texaco and reviewed by the MOE, in consultation with the Ministry of Labour. Final approval for the Shell clean-up, with specific objectives for the substances of concern, was given by the MOE in 1988.[27]

Major Clean-ups To Date

During the late 1980s clean-ups in Ontario have included a coal-tar contaminated site in Ottawa, discovered during construction of a transit line, at an estimated cost of $18 million; a PCB clean-up in Pottersburg Creek, near London; another coal-tar site in Kitchener-Waterloo, again resulting from a redevelopment plan and with a price tag of $2 million; and a clean-up on Berkley Street, in Toronto, at a cost of $2.5 million.[28]

The Department of National Defence has initiated a waste destruction program to be undertaken at Canadian Forces bases in different parts of the country. It plans to undertake destruction of fifty tonnes of mustard gas at Canadian Forces Base Suffield, in Alberta. In late 1989, DND began a program to incinerate 3,500 tonnes of PCB wastes brought from a number of northern federal sites to Goose Bay, Labrador. The PCB destruction, the first in Canada done by means of a portable incinerator, was completed in August, 1990.[29]

In 1978 the town of Smithville, located close to the site of the proposed OWMC facility in the Niagara region of Ontario, sold land to D&D Disposal, a company that began operation of a waste transfer station. PCB-contaminated wastes were stored at the site, awaiting final destruction by means of a new process the company hoped to develop.

Since there were almost no other disposal options available, the Smithville site had become, by the early 1980s, the largest storage depot for PCBs in Ontario. But the company never managed to develop a disposal plan for the wastes stored there, and when it turned to the option of sending the wastes to Scotland for destruction in that country, it failed to gain approval for export.

In 1986 D&D Disposal went bankrupt and the MOE assumed responsibility for maintenance of the badly polluted site. In 1987 it was found that the town's drinking water supply was threatened with contamination and since then Smithville has relied on other sources, including trucked water. The MOE had spent $7 million on testing and maintenance by 1988 and had signed a contract for disposal, using mobile, high-temperature methods. The incineration was given a Certificate of Approval on July 11, 1990. Total cost of the clean-up, which will be borne by the Ontario taxpayer, is expected to be approximately $50 million.[30]

In November, 1989, the MOE released a report stating that the PCB wastes had migrated down and contaminated the bedrock under the site. If these wastes are not cleaned up, the report said, they "could cause unacceptable concentrations of dissolved contaminants to the groundwater for decades." Unfortunately, there is no technology in existence for clean-up of waste at that depth. The MOE has begun a program to develop the technology over the next five years. The cost estimate for such a program of bedrock clean-up is in the neighbourhood of $100 million.[31]

The largest clean-up operation undertaken by the federal government to date is the ten-year, $50 million program intended to excavate and incinerate 700,000 tonnes of coal tar contaminated with polynuclear aromatic hydrocarbons and other substances, the product of almost a century of coke oven operation by the Sydney steel plant. The impetus for this program was not primarily an environmental concern, even though the pollution of Sydney harbour was severe enough to require closure of the lobster fishery in 1981. Rather, the clean-up was started as part of a joint federal-provincial plant modernization program initiated in 1981. Federal funding for the program comes from the Department of Regional and Economic Expansion, not Environment Canada. A contract for on-site construction of a $16.5 million incinerator has been awarded, applications submitted for Nova Scotia environmental approvals, and it is anticipated that clean-up operations will begin in the spring of 1991.[32]

Storing Up Problems for the Future

Statistics Canada, when it provided the $100 to $500 billion cost estimate for the forty-two Great Lakes Remedial Action Plans, went on to observe that the cost was so high as to be close to prohibitive, saying that it was a price that possibly "cannot or will not be paid." The obvious point was then made – "the lesson is clear" that there must be "a redoubling of efforts aimed at prevention of further degradation."[33]

As discussed below, pollution regulation has advanced to the point that the most obvious abuses, which in the past contributed to our present clean-up problems, are no longer tolerated. This does not mean, however, that the problem of remediation is limited to cleaning up old pollution or that clean-up is a one-time task. Until we stop pollution we will always need clean-up programs.

Each year we create future clean-up problems by discharging millions of tonnes of toxic substances to the environment, a portion of which collects in such quantities and at such locations as to require remediation. We are busy cleaning up old landfills but we are also busy creating new ones – undoubtedly better engineered and with many more environmental safeguards than in the past, but also accepting much greater volumes and varieties of toxic substances than ever before. The question that must be asked is whether a simple doubling of our present pollution prevention efforts will be sufficient.

CHAPTER 11

Setting Standards

Preventing Pollution

Having reviewed efforts to clean up past pollution, we now turn, in this chapter and the next, to the four topics central to preventing new pollution:

- the information available to environment departments as they regulate pollution;
- the way in which governments set standards limiting the total quantities of pollution discharged each year;
- the process for licensing new sources of pollution and requiring reductions from existing sources, which is the means by which most standards achieve legally enforceable status;
- the way governments attempt to ensure that pollution standards are in fact obeyed.

In summary, preventing pollution consists of two factors – setting standards and implementing them.

The Information Base

In 1986 Ontario Environment Minister Jim Bradley attempted to enforce pollution reduction requirements, first imposed in 1982 with a four-year deadline for compliance, on the Kimberly-Clark pulp mill located at Terrace Bay on the north shore of Lake Superior. The company said it could not possibly afford any reductions and would be forced to lay off employees if the 1982 order were not amended. During the ensuing controversy the minister both ordered a forensic audit of the Kimberly-Clark books and appointed an Experts Committee on the regulation of kraft mill discharges in the province. That Committee, made up of a toxicologist, an economist, and an expert on the pulp and paper industry, provided in 1988 one of the first independent examinations of a pollution source (in this case, organochlorine discharges, of which dioxins form a part, from the nine kraft pulp mills in Ontario), indicating the steps that could be taken to reduce the problem and the economic costs such action would impose on the industry. Armed with this data, the minister was able to, in his words, "call their bluff" and impose new regulatory requirements on the industry both in advance of his own MISA timetable and before similar action could be taken by the other jurisdictions that had begun to examine the problem of dioxin discharges.[1]

During this same period, while the minister was using independent data to force pollution reduction by a reluctant pulp mill, the Ontario Auditor-General took Bradley to task for relying on the regulated industry itself, rather than his own officials, for information on compliance with the newly imposed acid rain regulations.[2] The only defence the minister was able to offer was that his budget did not provide anything like the funds required to generate this kind of information.

These two contrasting incidents illustrate both what has to date been the norm in Canada and the potential for change. Traditionally in Canada the regulated industry supplies the information that the environment department, with limited funds and staff, then struggles to verify, interpret, and use to establish and enforce pollution limits. Any increase in the availability of independent, credible data obviously would be of considerable benefit for regulating pollution.

To regulate pollution successfully, government agencies need two types of information – (1) the physical nature of the pollution being regulated; (2) the social and economic impacts such regulation is likely to have. Both are equally important due to the unfortunate fact that cost to the regulated industry and larger society is almost always a more important criterion in determining regulatory action than is the environmental damage caused by pollution.

The empirical information needed by regulators can be divided into two major categories: (1) general information on the sources of various contaminants and the effects they cause as they move through the environment, and (2) more specific information on individual pollution sources. General toxicological information is generated by such government institutions as the Canada Centre for Inland Waters, established by the federal government in 1970 to undertake monitoring and research in all areas of water quality, and by scientists working in universities in Canada and other countries. During the past two decades governments have worked to establish "base-line" or "state of the environment" information, which can be used in establishing regulatory objectives and in measuring progress toward their achievement.

The first work of this nature, done earlier in the century, was undertaken largely in the resource management field – geologists mapping terrain in the search for fossil fuel reserves, for example, or forestry companies accumulating information on potential timber yields. By the 1960s, when government began to assume a mandate for environmental protection, new institutions were created for this purpose. In the United States the Council on Environmental Quality was created by the Nixon administration to prepare annual surveys of the state of the American environment. That work was taken over, when Council funds were cut back by the Reagan administration in the early 1980s, by the Conservation Foundation, a non-profit environmental research organization. In recent years another non-government organization, the Worldwatch Institute of Washington, D.C., has done a very credible job of providing base-line information on a global basis, through its annual *State of the World* report. The OECD first published a survey of the European environment in 1979 and since then, in the late 1980s, France, Japan, the Netherlands, and Indonesia have published comparable works in their own countries.

Only one such survey has been published to date in Canada, the *State of the Environment Report for Canada*, released by Environment Canada in May, 1986. A second edition is scheduled for 1991. There has been one regional report, on the Atlantic environment, published by Environment Canada in 1985, and one province has undertaken a comparable survey – *L'environnement au Québec – un premier bilan*, released by the Quebec Ministry of the Environment in 1988.

Ongoing monitoring of different aspects of environmental quality, such as concentrations of dust, sulphur dioxide, and other contaminants in urban air, is done by many of the provincial environment departments. The Atmospheric Environment Service of Environment Canada operates a string of monitoring stations, tracking such things as acid rain movement from U.S. and Canadian sources. As mentioned, the IJC, working with American and Canadian environment agencies, publishes regular data on contaminant trends in the Great Lakes.

Source-specific information on pollution is provided almost entirely by the polluting industries themselves. A condition of most provincial licensing approvals is periodic monitoring and reporting to the environment department by the regulated industry. This is supplemented and verified by occasional spot-checks done by the environment department.

Industry is also responsible for providing other types of information. In Ontario, for instance, all industries generating hazardous waste must, since 1987, provide the Ministry of Environment with information on types and volumes produced. All provinces operate a manifesting system, which requires that information be submitted on all wastes sent for off-site treatment and disposal. Pollution spills and accidental discharges must by law be reported immediately to the provincial environment department.

Although considerable attention is paid to the economic implications of pollution regulation, this information is generated for the most part on an informal basis. When Ontario introduced the MISA program to further regulate water discharges in 1986 it undertook to prepare economic impact predictions prior to introducing regulations under the program, a number of which have now been completed. Such information is also prepared in connection with the environmental assessment process. For the most part, however, governments rely on the regulated industry to provide such information and have almost no programs or staff in place to provide it for themselves.

The physical data and socio-economic information on which regulation is based are limited and to some degree uncertain and ambiguous, with interpretation inevitably being influenced by the assumptions and interests of the different parties – environmentalists and industry will seldom reach the same conclusion on the severity of risk posed by a particular pollution source. This means that for the general public and its elected representatives, who must make decisions in the face of both uncertainty and heated political conflict, the credibility of the source of information is of key importance. At present there are very few neutral sources of information on either the physical or economic aspects of pollution. Any efforts to provide neutral sources of information – perhaps by establishing an independent body, funded and managed by all parties – would be beneficial.

The Importance of Standards

Pollution regulation, despite all its complexities, consists essentially of two things – setting standards and enforcing them. Standard-setting is the process of deciding how much pollution will be allowed to enter the environment each year. Thus it is through the standard-setting process that governments, and the larger society they represent, make the final trade-off between the goal of environmental protection and other, conflicting, economic and social objectives. If we set the standard so as to allow x tonnes of pollution per year, we are told by ABC Industrial that the plant can continue to operate with the existing staff and indeed might even be able to expand and provide more jobs. But if we change the standard so that only half that amount is allowed, the plant, to reduce its pollution, will have to either shut down, possibly to reopen in another jurisdiction, or cut back on production. It will lay off all or some of its workers and will contribute that much less to the local economy.

Are we willing to pay that price? Who, in fact, will pay it – the company shareholders? the laid-off workers? Who pays the price of *not* moving to the stricter standard – the loon whose eggshells have become so thin it is unable to reproduce? the child playing in her polluted backyard whose blood-lead level is higher than that of her friend who lives on the other side of town? Most important of all, who sets the standard? What criteria do they use to judge the competing claims of the shareholders, the loon, the child, and the laid-off worker?

Although it lies at the heart of the pollution prevention process and is of vital importance to Canadians, standard-setting has traditionally been portrayed as a technical, objective process for which only scientists and engineers have the qualifications and expertise required to participate – a process somehow removed from politics. Nothing could be farther from the truth, for here the most intensely political decisions of all those surrounding pollution – who pays and who benefits – are made.

Types of Standards

The term "pollution standard" refers to the quantities of different types of pollution that may be legally emitted to the environment. This is distinguished from a non-enforceable "objective" – for instance, the objective set by the Canadian government that there be an average concentration over one hour of no more than 400 micrograms of nitrogen dioxide per cubic metre of air.[3]

Legally enforceable standards may directly limit pollution discharges by stipulating concentrations or quantities of pollution in the effluent (termed "emission standards"); may specify a maximum allowable ambient level or effect (which is less common); or may stipulate design and operation requirements, such as the thickness and porosity of the clay liner of a municipal landfill, which are intended to indirectly limit discharges (referred to as "design standards").

Emission standards governing discharges to air and water are the crux of regulation, and may place limitations in several different ways:

- by banning a substance completely – an example is the ban placed on DDT in the early 1970s;
- by setting a maximum limit on the concentration of the pollutant in the air or water that makes up the effluent stream;
- by setting a maximum on the quantity of pollutant that may be emitted per unit of production – for instance, the recommendation of the Experts Committee on Kraft Mills, referred to above, that Ontario set standards to reduce the discharge of the nine mills in the province from the present average of 6.5 kilograms of organic chlorine per tonne of pulp produced to 1.5 kilograms;[4]
- by an absolute limit on the quantity that may be emitted over a given

period of time – for instance, Ontario Hydro, under the 1985 acid rain program, must reduce its total annual emission of sulphur dioxide from 390,000 to 175,000 tonnes by 1994.

Standards that set maximum concentration levels were felt to be sufficient at the beginning of the era of modern pollution regulation, when it was believed that dilution was a sufficient and effective means of reducing the toxic effects associated with pollution. Production ratios were also used. Basing pollution standards on the ratio of pollution, or waste quantities, to quantities of the finished product reinforces the existing incentive any business has to improve efficiency by manufacturing the final product with maximum use of the raw material, thus minimizing the portion of raw material that must be discarded. A significant portion of the pollution reduction achieved in such areas as pulp and paper and ore smelting has been motivated as much by a desire to improve efficiency and competitiveness, on the part of both industry and government, as by any concern for the environment.

The problem with both concentration limits and production ratio standards, however, is that they do not set any limit on the total quantity of pollution that can be emitted from a particular source. In both cases, as production increases the total quantity of legally allowable pollution also increases. In more recent years, particularly as attention has been drawn to the problems of persistence and bio-accumulation of some substances, the aim of standard-setting has shifted toward setting limits on total quantities emitted each year. It seems very likely that standard-setting will increasingly take this direction in the future, with the objective being to reduce total annual pollution quantities by some fixed portion – 25 per cent, 50 per cent, and eventually, to the point of virtual elimination.

Standards governing new polluting sources are usually more stringent than those imposed on manufacturing plants or other sources already in existence. New source standards are usually based on policies or guidelines of the environment department. These become legally enforceable standards when they are prescribed as conditions in the environmental approval given to a new plant. Since it is easier and less expensive to incorporate pollution control technology into the production design during the planning process than to add it after the plant is in operation, standards for new sources are usually more stringent than those imposed on existing ones. Standards requiring reduction of pollution from an existing operation can either take the form of a negotiated abatement program, which is not carried through to the point of being expressed by the environment department as a legally binding obligation, or as a legal obligation, usually taking the form of an administrative order (in Ontario, a control order). Orders are negotiated with the company before being issued, the only difference from a voluntary program being the availability to environmental officials, if they choose to use it, of prosecution as a means of achieving compliance with the emission standards set forth in the order.

Standard-Setting in Theory

Although they have only a limited relationship to what actually happens, the two theoretical approaches to standard-setting have been developed in very precise terms. The two approaches are very similar. The first, in which ambient objectives are established, followed by emission standards to meet those objectives, has as its starting point the pollution-receiving environment and then works backward to the limits set on each individual source of pollution. The other method, known as "risk assessment – risk management," starts with the particular toxic substance that poses a risk, measured almost exclusively in terms of risk to our own species, and then again works backward to each of the individual sources of that contaminant in order that the risk may be "managed." Brief descriptions of each ideal process follow.

Ambient Objectives – Emission Standards.

1. Establishment of objectives. The environment for which standards are being set is defined in some manner (average air quality in Canadian cities, a particular lake or river, etc.) and agreement then is reached on the use to which that environment shall be put and, therefore, the pollution objectives that should be established. For instance, if standards are being set for water quality in a particular lake or river, a decision is made as to whether that water should be clean enough to supply drinking water; not that pure but still good enough for swimming; or, perhaps, usable only for boating. Such theoretical discussions centre largely on objectives for human use but also consider such aspects as toxic effects on fish, other aquatic organisms, and vegetation.

2. Establishment of scientific criteria for meeting those objectives. Based on scientific research into the effects of different substances at different concentration levels and exposure rates, the maximum concentration levels of various pollutants at which the particular body of water can be used for drinking, swimming, boating, or any other desired objective must be determined.

3. Setting of ambient concentration objectives. Having decided on objectives and criteria for meeting them, officials must set concentration level objectives – which may be more conservative than the scientific objectives – for all or some of the toxic substances present in the ambient environment. (In the case of federal air pollution objectives, different levels are often set to meet such criteria as "desired," "acceptable," and "tolerable.")

4. Setting of emission standards. All of the sources of pollution in the particular environment in question must be identified and the limits set in

terms of either concentration levels or total quantities, on the amount of pollution each may emit, such that the total sum of their emissions will result in pollution no higher than the concentration levels set in the ambient objectives.

5. Implementation of the standards. As discussed in more detail below, the emission standards are made legally binding in regulations, orders, or licences and then, to a greater or lesser degree, these standards are enforced.[5]

As described, the process seems logical and straightforward. In fact, it is enormously complicated and difficult. If, for instance, we were to use this method to set objectives and emission standards for the waters of Hamilton harbour, we would immediately run up against a number of difficult questions. Who should and should not have a say in the decision on the water quality objectives for that particular piece of water? How can we possibly reach agreement among all the users of Hamilton harbour – the local industries that rely on it for waste disposal; the several millions of Canadians and Americans who live downstream from Hamilton and draw their drinking water from Lake Ontario or the St. Lawrence River; the citizens of Hamilton who use it for various forms of recreation; the out-of-town visitors who may only wish to gaze across its sparkling waters once a year? And what right do we grant other species that live in or drink the water?

Literally thousands of substances are polluting Hamilton harbour and science does not yet have anything close to a full understanding of the effects they have, alone or interacting together, on humans or other organisms. Do we set ambient objectives for each? How much would that cost and how long would it take? If time and money preclude that option, which ones do we concentrate on? If, since we have little choice, we make a somewhat arbitrary list of the ten "worst" substances and give them priority for action, how do we identify all the sources of those ten pollutants, particularly since some of them may be in New Jersey or Arkansas?

Having worked our way through all of these difficulties, however, we now come to the hard part. Suppose that we have reached agreement that there must be, to give a simplistic example, a total reduction of 50 per cent of the annual quantities of each of the ten polluting substances now entering the harbour, and we have drawn up a list of the major sources of those substances and found, thank goodness, they are all in Ontario and therefore subject to Ontario law. How do we then apportion that pollution reduction, and therefore the cost, among all the sources in a fair and equitable manner? While we are considering that problem we receive an application for approval of a new industrial operation that will discharge, by itself, an annual quantity equivalent to the 50 per cent reduction we are trying to allocate among existing sources. Do we refuse to give approval to that new plant and all the others that may follow it in the years ahead?

163

As can be seen, there are two major obstacles. The first is the limitations of our data base and the second is a lack of agreed-upon principles for allocating the costs of pollution reduction.

Risk Assessment – Risk Management.

As mentioned, this theoretical approach is almost totally concerned with human health and takes as its starting point the pollutants that pose health threats. It includes the following steps:

- risk identification – identify and then rank by degree of risk, based on such criteria as toxicity, persistence, quantity in the environment, and likely exposure rates, all (or as many as possible) hazardous substances;
- risk analysis – use available scientific information to determine what degree of risk is posed by a particular substance that has been given priority for regulation through the identification process above;
- risk assessment – through some process, which combines public opinion with the scientific work done in the first two steps, reach agreement on what level of risk (often expressed in terms of the additional number of cases of cancer per 100,000 people exposed to the substance at a given dosage over a given period of time) is acceptable;
- risk management – set and implement standards to ensure the acceptable level of risk will not be exceeded.[6]

Like the first approach, risk assessment immediately runs up against the problem of the limited information available to regulators. Regulatory authorities simply do not have enough information available on the sources and potential health and environmental effects of the literally thousands of polluting substances of concern today, yet we do not have the luxury of waiting until that information is available. Decisions must be made based on incomplete and constantly changing information. Moreover, these decisions may impose significant financial consequences on the polluter and at the same time are taken very seriously by those who feel their health is threatened or protected by the decision made. Thus, decisions on "acceptable" risk will be influenced as much by crass emotions of greed and fear as by the calm, analytical process described above.

Finally, because the objectives of the different parties are so different, it is almost impossible to reach agreement among all the parties involved. It is extremely unlikely that those who are exposed to a certain degree of risk as a result of pollution, but who do not gain in any way from that exposure, will accept any level of risk higher than zero. For instance, people asked to drink marginally contaminated water that poses a risk of one additional cancer case per 100,000, but who did not receive any of the financial benefit accruing to those who used the water for waste disposal, will likely refuse to accept that risk. By the same token, the polluter will refuse to accept the additional cost of ensuring what, it is repeatedly argued, is an impossible state of perfect absence of risk.

We have not yet put in place principles and mechanisms to decide, first, who should participate in such a decision and, second, how that decision should be made. Various methods have been tried, including a town plebiscite and a collective-bargaining type of mediation, but these have been on an experimental and *ad hoc* basis. Furthermore, standards are set for the most part by industry and government representatives meeting behind closed doors, which makes any discussion of the ideal participative and consultative process still a matter of largely abstract interest. To date, standard-setting has focused not on "acceptable risk" but on "acceptable cost."

It is not surprising that the Environment Council of Alberta, which produced one of the few studies done to date on the standard-setting process in Canada, prefaced its description of the ideal process by saying that "It should not be thought that the model represents what actually takes place . . . in fact, the standard-setting process we have outlined is probably not followed with any rigor anywhere in Canada."[7] The study went on to explain how practice deviates from theory:

> Generally, goals and objectives upon which standards are based are not clearly articulated. . . . A major reason for this lack of goal clarity is that all jurisdictions tend to run together the goal identification, criteria development and ambient standard specification steps in the standard setting process. This has the effect of obscuring the value judgments involved in goal and objective determination and emphasizing the scientific and technical aspects of the process.[8]

Standard-Setting in Practice

The ideal process for setting standards, described above, begins with an examination of the environment and then works backward to some form of limitation on each polluting source. In a formal sense, the first standard-setting exercises followed that principle. In actual practice, however, the process has more often worked in the opposite direction – starting with an examination of the polluting source and the economics of reducing pollution and then moving on to set emission standards without ever examining the receiving environment.

Legislation such as the health laws of the first half of the twentieth century or the 1957 Ontario Water Resources Commission Act set forth generalized prohibitions on air and water pollution that might be dangerous to human health. When environmental objectives and standards were first set in the 1960s, knowledge of the effects of various toxins was largely limited to study of human exposure, through the related disciplines of medicine and occupational health. Thus when governments began to set standards for discharge to air and water, they turned to the one body of data available, albeit a limited one, to set concentration levels that would have "no adverse effect" on human health.

The first standards setting specific limits on discharges of particular substances were contained in regulations adopted by the Ontario government in 1967 under the authority of the Air Pollution Control Act. Maximum concentrations for thirteen substances were established. The concentration levels were measured not in the effluent stream but "at the point of impingement," the point at which the air emitted from a factory chimney or other source first encountered the ground, or a neighbouring building, or any other object – this was intended to allow the standard to take into account dilution of the substance, estimated on the basis of mathematical modelling, as it was carried from the polluting source. The concentration levels were set on the basis of "professional opinion related to the compound's effect on human health, animals, vegetation and general aesthetics including dust and odour. . . . [to achieve the objective of] the concentration having no or minimal adverse effect."[9] The number of substances regulated under what became, in 1972, Regulation 308 of the Ontario Environmental Protection Act was increased to twenty in 1972 and to 100 in 1974. These Ontario standards are set forth in regulations and thus automatically apply to any source of air pollution, unlike most standards that achieve their legal status through incorporation as conditions in the licence governing that source. Ontario has set policy objectives for over 100 other substances that form the basis for licensing conditions but are not themselves directly enforceable.

The Ontario ministry has been working to revise the system of air pollution standard-setting since 1983, with the objective of moving from point-of-impingement standards to "best-available-technology" standards that will cover a wider array of contaminants. A draft air pollution regulation based on this new approach was released for public discussion by the Ontario ministry on August 16, 1990. Like the water standard-setting program under MISA, the criterion used is not quality of the receiving environment but the "availability" of technology and whether or not it is "economically achievable."

Ontario, Newfoundland, and Manitoba are the only Canadian provinces to set air standards by means of point-of-impingement concentrations set in regulations. All other provinces rely primarily on ambient and emission guidelines and policies, for the most part based on guidelines developed by the federal government through federal-provincial or federal-provincial-industry task forces, which become enforceable when set as conditions of licences. Saskatchewan is the one province to set directly enforceable ambient standards – maximum concentration levels for such things as particulates, oxidants, nitrogen dioxide, and any pollution "that results in discharge of air contaminants, alone or in combination with the same contaminant from another source, that causes a concentration of an air contaminant in excess of the prescribed ambient standard for that contaminant, is prohibited."[10]

During the 1970s Environment Canada set emission standards governing air pollution from four industrial sectors – lead emissions from secondary lead smelters; mercury from chlor-alkali plants (which produce chlorine and caustic soda); asbestos from mining and milling; and vinyl chloride from vinyl chloride manufacturing (used in making synthetic fibres).[11] Environment Canada either directly enforces these standards or they are enforced by the provinces. Codes of practice, which are not directly enforceable, were set for several other industrial sectors during the 1970s, with the expectation that they would then be incorporated into provincial regulations. The federal government was instrumental in developing acid rain standards, but direct implementation is done through provincial regulation. More recently, because of the international nature of the issue, the federal government has played a leading role in developing standards set in regulations under CEPA aimed at the phased elimination of ozone-destroying CFCs.

The federal government has set directly enforceable standards for lead in gasoline – 0.77 grams per litre in 1976, reduced to 0.26 grams per litre effective December 1, 1990, and has also regulated motor vehicle emissions, under the authority not of the Clean Air Act but of the Motor Vehicle Safety Act, administered by Transport Canada, since 1971. Standards governing quantities of nitrogen oxides and volatile organic compounds are set on the basis of quantity emitted per mile travelled, which, like the production ratio approach, does not limit total loadings. As the number of cars in Canada increases, so, too, does the number of miles driven each year, and therefore the total quantity of motor vehicle pollution. This problem was cited as the basis for a planned tightening of those standards announced by Environment Canada in 1989.[12] These federal standards apply only to the manufacture of new vehicles, while the task of ensuring that in-use vehicles continue to comply with the standards is left to the provinces.

The first standards directly limiting discharge of toxic substances to water were phosphorous concentration limits set by Environment Canada in 1970 under the newly proclaimed Canada Water Act, described in Part II. Interestingly, these standards, like the acid rain regulations, resulted not so much from human health fears as from concern for the natural environment itself. Direct federal standards for such things as pulp and paper, petroleum refinery, and chlor-alkali plant emissions to water were then set at intervals during the 1970s on the basis of federal-provincial-industry consultations, with enforcement done either by Environment Canada or by the provincial environment department.

For the most part provincial water discharge standards are not set forth in regulations but in guidelines, which provide the basis for individual-case standard-setting using the instrument of conditions attached to the licence or approval. Ontario, for instance, in 1976, developed a policy document, *Objectives for the Control of Industrial Waste Discharges*, followed two years later by the Blue Book, *Water Management: Goals, Policies, Objectives and Implementation Procedures of the Ministry of the Environment.* Both were further development of the water quality objectives originally developed by the OWRC. The Blue Book sets forth fifty-two ambient water quality objectives for such things as temperature, turbidity, and PH and for specific substances, such as hydrogen sulphide, oil and grease, cadmium, copper, iron, lead, selenium, zinc, various pesticides, and a number of industrial organics. Such ambient objectives are intended to provide the "starting point in deriving waste effluent requirements."[13] The ambient objectives chosen by Ontario were derived not from direct examination of the receiving waters but almost entirely from standards developed by other jurisdictions – primarily the U.S. Environmental Protection Agency, the IJC, and the federal government.[14] Drawing from similar sources, the other provinces have also established guidelines that are then used to set enforceable standards during the licensing process.

Another guide for provincial licensing authorities is the federal Health and Welfare Drinking Water Guidelines, which provide maximum concentration levels for some fifty substances. The guidelines were first established in 1968, and revised in 1978 and again in 1987.[15] Ontario is in the process of setting new standards governing industrial discharges to water through the MISA program, described in Part II. These standards will be derived not from environmental criteria but from industry-government negotiations that will determine, for eight industrial sectors, what is the "best available technology economically achievable" (termed BATEA), which in turn will be used to determine load-limiting standards.

In one sense, the move in Ontario from the ambient-based standards of the 1978 Blue Book to the technology-based standards of the 1986 MISA program appears to be a step backward. However, several aspects of the MISA program suggest that, once implemented, its standards will result in significant load reductions. The emission standard-setting is preceded by a year of monitoring toxic emissions, thus giving the Ontario government far more accurate information on which to base standard-setting than it has had before. Public access is provided, in at least a limited sense, through an advisory committee with public-interest representation and the program is intended to meet the policy objective, stated by the minister in 1986, of

"virtual elimination of toxic substances." The minister said that he anticipated a 50-70 per cent reduction in annual loadings from the "first round"
of MISA standards.[16] Whether or not such objectives are achieved will
depend on the future of pollution politics in Ontario and the resultant
weakening or stiffening of the government's resolve as it bargains with
industry over the definition of "economically achievable." This is particularly the case since the ministry, after four years of work on the MISA
program, has not publicly stated what criteria will be used to decide what is
and what is not "economically achievable."

Some attempts have been made in Canada to set standards governing
individual substances, regardless of their point of origin, following the
procedure of the "risk assessment" model. Under the federal Environmental Contaminants Act, passed by the House of Commons in 1975 and then
incorporated into the new Canadian Environmental Protection Act in
1988, standards governing import and use of PCBs and a few other substances have been set. In February, 1989, the federal minister announced
that an advisory panel had designated forty-four substances for the Priority
Substances List of CEPA. Those substances, over the next five years, will be
subject to detailed assessment intended to result in standards governing
their use and discharge to the environment. A similar exercise was initiated
in 1983 by the Ontario Ministry of the Environment when it established the
Hazardous Contaminants Branch, with a mandate to establish substance-
by-substance standards, but little progress has been made.

In summary, the process used to set standards in Canada during the past
twenty years has been governed largely by the following three characteristics:

• Legally enforceable standards are set primarily through the process of
licensing each individual source of pollution, based on objectives and
guidelines that are then modified to fit the particular circumstances.
• Standards have been set not primarily as a result of objective and empirical study but as a result of bargaining between government and industry.
That bargaining takes place at two levels: on an industry-wide basis,
when guidelines and policies are set, and on an individual-plant basis
during the licensing process.
• This bargaining is done almost completely behind closed doors.

The secretive nature of the process was established by the Alberta Environment Council study of 1982, which reported that "There has been no
public involvement in the development of Federal air and water standards"
and that "There is essentially no public role in ambient or emission standard setting in Alberta, Saskatchewan or Ontario."[17] The one exception to
this approach, the study noted, was British Columbia, which in the late
1970s established a series of consultative inquiries. Since that study was

completed the process has become at least marginally more open. Ontario has consulted with the public, through establishment of a commission of inquiry in 1985, on standards governing operation of mobile PCB incinerators and, as mentioned, in 1986 provided for ongoing public review of the MISA process. However, there is still no guaranteed public access to the negotiation of Certificates of Approval in Ontario, other than of waste management sites that require a public hearing under the Environmental Protection Act and now also require Environmental Assessment Act approval. The 1989-90 process of revising federal pulp and paper effluent standards has been undertaken by Environment Canada with minimal public participation. The major study done by the department, which prompted the standard-setting process, only became public because it was leaked in 1988 to Greenpeace and the *Vancouver Sun*. Public information sessions were held across the country in the spring of 1990 but the standards had already been set by then.

The bargaining nature of standard-setting has been documented by the one other major examination of the process carried out during the past decade. As part of its 1980 study of regulatory activity and its impact on the Canadian economy, the Economic Council of Canada commissioned a series of detailed examinations of environmental regulation in such areas as toxic chemicals, B.C. lumbering and its water quality impacts, sulphur dioxide, and pulp and paper regulation. A summary document, *Environmental Regulation in Canada: An Assessment of the Regulatory Process*, was then prepared by Andrew Thompson, director of the Westwater Research Centre at the University of British Columbia. Thompson reported that all the case studies had found that "bargaining is the essence of the environmental regulatory process as it is practised in Canada," noting that bargaining was the method not only of setting standards but also of deciding whether or not they would be enforced. "Rules stated in statutes or regulations are merely points of departure for negotiating modifications of behaviour; and 'compliance' or 'non-compliance' means 'agreement' or 'disagreement.'"[18] Thompson concluded that environmental regulation was carried out through a constant series of negotiations, both between government agencies and industries and among different government jurisdictions and departments, simply because the information to set clear rules and require that they be obeyed was not available.

> The reasons why bargaining and negotiating characterize the process of environmental regulation, even in cases where the command/penalty mode of legislation suggests a more formal, adversarial style, are believed to lie in the knowledge gaps and uncertainties that pervade environmental issues. . . . Homicide can be defined in particular degrees, and penalties for homicide can be enforced with predictable

certainty. But the fisheries officials who drafted legislation that prohibited putting slash, stumps or other debris into water frequented by
fish knew very well that this prohibition could not be automatically
enforced. To do so would be scientifically and technically unreason-
able and politically unacceptable. The difficulties are that it is unclear
in what circumstances such debris is harmful to fish (though in some
cases it is clearly harmful), it is unclear what alternate technologies
are available for avoiding the putting of debris in water if logging and
land clearing are to be permitted, and it is impossible to determine if
the harm to fish will outweigh the social benefits derived from the
logging or clearing land. Consequently . . . standards or objectives
. . . must be negotiated in the circumstances of each individual case.[19]

Thompson went on to note that environmental regulation of pulp mills in
Ontario had been "of limited effectiveness" and that in the case of sulphur
dioxide bargaining "the government official is hopelessly 'outgunned' . . .
sometimes bargaining with industry about 'ability to pay' considerations
such as byproduct marketing with respect to which there is neither mandate,
technical ability nor experience."[20]

CHAPTER 12

Implementing Standards

Abatement and Approvals

An environment department wishing to reduce pollution from a given source will rely first on discussion with officials of the industry, which may then lead to a formalized program for abatement, albeit one with no legal teeth, known in Ontario as a "program approval." As long as it is operating in compliance with the terms of the abatement program the industry in question will not be prosecuted.

The next step, if the regulatory agency believes satisfactory results have not been achieved, is to incorporate that program into a legally binding order, in Ontario a "control order." While such an order mandates changes in procedures to reduce pollution, the Ontario ministry, for example, also has the power, under the Environmental Protection Act, to issue a stop order, which requires the industry to cease operations until the pollution problem has been resolved. All the provinces have similar powers to issue administrative orders. The regulated industry has a right of appeal when an order is issued, in Ontario to the Environmental Appeals Board.

Whether a voluntary program or binding order, the actual extent of pollution reduction achieved is the outcome of private negotiations between the polluter and government officials. As is the case in standard-setting (which in effect this process is), the company has far more technical expertise and information than does the regulatory agency and, since the outcome of the process is so critical to its financial fortunes, is willing to devote far greater staffing and financial resources to the process than is government.

Ontario has introduced at least some public access to the program during the 1980s. Before a control order is imposed, but after its terms have been settled between ministry staff and the industry in question, a public consultation session is held to provide information and seek the views of interested members of the public. Unlike such procedures as environmental assessment, in which interested parties are given an opportunity to state their case before a neutral board before it makes a decision, this form of consultation, coming at the end of the process, does not provide any real opportunities to influence the outcome. It has been described, by one author at least, as a "sham or public relations gesture."[1]

Approvals Given to New Pollution Sources

The approvals process can involve either one or two steps: (1) a licensing approval resulting in the issuance of a permit specifying pollution limits; (2) an environmental assessment that attempts to predict pollution effects, often considers alternative approaches that would better protect the environment, and may also involve a public hearing before some form of administrative board. All sources of pollution require licensing approval from the provincial environment department; the additional requirement of environmental assessment is only imposed in certain instances. In Alberta, for instance, major resource developments such as refineries and petrochemical plants require an environmental assessment in addition to licensing approval. The circumstances in which an environmental assessment is required, and the form it takes, vary considerably from province to province.

All provinces require that approval be obtained under authority of their environmental legislation – e.g., the B.C. Waste Management Act, the Alberta Clean Air and Clean Water Acts, the Manitoba Environment Act, the Quebec Environmental Quality Act, the New Brunswick Clean Environment Act – before any potential source of pollution or waste management system, municipal or industrial, can be put into operation. Application is made by the company or municipality, with documentation provided on the steps that will be taken to ensure compliance with relevant policies or regulations. Often there is a process of negotiation, usually without public access, and agreement is reached on allowable pollution levels. Those levels will then be specified in the permit or certificate issued to the company. A mechanism is provided for appeal by the regulated industry, usually to an administrative board, of the conditions of the permit. Breach of the conditions of the permit leaves the operation open to prosecution. Often the regulated operation will be required to undertake regular monitoring of pollution levels and to report to the environment department on the result. In Alberta, licences are issued only for a five-year period and must be renewed at the end of that time. This provides the regulatory agency with the opportunity to impose new conditions reflecting changes in technology or pollution objectives. Other provinces, such as Ontario, impose no such requirements.

Although more attention and public discussion is focused on approvals that go through an environmental assessment process, simply because public hearings catch the eye of the media and public, the vast bulk of the total pollution entering the Canadian environment each year is regulated under the licensing process alone, without the benefit of public scrutiny. For example, "In 1985/86, the [Ontario] Ministry issued about 5,000 certificates for such items as waste hauling and treatment systems, water discharges, waste treatment facilities, industrial and commercial discharges and pesticide spraying."[2] In comparison, during the period from 1976, when the Act was proclaimed, to March, 1985, a total of forty-four projects were approved under the terms of Ontario's Environmental Assessment Act.[3] Although by 1990 more projects were coming under this Act, the great bulk of approvals in Ontario are still under the authority of the Environmental Protection Act alone. Since it is the Act used to give approval to the vast bulk of the pollution that enters the provincial environment each year, it would seem reasonable to examine publicly the criteria used for EPA approvals, consistency of its application, public access under the Act, and such related issues. Unfortunately, the attention of the environmental lobby and others remains firmly fixed on the much less used Environmental Assessment Act.

Recommendations to improve public access to the Alberta licensing procedure were made in 1988 by the Review Panel on Environmental Law Enforcement. The panel noted that "The present licensing system is a closed system wherein license conditions are determined by negotiation between the government and the applicant. . . . There is no public notice upon the receipt of an application for a license and there is no opportunity for public input into the decision to issue a license or the conditions of the license."[4] The panel recommended that all applications for a licence under the Alberta Clean Air Act and Clean Water Act be published in newspapers; that information, other than proprietary information, be provided to the public on the application and an opportunity for public comment provided; and that terms of the licence be available to the public after it is issued.[5] As of 1990, the Alberta government had not acted on those recommendations, although some will be incorporated in the consolidation of environmental legislation being undertaken in that province.[6]

Although for the most part it does not directly regulate pollution discharges, the federal government does have licensing approval powers over toxic substances, more generally in the form of products than of wastes or pollution, through the 1975 Environmental Contaminants Act, now the 1988 Canadian Environmental Protection Act. New chemical substances that will for the first time be manufactured or imported must receive approval under the terms of CEPA.

Environmental Assessment

All provinces and the federal government require that in some cases, the circumstances of which vary greatly from jurisdiction to jurisdiction, an environmental assessment also be conducted in addition to the standard licensing approval. This requirement for environmental assessment is set out in specific legislation or is simply a matter of policy. Those jurisdictions, as of 1990, that have enacted specific legislation devoted to environmental assessment are:

Ontario:	Environmental Assessment Act (1976)
Alberta:	Land Surface Conservation and Reclamation Act (1980)
Saskatchewan:	Environmental Assessment Act (1980)
Newfoundland:	Environmental Assessment Act (1980)
Nova Scotia:	Environmental Assessment Act (1988).[7]

In the other provinces, the basic environmental legislation contains provisions allowing the minister to require in certain circumstances that an environmental assessment be carried out.

Hearings may be held before standing boards or specifically appointed committees or panels: in Saskatchewan a special Board of Inquiry is appointed when needed; in Manitoba the Clean Environment Commission handles assessment; in Quebec, the Bureau d'audiences publiques sur l'environnement has jurisdiction; and in Nova Scotia the Environmental Control Council oversees environmental assessment. In most cases these boards only have power to recommend, with the final decision made by the relevant minister on the advice of his department. Under powers granted to the Ontario Environmental Assessment Board in 1988, the Board in that province has decision-making powers in its own right.

Federal Environmental Assessment Review Process (EARP)

The federal government first introduced environmental assessment through establishment of the Federal Environmental Assessment Review Office (FEARO) in 1973. FEARO was established by policy only, through a cabinet decision with no legislative basis. The process was intended to allow assessment of projects undertaken or funded by the federal government or to be done on federal lands. The greatest weakness – aside from the lack of a legislative base – of the federal process is that it is done on a "self-assessment" basis, in which the initiating department (such as Transport

Canada planning a new airport) *itself* decides whether or not an assessment is required. Critics of this process argue that the decision to hold an assessment with public hearings should be made by the Environment Minister, not the minister whose own department is obviously interested in seeing the project go ahead as planned.

The process was clarified, although not substantially changed, when the federal government in 1984 adopted guidelines for EARP, through an order-in-council under the Government Organization Act. Court decisions in 1989 and 1990 held that the guidelines mandated environmental assessments for the Souris River and Oldman River dams. Another court action attempting to force environmental assessment of the Via rail funding cuts, which had been brought by the city of Thunder Bay, Greenpeace, and an NDP MP, failed in July, 1990.[8]

Responding to public criticism, then federal Minister Tom McMillan published a discussion paper in 1987 titled "Reforming Federal Environmental Assessment," which called for public comment in such areas as the self-selection basis and the need for a legislated process. As part of the 1988 election campaign, McMillan then announced, on October 20, 1988, that EARP would be legislated and made mandatory for "every federal undertaking and every undertaking on federal land."[9] On June 18, 1990, Robert de Cotret, who succeeded Lucien Bouchard as Environment Minister when the latter resigned in May, introduced the promised Canadian Environmental Assessment Act in the House of Commons. The new Act, if passed, will vest power to hold a public review in the Environment Minister, although the final decision on project approval will remain with the minister whose department would oversee the proposed project. Critics argue that the legislation is weaker than the 1984 order and is thus an attempt by the federal government to water down its own environmental legislation, which has, in effect, been forced on it by the courts.

The type of federal undertaking to which the new legislation applies will not be clear until it is enacted and regulations are written. This has led to fears on the part of environmentalists that the legislation may have a narrower scope than do the present cabinet guidelines.[10] It is likely that the applicability of the new Canadian Environmental Assessment Act will be a major source of conflict between the provinces and the federal government, among federal departments, and between the environmental lobby and the federal government in the next few years.

Intervenor Funding

One of the most important issues in the approvals process is public access. As set out in the discussion of standard-setting, in closed-door bargaining the proponent is in a position of strength. One way this can be changed is to provide more public access. This in turn raises the issue of funding, since access without resources is of little value. Environmental approvals invariably rest on complex and detailed scientific and technical issues, which can only be successfully addressed by public intervenors if they have sufficient funds to hire their own hydrogeologists, toxicologists, and other experts who can review and comment on the technical documents submitted by the proponent. Unfortunately, public-interest representatives, whether citizen groups formed to fight a particular development proposal or the professional environmental organizations, simply do not have the financial resources needed. One organization, the Canadian Environmental Defence Fund, was established in the early 1980s specifically for the purpose of raising funds to assist citizens involved in litigation or approvals, but it by no means can provide all the funding needed. The only real answer is to provide funding through government or to require the proponent, as part of the cost of gaining environmental approval, to fund at least some portion of intervenor costs.

During the past two decades this principle has increasingly come to be accepted in Canada. The first intervenor funding, amounting to $1,773,918, was provided by the Berger Inquiry of the mid-1970s,[11] followed by the Ontario Porter Commission on Electric Power Planning. In 1980 a special Parliamentary Committee on Regulatory Reform recommended that "public interest group participation in the federal regulatory process be encouraged and supported by higher levels of financial assistance."[12] By the early 1980s there was only one established program of intervenor funding, the resource development process regulated under the Alberta Energy Resource Conservation Act.[13] In the mid-1980s the Ontario Environmental Assessment Board sought to award costs to intervenors in advance, instead of at the conclusion, of a public hearing, but this action was appealed to the courts and disallowed. In 1988 Ontario introduced the Intervenor Funding Project Act, a three-year pilot project to provide funding for hearings before three administrative boards: the Environmental Assessment Board, the Ontario Energy Board, and the Joint Board (boards hearing both environmental and land-use cases under the Planning Act). Prior to that the Ontario Ministry of Environment had introduced its own funding program, under which $50,000 was provided to intervenors for a hearing on regulations governing mobile PCB destruction facilities, $3.2 million for the Ontario Waste Management Corporation hearing that began in the fall of 1989, and initial funding of $300,000 plus $450,000 annual funding for the MNR timber management hearing being conducted by the Environmental Assessment Board in northern Ontario.[14] The proposed federal Environment Assessment Act also includes provisions for intervenor funding.

Once the principle of intervenor funding (and therefore meaningful public participation) is established, the next challenge facing the environmental community will be to extend the scope of the entire assessment process. As noted above, assessments are held in an almost insignificantly small number of cases, and those are almost all public-sector projects. There is almost no requirement, anywhere in Canada, that private-sector undertakings receive assessment approval. Guaranteeing public access to the assessment process will be of little significance until that process, instead of licensing approvals, becomes the major vehicle for considering and approving all new polluting sources.

A further challenge is the extension of assessment processes to include not only physical projects, such as construction of a pipeline, but policy decisions, such as relative public spending on railways and highways, which have direct environmental implications. Although the concept has been endorsed both by the federal-provincial Task Force on Environment and Economy and in the June, 1990, federal assessment legislation, it still has a long way to go to become an accepted reality.

Enforcement

On December 4, 1989, NDP environment critic James Fulton rose in the House of Commons and read from a leaked Department of Fisheries memorandum, prepared by O.E. Langer, head of Habitat Management, Fraser River, Northern B.C. and Yukon Division, which stated that "we have been known for charging individuals for spills of deleterious substances (often accidental and less than a few gallons) and then continually ignore the daily discharge of millions of gallons of toxic effluent from a mill next door. This often results in the small guy or minor offence getting prosecuted and the large corporation getting some degree of 'discretionary immunity.'"[15] The Minister of Fisheries, Tom Siddon, rejected calls for his resignation and called in the RCMP to investigate the leak. He also rejected calls for an independent inquiry into federal enforcement practices, issued by a coalition of B.C. fishermen, natives, environmentalists, and forestry workers. The *Vancouver Sun*, on December 6, 1989, offered the following editorial comment:

> The reaction of the federal department of fisheries and oceans to the exposure of its failure to prosecute large corporate polluters under the Fisheries Act illustrates the depth of the scandal. The first thing the department did was to call in the RCMP. To charge the polluters? No. To investigate why they haven't been charged? No – to find out who blew the whistle by leaking an internal report that large polluters are going unpunished. . . . No matter how much the DFO tries to cover up the smell of dead fish, the whole business still stinks all the way to the top.[16]

This scandal broke one year after Environment Canada's Sinclair report, also a leaked document, documented that the pulp and paper industry has been out of compliance with federal and provincial discharge standards continually during the past two decades. In that same year, on March 28, 1988, the Ontario Environment Minister, Jim Bradley, stated that "It is a disturbing situation when my ministry must report, as it did last October, that 101 out of 154 industrial dischargers failed to meet discharge requirements. Furthermore, this report reflected no significant improvement over the previous year's performance."[17] Bradley's remarks echoed those of his federal counterpart two years earlier: "Land-based sources of pollution have not been prosecuted, under the Fisheries Act or under any other Act administered by the federal Environment Minister, for the tons of chemicals being discharged into the St. Lawrence River every day – not a single prosecution by Environment Canada in the past decade in that vast and highly populated area."[18] Nor yet were provincial authorities acting to enforce provincial regulations in Quebec. According to a report issued by the Canadian Environmental Advisory Council in 1987, from 1972 to the date of the study "under provincial regulations [pulp mill regulations under the Quebec Environmental Quality Act], only one case has been prosecuted."[19]

Thus, not only leaked documents but also speeches from ministers and government studies have documented the failure of federal and provincial environment departments to enforce their own laws and regulations. This raises doubts about the whole system of pollution regulation, from gathering data to setting standards and issuing orders and approvals. What is the value of all that activity if, at the end of the day, polluting industries know that they can safely ignore environmental regulations?

Past and Present Enforcement Practices

From the mid-1860s to the turn of the century repeated attempts were made by those using the Ottawa River to prod the federal government, presumably under the terms of the 1868 Fisheries Act prohibition of discharge of material deleterious to fish, into taking action against the lumber companies that were dumping sawdust into the Ottawa River – within sight of Parliament Hill. The rotting sawdust produced methane gas, which periodically exploded in the river. As is so often the case in pollution battles, it required a large-scale event to finally bring about action. In 1897 one such explosion threw a local farmer from his boat, drowning him in the river. Government action was finally taken, at which point

... the largest mill operator in the country resisted regulation and, in the face of government prosecution, announced he would pay any fines imposed until an injunction was issued, at which time he would close down his business and throw up to 2,000 men out of work. Eventually it took the personal intervention of the prime minister of the day, Wilfrid Laurier, to obtain a delay in Department of Justice

proceedings for an injunction to persuade this particular businessman to obey the regulations regarding sawdust pollution.[20]

This pattern of government reluctance to enforce pollution reductions
when economic interests were at stake was repeated in 1946 when the KVP
Lumber Company opened a pulp and paper mill on the Spanish River, in
Ontario, emitting sufficient pollution to kill the fish and wild rice downstream and to make the water unsuitable for swimming or drinking. Downstream landowners took the company to court, in 1948, seeking both
damages and an injunction to prevent the polluting activity. Chief Justice
McRuer granted the injunction but suspended it for six months, presumably to give the company time to voluntarily reduce its polluting activities.
The company lost successive court appeals, but while the courts were not
willing to come to the aid of the polluter the government of the day was. The
Ontario government of Leslie Frost passed an amendment to the Lakes and
Rivers Improvement Act, which had the effect of requiring that when a
court was considering a pulp and paper mill injunction, it must take into
account the economic implications of such action. When the Supreme
Court ruled that the legislation could not apply retroactively to KVP, the
government passed the KVP Company Limited Act, which came into force
on April 31, 1950, and "dissolved every injunction 'heretofore granted'
against the company restraining it from polluting the waters of the Spanish
River."[21]

At the time of the KVP case the only enforcement method available was
the type of common law action – individuals going to court to seek an
injunction or damages – used in that case. Only with the creation of the
Ontario Water Resources Commission in 1956 did the government have
another method – enforcement of regulatory requirements.

The term "enforcement," with its connotations of rigorous action taken
by the government to ensure that polluters obey the strict letter of the law, is
relatively new in the world of environmental regulation. In the 1970s and
1980s, after passage of modern environmental legislation, the general government objective in Canada was not law enforcement but pollution
"abatement," meaning at least some reduction in pollution quantities from
a given source, brought about through a negotiated agreement. Standard-
setting and enforcement were both matters of closed-door negotiation of
technical details surrounding the amount of reduction that could be
achieved. The implicit criteria for establishing an amount was, basically,
the point at which the company would balk, break out of the private
discussions, and accuse government of threatening jobs. It has been
argued, as noted above, that this method of negotiation was necessary
because the whole process of pollution prevention was so new that governments had little information and could not arbitrarily apply standards in

the absence of discussion with the regulated industry. The industry, after all, was almost the sole source of information – although far from being an objective one – on what could or could not be done. There is some merit in this argument. What has no merit, however, is the government position taken during the 1970s that once these negotiated standards were put in place by administrative order, non-compliance by the industry in question was not a sign that the company was breaking a law and that enforcement action was required but that *the standards were too strict and accordingly should be renegotiated.* This approach was demonstrated over and over again, throughout the decade, as deadlines for compliance were met and extended repeatedly, without any attempt to prosecute.[22]

An explicit statement of this policy of using negotiation in preference to prosecution, coming as late as 1987, is provided in an Environment Council of Alberta report, *Improving Enforcement of the Clean Air Act and the Clean Water Act*, which states:

> The current enforcement policy favours negotiation over the more arbitrary methods provided by the Act and Regulations. This policy has attracted considerable public criticism. Because industry representatives are involved in selecting the appropriate control technology, setting emission standards and negotiating licence conditions, a high rate of compliance should be expected and further negotiation at the enforcement stage is not warranted.[23]

An example of the type of public criticism referred to came from John Younie, environment critic for the provincial NDP, who offered up some damning statistics on the Alberta enforcement record: "Between 1972 and 1984, Alberta Environment has successfully prosecuted only 41 polluters. The fines given out over these 12 years amount to only $28,750; the average fine being $701."[24]

The Alberta record is consistent with that of other jurisdictions. The Desfossés review of Environment Canada found that prior to 1986 there had been no prosecutions under the Canada Water Act or the Environmental Contaminants Act, only two under the Clean Air Act, and three under the Ocean Dumping Control Act. Environment Canada would argue, of course, that this inaction is simply consistent with arrangements since 1975, whereby direct regulatory activity was delegated to the provinces and, since 1978, enforcement of the Fisheries Act was under the jurisdiction of the newly formed Department of Fisheries and Oceans. The problem with this defence is that virtually no enforcement action was taken by these bodies either. Peter Pearse, in the 1982 report of the Commission on Pacific Fisheries Policy, pointed out that "in the last four years more than 90 per cent of convictions have resulted in fines of less than $500 or no fines at all." He noted as well that:

Participants at the Commission's hearings repeatedly expressed serious misgivings about the Department of Fisheries and Oceans' performance in enforcing the laws and regulations it administers. They referred to the Department's tolerance of blatant violations, lack of support for the enforcement effort and inadequate training of fishery officers. . . . the Commission's review of the Department's policies and procedures have persuaded me that the enforcement program has been suffering from neglect.[25]

The provincial record is equally abysmal. A task force established in 1981 by the British Columbia government to investigate pollution of the Fraser River found that in approximately half of the cases investigated illegal discharges were being made.[26] In 1983 the Ontario government commissioned Peat, Marwick to do a study of economic incentives as a means of achieving pollution abatement. The consulting firm found that the low rate of prosecution and the low fines that resulted when companies were prosecuted meant that it was cheaper to pollute than to install the pollution control equipment needed to ensure compliance:

From the point of view of these and other large polluters, compliance costs usually far exceed non-compliance costs. Company managers thus have strong economic incentives to delay and procrastinate even if these tactics result in an occasional prosecution.[27]

The Canadian Environmental Advisory Council, in its 1987 study, found that in the period 1970-77 there was "uneven application of sanctions [by Environment Canada] despite a pattern of persistent, nation-wide non-compliance with federal standards for liquid effluent."[28] The report cited the Lynn Heustis study, *Policing Pollution*, which found that when prosecution does occur it is more often in the case of spills rather than in regard to continuous discharges that exceed legal limits. The same charge had been made in the leaked DFO memo of 1989, and has also been made by the Conservation Council of New Brunswick vis-à-vis federal enforcement in that province: "prosecutions are generally launched against industrial polluters only when a spill or other acute episode of pollution has had a rapid and highly visible impact on the environment, such as in the case of a fish-kill – not for chronic non-compliance with environmental regulations."[29] The Conservation Council went on to document the failure of the New Brunswick government to enforce its provincial legislation, reporting that up to 1985, the last year for which statistics were available, there had been no prosecutions under the 1977 Beverage Containers Act, one under the 1973 Pesticides Control Act, and nine under the 1973 Clean Environment Act. As the Council noted, "Many of the most well known cases of pollution have never been prosecuted."[30]

An indication of the current status of enforcement in a number of Canadian jurisdictions is provided in the following table:

Table 2
Prosecutions, Convictions, and Fines under Pollution Legislation

1. Federal
Environmental Contaminants Act
1985: none
1986: none
1987: 2 prosecutions, 1 conviction ($2,000 fine)
1988: none
Fisheries Act
1985: 48 charges, 9 convictions (average fine: $3,700)
1986: 33 charges, 12 convictions (average fine: $7,830)
1987: 32 charges, 29 convictions (average fine: $1,730)
1988: 21 charges, 16 convictions (average fine: $3,180)
Ocean Dumping Control Act
1985: none
1986: 1 charge, no convictions
1987: 8 charges, 8 convictions (average fine: $22,500)

2. British Columbia
Waste Management Act
April 1, 1988 – March 30, 1989: 149 charges; 87 convictions (average fine: $914.53)

3. Alberta
Clean Air Act
1983: 8 charges, 5 convictions (average fine: $550)
1984: 1 charge, no conviction
1986: 2 charges, 2 convictions (average fine: $1,000)
1988: 2 charges, 2 convictions (average fine: $1,125)
Clean Water Act
1983: 1 charge, 1 conviction ($1,500 fine)
(Nov.9/89 press release states that since Jan. 1, 1989, there has been one conviction, "resulting in a fine of $30,500")

4. Ontario (all environmental legislation)
1985-86: 86 prosecutions, 71 convictions (average fine: $8,530)
1986-87: 179 prosecutions, 138 convictions (average fine: $5,694)
1988-89: 211 prosecutions, 170 convictions (average fine: $6,212)
1989-90: 265 prosecutions, 164 convictions (average fine: $17,444)

5. *New Brunswick*
Clean Environment Act
1988-89: 5 convictions (average fine: $1,310)
1989-90: 8 convictions (average fine: $131)

6. *Nova Scotia*
1987: 5 convictions under Water Act (average fine: $980)
1 conviction under Environmental Protection Act ($1,700 fine)
1988: 4 convictions under the Water Act (one fine of $10,000; other three totalled $700)

SOURCES: The information supplied in this table is necessarily representative rather than comprehensive. Letters dated October 18, 1989, were sent to Environment Canada and nine provincial ministries of the environment (the same information had previously been assembled for Ontario) asking for information on prosecutions, convictions, and fines over the past decade. Replies were received from Environment Canada, no date, and the ministries of British Columbia, no date, Alberta, November 24, 1989, New Brunswick, November 10, 1989, and Nova Scotia, no date, providing the information set out above.

Separating the Abatement and Enforcement Functions

The difficulty with any discussion of enforcement methods, in the environment field or elsewhere, is the lack of information on compliance levels. Since those breaking the law are unlikely to disclose their activities it is often impossible to do more than estimate the proportion of industrial operations that are out of compliance. This in turn makes it difficult to say with any certainty which methods of inducing compliance are most likely to produce the greatest return on investment for the regulatory agency. It might be assumed that the limited number of prosecutions and convictions, combined with low fines, is an indicator of extensive non-compliance but this assumption cannot be proven. One school of thought argues that a low prosecution rate is in fact a sign of *successful regulation*, since use of the "blunt instrument" of court action is admission of failure on the part of the regulatory agency to achieve compliance by using the various other methods available to it.[31]

The various techniques used by government agencies to achieve compliance with regulatory requirements cover a broad range:

- inform the regulated industry of the requirements;
- encourage voluntary use of environmental compliance audits;
- provide advice, technical assistance, or financial assistance to help in bringing operations into compliance;
- impose environmental monitoring and reporting requirements;
- negotiate a formal, but not legally binding, abatement program;

- issue formal warnings;
- impose requirements in the form of an administrative order;
- prosecute non-compliance with terms of the licence, order, or regulations.

In theory, the regulator works through this spectrum of options in each case, always relying on the threat of prosecution but using it only as a last resort. For that threat to be effective, of course, the regulated industry has to believe not only that prosecution will be undertaken but also that court action very possibly will result in a penalty that outweighs the financial benefits of non-compliance. The point made in the Peat, Marwick study cited above was that for many industries in Ontario in the early 1980s it was cheaper to pollute and pay the occasional fine than to pay the capital and operating costs necessary to bring operations into compliance.

As seen in Table 2, the level of fines imposed by the courts at present are unlikely to act as a major deterrent, particularly for larger firms.[32] It is sometimes argued that a financial penalty is only one deterrent and that others, such as the bad publicity associated with a successful prosecution, are more likely to influence corporate behaviour. Some American courts have imposed penalties consisting of both fines and the requirement that the company take out a full-page ad in the local newspaper, informing readers of its environmental wrongdoing. Another penalty is to impose personal liability on officers and employees of the company, an approach that has been used to a limited degree in Canada to date.

By far the most successful step in achieving compliance has been the decision by Ontario to provide different departments and staff to implement the abatement and enforcement functions, combined with a significant increase in staffing for the enforcement function.

The minister of the day, Harry Parrott, announced to the Ontario legislature on October 16, 1980, that his ministry had created a "highly trained environmental police force" to deal with the "serious issue of illegal and unsafe disposal practices for liquid industrial waste."[33] Establishment of this additional staff complement of thirteen investigators, known as the Special Investigations Unit (SIU), was the first time that any Canadian jurisdiction had provided an investigation capability beyond that of the monitoring and inspecting done by abatement staff. At the same time two new solicitors were added to the Legal Services Branch of the ministry to assist with the anticipated increase in prosecutions.

Ontario took the next step in June, 1985, during the short-lived government of Frank Miller, by announcing the creation of a new branch, in essence an expanded SIU, termed the Investigations and Enforcement Branch. Seventy additional staff were hired, for the most part investigators, many of them with backgrounds not in waste management or waterworks engineering but in police enforcement.[34] Using search and seizure powers the Branch conducts early-morning, unannounced raids on industrial operations, a far cry from the early 1970s when MOE staff would wait patiently outside the Inco gate while the company decided whether or not it would grant admittance.[35]

Although the separation of abatement and enforcement was established under the Tories, the new government of Premier Peterson pledged to double the Enforcement Branch budget. For the 1988-89 fiscal year the staff complement of the Branch was 100 (up from the thirteen of the SIU in 1981) and the budget was $4,491,800. The significance of this change is twofold. First, the simple increase in staffing allows an increase in prosecutions and resulting convictions (thirty convictions in 1981 when the SIU was formed in comparison to 170 in 1988-89). More importantly, though, the ministry is now able to move through the spectrum of compliance techniques, set out above, without the difficulties inherent in asking the same abatement officer to change from a negotiating, assisting role of interaction with a particular company to a prosecutorial role and then back again. By creating a separate enforcement branch, abatement staff can continue to assist – as long as the company operates within the law. As soon as non-compliance is suspected, however, investigation is done by a completely separate group of officials who have no ongoing relationship with the company in question.

Why did Ontario make this change? In his 1980 speech, Parrott referred to the increased "temptation for illegal disposal" resulting from the fact that Ontario was then eliminating the landfilling of liquid industrial waste but had not yet provided "appropriate treatment facilities." More stringent enforcement was required. At the same time, the courts had created the "due diligence" defence, allowing a polluter to avoid conviction if it could be proven that all reasonable care had been taken. More investigators were needed to give the prosecutor information on a company's operations so that such a defence could be counteracted in court. Although the environmental movement during the period 1980-85 was calling for more enforcement, the creation of a separate enforcement branch grew out of the 1980 SIU and was not the result of a specific policy proposal advanced by the environmental lobby.

During this period pressure was also mounted in Alberta for a change in enforcement practice. In 1982 and 1983 the Alberta Environment Department undertook a highly publicized prosecution of Suncor Inc., which resulted in a conviction in May, 1983, under the Fisheries Act, for an oil spill to the Athabasca River. The Alberta Environmental Law Centre published an analysis of the case, citing public concern over statements by the Alberta minister that his government "prefers to negotiate infractions of laws rather than prosecute them."[36] The Law Centre maintained the pressure by convening in 1985 a national conference on enforcement of environmental law, which was followed by the creation by the Alberta government, in 1986, of a special panel to review measures that might be taken. The panel in 1988 recommended establishment of an investigations and enforcement branch within the Pollution Control Division, following the Ontario model. In a press release dated November 9, 1989, the Alberta Environment Department, still in a defensive mode, stated that there was a need to provide information "clarifying media reports of enforcement actions taken by the Department in 1989" and promised a "complete reorganization of the Pollution Control Division" accompanied by "new legislation."[37]

The one other jurisdiction to review its enforcement procedures is the federal government. During development and passage of the Canadian Environmental Protection Act in 1988, the federal department came forth with a comprehensive compliance and enforcement policy and announced the commitment of additional funding for enforcement. It is not yet clear, however, to what extent the federal government will itself enforce the Act and how much will be done by the provinces. As noted, this issue has been the subject of private negotiation between the federal and provincial governments since 1987 and has not yet been resolved.

In summary, the following elements are needed to improve the record of Canadian governments in enforcing their environmental legislation:

- a policy decision that full compliance will, in fact, be required and that such things as the failure of the pulp and paper industry to comply with the 1971 water discharge requirements or the documented failure of Ontario industry (and in all likelihood, that of all other provinces) to comply with water discharge requirements will no longer be tolerated;
- significant increases in the funding and staffing provided both the abatement and enforcement functions;
- separation of the two functions through creation of enforcement branches, following the Ontario model.

Until these steps are taken Canadian governments have no assurance that their environmental laws and regulations are, in fact, obeyed.

Waste Management

The bulk of the industrial hazardous waste generated in Canada each year, which is discharged to the air, rivers, lakes, and sewers, is managed by the system of pollution regulation described above. A further regulatory system manages the remaining hazardous waste (that portion that is contained, perhaps treated, and then transported to off-site or on-site disposal – probably less than 25 per cent of the total), plus industrial and commercial non-hazardous and household waste.

Federal jurisdiction over waste management is limited to ocean dumping, regulated under the Ocean Dumping Control Act, and international and interprovincial shipment, regulated by the Transportation of Dangerous Goods Act. Beyond these domains, the federal government plays only a co-ordinating role, working toward harmonization of provincial regulatory requirements. Although the primary regulatory responsibility rests with the provinces, municipalities still play a very significant role, both through regulation of hazardous waste sewer disposal, which accounts for a quarter of the total generated each year, and provision of solid waste disposal facilities.

Prior to 1984, the federal co-ordinating role was provided by the Waste Management Branch of Environment Canada. After the Branch was reduced in size, as a result of the Mulroney government expenditure cuts, the Canadian Council of Resource and Environment Ministers, now the CCME, took over this responsibility. In March, 1987, the environment ministers released their Action Plan for the Management of Hazardous Wastes, which was a plan for co-ordinated action by the provinces in the following areas:

- standardization of provincial waste classification systems;
- development of guidelines, to be used by the provinces as regulations under their environmental legislation, for operation of hazardous waste disposal facilities;
- development of guidelines, again for use by the provinces, for decommissioning industrial plants;
- harmonization of provincial manifesting systems;
- development of a national contaminated site clean-up program;
- promotion of hazardous waste reduction, recycling, re-use, and recovery.

The plan is still in the process of being implemented.

Classification

The foundation for waste regulation is the system used to classify wastes in terms of their toxicity and potential for adverse environmental impact. Regulatory agencies in Canada and other jurisdictions have by now developed sophisticated classification systems of several hundreds of categories. The most important distinction, however, is simply whether a waste is classified as "hazardous" or "non-hazardous"; those wastes classified as "hazardous" are governed at all stages in their life cycle – from initial generation through storage, transportation, and disposal – by a separate, and more rigorous, regulatory system than that used for non-hazardous wastes.

Hazardous wastes are defined primarily by regulations under the federal Transportation of Dangerous Goods Act. These regulations were developed through industry-government consultation between 1980, when the Act was proclaimed, and July 1, 1985, when the regulations finally came into effect. Waste classifications set forth in the environmental legislation of each province are largely based on those of the federal Act. Prior to 1985 most provinces had generalized definitions of hazardous waste, but they then moved to replace them with the more detailed and specific listings of the federal regulations.[38] Radioactive wastes, on the other hand, are regulated directly by the federal government under the authority of the Atomic Energy Control Act.

Storage and Transport

Each province regulates how hazardous wastes are stored, stipulating security measures, container design, labelling, fire protection, and other aspects with bearing on human and environmental safety. Since the disasters of the Montreal PCB fire and the Ontario and Quebec tire fires of 1990, considerable attention has focused on the adequacy of storage regulations and their enforcement. Storage is of particular importance for PCB and radioactive wastes, for which there are no approved methods of disposal at present. In these cases storage *is* the disposal method.

During the past few years the problems of groundwater contamination caused by leaking underground gasoline storage tanks have caused concern. It has been estimated that there are between 7,000 and 35,000 leaking underground tanks in Canada.[39] The Canadian Petroleum Association has undertaken a program to develop guidelines for tank installation and replacement. Regulation is done not by environment departments but by such bodies as the Ontario Ministry of Consumer and Commercial Relations, under the authority of the Gasoline Handling Act.

Industrial wastes moved off the owner's property are carefully monitored by provincial environment departments through a "waybill" or "manifest" system. The purpose of the system is to guard against unlawful off-site disposal by ensuring that a record is supplied to government of each waste shipment. The owner, transporter, and disposer of the waste, usually three separate companies, are each required to complete the appropriate section of the manifest form, providing information on quantity and classification of the wastes in question. Copies of the manifest must be forwarded to the waste management branch of the environment department, which is then in a position to monitor the off-site movement. This is done, for example, by comparing the quantities shown as being disposed of with the quantities shown as originally leaving the factory gate. The only weakness in the system is the sheer volume of waste shipments that government agencies, with limited resources, have to monitor. It is not clear what portion of the manifest forms provided to waste management officials each year actually receive detailed scrutiny.

Transport of hazardous waste across the Canada-U.S. border, in the neighbourhood of 100,000 tonnes per year, is governed by a Canada-U.S. agreement that came into effect November 8, 1986. Under the agreement, the exporting country is obliged to inform the importing country of each proposed shipment, and the receiving country can then decide whether or not it will accept the shipment.

Treatment and Disposal

The regulation of both hazardous and non-hazardous waste disposal has become extremely rigorous over the past twenty years. In almost all instances annual or semi-annual monitoring must be done of air and water quality on the disposal site and every method made to guard against off-site pollution. This tightening of regulatory requirements, combined with increased resistance from citizens living in the vicinity of waste disposal sites, has made it increasingly difficult to establish new disposal sites, either for municipal garbage or for hazardous wastes. This means that less adequate disposal methods continue to be used – such as pouring untreated liquid wastes directly into a river or prolonging the life of a dated, leaking municipal landfill – simply because there is no alternative.

Although regulatory requirements direct hazardous wastes to appropriate disposal destinations and all disposal methods are closely regulated, there has been no attempt to use regulatory or other instruments to influence disposal pricing. Disposal pricing is a vital waste management tool, since it, more than anything else, determines the incentive the generators of waste have to reduce quantities produced each year. It is likely that during the next decade B.C., Manitoba, Ontario, and Quebec will join Alberta in providing publicly owned hazardous waste disposal facilities. This means that prices, for those facilities at least, will be set by government agencies. To date, however, there has been no attempt to use surcharge taxation or regulations to increase disposal prices. Solid waste disposal prices have increased in Ontario in recent years but this has been due to a shrinking supply of landfill capacity rather than any government policy.

Reduction, Re-use, Recycling, and Recovery

Reduction. There are no regulatory requirements to reduce the quantities of either hazardous or non-hazardous waste produced each year. In some cases, pollution emission standards will have the indirect effect of achieving reduction, since the need to change production processes in order to produce less waste will assist in meeting those requirements. (An example is pulp and paper discharge standards, which in combination with government financial incentives for plant modernization have reduced the portion of each tree that, after being chopped and shredded, is discharged to the river as waste.)

In the area of solid waste, attention has been paid to reducing the quantity of packaging produced each year and that immediately becomes waste. The National Task Force on Packaging, convened by the CCME and with representatives from all sectors in 1990, recommended a number of steps that could be taken to reduce packaging, but it shied away from recommending that they be incorporated into law.

To date, however, no jurisdiction has introduced, or even considered, legally enforceable requirements to reduce waste. The federal government since 1970 has provided financial assistance – under the Development and Demonstration of Resource and Energy Conservation Technology program, administered jointly by Environment Canada and Energy, Mines and Resources – for the development of new technologies to reduce waste and increase energy efficiency. Financial and technical assistance in industrial waste reduction and recycling is provided by the Ontario government.

Re-use. Regulatory requirements to re-use materials that otherwise would become waste have been limited to soft drink, beer, and milk containers. As discussed in Chapter 14 below, a number of provinces introduced "bottle bills" in the 1970s but they have been difficult to enforce and have for the most part been relaxed. No attempt has ever been made to require that liquor, other than beer, be sold in re-usable bottles.

Recycling. Although considerable attention has been paid to recycling in recent years, governments have relied completely on the voluntary efforts of industry and householders to recycle wastes. Aside from a few municipal by-laws, there have been no regulatory requirements to recycle.

Industry recycling has been encouraged through establishment of Canada and Ontario waste exchanges. Industries are invited to list wastes they must dispose of with the exchanges. Others, who may be able to use such wastes as raw materials, are then provided with an opportunity to contact the disposer and receive the wastes without charge. The Canada Exchange recycles approximately 25,000 tonnes a year, which accounts for a relatively small portion of the 8-million-tonne annual production of hazardous wastes in Canada.[40]

Household recycling, based on source separation of bottles, cans, and plastics combined with curbside pick-up service, has in the past few years been established in communities in B.C., Alberta, Ontario, Quebec, Nova Scotia, and New Brunswick. Citizen participation rates have been high and such programs have reduced the quantities of solid waste going to landfills by anywhere from 2 to 15 per cent. Since recycling programs normally only serve homes, and not apartment buildings, and since residential waste accounts for only 33 per cent of the solid waste generated each year (commercial and industrial account for 37 per cent and construction the remaining 30 per cent of solid waste) there is a limit to how much such programs can achieve. They are further hampered because governments have introduced no regulatory or fiscal measures to ensure a market for the recyclable materials, such as a surtax on virgin paper, collected through such programs.

Recovery. During the past decade waste recovery has been approached primarily in terms of generation of energy (such as steam for heating buildings or electricity) from incineration of municipal garbage. In the late 1970s Energy from Waste (EFW) was hailed as the answer to both the energy crisis and the pending shortage of landfill capacity, and a number of such plants were built in both the U.S. and Canada. Since then, an effective resistance has been mounted by the environmental movement, which argues that EFW suffers from two major drawbacks. The first is that inciner- ation produces new contaminants that would not exist if materials like plastics, which generate contaminants when burned, were landfilled. The argument is made that even high-efficiency combustion, which can achieve a destruction rate of something like 99.9 per cent of the dioxins and other substances of concern, will still contribute, through the remaining 0.1 per cent, a significant and ongoing amount of pollution. The other and per- haps more telling argument is that incineration provides no incentive to reduce the quantity of municipal garbage initially produced. In fact, it has the reverse effect, providing an incentive to maintain high waste quantities because the facility, whether publicly or privately owned, must generate sufficient revenues, through sales of energy, to offset the high capital cost of construction. This can only be done by maintaining a high volume of waste going into the plant each year. The other alternative – generating revenue through increased disposal pricing – is not yet considered a viable policy option.

The other form of recovery being given active consideration is the composting of organic wastes. Individual households are being encouraged to do this on their own but no large-scale programs have yet been implemented.

CHAPTER 13

Does the System Work?

The system of pollution regulation described above can be said to "work" only if it achieves two objectives. The first, of course, is the reduction of pollution quantities to the point that environmental harm no longer occurs. But just as important is the objective of doing so in a manner that does not unduly compromise other social objectives. If we were to divert virtually all government spending to pollution regulation, or strip polluters of their rights to due process when prosecuted, we could solve the problem overnight. But we would do so at the expense of other equally compelling needs for government spending or of our hard-won principles of justice.

For this reason a regulatory system or government program can be usefully judged by three criteria – effectiveness, efficiency, and fairness. For a system to be effective it must actually achieve its stated goals – in this case, reducing pollution to the point that it does not cause environmental harm. Efficiency refers to the cost, to both government and regulated industry, imposed in meeting that objective. Fairness focuses on the extent to which regulation is carried out in an even-handed, non-discretionary manner with no special favours given.

By these criteria, does the system work? The short answer is that the system meets one of the criteria and fails the other two. Pollution regulation is probably as efficient as any other regulatory system, but given the unique characteristics of each it is impossible to make comparisons. The Nielsen Task Force review of Environment Canada recommended the establishment of "simpler, but more effective, organization and management structures" but did not suggest that management at the time of the study, 1985, was glaringly inefficient.[1]

Pollution regulation obviously fails to meet the fairness criterion. The very nature of the system, which is based on case-by-case negotiation of both standards and their enforcement, dictates that it cannot be applied evenly and in a non-discretionary manner to all industries. If it were, what would be left to negotiate? As the system reaches maturity over the coming decade the greatest challenge is to transform this inherently discretionary system into one that is accessible and accountable, and, just as important, that finds acceptance in the eyes of the regulated industry by ensuring clarity, predictability, and even-handedness.

Finally, the discussion above shows that the system is not effective. While the environment is better protected today than it was twenty or thirty years ago, it still suffers from the ongoing impacts of pollution generated each year. In some areas the system clearly is effective. The landfilling of solid waste, because of regulatory requirements, is for the most part carefully controlled to minimize environmental impacts. Industrial hazardous wastes, on the other hand, are still primarily discharged untreated to sewers, lakes, or rivers. The effect of air pollution on forests and crops is too widespread and damaging to conclude that regulation in that area has met its goals. The evaluation of the state of the Great Lakes ecosystem done by the Conservation Foundation and the Institute for Research on Public Policy (IRPP) reached these conclusions:

> Air quality probably has improved over the past two decades because of declines in emissions of various pollutants. Quality still is unsatisfactory in many areas ... more reductions in emissions are needed. ...
>
> Although concentrations of some pollutants meet ambient water quality standards, concentrations are still high enough to cause serious contamination problems in fish and other wildlife. ...
>
> Preventive activities are in their infancy, so groundwater quality is degenerating.[2]

Thus, after something like a quarter-century of regulation by American and Canadian governments, the Great Lakes ecosystem is still polluted. We have to conclude that the regulatory system "works" in that the environment would be in much worse shape with no regulation, but it has still not met its basic objective of preventing environmental damage.

The Failure To Reduce Quantities

The basic problem is that the regulatory system has placed some limits on the discharge of toxic substances but in many cases those limits are still far too high. This is hardly surprising, since the chief criterion used in pollution regulation has always been cost to the polluter, not benefit to the environment. Until very recently the policy objective, notwithstanding political rhetoric, was to negotiate abatement programs that would achieve at least some pollution reduction but without any effect on the firm's profitability or ability to provide employment. As we shall see in Chapter 15, the federal regulation of pulp and paper mill discharges to water, introduced in 1971, was exactly such a program and, not surprisingly, by the 1980s, after more than a decade of regulation, had still achieved only marginal pollution reductions. The Canadian acid rain program, on the other hand, implemented in 1985, had from the outset a policy objective of 50 per cent reduction in sulphur dioxide emissions. By 1994, a decade after program implementation, this objective will have been achieved.

It would seem, therefore, that the first step in making pollution regulation work is a move from an objective of unspecified abatement to specific reduction targets. This is precisely what has happened in such areas as CFC emissions, pesticide uses, and solid waste diversion from landfill. The question that must be addressed is whether the existing system is capable of meeting these new objectives. A number of authorities in industry, government, and academe have suggested in recent years that it is not and that we must introduce new, flexible, and more sophisticated means of influencing the behaviour of polluting agencies.

Do We Need New Instruments?

The present system for setting and enforcing pollution emissions is sometimes referred to as one of "command and control." Although perhaps it might better be described as one of "private discussion and negotiation," the inference in the label is clear. Pollution regulation smacks of the rigidity and unwieldiness of the centrally planned economies of the Soviet bloc, which have now so convincingly demonstrated their failure either to meet the basic needs of their citizens or to protect their environment. Thus it is argued that instead of "command and control" we need "market-based" approaches. In the words of one study these are characterized by "relying on the decentralized and largely independent decisions of pollution generators. Environmental objectives are achieved through the response to governmentally imposed changes in the costs polluters face in using certain inputs and/or in disposing of waste products."[3] As well as being decentralized, the market-based approach, also described under the heading of "economic instruments," relies on voluntary instead of legislated action: "Market-based incentives are different from the traditional command and control approaches, which impose fixed emission limits on individual sources, in that they rely on voluntary decisions by polluters."[4]

The major economic instruments that have been considered and implemented in some European and American jurisdictions during the past two decades can be described as follows.

Effluent fees are the system in which industries are allowed to discharge a pollutant up to a particular load-total or concentration level and then are charged a per unit or sliding scale fee for all pollution emitted above that amount.

Tradeable emission permits are used in a system in which government sets a limit on the total quantity of a particular form of pollution that may be emitted in a given geographic area – e.g., x tonnes of sulphur dioxide per year in a circle of y miles diameter or a given jurisdiction – but then does not proceed to the next step of imposing emission limits directly on each of the sources within that area. Instead, those sources are allowed to buy and sell "emission rights," initially granted to each on the basis of existing sources and total quantity of reduction required to meet the standard imposed on the area as a whole. Thus if a new industry wishes to begin operations that will add to the total annual sulphur dioxide loading in the area it will have to "buy" that right to pollute by financing reductions implemented by the existing sources. Also included under this heading are such concepts as "banking emissions," in which a polluter whose emissions are below the regulatory standard in one year can "save" the allowable emission quantity not used and add it to the allowable quantity emitted in the following year.

Waste disposal pricing encourages the generator of either household or industrial wastes to be more efficient and less wasteful by charging more for waste disposal; under such an approach governments would influence disposal pricing either by increasing disposal fees at publicly owned facilities or by imposing a tax or surcharge on private facilities.

Input fees, unlike waste disposal pricing, which increases cost to the polluter at the back end of the process, increase costs at the front end on polluting substances. The best-known example is the U.S. Superfund clean-up program, which is financed by a tax on forty-two different petrochemicals used by industry. Another example is the carbon tax, "an excise tax on the carbon contained in fossil fuels," which is advocated by environmentalists in Canada. All such pricing and taxation programs have a dual objective of influencing the behaviour of the polluter through pricing and of generating government revenue to be used to finance environmental protection programs.

Deposit-refund is a program intended to encourage re-use and recycling, the best known being the deposit placed on pop or beer bottles, which is then refunded when they are returned.

All of these approaches are systems to be implemented by government agencies, usually as a supplement to existing regulatory methods. A different approach, in that it does not rely on government action, is increased private property ownership of natural resources. It is argued by some that the "tragedy of the commons" occurs because no one owns the commons and therefore no one has an incentive to protect it. This argument has been advanced most recently in Canada by Walter Block of the Fraser Institute. Block argues that polluters have been shielded from full liability for the effects their pollution has on property held by others, starting in the nineteenth century with English court decisions which held that farmers could not sue for damage to crops caused by fires started by sparks from locomotives because the rail system served a larger public good. In the best tradition of "polluter pay," Block argues that legislative reforms should be enacted to increase the ability of private property-owners to sue for pollution-caused damage and that we should then rely on private litigation, instead of government regulation, to reduce pollution.[5] As noted, the environmental community for many years has pressed for an "environmental bill of rights," one part of which would give increased powers to the private citizen to institute private prosecutions and common law actions. Block parts company with the environmentalists, however, when he suggests that private litigation replace government regulation as the means of protecting the environment.

Using the example of the *Exxon Valdez* oil spill, Block points to the need to increase the liability to which Exxon is exposed in such an instance and then goes on to make a somewhat surprising suggestion. "Why not carry the privatization trail blazed by Margaret Thatcher even further and privatize what now seems to be unprivatizable, that is, the oceans and seas and other large bodies of water into which oil can spill? ... If people owned various patches of the ocean, they would have an economic incentive to protect their holdings. For example, they might well insist that any ship passing through their property with a cargo of oil be double-hulled."[6] Block admits that the proposal "will appear to many as science-fictionish, idiosyncratic, lunatic, or just plain ludicrous," but he does not offer any practical suggestions that might mitigate those views. He does not suggest who would sell, who might buy, how their property would be demarcated, or how, indeed, the new owners might control use of the ocean property by others.[7] (This suggestion by no means represents Block at his most ludicrous. He goes on to a lengthy diatribe against David Suzuki and then departs even further from the field of economic theory by launching an attack on the animal rights movement. Block is unwilling to accord any rights to animals until they begin to "respect the rights of human beings," by which he means that the larger mammals, such as bears and lions, should change their ways and stop attacking us. Until they do, "Why should we do more for the lion ... than it is willing to do for us?"[8])

The concept of market-based approaches, particularly in the form of effluent charges, was advocated by economists in Canada during the 1970s and 1980s but no real interest was shown by governments, the environmental community, or business. For instance, the 1985 conference on environment organized by the Economic Council of Canada, presumably one organization that would have an interest in such an approach, did not devote any time to the subject. Recently, however, both business and industry have begun to suggest that such an approach is needed. The following statement by Roy Aitken, executive vice-president of Inco, exemplifies this recent interest:

> Without doubt there is a place for regulation. One need only look at the ecological disaster of the *Exxon Valdez* oil spill off Alaska to see the need. . . . But until recently, regulation and legislation have been essentially the only game in town. Now governments are looking for new tools to achieve more efficient and effective environment/ economy integration: economic mechanisms such as contaminant charge schemes; tradeable emission discharge rights; investment tax credits for exceeding environmental standards. . . . The concept of incentives to industry to make changes may be distasteful to some. It runs counter to the "Polluter Pays" slogan. But that is an old-fashioned idea. It fails to recognize that we are all polluters. . . .[9]

The C.D. Howe Institute, although not going to quite the lengths of its more right-wing counterpart, the Fraser Institute, has also endorsed this approach. In a 1990 publication, the Institute acknowledges the need for a "framework law" but goes on to say that "a 'command-and-control' approach will not work" and insists that "a market-based incentives and pricing approach must be central."[10]

Government interest in the subject is reflected in the 1990 Environment Canada *Green Plan* discussion paper:

> The Government believes that economic instruments can be an effective complement to, and in some cases a substitute for, environmental regulation. However, given limited experience in Canada and other countries with such instruments, the Government believes that further work is needed to assess fully the merits of using economic instruments in pursuit of environmental objectives.[11]

Canada's *Green Plan*, released December 11, 1990, states that "In 1991, the Government of Canada will establish a program to support practical research into the use of economic instruments. . . ."[12]

Since new instruments will require considerable study and consultation before they can be introduced, there is a very real danger that this will provide an excuse for further inaction. The Reagan administration consistently said more scientific study was needed before action could be considered on acid rain. Is Canada now going to say we need more study on instruments before action?

The other weakness in the case for economic instruments is that no analysis done to date has demonstrated any inherent inadequacy in existing instruments. It is true that the task of setting and enforcing standards is extremely difficult, but such approaches as effluent charges or tradeable emission rights still require that exactly the same decisions as to quantities of allowable pollution be made and enforced. Thus we still have all of the difficulties, and administrative costs, of the command and control system but to them would be added another layer of bureaucracy to administer the various economic approaches.

The one significant market approach that does make sense, because of its basic simplicity, is energy and waste disposal pricing. Other than this, however, economic instruments or claptrap theories about privatizing resources are pitfalls to be avoided. The existing system has failed to date because there simply has not been the political will to use it and to impose the true costs of environmental protection on polluters, consumers, or workers. Now that the necessary will has been summoned forth by changing public attitudes, there is no need to spend time and effort in devising new approaches. We must simply use the ones we have. The study *Great Lakes: Great Legacy?* concluded that existing legal and administrative mechanisms were capable of meeting the challenge of environmental protection in the Great Lakes ecosystem, even though the basin is divided by an international border. "One positive note is the fact that the institutional wherewithal already exists to integrate environmental quality efforts and eclipse the crisis management mode of environmental protection. . . . What is needed to rescue the Great Lakes region from its continuing environmental decline is the will to act and the discipline to take a long-term perspective."[13]

The most important step needed to strengthen the existing regulatory system is to provide significantly increased financial and staffing resources. Beyond that, steps must be taken to increase both public access and the accountability of government and industry. Closed-door discretionary bargaining must be replaced with clear-cut rules, evenly applied. But the system by no means need be abandoned. It worked for phosphorous and acid rain and, although the challenge is more difficult, can work for all other pollutants as well.

PART IV

From the Green Garbage Bag to the Stratosphere

The chapters here tell the stories of our attempts to limit the damage caused by five types of pollution – municipal garbage, industrial hazardous waste, pulp mill discharges to water, acid rain, and CFCs. The purpose is to illustrate by means of these specific case studies the regulatory system – and the political controversies endemic to it – outlined in the previous chapters.

The topics were chosen to ensure that the full spectrum, of both air and water pollution and solid and hazardous waste management, was included. A more important factor in their choice, however, is the fact that they represent the full range of jurisdictional authority – the roles of all governing bodies, from town or city councils to the United Nations, are discussed.

Some of these are success stories – most notably acid rain but also negotiation of the Montreal Protocol, a success in that it was the first time the international community agreed to take common action to reduce pollution emissions, despite the fact that the standards agreed on were immediately seen as too lax. Others, in particular our failure after ten years of trying to provide treatment and disposal capacity for the hazardous wastes we produce each year, are undoubted failures.

CHAPTER 14

Where Do We Put the Waste?

Ontario Solid Waste Management

Solid waste management offers an excellent paradigm for understanding both hazardous waste and air and water pollution issues, because it differs from them only in its visibility:

> At its root all pollution is garbage disposal in one form or another.... If you took a bag of garbage and dropped it on your neighbour's lawn, we all know what would happen. Your neighbour would call the police and you would soon find out that the disposal of garbage is your responsibility ... but if you took the same bag of garbage and burned it in a backyard incinerator, letting the sooty ash drift over the neighbourhood, the problem gets more complicated.... And when the garbage is invisible to the naked eye, as much air and water pollution is, the problem often seems insurmountable.[1]

This visibility allows us, in the case of municipal solid waste, to focus clearly on the issue that is central to management of all types of waste – how can governments achieve at the same time the two largely contradictory objectives of both reducing quantities generated each year and providing environmentally secure disposal capacity for the remainder? From an environmental perspective, waste reduction – not generating waste in the first place – is the only sensible policy option. The less waste we produce, the fewer resources we consume and the less pollution we cause through its disposal. The environmentalist is also concerned, however, to minimize pollution effects by providing good disposal methods instead of bad for the remainder – for instance, properly engineered and operated landfills instead of the leaky, smelly garbage dumps of the past. But if there is enough disposal capacity there is no incentive to reduce the amounts generated. Providing that incentive either by the economic means of disposal pricing or through legislation and regulation carries a political price that elected representatives in Ontario and the other Canadian provinces have been unwilling to pay. This theme – the connection between reduction and disposal – underlies both the following story of the failure of successive Ontario governments to resolve the steadily worsening solid waste crisis in that province and our national failure to provide hazardous waste disposal capacity.

Waste Management in a Shambles

The municipality of Halton Region, located just west of Lake Ontario, was created by Ontario in 1974 as part of its program to consolidate small municipalities into regional governments. Prior to amalgamation, the municipalities that made up Halton Region had owned and operated their own landfill sites. After 1974, in keeping with its new mandate for regional waste disposal, Halton began a search for one large site. In 1977 it rejected a proposal to establish a site in Burlington, on land owned by the National Sewer Pipe company, and instead selected a site near the town of Milton. The site was approved by the Ontario Municipal Board in 1979 but local citizens and Milton officials strenuously fought the proposal. Milton council refused to amend its official plan or pass the necessary zoning; the matter was then litigated, which resulted in the court disallowing the choice of the Milton site.

The Region returned to the drawing board and launched, in August, 1982, a Waste Management Master Plan process, carried out under the provisions of the Ontario Environmental Assessment Act and intended not just to site a landfill but to develop a comprehensive plan, including the three R's and possibly disposal by incineration as well as landfill. During this time National Sewer Pipe, still seeking the enormous profits that can be made by obtaining a Certificate of Approval for a landfill, continued to press for use of its Burlington site, carrying out hydrogeological studies which, the company claimed, supported its case.

By October, 1985, Halton had completed its plan and submitted an environmental assessment to the ministry for approval. The plan called for recycling and construction of an energy-from-waste incinerator after 1996 and offered a selection of two possible landfill sites: the National Sewer Pipe lands in Burlington and the Milton site, which had been ruled out by the court six years earlier. The Region preferred the Burlington site but, in what became a major point of controversy during the hearing, submitted both, saying that either was suitable and leaving the decision to the Environmental Assessment Board. Shortly afterward the existing landfill, which had met the Region's needs since the 1970s, became full, and because a decision had not yet been reached on its replacement, Halton took the unprecedented step of trucking its solid waste into the United States, to be incinerated at the Occidental facility in Niagara Falls, New York.

The hearing on the two proposed landfill sites was held under the Consolidated Hearings Act, because approvals were required both for zoning, under the Planning Act, and for environmental acceptability under the Environmental Assessment and Environmental Protection Acts. They began May 5, 1987, before a Joint Board, consisting of H.H. Lancaster of the Ontario Municipal Board and D.J. Kingham of the Environmental Assessment Board. Parties to the hearing were the Region (the proponent), opponents of the Milton site – the Town of Milton, the Milton Area Citizens Coalition, and NSP Investments, owners of the Burlington site, still pressing to have their site chosen, and those favouring the Milton site – the city of Burlington and the West Burlington Citizens' Group, both fighting to keep the landfill out of their backyard.

The Joint Board, after chastising the Region for offering a choice of two sites without itself making a selection, issued its decision in favour of the Milton site almost two years later, on February 24, 1989. The decision came after 194 gruelling days of listening to expert witnesses argue over the hydrogeology, ecology, social and economic impacts, and every other conceivable detail of the two rival sites. That decision was then appealed to cabinet by those fighting against the Milton site. In March, 1989, cabinet confirmed the Joint Board decision.[2]

The process cost millions of dollars, locked Halton citizens for two exhausting years into what the Board termed a "bitter crossfire of rival communities," and engaged the abilities of hundreds of capable environmental professionals. And what was achieved? No fundamental issues were advanced or clarified, no precedents of environmental law were set, and the benefit to the natural environment, by selecting one site over another, was marginal at best. There has to be a better way to decide what to do with our garbage.

Unfortunately, this scenario is being played out repeatedly in every part of the province. Efforts to reduce waste quantities have failed completely – per capita waste generation increased 25 per cent during the 1980s;[3] existing landfills are filling up; the approvals process for new landfill sites is mired in confusion and bitterness. In 1987 the ministry closed a leaking landfill site in Tiny Township, on Georgian Bay, and ordered Metro Toronto to accept the 25,000 tonnes of waste that had been going there. Tiny Township and neighbouring municipalities had been engaged in a Waste Management Master Plan for ten years, at an expenditure of $10 million, but their proposed site was rejected by the Environmental Assessment Board in 1989. The Board's rejection was based not on potential pollution from the new site but because the assessment process had been flawed. The previous year Peel Region, northwest of Metro, had imposed a temporary freeze on all land development approvals, on the basis that it could not guarantee waste disposal capacity for new development when it was told by the MOE, in the fall of 1988, that the waste management plan it had been developing since the early 1980s was inadequate. The Region of Ottawa-Carleton, in light of the Board decision on Tiny Township, ordered a review of its own Master Plan process, which to that point had taken six years and $1.2 million and in January, 1990, decided to start all over again to correct flaws in the process that, it was assumed, would result in EA Board rejection of the planning process, whatever it might be. The Ottawa Region chief administrative officer made this comment to the regional council:

> One of the extraordinarily confusing concepts in the process of waste management planning is the distinction which has been made between waste management master planning and environmental assessment. There appears to be no general agreement among staff of the Ministry of the Environment as to whether this distinction really exists or whether it is a distinction made purely for government funding purposes. . . .
>
> The Ministry of the Environment's position . . . can only be gleaned from general policy statements made by MOE staff and from public statements of the Minister reported in the press. . . . [4]

The *Ottawa Citizen* echoed this complaint, pointing to the problem of "confusing signals from Queen's Park (does anybody know, even now, its policy on incineration?)."[5] Then in June, 1990, the Ontario cabinet overturned the EA Board decision on Tiny Township, ordering new studies and a new hearing, but without itself choosing a site. All of this was played out against the background scenario of Metro Toronto and surrounding regions, generators of some 3 million tonnes a year, desperately thrashing and flailing as they approached the 1992 deadline by which their existing landfills would reach capacity.

In March, 1989, the Association of Municipalities of Ontario issued a report stating that the environmental assessment process for waste planning "is too cumbersome . . . too uncertain . . . takes too long to complete . . . [and] is inordinately expensive." The report used understatement to note that "there is little in the way of broad provincial policy to assist in guiding or forming the framework within which municipalities can plan for waste management."[6] Pollution Probe was more blunt. In the summer of 1990 Probe issued a report stating that "Ontario is currently confronted with a waste management crisis. . . . However, the province has taken no substantive action."[7] A month earlier the Ministry of the Environment had issued its own report, admitting that "waste disposal capacity is not meeting ... demand ... 160 landfills have less than two years of approved remaining capacity," and concluding that "current waste management practices are inadequate."[8]

How did Ontario get into this mess? To answer that question we need to review the main components of waste management and then turn to the beginning of the story – the first efforts by the environmental community in the late 1960s to promote recycling of cans and bottles.

Components of Solid Waste Management

Ontario each year produces somewhere between 10 and 14 million tonnes of solid waste, of which approximately one-third is household garbage and the remainder is commercial and industrial solid non-hazardous waste. Ontario citizens produce more waste, per capita, than do those of any other nation. This waste is disposed of in 1,400 landfills and five energy-from-waste incinerators.[9] Jurisdiction over solid waste management is divided between three levels of government. The bottom tier municipalities pick up the garbage, regional municipalities dispose of it, and provincial authorities, both administrative agencies such as the Ontario Ministry of the Environment and quasi-judicial bodies such as the Ontario Municipal Board and Environmental Assessment Board, regulate the process, using environmental and land-use planning legislation.

Until recently, since there was no concern for environmental impacts, solid waste disposal, by burning or burial, was virtually free and disposal capacity virtually unlimited. Nobody thought much about the problem. During the 1970s and 1980s, however, the introduction of progressively more rigorous environmental regulation made both burning and landfilling much more difficult; apartment incinerators, for instance, have been disallowed, while regulations intended to prevent groundwater pollution and the vagaries of the environmental assessment process have made siting a new landfill a long, difficult, and uncertain process. As a result, available disposal capacity is rapidly being depleted. As disposal capacity becomes limited, the laws of supply and demand inevitably mean that disposal pricing, the "tipping fee" or charge per tonne for landfilling or incinerating waste, will eventually increase. In the period 1988-91 Metro Toronto increased the per tonne price it charges private haulers who dump in its Keele Valley landfill from $18.50 to $85 to $150.

In theory, this increased disposal cost will lead to reduction of waste, since as disposal capacity becomes a scarce and therefore more expensive commodity, those wishing to dispose of waste will have an economic incentive to produce less of it in the first place. In fact, as is the case in most other areas of activity, the working of the marketplace is distorted by government action.

First, a municipality operating a landfill will not necessarily pass all the costs, including the cost of environmental impairment, along to the users; second, government action in regulating disposal has created the initial scarcity and therefore demand. Environmentalists applaud the shortage of disposal capacity because it forces municipalities and others to think seriously about reducing waste quantities. But is this disposal shortage – which leads to the kinds of costly, frustrating, and bitter wrangling described above – the only way we can find to produce less garbage in the first place?

In every aspect of waste and pollution management, government regulation both creates and drives the marketplace. However, if we do not have a functioning market to allocate supply and demand, nor do we have comprehensive government policy to achieve the same end. The fact that responsibility for disposal and regulation is divided between two jurisdictions makes integrated planning difficult, but, as we shall see, the real problem is that successive provincial governments have not yet been able to develop and implement a coherent policy.

From the Pop Bottle to the Blue Box

Before the modern environment era, but not that many years ago, a two-cent deposit was sufficient incentive to bring pop bottles back into the store where they could be returned to the manufacturer to be cleaned, refilled, and sold again – as many as fifteen or twenty times – before reaching the end of their useful life. Before the terms had been coined the marketplace, in the absence of regulation, supplied an "economic instrument" that successfully achieved the second in the hierarchy of waste management options – "re-use."

In the late 1960s, as the modern environmental movement was coming into being, much of the concern over pollution – before the days of acid rain or stratospheric ozone depletion – centred on litter and waste. Today municipal waste is a hot issue because nobody wants a landfill in his or her backyard. Then it was prompted by a more altruistic concern over resource consumption than any shortage of disposal capacity. The environmental movement adopted recycling as one of its primary goals and established recycling depots for conscientious citizens to drop off their bottles and tin cans. Since there was almost no government support given for such programs, capital and operating costs had to be met from either charitable donations or revenue generated by sale of the recycled goods.

These early recycling efforts failed for several reasons. Recycling depots relied on citizens not only to segregate their garbage but also to transport materials to the depot, an effort only a minority were willing to make, thus limiting the percentage of total recyclable materials that could be attracted. A far greater problem, however, and one that present-day recycling programs have still not solved, stems from the fact that recycling depends on the existence of a market for raw materials in the form of used glass, cans, or newspapers. No attempt was made by governments, through regulation or fiscal policy, to expand the market for recycled materials, with the result that these programs were almost all killed off during the course of the 1970s by such things as the vagaries of newsprint pricing, which often made new paper cheaper than recycled.

Recycling, however, was only one objective. Eliminating the production of waste in the first place – reduction – was always the priority goal, followed by re-use. In the case of the latter, attention centred on pop bottles. The October, 1970, newsletter of the newly formed Pollution Probe informed readers of the Probe campaign for increased use of refillable containers and urged them to write letters to government and industry and then, in the spirit of the times, to move to direct action: "fill your [shopping] cart and ask for soft drinks in returnable bottles; if you can buy none in the brand you want then leave your cart in the aisle, not at the check-out counter (that antagonizes other customers)."[10]

Similar battles were being fought in the United States. In 1972 Oregon became the first American state to pass a "bottle-bill," requiring that a deposit be paid for returned soft-drink bottles. Vermont, Michigan, Maine, Connecticut, and Iowa followed suit, in the face of strenuous opposition. "In the years after the Oregon law was passed, proposals to extend it sparked intense political controversy. Container manufacturers bitterly resisted the drive for returnables ... organized labour in steel, aluminum and glass also protested."[11]

Such lobbying in Ontario produced results. In 1976 the Ontario government developed regulations requiring that 75 per cent of all soft-drink containers be refillable.[12] The regulations prohibited sale of soft drinks in aluminum or plastic containers, based on the theory that source separation recycling would not work if too many different materials were used. The Ministry of Environment had taken a first step, and moreover one that was clear and decisive, in the use of regulations to reduce waste quantities. Unfortunately, it has never taken another one since. As is so often the case, the initiative was not successful because the regulations were not strenuously enforced. "This approach failed because the MOE did not have enough personnel to check out refillable levels at all stores."[13]

During this period of the late 1970s, while non-profit (and some municipal) recycling efforts were faltering and non-refillable containers were proliferating illegally on store shelves, available disposal capacity was being constrained by new regulations governing landfill design and use. The ministry was working to eliminate landfills that leached pollution directly into groundwater. In 1980 the Environmental Assessment Act, passed in 1976 but only with application to provincial projects, was extended to municipal undertakings, which complicated the process of siting new landfills. While EPA approval had provided for a public hearing before the Environmental Assessment Board, the addition of the EAA approval meant that municipalities had to demonstrate that they had considered alternative waste management options instead of simply applying for permission to open another landfill.

By the 1980s the number of alternatives had increased. In 1981, the first experimental curbside recycling program – using the now familiar blue boxes with the slogan "We Recycle!" – was started in Kitchener and immediately demonstrated gratifyingly high participation rates. At the same time, garbage incineration, in the form of energy-from-waste (EFW) plants, was attracting the attention of municipal works departments. The concept of using garbage to generate energy seemed too good to be true, since it solved two problems at the same time. One such plant was approved and built in London, Ontario, and Toronto and other municipalities began to plan for others.

On June 13, 1983, Keith Norton, then Minister of the Environment, introduced his "Blueprint for Waste Management in Ontario," the first comprehensive policy statement since his predecessor, Harry Parrott, introduced his seven-point program in September, 1978. The "Blueprint" addressed both hazardous and solid waste and, in the case of the former, embodied a number of new and worthwhile initiatives. For the first time hazardous waste generators were told they would have to provide the MOE with regular information on quantities and types of wastes produced each year, thus giving government the first reliable data on the scope of the hazardous waste problem in the province. The waybill system, used to keep track of the transport of hazardous wastes, was strengthened and the system of classifying wastes under Regulation 309 of the EPA was clarified and improved.

Municipal waste policy was less clear-cut. Municipalities were told that they must undertake comprehensive waste management planning, co-ordinated with other land-use planning and subject to approval under the Environmental Assessment Act. The minister also stated that the "Four Rs . . . must and will be a major part of waste management in our province . . . [representing] the greatest challenges we face in bringing new life to waste management in this province."[14]

The policy document contained absolutely no provisions for actually *achieving* reduction or recycling objectives, however. The "Blueprint" lacked any realistic discussion of the steps to be taken to make reduction and recycling a reality – provision of adequate financial and staffing resources, at either the provincial or municipal level; some means of influencing the recycling market through regulatory requirements, subsidies, disposal pricing, or other mechanisms; and, ultimately, at least some consideration of legislative steps to reduce waste volumes. Norton urged industry and the public to work voluntarily toward the achievement of reduction and recycling objectives and pledged government leadership in such areas as increased purchasing of recycled paper. He "propose[d] for discussion" the possibility of a disposal fee to provide an incentive for reduction and to generate revenues to fund four-R activities but cautioned that "considerable discussion and review of the disposal fee concept is essential" before it could be actually introduced.[15] Norton made no mention of the fact that while the "Blueprint" was being prepared his government, under intense lobbying from the aluminum industry for a change in the regulations prohibiting aluminum soft-drink cans, was getting ready to abandon the one regulatory beachhead established during the past decade.

By the fall of 1982, the MOE had received fourteen separate proposals from industry for changes to the soft-drink regulations, including one from Alcan, the aluminum manufacturer, which badly wanted access to the soft-drink can market. Alcan offered, in exchange for dropping the ban on aluminum containers, to provide financial support for what was coming to be seen, after the successful Kitchener experiment, as the next logical step in recycling – curbside pick-up, with the regular garbage collection, of recyclable materials. In October, 1982, the Recycling Council of Ontario submitted a brief to the ministry supporting the Alcan proposal. In December of the same year the MOE released for discussion a Green Paper, setting out different options.

In January and February of 1983, the steel and aluminum industries squared off and started swinging. The steel industry released a report estimating that 3,500 jobs would be lost if the regulations were changed to allow aluminum cans, which was then countered by the Alcan claim that the entire can-making industry in Ontario only employed a total of 1,200 people, of whom only forty-three would lose their jobs if the Alcan proposal were adopted. In May, Alcan joined forces with Domglas Inc., Consumers Glass Co., Ontario Paper Co., and Twinpak Inc. to form the Recycling Support Council, which then provided financial support for a recycling demonstration project in Burlington. In November the newly formed Council announced that it would contribute $1 million toward the cost of curbside recycling if the regulations were changed. In that month the steel industry formed the Canadian Tin Plate Recycling Council, with a mandate to promote the recycling of steel cans. The wrangling continued through 1984 and into 1985 as environment ministers came and went – Andy Brandt had replaced Keith Norton in June, 1983, and was himself replaced by Morley Kells in March, 1985, just before the Ontario election. Susan Fish held the position during the brief tenure of the Frank Miller minority government from May to June. When the Liberals took power Jim Bradley became minister. By August, 1985, the environmental community was split over the issue with Pollution Probe, attracted by the offer of private-sector funding for recycling, and the Recycling Council of Ontario, as it always had been, committed to the Alcan proposal, while CELA, the Federation of Ontario Naturalists, and others called for a 100 per cent refillable objective, with mandatory deposit regulations. The new minister sided with Pollution Probe and in December, 1985, the regulations were amended. Aluminum cans would be allowed as of 1987 and the requirement to provide refillable containers relaxed, provided that recycling targets were met.[16]

Ontario Multi-Material Recycling Incorporated was established in 1986 by the soft-drink industry as the vehicle to provide the promised funding for curbside recycling. Costs were to be divided evenly between OMMRI, the MOE, and the participating municipality. In 1986 OMMRI set its recycling contribution at $2 million per annum, a figure that matched that year's MOE recycling budget. In 1987, after a study commissioned by Coca-Cola Ltd. of the capital funds needed for recycling, that contribution was increased to $20 million over the three-year period 1987-90, or approximately $6.6 million a year. Presumably the financial benefits accruing to the industry as a result of the 1985 change in regulations were such that it could swallow a tripling of the cost without a murmur.

Metropolitan Toronto councillor Richard Gilbert, writing in the *Toronto Star* of March 17, 1989, has said that "Meanwhile, the soft drink industry is laughing all the way to the bank. Some $20 million is being put into the Blue-Box programs but three or four times that amount is being saved through not having to provide refillable containers and operate a deposit system." Gilbert went on to point out that the 1985 regulatory amendments had the effect of shifting the government policy focus almost completely to recycling, the third in the preferred hierarchy of waste management options. He pointed out that "recycling glass and other materials always causes more pollution, energy use, and waste than re-using items made from the materials" and concluded by saying that "Ontario should not be settling for the third best method of waste management."[17] By the summer of 1990 the blue box program was serving approximately 2 million Ontario households and diverting some 260,000 tonnes away from landfill disposal. This represented some 2 per cent of the 10-14 million tonnes produced in the province that year.[18]

On March 10, 1989, Environment Minister Jim Bradley announced an Ontario policy objective of 25 per cent diversion from landfill by 1992 and 50 per cent by the year 2000. However, like the 1983 "Blueprint," he did not announce any use of regulatory powers to achieve these objectives, such as requirements for the use of recycled paper. Instead, Bradley said that he would "urge municipalities to charge true cost tipping fees" and would introduce legislation "clarifying the province's powers to make 4Rs activities mandatory" should his attempts at moral suasion not prove successful. This legislation, it should be noted, had been promised each year since

1986. MOE spending devoted to reduction, re-use, and recycling had increased substantially since 1983 but nothing else had changed.[19]

On October 5, 1989, Alan Tonks, chairman of Metro Toronto, issued a statement saying that he and the chairmen of York, Peel, and Durham regions had met with the minister to tell him the targets were "impossible to meet . . . unless there is some very strong legislative action taken by the provincial government."[20] The problem is very simple – in the absence of regulatory action, there is insufficient demand for recycled materials and no other incentive. During 1989 the price for used newsprint, which constitutes close to three-quarters of all recycled materials, dropped from $45 a tonne to between $5 and $10. Since some municipalities were paying as much as $23 a tonne for blue box collection, the incentive to expand recycling from the present 2 per cent to the proposed 25 per cent over three years is distinctly absent.[21]

However, while ministry officials met with newspaper publishers and called on them to "take their share of responsibility by injecting money into expanding the Blue Box program," there was no suggestion that regulatory powers might be used to require use of recycled paper. On February 19, 1990, the minister announced that the newspaper and food products industries had joined OMMRI and would both provide funding and undertake voluntary measures toward reduction, re-use, and recycling. If the offer of money to stave off regulation had worked for the soft-drink industry, it obviously could work for others as well.

The Ontario government took no legislative steps to reduce waste quantities, nor did it do anything to improve the disposal approvals process. A ministry task force, appointed in 1987 to make recommendations for improvement of the administration of the Environmental Assessment Act, did not report until January, 1991, when it released a discussion paper. Another government task force, this one not in the MOE but in Treasury and Economics, reported involuntarily in the fall of 1989 when its draft report on potential changes to both land-use and environmental assessment legislation, intended to speed up development, was leaked to the environmental community. Environmentalists charged the Liberal government with plans to gut the Environmental Assessment Act, and confusion over the real intentions of the Peterson government persisted.[22] Adding to this confusion was a lack of a clear policy statement by the government on incineration. The Ministry of Environment seemed to be opposed, as indicated by the fact that the fourth "R," recovery, had been dropped from its lexicon,[23] but the Ministry of Energy continued to provide grants for EFW planning.

Metro Garbage

As municipalities throughout the province continued to flounder in the difficulties of meeting their own waste management needs they also increasingly began to look over their shoulders, wondering if they might figure in the plans of Metro and its neighbours. In 1980, when Metro approved its most recent Solid Waste Master Plan, disposal capacity was provided by landfills in nearby Pickering and an aging incinerator on Commissioners Street in east Toronto. Negotiations were under way for the purchase of a mammoth, 20-million-tonne landfill, known as the Keele landfill, near the town of Maple northwest of Metro, and the city of Toronto was beginning to develop plans for a new energy-from-waste plant, to be located in South Riverdale, not far from the existing Commissioners Street incinerator. The Keele site began operations in 1983, with the expectation that it would provide capacity through to the end of the century. Annual disposal quantities at that site were much higher than expected, however, presumably because waste was diverted to it from other landfills that were closed because they either reached capacity or failed to meet increasingly stringent environmental regulations.

By 1985 Metro officials began to realize that planning for new capacity would have to begin much earlier than had been anticipated. Unlike the process that produced the 1980 plan, however, this effort, because of the requirements of the provincial Environmental Assessment Act, would have to be carried out in full consultation with all affected parties, including the environmentalists pressing for increased reduction and recycling, stores and industries concerned about their disposal costs, and citizens in York and Durham regions worried that their communities might end up on the receiving end of some 3-4 million tonnes a year of solid waste. It was eventually decided that the planning process would be undertaken jointly by Metro, York, and Durham, co-ordinated by the Metro Works Department. By mid-1987 a full-blown consultative process – known as the Solid Waste Environmental Assessment Process, or SWEAP – was under way, with municipal staff, citizens, and consultants diligently examining the esoterica of bottle recycling, backyard composting, economies of waste-derived energy sales, and related topics.

By 1988 it was starting to become apparent that this process could not be completed before Keele and the other Metro sites filled up, particularly since the existing incinerator on Commissioners Street was coming under increasing public pressure to cease operations, due to air pollution, and the new incinerator proposed by the city was rapidly losing support at City Council in the face of determined citizen opposition. An interim solution, undoubtedly another landfill, would have to be found.

The search for an interim site began with public meetings in the fall of 1987 in Durham Region, the municipality to the east of Metro, to discuss possible use of the Metro-owned Brock South site. Not surprisingly, Durham citizens and municipal politicians objected strongly to Metro once again looking to dump its waste outside its borders without even going through the motions of looking for a site within Metro Toronto itself.

By the summer of 1988 the pressure on Metro was becoming intense. At the accelerated rate of dumping, the Keele site was expected to be full by 1992. Negotiations for an interim site outside Metro were stalled and the provincial minister, Bradley, announced that the choice of an interim site would require the same Environmental Assessment Act approval – a process guaranteed to take a minimum of three years – as was the longer-term search being conducted under SWEAP. The one possible site within Metro, the Rouge Valley in Scarborough, was being defended strongly by the Save the Rouge Valley committee, a citizens' group that had been fighting to save this last major piece of green space in Metro for at least a decade. The group's efforts got a major boost when the federal minister, Tom McMillan, flew into town during the pre-election summer of 1988 to announce the availability of federal funding to purchase the Rouge for a park.

Earlier that year, with a municipal election scheduled for November 14, local politicians, both on Toronto and Metro councils, had begun pressing harder for a shut-down of the aging Commissioners Street incinerator, built before the development of high-tech air pollution controls and an acknowledged source of air pollution in the already contaminated South Riverdale part of Toronto. The plant burned 150,000 tonnes of garbage a year and, according to a 1987 Toronto Board of Health report, emitted to the surrounding air 322 tonnes of hydrogen chloride, 100 tonnes of fly ash (which included, among other toxic contaminants, 5.4 kilograms of dioxins and furans), and 1.2 tonnes of lead.[24] In May, 1988, Metro Council had bowed to political realities and ordered the plant to cease operations on July 1.

Both SWEAP and the interim site search continued through the fall of 1988, but by the end of that year two new developments had become apparent. First, the provincial government had become directly involved in the regional negotiations, sending a senior civil servant, Gardner Church, to engage in shuttle diplomacy among Metro, Durham, York, and Peel politicians and staff. By February, 1989, it was announced that the regions were meeting on a regular basis and then, on March 14, 1989, Premier Peterson and the regional chairmen announced creation of the Greater Toronto Authority, a body chaired by Church and made up of the regional chairmen, endowed with a mandate to search for a long-term, regional solution to the waste disposal problem.

Second, it had become clear that the private sector was keenly interested in the potential billion-dollar Metro waste disposal market and that government thinking, at least at the provincial level, was inclined toward a private, rather than public, solution. In the spring of 1989, as the GTA was being formed, Laidlaw, in concert with CP Rail, advanced a proposal to send Metro waste to Kapuskasing, some 500 miles north, where it would be recycled, incinerated, and landfilled in a mega-facility to be constructed there. Cost estimates of $150 to $200 per tonne were mentioned. At the same time there was a flurry of press interest in private meetings held between Premier Peterson and his staff and Marco Muzzo, a land developer who was considering a move to the garbage business. The GTA announcement on March 14 set out the intent to invite proposals from the private sector for a waste management system, to be operational after EAA and other approvals were obtained, with a target date of 1996. To handle waste disposal between the filling of the Keele site in 1992 and 1996, each of the regions had agreed to nominate one site within its borders (forcing Metro to again consider the Rouge), one of which would then be selected by a yet-to-be-determined process. In the summer of 1989 Premier Peterson, overriding the statement of his Environment Minister the previous summer, said the interim site would not be subject to Environmental Assessment Act approval, requiring only consideration under the less onerous Environmental Protection Act.[25]

By the summer of 1990, when the Liberal government was defeated at the polls by the NDP, led by Bob Rae, the situation was still much the same. The Greater Toronto Authority was coming into being, with a mandate not only for waste management but also for regional transportation and planning issues, but the form it would take or its role relative to either the province or regional municipalities was still not clear. Metro and the regions still had neither interim nor permanent capacity, although they were actively seeking to purchase existing approved capacity in other parts of the province, and two interim landfill sites, one in Peel and one in Durham, had been scheduled for EPA hearings in November and January.

On November 21, 1990, Ruth Grier, newly appointed NDP Minister of Environment, rose in the Ontario legislature to announce her government's solution to the Ontario garbage crisis. Her announcement included several vaguely outlined waste reduction measures; changes to the Environmental Assessment Act process; and creation of a "new public sector authority" to "search for and select a waste disposal site" for the GTA regional municipalities, but without the exemption from EAA approval granted by former Premier Peterson and use of emergency powers, if necessary, to extend the life of the existing sites being used by Metro, Peel, York, and Durham. The regional councillors welcomed the statement, jubilantly announcing that they were off the hook and the province now had to find them a landfill, but nobody else rejoiced. Residents in the vicinity of the existing sites and the proposed new interim sites worried that they might lose any say in the process through use of emergency powers. Environmentalists complained that the NDP had not acted on its pre-election promise to ban incineration. Nobody understood the role of the "new authority," or whether it meant solid waste disposal had now become a provincial responsibility. The EPA hearings scheduled for the two interim sites were cancelled and everybody settled back to wait for the next announcement.

The government might have changed but the fog of confusion surrounding garbage disposal in Ontario had not yet lifted.

The Failure to Provide Hazardous Waste Treatment and Disposal Capacity

At one a.m. in the darkness and fog of the morning of August 24, 1989, the crew of the Soviet freighter *Nadezdha Obukhova*, a few hundred yards away from barricades separating Quebec provincial police and several hundred angry Baie Comeau citizens, began unloading their shipment of fifteen large white containers containing PCB-contaminated oils. Earlier that evening, Superior Court Judge Paul Corriveau had agreed to hear an application the next morning for an injunction to prevent the unloading of the wastes, and notice of that decision had been conveyed by bailiffs to both Hydro-Québec, owner of the storage site to which the wastes were en route, and Dynamis Envirotec Inc., the company handling the wastes under contract to the Quebec government. When the citizens behind the barricades saw that unloading had indeed begun, despite the serving of notice, they hurriedly awakened Judge Corriveau at his home. The judge issued a formal injunction ordering the work stopped and the containers returned to the deck of the freighter. This injunction was given to Dynamis official Martin Clermont, in Baie Comeau, at 3:40 a.m. and to the ship's captain at 4:01 a.m. – after all the containers had been transferred to the dock. By 4:30 a.m. the *Nadezdha Obukhova* had quietly slipped her moorings and was stealing down the St. Lawrence.[26]

The PCB-contaminated wastes unloaded under cover of darkness on the Baie Comeau dock had for a large part of the previous decade been sitting in a warehouse owned by Marc Levy in St.-Basile-le-Grande, forty kilometres southeast of Montreal. Almost exactly a year earlier, on August 23, 1988, the warehouse had caught fire, sending clouds of oily, poisonous smoke drifting over the neighbourhood and forcing the evacuation of some 3,000 local residents, who spent the next eighteen days in temporary shelters before Quebec and federal health and environment officials informed them that the PCB levels in their homes did not represent a health threat. During the course of the next year, the Quebec government paid out a total of $12.7 million dollars in settlement of claims for crops that had to be destroyed, lost wages, and other damages caused by the fire.[27]

That PCB fire, coming as it did shortly before the federal election of November 21, 1988, turned public attention yet again to the vexed question of hazardous waste storage, transport, and disposal. Media stories across the country drew attention to the fact that PCB wastes were in storage in at least 1,600 different sites, scattered in cities and towns from the Atlantic to the Pacific, awaiting disposal. The immediate response of the federal minister, Tom McMillan, was to point out that the provinces bore responsibility for regulating storage and that federal responsibility was limited to developing non-enforceable guidelines that provincial agencies could, if they so chose, use as a basis for their own regulatory requirements.[28] Perhaps sensing that this washing of hands was not the most politically astute gesture, McMillan then shifted to a different tack and announced that his department would use the new regulatory powers of the Canadian Environmental Protection Act, just proclaimed a few months before, to regulate PCB storage sites directly. The standards were drawn up during the month of September and all of the provinces (with the exception of Prince Edward Island), presumably motivated by the familiar desire to protect their jurisdictional turf, applied for "equivalency" exemption, following the procedure established under CEPA, on the grounds that their own storage regulations were as stringent and would be as diligently enforced as the new federal standards.[29]

In early 1989, while Environment Canada was back-pedalling from its pre-election foray into a direct regulatory role, the Quebec government turned its mind to the problem of what to do with the remaining PCB wastes still sitting in what was left of the St.-Basil warehouse. Immediately after the fire the Alberta government, owner of the Swan Hills facility, the only one in the country licensed to dispose of PCB wastes, had generously offered to exempt the St.-Basil wastes from its ban on imports from other provinces. However, Quebec-Alberta negotiations over methods of containment and transport had broken down and the offer had been withdrawn. This was followed by Quebec's announcement that a new solution had been found when, in July, 1989, a $7.9 million contract was signed with Dynamis Envirotec, Canadian agent for ReChem International, to have the wastes shipped to Great Britain, for treatment and disposal at the ReChem facility in Pontypool, Wales.

Unfortunately for ReChem, the Quebec government, and the citizens of Baie Comeau, Greenpeace U.K. was that summer engaged in a campaign to protest the increasingly large quantities of hazardous wastes imported each year by Britain for treatment and disposal. Thus in August, when the wastes arrived in Britain by Soviet freighter, it was met by Greenpeace inflatable boats and dockside protesters carrying signs with such messages as "No thanks. Take it back." Dockworkers refused to unload the ship, leading port authorities to refuse it entry, and within hours the ship was on its way back to Canada. On August 16 Quebec Environment Minister Lise Bacon announced that the wastes would be held in temporary storage at the Hydro-Québec storage site in Baie Comeau, where they were unloaded in the early morning darkness of August 24.[30]

In explaining its reasons for protesting the shipment of Quebec waste, Greenpeace representative Sue Adams said, "Our hope is that all industrial countries, including Canada, take responsibility for their own waste."[31] Presumably, Greenpeace was not simply trying to keep the wastes out of Britain's backyard but was working on the theory that if export was not available as a disposal option more attention would be paid to reducing quantities of wastes generated in the first place. Prime Minister Mulroney seemed to agree with Adams when he said shortly afterward that Canada should dispose of its own wastes. Acting on this new policy directive, federal authorities took legal action in an attempt to prevent further exports by Quebec of some portion of the St.-Basil wastes. This attempt was unsuccessful, however, and eventually some were shipped to France for treatment and disposal. On November 6, 1989, federal Environment Minister Lucien Bouchard announced that regulations would be brought in under CEPA by March, 1990, banning all overseas exports of PCB wastes.

Thus by 1990 Canada had arrived at a situation in which 24,000 tonnes of PCB wastes were in use in electrical transformers or sat in storage, awaiting treatment and disposal. Prior to a 1980 import ban, 40,000 tonnes were brought into Canada; the remaining 16,000 tonnes are assumed to have already entered the Canadian environment. Export to disposal sites outside the country was no longer an option; export from other provinces to Alberta, site of the only licensed disposal facility in the country, was not an option; and approval and construction of treatment and disposal facilities in other parts of the country still seemed to be a distant hope. Attempts to establish such a facility in British Columbia had bogged down in 1984 and were only beginning to get back on track; the Manitoba Hazardous Waste Management Corporation, established in 1986, was still in the early stages of searching for a site; the Quebec public had just been told by government officials, at public hearings of the hazardous waste inquiry established after the PCB fire, that it was still in the "stone age" of waste management and that some 250,000 tonnes of waste a year were dumped illegally in the province;[32] in Ontario, Environmental Assessment Board hearings on the feasibility of the Ontario Waste Management Corporation plans to build a facility had only just begun, and these hearings were expected to last up to two years. The successful destruction at Goose Bay by the Department of National Defence and the destruction at Smithville, planned by the Ontario government, were the only rays of light on the horizon.

If the only environmental threat came from PCB wastes – which are for the most part in some form of secure storage and are now generally agreed to be relatively benign, in comparison to many other toxic substances – Canada's failure to provide treatment and disposal capacity would be a less serious matter. But PCBs, which never were produced in this country and have not been imported since 1980, represent only a tiny fraction of the problem. Each year Canadian industries generate approximately 8 million tonnes of hazardous wastes. Somewhere in the neighbourhood of one-tenth of that amount is recycled or treated in some manner to reduce its toxicity before disposal. The remainder is discharged to the environment, either through landfilling (from which it eventually seeps its way through to groundwater), by discharge to sewers (from which it finds its way to lakes or rivers, having passed through sewage treatment plants not designed to cope with industrial wastes), or by being poured directly into rivers or lakes, with or without some form of pre-treatment. One way or another, some 5 or 6 million tonnes of hazardous waste pollute Canadian waters, *each year*, while we continue to grope through the difficulties of providing adequate treatment and disposal capacity. That process began on September 28, 1978, when Ontario Environment Minister Harry Parrott stood up in the legislature and made the first commitment by a Canadian government to provide a treatment and disposal facility. Between that date and Bouchard's announcement eleven years later, many Canadian governments have made similar commitments. Why is it that after twelve years Ontario and other Canadian governments, with the exception of Alberta, have been unable to do what they said they would do?

Perhaps the most useful way to address that question is to look at the success stories. What treatment and disposal capacity has been put in place and what allowed it to happen? A major category of disposal is what is referred to as "on-site" – methods of reducing toxicity and then disposing of wastes, through incineration or landfill, on the company property. The phrase is taken also to include such disposal methods as discharge to sewers, rivers, and lakes, with or without preliminary treatment, and so it is impossible to say what portion of waste going to on-site disposal is dealt with in an environmentally sound manner. However, by now almost all privately owned disposal methods are licensed by regulatory authorities, which means that at least some attention is paid to environmental impacts. A greater portion of the waste produced each year goes to on-site than to off-site disposal. For instance, Alberta is estimated to produce a total of 80,000 to 100,000 tonnes of hazardous waste a year, but the Swan Hills facility has an annual capacity of only 15,000 to 20,000 tonnes – thus the ratio of on-site to off-site disposal is approximately 5:1. Ontario, on the other hand, produces approximately 4 million tonnes per year, while the proposed OWMC facility will handle, initially at least, 150,000 tonnes – a ratio of about 27:1. That proportion will change, hopefully, if methods such as sewer disposal are increasingly restricted.

At present there is a chicken-and-egg relationship between off-site disposal capacity and pollution regulation. If the capacity is not available, industry will argue against regulatory action restricting current disposal methods; at the same time, without regulations to drive the waste to an off-site disposal facility the volumes treated will not generate revenues sufficient to justify the original capital investment, regardless of whether it is privately or publicly owned. This has been a major hindrance to provision of off-site capacity, but once provinces like Ontario, B.C., and Manitoba provide their own plants, pressure will grow for increasingly stringent regulation of on-site disposal.

The private sector can boast of a few successes in providing off-site disposal – most notably the Stablex plant at Blaineville, Quebec, and the Laidlaw facility at Sarnia, Ontario, which together probably accommodate something in the neighbourhood of 200,000 tonnes a year. Other private-sector ventures, such as the D & D Disposal company located in Smithville, Ontario, and the infamous St.-Basil PCB "disposal" firm, have been disastrous failures, with the taxpayer left to pick up the tab after the company has gone into bankruptcy.

The Alberta Success

The Alberta facility is the major Canadian success story to date, particularly since the town of Swan Hills, instead of fighting a NIMBY battle, actually *invited* Alberta to locate the plant there. (It should be pointed out that the plant is twelve miles from the town and that nobody lives in the immediate vicinity of the site, factors that may have contributed to this receptivity.) As was the case in Ontario, direct government involvement in hazardous waste disposal was prompted by public objections to private-sector proposals, in this case a 1979 application to site and operate a plant near Fort Saskatchewan, Alberta. The Alberta government responded by placing a moratorium on disposal siting, either public or private, until a comprehensive plan for waste management had been put in place. Background studies on waste types, quantities, and options for disposal were prepared and during 1980 sixteen public hearings, under the auspices of the Environment Council of Alberta, were held in different locations. Out of that process came a recommendation, made to the Alberta government in 1981, to establish a Crown company to undertake a site search and then proceed to contract with a private-sector firm to construct and operate the treatment and disposal facility. The siting process was carried out from 1981 to 1984 by the Alberta Environment Department, working in conjunction with regional planning commissions. After constraint mapping to eliminate sites unsuitable for physical or social reasons – a high risk of groundwater contamination; proximity to historical sites; population density; etc. – communities interested in receiving the benefits associated with the plant, such as employment and lower tax assessment, were invited to indicate interest. Initial examination was made of fifty-two possible sites, of which three-quarters, after local discussion, declined to continue the process. The remainder asked to be considered in more detail. Eventually five possible communities were in the running, each of which then held a local plebiscite. Swan Hills, 125 miles northwest of Edmonton, had a 60 per cent voter turnout in September, 1982, with 79 per cent voting in favour of the facility.

In 1984 the Alberta Special Waste Management Corporation was created, which in turn contracted with Bow Valley Resource Services for a joint-venture ownership – 40 per cent public and 60 per cent private – of the $50 million plant. The government owns the site, provided utilities and roads, and has guaranteed Bow Valley a 15 per cent rate of return on its $27 million investment. The 1979 siting moratorium has been maintained, which means this is the only off-site facility in the province. After the May, 1985, Kenora PCB spill, the Alberta government declared it would no longer accept out-of-province wastes and has not imposed any regulatory requirements that certain classes of waste, now going to on-site disposal, be shipped to Swan Hills. Nor has Alberta yet imposed a policy of charging high disposal prices to encourage waste reduction. As a result, the plant has lost money each year since it opened in 1987, with Alberta government payments in 1987 and 1988 to Bow Valley, to meet the guaranteed rate of return, totalling $32.7 million. The Alberta polluter is not yet paying, and is not expected to until the early 1990s when the plant will likely break even for the first time.[33]

British Columbia and Manitoba

The first step taken by British Columbia to provide off-site disposal capacity was a 1979 study of waste management needs, undertaken jointly with the other western provinces, the territories, and the federal government. This provided an estimate of 70,000 tonnes of hazardous waste generated in the province each year. In 1980, a Hazardous Waste Advisory Committee was established, and in 1981 the Committee reported on the regulatory framework needed to govern waste generation, transportation, and disposal, which led to adoption of the B.C. Waste Management Act in November, 1982. The government then invited private-sector proposals for the construction and operation of a facility, preferably at no cost to the province. In September, 1983, the B.C. government announced that two possible sites had been selected for hazardous waste landfills, which, not surprisingly, sparked local opposition to the process. At the same time, arrangements were concluded with the Genstar/IT Corporation, based on use of an existing cement kiln in the Vancouver area for incineration, and with projected capital costs between $5 and $10 million. In July, 1984, however, after conducting its own survey of wastes generated, the company pulled out of the deal, saying that low volumes (estimated at 15,000 tonnes a year) projected to come to the plant made the venture economically unfeasible, particularly in light of the fact that the potential market had been restricted by the government decision not to allow imports of hazardous waste into the province.[34]

Immediately prior to the collapse of this initiative, a number of environmental organizations, including WCELA, Greenpeace, SPEC, several Indian bands, and labour unions, had formed the Hazardous Waste Management Coalition, which, in the fall of 1984, recommended that B.C. begin the planning process over again, this time based on full public consultation and selection of site and private-sector operator only after more detailed study of the province's waste management needs.

In February, 1987, the B.C. government appointed a Special Waste Advisory Committee with a mandate to review waste management needs and invite proposals for a joint-venture operation. In 1988, the Committee recommended Envirochem Services, a Canadian-American consortium that changed its name to B.C. Special Waste Services Inc. and proposed a facility in the Ashcroft-Cache Creek area, one of eight B.C. communities that had indicated in 1987 they were interested in being considered for such a site.[35] On December 5, 1989, the B.C. government announced a "new strategy" to manage the annual quantity of hazardous waste generated in the province, now estimated to be 110,000 tonnes, plus the more than 400,000 tonnes held in storage. The strategy consisted of establishment of a treatment facility and efforts to encourage reduction, re-use, and recycling.[36] In May, 1990, Environment Minister John Reynolds introduced legislation to establish the British Columbia Hazardous Waste Management Corporation. As of August, 1990, this new corporation had not yet begun to plan for construction of a treatment and disposal facility.[37]

Nor yet is Manitoba any further ahead. Manitoba established its own hazardous waste management corporation in 1986 but as of 1990 a treatment facility had not yet been built. The approximately 20,000 tonnes generated each year go to sewers or receiving waters, with some going to a "temporary storage facility" at Gimli, which was established in the 1970s.[38]

Ontario

The announcement in September, 1978, that the Ontario government would no longer rely exclusively on the private sector to provide off-site capacity was followed, in 1980, by creation of a Crown corporation, headed by the best-known environmentalist in the province, Dr. Donald Chant. The Ontario Waste Management Corporation (OWMC), the government announced, would build and operate a site on government-owned land in the South Cayuga area. This decision to forgo a search for an environmentally and socially acceptable site, but to choose the site simply on the basis of land already owned by the province, went some way to reduce the stock of good will and credibility initially provided by Dr. Chant's appointment.

Further scepticism was engendered when it was announced that because of the urgent need to put such a plant into operation, the proposal would be exempted from the need to gain approval under the Ontario Environmental Assessment Act. Instead, public hearings would be held before a specially appointed board under the terms of the Environmental Protection Act, thus limiting scope of the approval process to the physical nature of the undertaking and its potential effect on the biological environment, with no requirement to consider alternative means of achieving the objective of the undertaking.

Hydrogeological studies of the proposed site led Dr. Chant to conclude that the potential for groundwater pollution and flooding were of sufficient concern that the site should be rejected. Hence, the OWMC announced in 1981 that it would begin an open, consultative, Ontario-wide search for a site. In September, 1985, after an exhaustive process of public consultation, the OWMC announced its choice of West Lincoln, located in the Niagara region of Ontario, as the site for its proposed facility. Unlike Alberta, as the choice began to narrow in on West Lincoln, local opposition became heated. Immediately before that, the newly elected Liberal government, as one of a number of steps taken to establish its environmental *bona fides*, had designated the OWMC process under the EAA.

Finally, in 1989, after a certain amount of sparring between the Corporation and the Ministry of the Environment, the OWMC released in final form its environmental assessment – a 22-volume, 7,000-page appraisal of the need for off-site treatment and disposal, review of alternatives and alternative methods, and rationale for the preferred site and proposed $500 million plant. The cost to the Ontario taxpayer for this planning exercise, from 1980 to 1990, was approximately $80 million – more than half again the cost of *building* the Alberta plant. And the process is far from over. The OWMC faces stiff opposition at the Environmental Assessment Board hearing, not only from local residents in the vicinity of West Lincoln but also from the local municipality, a coalition of environmental organizations, and its major commercial competitor – Laidlaw Environmental Services. A total of approximately $500,000 has been provided to the opponents, including the Region of Niagara, to allow them to hire both legal representation and experts to review the technical studies of the assessment.

The question that has not yet been answered during the Ontario planning process – the same one that has vexed all the provinces – is whether or not there will be sufficient demand for OWMC services to meet capital and operating costs. In addition, since Ontario, unlike Alberta or B.C., has an existing private-sector treatment operation, it is not known how the public- and private-sector agencies will divide the market. Will the OWMC, like Bow Valley, operate with an annual subsidy and thus attract wastes through low disposal pricing? Or will Ontario, as part of an overall waste reduction strategy, follow a policy of coupling high disposal prices with regulatory requirements that at least some classes of waste be sent only to the OWMC plant? Although such issues have been raised by the environmental community, they have not to date been publicly addressed by the Ontario government.

The first task for governments in the field of waste management is to ensure that those who produce waste no longer use the environment as a receptacle for unlimited disposal. In the case of solid waste that has largely been achieved – comprehensive standards governing design and operation of solid waste landfills have been put in place and other forms of disposal, such as apartment incinerators or energy from waste plants, must now meet fairly rigorous air pollution standards. Unfortunately, this is not the case for hazardous waste, which, ironically, poses a greater environmental threat than does municipal garbage. As we have seen, most of the hazardous waste produced each year is poured directly into lakes, rivers, sewers, or landfills.

Canadian industry disposes of its hazardous waste in this manner because it has no choice – the country does not have enough disposal capacity to accommodate even a fraction of the waste it produces each year – and because there is virtually no incentive, in the form of either legal sanctions or financial rewards, to dispose of hazardous waste in an environmentally acceptable manner or to reduce the quantities initially generated. The next task obviously is to provide hazardous waste treatment and disposal capacity *and* to close off existing disposal options. Although the first step probably will be taken, there is no guarantee of the second. It is likely that at some point during the coming decade B.C., Manitoba, and Ontario will join Alberta in having publicly owned treatment facilities. But will they actually be used? Unless governments in those provinces are willing to limit existing disposal options severely, these facilities will become underutilized white elephants.

The other side of the equation – reduction of waste quantities – gives even less cause for optimism. The history of recycling, reduction, and re-use in Ontario demonstrates two things – the eagerness of individual citizens to take personal responsibility for reducing environmental damage caused by their waste, and the equally great eagerness of the Ontario government to avoid any action that would impose costs on commercial and industrial waste generators. Despite the prevailing interest in "economic instruments," governments have shown no interest in using the one such instrument that is simple and at hand – increasing solid and hazardous waste disposal costs enough to provide a real incentive for reduction.

CHAPTER 15

Setting Standards for the Pulp and Paper Industry

The Difficulties of Regulating the Industry

In 1804, when England's timber trade with the Baltic countries was inter-rupted by the Napoleonic Wars, she turned to British North America to supply masts for the Royal Navy. Logging and export of timber quickly became a major staple of the pre-Confederation economy and the spring log drive, with fleet-footed lumbermen dancing lightly over white water, became a part of the Canadian mythology. In the 1840s the technology for making paper from wood pulp, instead of cloth, was developed and the first chemical pulp mill was built at Windsor, Quebec.

By the time of the First World War the demand for newsprint in Ameri-can cities had led to the establishment of pulp and paper mills across the country and the industry had become one of Canada's leading employers. That position was maintained through to the late 1980s when the industry, with 149 mills located in almost every province, was Canada's leading manufacturer, exporting 23 million tonnes of product, valued at $14 billion (second only to steel exports).[1] The industry was also responsible for approximately half of the total water used for Canadian manufacturing processes and had maintained its position as one of the major sources of air and water pollution in the country.

The technology of making paper from wood pulp has continued to evolve during the past hundred years as the essential objective – separating the wood fibres from the other materials that make up the tree trunk, in particular lignin, a resinous adhesive that gives the trunk its strength – has been pursued by a variety of mechanical and chemical processes. The original mechanical processes of grinding logs into pulp were virtually pollution-free but produced damaged fibre and, in consequence, weak pulp. During the latter part of the nineteenth century mechanical chipping and grinding was supplemented by a number of chemical processes until, by the 1930s, the kraft process, which used sulphate processing to produce a dark brown pulp, had been established as the cheapest production method. The dark pulp is then bleached, using chlorine bleaches. This part of the process "could easily be assumed to be the main cause of much of the pollution that comes from the pulp and paper industry."[2]

Pulp and paper mills were originally established on rivers, to gain access to a power supply, to provide the very large quantities of water needed for soaking and pulping the wood, and to allow for easy waste disposal. Although the location of some mills today allows hook-up to a sewer system, 122 mills still discharge wastes directly to water. The wastes discharged consist of those parts of the original lumber not used and the variety of chemicals used in and produced (a mixture that is still far from fully understood) during the pulping and bleaching processes. As production efficiency has increased over the years, pollution in the form of wood wastes has been reduced. (This increased efficiency has been driven more by the competitive need to maximize use of the tree that forms the raw material for the process and thereby to minimize the amount of waste, than by environmental concern on the part of the industry or regulatory pressure brought to bear by provincial and federal agencies.)

In 1971, when the first standards were developed, pulp and paper pollution was divided into three categories:

• total suspended solids – bits of bark and wood not used in the process;
• biological oxygen demand (BOD) – organic wastes that consume oxygen in the receiving waters, thus injuring or killing aquatic life through oxygen deprivation;
• acute toxicity – the unknown mix of chemicals lethal to fish and other organisms in the immediate vicinity of the effluent outfall.

Attempts to regulate pulp and paper mill pollution over the past two decades have been impeded by two major political factors. The first is the relative invisibility of the industry. The mills are located for the most part in isolated areas and their names are not associated with products recognized by the general public. This means that public opinion, a powerful factor in the motivation of corporate behaviour, particularly when court convictions and fines are both infrequent and of a low dollar value, is not a factor. Second, because the mills are so often located in one-industry towns, job blackmail almost always works – the employees, the citizens of the town and surrounding area, and their elected representatives at all government levels will tend to support the company when it threatens to close down instead of spending money on pollution control.

The other inherent difficulty of regulating pulp mills is the division of responsibility between two levels of government. Most mills operate under provincial rather than federal standards, and in many cases where federal standards are applicable they are enforced by provincial rather than federal officials.

Thus, after twenty years of provincial and federal regulation and after receiving literally billions of public money in grants and tax exemptions intended to assist with pollution control, the majority of mills still do not meet federal toxicity standards and the industry remains one of Canada's largest polluters. Why has the federal government been unable, during the past twenty years, to implement its water discharge standards?

Development of the Federal Standards

In 1950, when Ontario passed special legislation to protect the KVP mill on the Spanish River from the threat of a court injunction to stop polluting the river, pulp pollution was considered a sign of prosperity, not a cause for concern. By the 1960s, however, attitudes had changed to the point that some form of abatement was being pursued by provincial bodies and, at the federal level, by the Department of Fisheries and Forestry.[3] The results achieved, however, were minimal and during the late 1960s, as the federal government prepared to take regulatory action to protect Canadian rivers and streams, pulp and paper pollution was the first major target. The legislative vehicle used was the Fisheries Act, not because it was particularly well suited to the task but because protection of fisheries was the one area, under the terms of the Canadian constitution, most clearly in the federal rather than provincial domain. Robert Shaw, the first deputy minister of the new department, explained: "The department [Environment Canada] was based on the Fisheries Act because fisheries, according to the Fathers of Confederation, were a federal responsibility."[4]

Staff of the Fisheries Branch of the then Department of Fisheries and Forestry in August, 1967, prepared a paper titled "Proposed Program of Pollution Control and Anti-Pollution Research in the Fisheries Environment." Discussions at a staff level were held with the Department of Energy, Mines and Resources and the Department of National Health and Welfare, followed in March, 1968, with creation by cabinet of a high-level, interdepartmental Committee on Water to co-ordinate federal water pollution control policy.[5] A memorandum advocating amendment of the Fisheries Act to provide regulatory power over pulp and paper discharges to water was submitted to cabinet on January 9, 1969, followed by public hearings on water pollution in British Columbia, conducted in April of that year by the House of Commons Standing Committee on Fisheries and Forestry. Cabinet approved the proposed amendments during the summer of 1969 but conflict arose over which department, Fisheries or Energy, should have jurisdiction and which legislation, the Fisheries Act or the Canada Water Act, still in the process of being drafted, should be used. The amendments for that reason did not receive first reading until April 10, 1970, and did not receive royal assent until June 16, 1970.[6]

In April, prior to this enactment, staff of the Department of Fisheries, which became part of the new Department of the Environment in July, 1971, had established a task force to develop the regulations. The first issue faced by the task force was whether to base standards on the assimilative capacity of the receiving waters, that is, the extent to which the river or lake the mill used for waste discharge was already polluted and what reduction in pollution was needed to restore the environmental health of the waters, or simply to focus on the reductions that could be achieved by requiring changes in the technologies of pulping and papermaking. The first approach was rejected almost immediately because "there were simply not enough data of sufficient quality available on which to assess assimilative capacities."[7] The preferred approach was confirmed in a speech given by the new minister, Jack Davis, in October of that year, which made it clear that, in his mind at least, standards should be based on the most practicable levels of technology. Davis said that the purpose of the new federal regulations was not to supplant the provincial role but to provide minimal national standards that would act to prevent the creation of "pollution havens." The minister then went on to clarify a key issue – the standards, once adopted, would apply immediately to new or expanded mills but not to existing mills, since they would need time to phase in the necessary production changes. Thus technology (and therefore cost) would be the criterion, not environmental quality, and even it would not apply to existing mills.

By the time of the minister's speech the task force had developed draft regulations, although without having undertaken any consultation with either the provinces or the industry, let alone the general public, and relying completely on data supplied by a 1960 American report on pulp discharges. The draft regulations were severely criticized by other government officials, who questioned the validity of the data on which they were based, with the result that in January, 1971, a new regulations development team was created, this time including representation from industry and the provinces, although still not the public. The team was told by the minister that the "best practicable technology" method was not to be questioned and that their role was simply to revise the numbers in the October, 1970, draft.[8] This group worked during the course of the summer, with the industry representatives as the only source of information on what reductions "practicable technology" could or could not achieve. "A key input to this process was the information on effluent loadings and levels of technology provided by the CPPA [Canadian Pulp and Paper Association] representatives on the Team. It should be noted that the government officials had no way of checking into the veracity of this information. . . . "[9]

The regulations became law, at least for new mills, in November, 1971. They set numerical limits on the quantities of solids and BOD materials that could be discharged in proportion to quantities of production, thus placing no absolute limits on loadings to the environment. The regulations also set a limit on the concentration of toxic substances in waste-water, but again no limit was placed on total quantities that could legally be discharged. The regulation provided for a test of acute toxicity in the following manner: "It is a pass/fail test that requires that local fish to [*sic*] be placed in a tank comprised of 65 percent effluent from a mill's outfall and 35% freshwater for 96 hours. If at least 80 percent of the fish survive, the effluent from the mill is considered non-toxic."[10]

Enacting the effluent standards in law, of course, is only the first part of the process – they must then be implemented in the real world. Beginning this process in late 1971, staff of the Department of Environment, already hampered by limited staffing and financial resources, immediately encountered two difficulties: (1) the strong reluctance of the pulp and paper industry to spend money on anything other than production changes that would reduce the cost of production, and (2) the unwillingness of their provincial counterparts to allow a direct federal regulatory role within their jurisdictions. Thus, effluent monitoring was done for the most part by provincial, rather than federal, environment departments. The process has been described as follows:

> The effluent monitoring program is carried out using two mutually supportive techniques. The first is an industry self-monitoring program that requires each mill to measure and keep records of its discharge flows, and to sample for BOD, TSS and toxicity to fish. The second is a program whereby employees of government randomly take samples of all mill discharges and conduct laboratory analysis of the samples. The vigour with which the monitoring activities are conducted varies across the country, because such monitoring is undertaken either through or in cooperation with provincial or local authorities. The degree of cooperation between federal and provincial authorities differs according to the relationships established at the regional level.[11]

During the 1970s staff of Environment Canada and, after 1978, the separate Department of Fisheries worked to implement the standards, both directly and through provincial regulations, which in theory (although not in fact) were at least as stringent as the Fisheries Act standards. Prosecution was not used as a means of achieving compliance, nor were standards applied on an across-the-board basis. Instead, the process degenerated to a grinding, mill-by-mill series of negotiations. Not surprisingly, since each mill knew that it had to drive at least as hard a bargain as its competitors in the other mills, progress was slow.

By 1984, when Environment Canada published its *Status Report on Abatement of Water Pollution from the Canadian Pulp and Paper Industry (1982)*, the Canadian public learned that from 1969 to 1982 total suspended solids discharged by all mills in the country had declined by 59 per cent, from an average of forty-nine kilograms per tonne of pulp produced to an average of twenty-two kilograms. The 1971 regulations, however, required an average of ten kilograms per tonne. During that same period, BOD discharges had declined by 42 per cent, but were still not in keeping with the regulatory requirements – by 1982, total BOD discharges were calculated to be 2,439 tonnes per day, down from 4,235 in 1969, but the maximum allowed by the regulations was 1,816 tonnes per day. The report further stated that only thirty-four mills were in compliance with the toxicity requirements in 1980, and by 1982 that figure had only increased to thirty-six. The report noted that "A large number of mills do not yet have toxicity compliance schedules."[12]

This lack of progress could not be attributed to a failure to provide the Canadian pulp and paper industry with assistance. Although "polluter pay" was the policy espoused by the Canadian and provincial governments during this period, in actual fact considerable public money was spent to help the pulp and paper industry reduce its pollution loadings. The trend had started with a paper presented by the CPPA to the 1966 CCRM conference, Pollution and Our Environment, suggesting that the industry be given assistance in meeting the costs of pollution reduction. In 1968 the CPPA submitted a detailed brief to the Department of Energy, Mines and Resources, putting forth a more explicit request for financial assistance in meeting pollution control requirements. This request was refused, but during the next two years the government position began to soften: "It is apparent ... from the record of discussions between the DEMR and the Ontario government, that, by the spring of 1970, the DEMR was giving serious consideration to a wide range of incentives to encourage the pulp and paper industry to reduce pollution, while still insisting publicly that the industry would be required to meet the full costs of pollution control."[13]

The industry was already eligible for assistance under the Accelerated Capital Cost Allowance program of 1965, which both provided a rebate of the federal sales tax on pollution control equipment and allowed depreciation of capital costs over a two-year period. In 1971 a program specifically intended to benefit the pulp and paper industry, the Co-operative Pollution Abatement Research program, was introduced to assist with the cost of developing new pollution control technology. Between 1971 and 1979, when the program ended, $10.6 million was given to the industry by the federal government. Under a similar program, titled Development and Demonstration of Pollution Abatement Technology, introduced in 1975, another $3 million was given to industry.[14]

This was not enough, however, according to the industry. In 1976 Abitibi-Price stated in its annual report that "irreparable harm" would be done to the Canadian industry "if compelled to devote too high a per centage of its available capital to environmental projects."[15] This appeal was successful. A 1978 report of the Department of Industry, Trade and Commerce concluded that the industry could not meet foreign competition without government assistance, while an Ontario government task force also called for assistance, pointing to the effect that threatened plant closings would have on "vulnerable communities."

Between 1979 and 1985, $544 million was provided to the industry by the governments of Canada, Ontario, Quebec, New Brunswick, Nova Scotia, and Newfoundland under the Pulp and Paper Modernization Grants Program, a program intended to provide capital funding to make Canadian pulp and paper more competitive in the face of competition from the United States and the Scandinavian countries. This money was combined with industry capital investment for a total spending during the six-year period of $3.1 billion on plant modernization. Approximately 18 per cent of this total was spent on pollution abatement.[16]

Capital spending by pulp and paper plants on pollution reduction during the 1970s and early 1980s was concentrated primarily on improving the efficiency of the process by using a greater percentage of the raw material – the tree – entering the plant, which had the result of both decreasing production costs and reducing the amount of wastes – both solids and BOD – discharged to the receiving water. This is hardly surprising, since the industry had both a direct financial incentive to improve efficiency and was, in addition, in receipt of considerable public assistance. The situation was different in the case of toxicity controls, however. There, industry had no financial incentive, nor was it compelled with any urgency by government to act. Pressure to move in this area has only come in recent years, in response to the emotive power of the word "dioxin."

Dioxin and Greenpeace

The term "dioxin" is used to refer to a group of seventy-five different compounds that are formed from a "basic nucleus of two benzene rings, bonded together by oxygen atoms." The dioxin compounds that have received the most attention to date are those containing chlorine atoms, in particular a substance named 2,3,7,8-tetrachlorodibenzo-p-dioxin, known as TCDD. During the nineteenth century it was known that an unidentified substance was responsible for the skin disfiguration chloracne in plants producing chemicals such as chlorine gas. By the 1950s this substance had been identified as present in the weed-killer 2,4,5-T, which, with another closely allied substance, 2,4-D, was used during the Vietnam War as the herbicide Agent Orange.[17] Although in the early part of the decade attention was focused primarily on dioxin itself, by 1989 it had become clear that the term, more than anything, was a symbol for a whole array of largely unknown toxins described as "chlorinated organics." Toxicologist John Sprague has described the situation thus:

> You think back to all the big environmental scares of the past. You think back to the '60's: DDT is an organochlorine; PCB is an organochlorine. They were all over the world before we even realized we had a problem. The toxicity of PCBs is something of a question, but we know they're not good for us. Chlorinated dioxins are an organochlorine. The more chlorine in them, the more toxic, the more bioaccumulative, they tend to be.[18]

In late 1980 the Canadian Wildlife Service, a division of Environment Canada, released a scientific study of dioxin contamination of herring gull eggs in the Great Lakes region. The federal Minister of the Environment, John Roberts, submitted the report to the U.S. State Department, urging the American government to "undertake a thorough investigation of dioxin pollution in the international waters which form the common border between the United States and Canada."[19] By 1983, a working group on dioxin had been established within the U.S. Environmental Protection Agency and in Canada the National Dioxin Action Program, staffed by Environment Canada, Department of Energy, and Health and Welfare, had begun. Both groups began to collect data on sources of dioxin in the environment, with hazardous wastes and incineration of solid waste as primary suspects. Samples taken from pulp sludges in International Falls, Minnesota, and Fort Frances, Ontario, were found to contain 414 parts per trillion of dioxin.[20]

Prompted by these findings the EPA, in conjunction with the American pulp and paper industry, launched in May of 1986 what became known as the "Five Mills" study – a sampling of effluent from mills in Minnesota, Maine, Oregon, Texas, and Ohio. By September, 1987, the EPA, based on results from the sampling program, was prepared to begin for the first time placing direct limits on quantities of dioxins in mill effluent.[21] The American Paper Institute, for its part, was preparing a major public relations effort to minimize media reporting on health threats associated with the mill waste.[22]

While some dioxin sampling was being done in Canada during this period (dioxin was again found in great blue heron eggs in Crofton,

Vancouver Island), public attention was focused, in the fall of 1986, on the first environmental crisis encountered by the new Liberal government in Ontario. As discussed previously, October 31, 1986, was the deadline for complying with the fish toxicity requirements of a 1982 control order imposed on the Kimberly-Clark plant in Terrace Bay, Ontario. When the company said it could not afford the cost of $20 million, the Ontario minister, Jim Bradley, ordered a forensic audit of the company's books and then, convinced the company was telling the truth, extended the control order deadline by three years. The environmental community protested vigorously, causing Bradley to reduce the extension to one year, which in turn prompted the company to threaten a shutdown – thus taking away 1,600 jobs in an area of high unemployment. Not surprisingly, workers, townspeople, and local politicians objected strongly to the pollution controls, with the result that a new order was negotiated with a 1989 deadline. The Ontario government also established what was known as the Expert Committee on Kraft Mill Toxicity.

Meanwhile, in August, 1987, Greenpeace published a report on pulp and paper dioxin contamination in American and Canadian mills that accused governments in both countries of withholding information and failing to take effective regulatory action. The following month Greenpeace launched another salvo, using documents leaked by a source in the American paper industry that raised the issue of possible dioxin contamination of such paper products as coffee filters, paper towels, and disposable diapers. This suggestion that hazardous wastes were found not only in the backyard but in the kitchen sparked a flurry of charges and counter-charges. The smoke still had not cleared two years later when George Petty, chairman of Repap Enterprises of Montreal, made one of the more memorable contributions to the dioxin debate, saying "A baby would have to eat 7,000 diapers a day to have a problem with dioxins – eat, not wear the goddam things."[23]

The issue of pulp mill dioxins was given a new urgency in Canada in January, 1988, on the day that Renate Kroesa, an industrial chemist specializing in pulp mill pollution on staff at the Greenpeace Vancouver office, made an appointment with Environment Canada officials to review with them – a few days before publicly releasing the results at a news conference – the dioxin presence Greenpeace had found in effluent from the mill located at Harmac, on Vancouver Island. Greenpeace had arranged to have the sample analysed by a Swedish lab and, based on the dioxin contamination found there, issued a news release warning the public not to eat fish or shellfish caught in the vicinity of the mill. This prompted Tom Siddon, Minister of Fisheries and Oceans, to announce that the program of sampling for dioxins and other organochlorines in pulp mill effluent, which had been under way for some time, would be accelerated.

In April, 1988, the Ontario government released the report of the Expert

Committee on Kraft Mill Toxicity, which took the position that the health threat posed by chlorinated dioxins had been overstated in the media, saying that "Chlorinated dioxins and furans may not be as toxic to humans as is commonly believed."[24] The Expert Committee suggested there was danger that the time and money of scientists and regulatory agencies would be devoted to this particular substance to the exclusion of other, equally significant, threats and pointed out that kraft mills in Ontario contributed an annual total of thirty-three tonnes of "organochlorines to the environment," of which dioxins formed an "infinitesimally small proportion."[25] The real problem, the Committee stated, was that 97 per cent of the chemical substances in that thirty-three tonnes had never been analysed or identified, leading to the inevitable question – "how many other subtle toxicants in bleach plant waste await discovery?"[26] The Committee recommended that instead of more time spent analysing dioxins or searching for other toxins in mill effluent, steps should be taken immediately to reduce the total quantity of organochlorine discharge:

> Dioxins have been found in almost all bleached kraft mill effluents analysed by laboratories with extensive experience in dioxins and similar substances. There does not seem any reason to wait for the discovery of other subtle toxicants in bleach plant waste. There are known methods for reducing organochlorine discharges, some of them economically advantageous, and others that are at least without severe economic penalty. It seems evident to us that Ontario mills should start now to significantly reduce their output of organochlorines.[27]

The report concluded with an estimate of the capital and operating costs associated with the measures recommended to reduce organochlorines and the ability of the industry to incur such costs. The cost would vary from mill to mill, of course, depending in large part on the amounts already spent to date on pollution control. It was noted, also, that "with the exception of the 1970-1974 period, profits in pulp and paper were in excess of those earned in the overall manufacturing sector" and that the industry has "undergone a 'boom' phase since 1985," leading to the conclusion that cost should not be an impediment to action.[28]

On May 16, 1988, as the Ontario government was beginning to consider action based on this report, the federal ministers of fisheries, health, and environment released preliminary results of the accelerated dioxin study, which to that date had focused on B.C. mills. They reported that "levels of dioxins and furans found in the edible portions of fish samples are not considered to pose a health hazard to consumers" but that "relatively higher levels of dioxins and furans have been identified in a few samples of prawns and crabs . . . taken near pulp mills in Port Mellon, Woodfibre and

Prince Rupert, British Columbia." It was announced that the sampling program had been extended to all mills using chlorine in the bleaching process.[29]

On June 28, 1988, the West Coast Environmental Law Association announced that on behalf of a number of B.C. unions and environmental organizations, including Greenpeace, the Sierra Club of Western Canada, the Western Canada Wilderness Committee, the Provincial Council of Women, the Canadian Association of Industrial, Mechanical and Allied Workers, Canadian Paperworkers Union Local #76, and Pulp, Paper and Woodworkers of Canada, it was pressing the provincial and federal governments to achieve the following objectives:

1. Adopt regulations or permit standards to eliminate the discharge of persistent, toxic chemicals, including organochlorines (such as dioxins and furans) from pulp mill effluent.
2. Achieve compliance with existing regulations and permits, and prosecute non-compliance.
3. Take leadership in promoting the availability and marketing of pulp and paper products bleached without chlorine.
4. Routinely release information on compliance and environmental impact regarding pulp mill pollution.[30]

The federal government, acting on further information provided by the dioxin sampling program, announced at the end of November that crab, prawn, and shrimp fisheries had been closed in the vicinity of three B.C. mills due to health threats associated with identified pollution levels.

The next spring, approximately a year after its release of the dioxin finding from the Harmac mill, Greenpeace received anonymously in the mail a copy of a report, dated July, 1988, titled *Controlling Pollution from Canadian Pulp and Paper Manufacturers: A Federal Perspective.* The report, known as the "Sinclair Report" after its principal author, William F. Sinclair, had been prepared during the period 1986 to 1988 as part of the internal, secret review and evaluation of federal efforts to reduce pulp and paper mill pollution since promulgation of the original Fisheries Act regulations in 1971. The general theme of the report was that, given the relatively low government expenditures to date, significant progress had been made in reducing quantities of solids, oxygen demanding substances, and toxins entering Canadian waters. In the fiscal year 1985-86, the federal government had contributed eighteen person-years worth of staffing to the task of "helping control pollution within the pulp and paper industry," representing approximately 16 per cent of Environment Canada's total pollution control effort that year. All provinces combined had contributed another twenty-eight person-years, representing 18 per cent of their effort. Total federal and provincial expenditure on pulp and paper pollution control for that year was estimated at $3.1 million.[31] In exchange for this "fairly modest on-going annual commitment of government revenue," governments had achieved the following reduction in pollution loadings from 1970 to 1985:

> solids – reduced from total daily loading of 2,100 tonnes to 800;
> BOD – reduced from total daily loading of 3,400 tonnes to 2,000;
> acute toxicity loadings – reduced from total daily loading of 8,800 cubic metres to 5,800.[32]

The report made very clear, however, that federal regulations were still not being met and that provincial regulations in almost all cases were weaker: "very major reductions in TSS and toxicity loadings could be achieved in British Columbia if federal standards were being met. . . . Toxicity loadings in Quebec could be substantially reduced if federal toxicity limits were being met. The loadings in every region could be reduced as a result of the nation-wide application of federal standards."[33] Although making every effort to be fair to the regulated industry, the report had no choice but to conclude that the pulp and paper industry in Canada had demonstrated "a lack of commitment . . . to meet government standards."[34]

Greenpeace immediately put together a press kit consisting of the most damning extracts from the report, with a covering news release headlined "Billion $ Giveaway Fails to Control Mill Pollution" and stating that:

> • the Canadian pulp and paper industry is more highly subsidized than its competitors – but has fallen far behind in pollution controls
> • laws passed in 1971 are violated daily by the majority of mills while the federal government turns a blind eye.[35]

The Alberta Approvals

At about the same time that Greenpeace was seeking to purify B.C.'s pulp and paper waters, the industry in Alberta ran afoul of the confusion of jurisdictions. In December, 1988, Alberta Premier Don Getty announced that his province had completed negotiations for a major expansion of the forestry industry. Based on new technological developments, the expansion was planned to harvest and use to make pulp the aspen trees that cover much of northern Alberta and which, until then, had been considered to have no economic value. Getty's announcement was for a total of "$3.4 billion in private sector forestry investment, assisted by government loans, guarantees and infrastructure aimed at doubling the size of the province's forestry sector by the mid 1990's."[36] The extent of this public assistance and the perceived low returns on the forest leasing arrangement, coupled with the fact that the deals had been concluded in secret, with no public notice or access, were the first factors to prompt scepticism. However, environmental impacts of the proposed expansion of Alberta's three existing pulp mills, plus construction of four new ones, soon came to the fore.

The negotiations had been in process since 1987, and by the spring of 1989 the Alberta government issued environmental and construction approvals to all of the new mills except for the Alberta-Pacific Forest Industries plant planned for the town of Prosperity on the Peace River. Four of the new plants were bleached kraft mills and for these the government insisted they meet "Swedish pollution standards."[37] When he announced approval of the Peace River Daishowa Canada Co. mill, in February, 1988, Forestry Minister LeRoy Fjordbotten had said the mill "will be the cleanest bleached kraft pulp mill in Canada, and it will be one of the most pollution-free in North America."[38] The standard imposed by Alberta was a maximum loading of 1.5 kilograms of organochlorine wastes per air-dried tonne, far lower than any existing mills in Canada, the U.S., or Sweden and in line with the maximum considered for the proposed new Ontario standards.

Nevertheless, the production ratio standards would still result in significant loadings. An article in the *Toronto Star* made the point that "Since the mill is scheduled to produce more than 1,000 tonnes of air dried pulp a day at least 1,500 kilograms of organic waste containing 300 chemical compounds – many of them untested – will enter the river each day."[39]

With such rigorous new-source standards, however, the industry and the Alberta government assumed that final approval for the Al-Pac plant would proceed expeditiously. However, because the Peace River crosses a provincial border, the federal government had no choice but to do its own assessment, in addition to whatever approvals process Alberta followed. The Federal Court decision of April, 1989, requiring federal environmental assessment of the Saskatchewan dam on the Souris River had changed the course of events. Newly appointed Alberta Environment Minister Ralph Klein threatened to litigate to protect Alberta's right to approve the project without interference from Ottawa but then agreed to a compromise solution. An assessment would be done by a joint federal-provincial review panel, with four of the seven members appointed by Alberta.[40]

The federal government had wanted the panel to investigate all aspects of forest management but deferred to the Alberta proposal that its mandate be limited to environmental impacts. As part of the negotiated terms of reference, however, Alberta conceded that the panel would investigate the *cumulative* effect of *all* the mills on the Peace and Athabaska rivers, not just the Alberta-Pacific mill seeking approval.

These negotiations were concluded and the Environmental Assessment Review Board appointed by July, 1989. Prior to that, in June, 300,000 Alberta citizens had signed a petition calling for a moratorium on the pulp mill developments. Opinion in the towns in which the new mills would be located was divided, with some welcoming the new prosperity and others opposing the mills because of the air and water pollution they would bring.

At the outset of the Review Board public hearings in July, Dr. Robert Lane presented the Environment Canada submission. He said that the assessment done by the company itself was "unacceptable" and that there was not yet enough information available to do a proper assessment of the cumulative impact of organochlorine and BOD discharges of the Al-Pac and other mills. He recommended that no approval be given until that information was obtained and another environmental assessment done. Lane went on to say that the federal government did not have the power to prevent approval of the new mill but would have power to enforce federal Fisheries Act standards once it was operating.[41] His submission, implying that the federal government wanted the project stopped, was a thunderbolt.

Alberta Environment Minister Klein immediately said Dr. Lane's submission did not represent the Environment Canada position and spent the afternoon on the phone with the Federal Environment Minister, Lucien Bouchard. At the end of the day, however, Bouchard issued a statement saying he supported Dr. Lane's review. In Alberta two conspiracy theories began to circulate. The first was that the Mulroney government was using the assessment to repay Alberta for holding an election on a Senate appointment, while the second was that the Ontario caucus in the Tory party had convinced the federal government to slow down the Alberta mills because they competed with Ontario pulp.[42]

In September, 1989, Alberta Environment released its own review of the company assessment, citing 231 deficiencies. During the fall public opposition in Alberta increased, with the Review Board public hearings providing a forum. The Alberta Medical Association condemned the quality of the company's health impact assessment and called for a moratorium; the project was opposed also by native bands, Alberta environmental organizations, the IJC, and the federal Department of Indian Affairs and Northern Development.

In March, 1990, the Review Board reported, recommending that the project be halted until more studies, expected to take two years, were completed. The Alberta government immediately endorsed this recommendation. Presumably the Getty government acted for two reasons – it had previously committed itself to acceptance of the Review Board recommendations, and the strong public opposition by that time focused on the project meant it would have been a major political problem to reverse that commitment.

The Alberta business community predicted the decision would mean investors would look to other provinces or countries. In 1988 Adam Zimmerman, chairman of Noranda Forest Inc., had said that in Alberta "they kiss [pulp companies] on both cheeks and give them grants."[43] In March of 1990 he said, "it means nobody's going to go near any new project unless they have an iron-clad understanding of what the rules and the protocol are. They'd be better off going someplace else."[44]

In December, 1990, however, after the company announced it would use a different pulping process, Alberta reversed its position, to the consternation of environmentalists, and approved the mill.

The New Federal Standards

Lucien Bouchard, after the Greenpeace release of the leaked Sinclair report in the spring of 1989, took two actions: damage control by releasing the full text of the Sinclair report; and a pledge, on March 15, 1989, that "a dioxin and furan regulation will be promulgated by the middle of next year" under the Canadian Environmental Protection Act.[45] A few months later both Ontario and British Columbia announced their intention to bring in regulations by December 31, 1991, limiting total discharge of chlorinated organic compounds to 2.5 kg per air-dried tonne of pulp. During the course of the year Alberta and Quebec also announced their intention to bring in new pulp mill standards. On June 22, 1989, the Canadian Pulp and Paper Association released an "Environmental Statement," committing the sixty member companies, among other things, to "operate facilities in compliance with all applicable regulations," while "recognizing that not all installations meet those objectives at this time."[46]

On January 3, 1990, Bouchard announced that Environment Canada would not only regulate dioxins and furans but also use "regulations or guidelines under CEPA to strictly control organochlorine discharges in bleach plant effluents" and amend the 1971 Fisheries Act regulations, making them applicable by 1994 to all mills regardless of their date of construction.[47] Using its clearly defined constitutional powers under CEPA, Environment Canada has stated that these new discharge requirements will be met through provincial regulation and enforcement where "equivalency" has been established, but if it cannot be so established, then directly by Environment Canada officials.[48] The new federal regulatory program has three components:

1. amendments to the Fisheries Act to set new limits for acutely lethal discharges, total BOD, and total suspended solids; by 1994 the 1971 regulations, which as of 1990 only applied to eleven mills out of the 155 in the country, plus these new standards will apply for the first time to all mills;
2. new regulations under CEPA to "virtually eliminate" dioxin and furan discharges, based on the criteria of discharges below the detection limit of "state-of-the-art technology"; again, this regulation is to be in force by 1994;

3. development of further regulations at an unspecified date in the future to "strictly control" organochlorine discharges.

It has been estimated that the new standards will require ninety mills to install secondary treatment facilities for waste water. The Canadian Pulp and Paper Association has said the cost of such modifications will be $5 billion but has not yet said whether or not it will ask for further government subsidies. Bill Andrews of WCELA has criticized the federal initiative on the grounds that "the new standards won't touch some of the most worrisome contaminants, a category of chemicals known as organochlorines."[49]

The issue of jurisdiction, which, as the Sinclair report made clear, so hampered the 1971 federal effort, has still not been resolved. In May, 1990, Environment Canada issued the following statement, clearly suggesting that both the federal and provincial governments will continue to regulate:

> The federal government will work to ensure that the requirements of provincial legislation, the Canadian Environmental Protection Act and the Canada Fisheries Act are enforced through administrative arrangements that will simplify delivery and at the same time respect the authorities imposed by each of the statutes. Working as partners, and concentrating efforts will allow both levels of government to address the environmental problems facing this industry at a much faster pace.[50]

It is impossible to tell from this statement which standards, federal or provincial, will be applied in any given province or whether federal or provincial officials will enforce the new federal standards in those areas where they take precedence over provincial standards. What has changed from 1971? That question cannot be answered until federal-provincial "equivalency" negotiations are completed, and it is impossible to predict when that will be in the post-Meech era. It is very unlikely, however, given both traditional provincial hostility to federal intrusions and the fact that B.C., Alberta, Ontario, and Quebec are all developing their own new standards, that the provinces will roll over and play dead.

CHAPTER 16

International Pollution

The two stories in this chapter deal with acid rain – a bilateral Canada-U.S. issue – and CFC emissions, a fully international air pollution problem. The politics of the Canadian acid rain program during the primary period when it was developed, approximately 1980 to 1985, consisted of two sets of negotiations, each of which influenced the other. The first was the Canadian-American diplomacy in which Canada attempted, unsuccessfully, to convince the United States to sign a treaty on transboundary air pollution that would then provide the framework for regulatory action in each country. The second was the series of negotiations, among the eastern provinces and the federal government, on allocation of the cost (both government subsidies to the polluters and the portion of the overall 50 per cent reduction in annual emissions that would be achieved in each province) of a sulphur dioxide reduction program. Political pressure brought to bear by the environmental lobby in Canada was a significant factor. Negotiation of the 1987 Montreal Protocol on the Ozone Layer, on the other hand, involved virtually no federal-provincial negotiation and was not the subject of the same lobbying pressure within this country.

Both the acid rain program and the 1987 Protocol were only made possible, however, by the success of the major players, both government and industry, in reaching agreement on allocation of the cost of the pollution reduction activity.

The Canadian Acid Rain Program

The term "acid rain" entered the English language in the late 1970s and during the next decade came to symbolize one of the best-known and most politically powerful environmental issues in Canada. Although the term refers to both sulphur dioxide and nitrogen oxide pollution, and is now used for a wide range of toxic air contaminants, most of the attention devoted to the issue over the past decade has focused on sulphur dioxide and the problem it poses when it is transformed to sulphuric acid during the time it is carried by air currents, often many days during which it may travel hundreds of miles from its original source to its point of touchdown. The effects of acid rain – acidification of lakes and streams to the point that, in worst cases, almost all aquatic life is killed off; gradual corrosion of buildings, automobiles, and other objects; synergistic combinations with other air pollutants with resulting damage to forests and crops; effects associated with the release of toxic metals, as water acidification levels rise, from the streambeds or soils in which they are held – are now well known and considered sufficiently serious by those on both ends of the political spectrum in Canada to warrant expenditure of considerable funds on the problem.

For the most part sulphur dioxide is emitted to the air in large volumes by a relatively small number of sources, such as the coal-fired electrical utilities in the Ohio Valley and ore-smelting mines in Ontario and Quebec, which makes efforts to curb emissions much easier. Political pressure can readily be brought to bear on a small number of known polluters, illegal activity can be detected more easily, and the mechanics of standard-setting, because only one substance is involved, are relatively straightforward. These unique characteristics of the issue go a long way to explain why acid rain is the major success story since the phosphorous reductions of the 1970s – "success" defined as government action that has significantly reduced the annual quantities of the pollutant in question emitted to the environment – in the battle against pollution in Canada. Nevertheless, the struggle against acid rain in Canada stretches over some thirty years, from the early 1970s, when the Ontario government first imposed regulatory requirements for emission reductions on the Inco operations in Sudbury, to 1994, when the reductions spelled out in the Canadian federal-provincial program of 1985 will come into full effect. The corresponding date for the U.S. program is the year 2000.

The story of the acid rain program carries considerable significance for pollution politics for a number of reasons, including the following:

- Through the acid rain studies of the mid-1970s, scientists in North America and Europe first became fully aware of the phenomenon of long-range transport of airborne pollutants.
- The political significance of this movement over hundreds and thousands of miles was the crossing of international borders, which had the effect of transforming air pollution from a matter of local or provincial jurisdic-

tion to one of international significance; in Canada, this has had the effect of drawing the federal government back into a policy area that, by the late 1970s, it had almost completely abandoned to the provinces.

- The issue illustrates clearly, for example through the Reagan administration's continued insistence on more research before taking legislative action, the inevitable connections between scientific data and analysis and public policy.
- The issue demonstrates the immense political benefits to be gained from an explicit, easily understandable objective – the reduction of average annual loadings to twenty kilograms per hectare.
- Movement was not possible on the acid rain issue in Canada without a political willingness to bear the necessary cost and agreement on the allocation of that cost – both between industry and government and between jurisdictions.

Sulphur Dioxide Pollution

In Canada, the acid rain issue has largely revolved around one primary source – the nickel mining and smelting operations carried out in the Sudbury area that produce large amounts of sulphur dioxide gas, both emitted from the ore itself during the smelting process and from the burning of sulphur dioxide-laden coal. The problem was recognized as early as the turn of the century, when the Ontario government first took action on Sudbury air pollution. In 1902 Ontario passed a regulation in connection with the establishment of forest reserves requiring that "no ores containing sulphur or other deleterious substances shall be roasted in the open air in any Reserve or treated in such a way as to expose the trees and other vegetation therein to injury."[1] The next intervention was taken to protect the polluter, not the environment. In 1915, the government responded to requests from Sudbury mining interests by including a clause in grants of crown land made to those settling in the Sudbury area, precluding them from taking legal action to obtain compensation for damages caused by "sulphur fumes."[2] In 1921 the Ontario government passed the Damage by Sulphur Fumes Arbitration Act, a mechanism to be used to settle claims for damage.

By the 1960s those driving north on Highway 69 knew they were entering the Sudbury area by the transformation in the landscape seen outside the car window – from the green of field and forest to a blasted moonscape of blackened rock with not a scrap of vegetation left alive. When NASA sent its astronauts to the Sudbury area to practise walking in an environment as devoid of life as any lunar landscape, the mayor of Sudbury publicly objected to this insult to his city and attention was graphically focused on the effects of sulphur dioxide air pollution. As a result of incidents such as this and the growing attention being paid to pollution throughout the

1960s, the Ontario government moved to regulate Inco emissions in two ways. First, in accordance with accepted wisdom of the time, it sought to neutralize the pollution by diluting it and spreading it over a wider geographic area. This was to be accomplished by encouraging Inco to build a higher chimney-stack on its smelter so that emissions would be carried greater distances before reaching ground and concentrations of pollution in the immediate area would be significantly reduced. Second, Ontario used the expanded powers of the 1967 Air Pollution Control Act to issue an order, in 1970, requiring a reduction of daily sulphur dioxide emissions from 6,000 tons to 750 to be achieved by 1978.

Inco did not publicly object to either requirement. The decision to build a tall stack had already been publicly announced by the company some fifteen months earlier and presumably it felt that the reduction to the 1978 figure of 750 tons a day, a figure pulled from the air and for which no rationale was ever provided by the Ontario government, was sufficiently distant that it could be safely ignored for the moment. The 1,250-foot "super-stack" was built and came into operation in 1972, and in 1973 Inco emissions were reduced, by means of a new mill that allowed increased separation of sulphur from the nickel ore before smelting, from 6,000 to 3,600 tons per day. As a result of these two initiatives, the environment in the local Sudbury area improved considerably in the next few years. During the 1970s, however, the focus of concern began to shift from effects on vegetation in the immediate area to more subtle impacts on water quality in areas far removed from the source of the pollution.

Acid Rain Becomes an Issue

Long before construction of the Inco stack, scientists in Canada and elsewhere had identified the acidification of lakes as a pollution issue and had begun to explore the possibility that it was connected to emissions hundreds of miles away, in an upwind direction. In Canada, research on possible connections between acid levels and declining fish populations was carried out in the 1960s on lakes in Ontario's Killarny Park, located not far from Sudbury. The issue was first drawn to public attention when a report on work done by Dr. Harold Harvey, a zoologist with the University of Toronto, was carried in *The Globe and Mail* of July 26, 1971. Inco immediately issued a statement denying any responsibility, saying that "a full 80 per cent of the sulphur dioxide in the atmosphere comes from organic decay" and that only "6 per cent [can be attributed] to smelting operations."[3]

Acid rain first achieved international recognition at the 1972 Stockholm Conference when Sweden presented a paper on acidification of lakes in that country, resulting from sulphur dioxide emissions originating in other countries, including England and Germany. During the next few years the pace of scientific research in Canada, the United States, and Europe was accelerated, with the result that by the time the Ontario Ministry of the Environment published such studies as *An Analysis of the Sudbury Environmental Study: Network Precipitation Acidity Data June-September, 1978* there was general scientific agreement on the nature and scope of the problem. The year before that, the issue had received its first prominent public airing in a series of articles written by reporter Ross Howard for the *Toronto Star*.[4] Acid rain was clearly established as a new issue, differing from the preceding concern over sulphur pollution in two respects – the focus, initially at least, was not on vegetation but on aquatic effects, giving rise to the politically powerful "dying lake" metaphor, and there was a growing realization that the sources of acidic pollution might be many miles away – even in another country.

From the outset, acid rain was seen in Canada as a bilateral issue, felt by many to be only the latest in a long series of transboundary insults from the south – starting with the American invasions of 1776 and 1812, and stretching through to domination of Canadian television and magazines in the post-war era. Interestingly, in light of the Canadian perception of itself as the injured party, the first shot in the Canada-U.S. acid rain border war was fired in May of 1978 when the U.S. Senate adopted a resolution objecting to the transboundary impacts associated with the proposed Ontario Hydro coal-fired electricity generating plant, to be located at Atikokan, 200 kilometres west of Thunder Bay and only fifty kilometres north of the international border.

The American government had already taken regulatory action governing sources within its own borders. In 1970 the U.S. Congress had enacted the Clean Air Act, which, as is the case in Canada, divides authority between the federal and state or provincial governments, although in the U.S. the federal government has far greater powers to require state action than is the case in Canada. Under the Clean Air Act, air quality objectives, expressed as maximum and average concentration levels and known as National Ambient Air Quality Standards, were established by the federal government for sulphur oxides, SO_2, particulate matter, CO, ozone, and lead. Achievement of these objectives was left to the individual states, which developed and applied emission standards for particular sources as required. In 1977 the Act was amended to require increased action by states that had failed to achieve national standards. In addition to these ambient and emission standards for existing operations, considerably more stringent standards, basically requiring installation of the best available pollution control technology, were developed for new plants. The rationale was that applying pollution abatement equipment to existing plants was far less cost-efficient than building it into the plans for new operations. Thus, within the established limits, air pollution would be allowed initially but would gradually be reduced as older plants were taken out of operation and replaced with those meeting the more stringent standards. The same rationale had governed implementation of the Canadian pulp and paper mill water discharge standards in 1971.

The New Source Performance Standards, intended to bring about emission reductions over twenty-five to fifty years, were used – along with arguments that scientific research had not yet established a clear causal link between American emissions and acidification of lakes in Canada – to resist calls by both Canada and U.S. environmentalists for emission-reducing legislation. An example is the following claim, made by an American author in 1988:

> The U.S. government has not taken, and needs not take, further legislative measures such as those recently adopted by Canada [the 1985 program, intended to reduce emissions by 50 per cent by 1994] or West Germany to reduce SO_2 emissions. U.S. industry will make those reductions as it upgrades its physical plant. Such piecemeal reductions are not the sort of grist for governmental pronouncements on new acid rain programs, but the "invisible hand" of a market economy works just as well and perhaps more efficiently than the whim of politics in this area.[5]

In July, 1978, the two countries established the Bilateral Research Consultation Group (BRCG), a mechanism to allow ongoing co-ordination of research and exchange of information between Canadian and American scientists. This began a process of increasingly closer co-operation on the issue, which culminated in the signing of the August 5, 1980, Memorandum of Intent, a commitment to work toward a Canada-U.S. agreement governing transboundary air pollution.

Regulation in Ontario

In the same month that Canadian and U.S. scientists began their formal collaboration, acid rain first blew up as a major political issue in Ontario. The cause was the announcement, on July 27, 1978, by George McGague, the newly appointed Minister of Environment for Ontario, that Ontario had extended until 1984 the 1978 deadline, established in the 1970 control order, for a reduction of Inco's daily emissions. The 1978 reduction requirement of 750 tonnes, the minister said, was "unjustifiable from an environmental perspective and unrealistic from a technical point of view." The public reaction was immediate and sufficiently strong to cause Premier Bill Davis to shuffle his new minister to another posting less than two months after his appointment, replacing him with Dr. Harry Parrott. The Resources and Development Committee then held public hearings on acid rain in February, 1979, accompanied by "almost non-stop media report-ing" that constituted "the Ontario and Canadian public's most concen-trated crash course in acid rain, government decision-making and corporate response."[6]

In the spring of 1979 environmental organizations in Ontario, stimulated by the failure of the Ontario government to enforce its 1970 order, began working with their counterparts in other parts of Canada and the U.S. to organize a major conference on the issue of acid rain. Groups such as the Ontario Sierra Club, the Federation of Ontario Naturalists, the Canadian Nature Federation, the National Parks and Conservation Association, and Friends of the Boundary Waters Wilderness began planning for a joint Canada-U.S. conference, titled Action Seminar on Acid Precipitation (ASAP). The conference was held in Toronto at the beginning of November. Although funding was supplied in part by both American and Canadian government agencies, the initiative for the event clearly came from the environmental community and, as the title suggested, the purpose was to plan action, not to exchange technical and scientific papers. A comparison between the ASAP conference and the Pollution and Our Environment Conference of 1966 – focused almost completely on the technical aspects of pollution abatement, organized by a government agency, and with almost no public-interest representation – gives a good indication of the changes in environmental politics during the intervening thirteen years.

In May of 1979 the federal Conservatives were elected and John Fraser, a former B.C. environmental lawyer, was named federal minister. The new minister's background gave him a personal commitment to the need for environmental protection not found in many of the provincial or federal appointments to the junior posting of environment. During that summer, Fraser began to draw public attention to the need for action on acid rain. The issue was kept before the public eye when, just before the ASAP confer-ence, the Canadian-American working group released its first report on current understanding of sources, transport, and effects of acid rain pollution.

The international commitment to deal with transboundary pollution was reinforced on November 13 when Canada, the U.S., and thirty-two mem-bers of the Economic Commission for Europe signed the Convention on Long-Range Transboundary Air Pollution, committing themselves to regu-lar exchanges of information and a co-ordinated approach to the problem. In April, 1980, the House of Commons Standing Committee on Fisheries and Forestry appointed a sub-committee on acid rain.

Negotiation of the Canadian Program

During the spring of 1980 the Ontario government began to move away from the position that it would only act "in co-ordination with other jurisdictions" – the Ontario position Premier Davis had consistently stated since the 1978 extension of the Inco control order. The Ontario government was under increasing pressure from environmentalists within the province and from the federal government, which was finding it difficult to ignore the American claim that Canadian calls for U.S. action, without doing anything to "put its own house in order," lacked moral authority.[7] After the brief Tory reign in Ottawa, the new Environment Minister, John Roberts, issued a statement in April, 1980, saying that federal studies showed Inco could reduce its emissions by half, using existing technology, at a cost of $400 million.[8] On May 1, 1980, the Ontario minister, Parrott, announced a new control order that immediately reduced allowable daily emissions to 2,500 tonnes and required a further reduction to 1,950 by 1983. This had no impact on Inco's daily operations because a slack world market meant that nickel production in Sudbury had been reduced and daily emissions were already at that level. No great hardship was anticipated since Inco had previously announced development of new production technologies that would allow a further 25 per cent reduction. However, Parrott's announcement gave an appearance of Ontario action, which was further strengthened in January, 1981, when the province imposed a 42.5 per cent reduction by Ontario Hydro in its combined sulphur dioxide and nitrogen oxide emissions. Hydro was given a three-year period to meet this new requirement, which was largely seen at the time as an election ploy to assist the Ontario Tories in gaining a majority in the election called for March 19, 1981.[9]

By October of 1980 Ronald Reagan appeared likely to defeat President Carter in the November U.S. presidential election and some Canadians were displaying a prescient concern for the effect that might have on American resolve to take joint action with Canada. John Fraser, now out of office but his interest in the issue unabated, began discussions with environmentalists of the need for some form of non-government representation of Canada's acid rain interests in Washington. These discussions led to formation the following year of the Canadian Coalition on Acid Rain, representing a number of Canadian environmental organizations.[10] The CCAR went on to become one of the most effective of all Canadian lobby groups, moving early into the use of direct mail, both for fund-raising and to stimulate letter-writing campaigns. As well, the group had continual direct access to both provincial and federal environment ministers and, as the issue increasingly moved there, to the Prime Minister's Office. The Coalition enjoyed two distinct advantages. First, approximately half of its annual $200,000-$300,000 budget was provided directly by the Ontario and Canadian governments, who were happy to fund an organization that furthered their own strategy of keeping public attention firmly fixed on the need for American action. No other Canadian environmental lobby organization, then or since, has received anything like that level of government funding. Second, its Board of Directors was led not by environmental activists who had descended from the 1960s counter-culture but by representatives of such organizations as the Muskoka Lakes Association, made up of affluent Torontonians who owned cottages in Muskoka – people familiar with the exercise of power who were confident that their usual ability to influence events could be transferred to what for them was this new and fascinating arena of pollution politics.

By the time that the Coalition had opened offices in both Toronto and Washington, in 1981, the spirit of Canadian-American co-operation on the issue had become badly frayed. As mentioned, the joint scientific initiative of 1978 had led to a comprehensive report on the problem in the fall of 1979, followed by diplomatic activity that culminated in the August, 1980, Memorandum of Intent. The mechanism established to negotiate a transboundary air agreement was the Canada-United States Co-ordinating Committee, which in turn had established five working groups to review and provide detailed reports on both the scientific and legal issues to be encompassed by an international agreement. The reports of these working groups were released in February and March, 1981, followed, on June 23, with the opening in Washington of formal negotiations between the two countries. By that time, however, the prospects for such negotiation were increasingly being cast in doubt by officials of the newly installed Reagan administration, who from the time of first taking power had been suggesting that more research was needed before any commitments to specific action could be made. The new Canadian minister, John Roberts, "repeatedly expressed concern that the United States was not living up to the provisions of the MOI." In April Roberts met with James Watt, Secretary of the Interior, who assured him that negotiations would begin on schedule and the administration would not give away any of its powers to control acid rain in the upcoming amendments to the U.S. Clean Air Act.[11]

After a preliminary exchange of views between the two governments, Canada began to develop a position on reductions in preparation for the next round of diplomatic talks, scheduled for February 25, 1981. To do this two things were necessary – a decision had to be made on the quantity of acid rain loadings deemed acceptable and then a further decision made on the reductions required to achieve that objective. At this stage the task was limited to deciding on a total emission reduction objective for all sources; allocation of cuts among the major polluting sources in both countries was not yet attempted.

Scientists in Environment Canada achieved the first task by plotting on maps all information gathered to date on acidification damage in eastern North America and rates of annual deposition. This led to the conclusion that for "moderately sensitive ecosystems" damage could be kept within acceptable bounds if no more than twenty kilograms of acid rain fell on each hectare per year.[12] The decision on what reductions would be required to meet that target was then made at a December, 1981, meeting in the boardroom of the Ontario Ministry of the Environment, attended by the federal minister, John Roberts, the Ontario minister, Keith Norton, and the Quebec minister, Marcel Leger, and their respective officials. Scientists from the Atmospheric Environment Service told the ministers that their computer modelling of Canadian and American sources and subsequent airborne transport led them to conclude that a reduction of between 30 and 70 per cent from 1980 levels was required. Splitting the difference, the politicians decided on a target of a 50 per cent reduction in both countries – of which, in Canada, 25 per cent had already been achieved by the Ontario regulations on Inco and Ontario Hydro.[13]

Accordingly, John Roberts announced on February 15, 1982, that "Canada is prepared to cut sulphur dioxide emissions in eastern Canada, including Manitoba, by 50 percent by 1990, contingent on parallel action by the United States."[14] This position was formally presented to the American government at a negotiating session on February 25, 1982. At the same time, Roberts asked his provincial counterparts to begin consultations on the reductions that would be required in each province to achieve the overall 50 per cent Canadian reduction.[15] The Canadian position was rejected by the American representatives, on the basis that available data did not support the 50 per cent reduction figure and that more research was therefore needed, at a session on June 15, 1982. The following year Canadian External Affairs Minister Allan MacEachen twice discussed the subject with his counterpart, U.S. Secretary of State George Shultz, and Canadian and American scientific papers were exchanged. At the same time provincial officials, at a series of meetings convened by Ontario, were developing computer models of the "optimal solution" for allocation of the Canadian cuts.

On August 12, 1983, Charles Caccia, a committed environmentalist, replaced John Roberts as Environment Minister in the final months of the Trudeau government. In response to both his own convictions and growing political pressure within Canada, orchestrated by the CCAR, Caccia made a cut in acid rain emissions his first priority. At the same time, the U.S. Environmental Protection Agency was for the first time developing plans for possible action to be taken in that country. In May, 1983, President Reagan had moved to stanch a political wound by dismissing the head of the EPA, Anne Burford, whose administration had been marked more by scandals over use of Superfund monies than by any action to protect the environment. She was replaced by the popular, and credible, William Ruckleshaus. During the summer and early fall of 1983 rumours were reaching Ottawa that Ruckleshaus was preparing a plan. Known as the "North-East

Option," it would achieve a 25 per cent reduction in U.S. emissions in the northeast at a cost of $10 billion, and it was rumoured this would be put on the table at the next Schultz-MacEachen meeting, to be held on October 24-25.

The annual meeting of the Canadian Council of Resource and Environment Ministers was scheduled to be held in Fredericton, New Brunswick, on September 29, immediately prior to the Schultz-MacEachen meeting. At that meeting Caccia was able to convince the provincial ministers that if the Ruckleshaus plan were proposed by the Americans in October, Canada would match the proposed cuts, despite the fact that an allocation of that reduction had not yet been negotiated among the provinces.[16] As it turned out, no American plan ever materialized, budget chief David Stockman having convinced President Reagan that spending billions of dollars to save fish in northeastern lakes was the height of fiscal folly.

Caccia, however, undeterred by this lack of the American stick with which to threaten the provinces, continued to press for a Canadian program. In February, 1984, he sought and received confirmation from Eugene Forsey that the Canadian constitution did indeed give the federal government power to regulate emissions directly, using the Clean Air Act, regardless of what action the provinces might or might not take.[17] Whether or not the Trudeau government would have incurred the wrath of the provinces by taking such action remains a moot point. On March 6, 1984, Caccia again met with his provincial counterparts, this time to discuss unilateral Canadian action. No progress was made during the morning discussions and the ministers then retired for a private and, as reported by those waiting outside the door, occasionally heated luncheon discussion, with no officials or aides present. It took some time, but the ministers emerged by mid-afternoon to announce that they had agreed to a unilateral 50 per cent reduction by 1994.[18]

When the Conservatives defeated John Turner's short-lived Liberal government in September of 1984, the Mulroney government was bound by the pre-election commitment, given to the CCAR, to bring in a Canadian acid rain program within six months of taking office. By this time there was agreement in Ottawa that government funds should be committed to the program, and the early winter of 1984-85 was spent in discussions with both polluters and the provinces on the workings of that assistance. Again, the Canadian desire to press for American action lent a sense of urgency. The first of the annual Mulroney-Reagan meetings, the "Shamrock Summit," had been scheduled for March 17, 1985. Political realities were such that Prime Minister Mulroney had no choice but to put acid rain on the list of pressing Canadian-American issues and he had stated, in a speech given in the House in early January, 1985, that Canada could not press for American cuts unless "our own hands are clean." Thus, on February 5, 1985, the federal and provincial ministers announced the Canadian program, following the lines of the agreement negotiated by Caccia the previous year, and on March 6 the federal government announced its assistance in meeting the 50 per cent target by spending up to $150 million, to be matched by provincial funds, on modernization of the smelting industry.

On June 26, 1985, the Liberal government of David Peterson took office in Ontario and the new Environment Minister, Jim Bradley, immediately began to develop the program committed to by his Tory predecessor, Andy Brandt. Peterson, like Mulroney, had also given a pre-election commitment to bring in a program within six months of taking office, and on December 17, after a series of negotiations with Inco, Falconbridge, Algoma Steel, Ontario Hydro, and the other major polluters, the Ontario government brought in regulations that would achieve a 67 per cent cut in emissions from sources within the province by 1994. During the next few years federal-provincial agreements were signed with all of the other eastern provinces, implementing the reductions – for instance, New Brunswick will cut by 16 per cent while Manitoba has agreed to 25 per cent – to achieve the 50 per cent Canadian program.

On November 15, 1990, President Bush signed the 1990 Clean Air Act, which requires that sulphur dixoide emissions in the United States be reduced by approximately half by the year 2000.

The 1987 Montreal Protocol

Ozone, when located at ground level, is a major component of urban smog and is directly responsible for both human health effects and damage to the natural environment. Ozone in the stratosphere, however, between twenty and thirty kilometres above us, absorbs a significant portion of the ultraviolet radiation from the sun that is damaging to many forms of life on earth.

In 1928 the DuPont chemical company began to search for a new chemical substance that could be used in refrigerators. The search was stimulated by the need to replace ammonia and sulphur dioxide, the substances used until that date, because they were highly toxic and inflammable. Researchers combined fluorine with carbon and one of the halogen elements to produce the new substance freon, which was stable, non-flammable, and non-toxic – clearly a more environmentally friendly product than those it was replacing. In the 1950s and 1960s the related compound, chlorofluorocarbons, began to be used as the propellant in aerosol spray cans.[19] Between 1960 and 1974, global production of CFCs for refrigeration, aerosol spray, and other uses such as cleaning electrical equipment, increased significantly.

In 1974, two atmospheric chemists at the University of California, Drs. Rowland and Molina, published a paper in *Nature* advancing their theory that CFCs over a period of fifty or more years would gradually drift up to the stratosphere and, once there, be broken down by the ultraviolet light to their constituent parts. The chlorine molecules thus released from CFCs would then begin a chain reaction with the ozone molecules, breaking them down to normal oxygen and chlorine monoxide, neither of which is capable of absorbing ultraviolet light. The product developed forty years earlier as a safe alternative to its more toxic predecessors, Rowland and Molina argued, was endangering life on earth.

Since 1969, an estimated 2 per cent of the ozone layer, on a global average, has been destroyed, which means that the amount of ultraviolet radiation reaching the surface of the earth has increased.[20] Scientists are concerned about increasing ultraviolet radiation in part because it is expected to increase skin cancer rates but also because of its effect on plant life, agricultural crop yields, and a variety of different ecosystems. Dr. Sayed Z. El-Sayed of Texas A&M University has studied the effects of ultraviolet radiation on phytoplankton in the oceans off Antarctica, finding that increased radiation slows the rate of photosynthesis and that increases above 10 per cent kill the tiny aquatic plants completely. Phytoplankton is eaten by small crustaceans, known as krill, which in turn are eaten by whales and other species. Dr. El-Sayed is quoted as saying that if ultraviolet radiation in Antarctica increases because of CFCs released to the atmosphere thirty or forty years ago, "we are going to be in some trouble. I can't predict how much trouble but it does not bode well. If anything happens to the krill, the whole ecosystem will absolutely collapse. We can say goodby to the whales, to the seals, to the penguins, et cetera."[21]

Increased ultraviolet radiation, however, is only a part of the environmental threat posed by CFCs. Chlorofluorocarbons are also one of the "greenhouse gases" that, along with carbon dioxide and methane, are rapidly changing the composition of the global atmosphere in ways that may result in a number of extremely severe consequences.

When Drs. Rowland and Molina discovered the ozone-destroying properties of CFCs in 1974, potential damage to the earth's ozone layer from stratospheric jet travel, such as the Concorde, was already a topic of public concern. Perhaps for this reason, action was taken in the U.S. very quickly, with attention focused on freons in aerosol cans. Oregon and several other states passed legislation regulating CFC use in aerosols, leading American CFC producers to look more favourably on federal legislation that, if nothing else, would provide uniform national standards instead of a crazy quilt of state legislation.[22]

Legislation prohibiting the use of CFCs in aerosols was passed in the United States in 1978, and Canada, in 1980, enacted regulations under the Environmental Contaminants Act prohibiting the use of chlorofluorocarbons in antiperspirants, deodorants, and hair sprays. In that same year the

European Economic Community took regulatory action in a different form, directed not at CFC users but at production totals. This EEC limit on total production capacity over the long term has been described as "a painless move, supported by European industry, which gave the appearance of control while in reality permitting undiminished rates of expansion for at least two more decades."[23]

By 1980, therefore, the battle lines for international action on CFCs had been drawn. American industry, already required by domestic regulation to eliminate a major portion of its aerosol production and quite happy to see the same requirements imposed on competitors in other countries, was facing producers in the United Kingdom, France, and Italy, allied with others, primarily in the U.S.S.R. and Japan, who were determined to resist any international movement for further controls.

The context for the multilateral negotiations on CFC controls was provided by the United Nations Environment Program, which in 1977 established the Co-ordinating Committee on the Ozone Layer, a vehicle for the exchange of information and co-ordination of action. Two international meetings convened that year to discuss ozone depletion and steps that might be taken beyond an aerosol ban. In April, 1980, the U.S., Canada, Sweden, Norway, Denmark, Germany, and the Netherlands called for all nations to reduce CFC emissions from all sources.[24] Although the American commitment to take further domestic regulatory action was badly weakened by the coming to power of the Reagan administration in that same year, the U.S. continued to press for some form of international action.

During the 1980s attention in Canada, on the part of both environmental organizations and the general public, was focused more on acid rain and contaminated drinking water than on depletion of the ozone layer. The pressure for some form of international action came primarily from the scientific community, as more evidence of ozone depletion began to accumulate, and from those diplomats and others pursuing the UNEP quest for an agreement. In May, 1981, UNEP announced plans for a global convention, followed in November by a meeting of legal experts to discuss the form a possible protocol might take. In January, 1982, twenty-four UNEP member nations again met to discuss a possible convention for the protection of the ozone layer. Progress was slow, however. During the next few years negotiations were, in the words of the chief Canadian negotiator, "characterized by very emotional debate, constant imputing of motives and aggravated by a lack of scientific consensus."[25] The European CFC producers and their national governments were suspicious of American motives, convinced that DuPont had secretly developed a substitute for CFCs it would reveal as soon as their production had been banned.

In 1984 the European Community had made a counter-proposal to the 1983 call for a ban on aerosol use by suggesting that any international agreement instead place limits on new production capacity. "Each side was backing a protocol that would require no new controls for itself, but considerable adjustment for the other," Richard Benedick has noted, because "The United States had already imposed a ban on non-essential uses of CFCs, but U.S. chemical companies were operating at close to capacity and thus would suffer under a production cap. Their European counterparts, on the other hand, had substantial underutilized capacity and could expand CFC production at current rates for another 20 years before hitting the cap."[26] In March, 1985, nations did, however, sign the Vienna Convention for Protection of the Ozone Layer, an agreement to continue to take coordinated action but with no commitments to specific reductions.

During this period scientific estimates of the potential extent of ozone depletion were far from unanimous and provided enough uncertainty to buttress the argument that there simply was not enough data yet available to justify the cost of reducing CFC production and use. That began to change, however, in the fall of 1984, with the first discovery, by a British research team using ground-based measurements, of the Antarctic ozone layer "hole," a finding soon confirmed by NASA satellite data. The political significance of the data came as much from the way it was conveyed to the public as from its substance. By August of that year television viewers were seeing satellite schematics of the Antarctic ozone hole with the evening news. "The [television] image was vivid and the message was too. The idea that the ozone hole, like a tiny puncture in a fragile eggshell, could signal the eventual demise of the earth's atmosphere shook many policy makers into action by early 1986."[27]

The political pressure, in both Europe and the U.S., for some form of action was continuing to grow, however, particularly when testimony at a U.S. Senate committee hearing in June explicitly linked CFC emissions not only to the detrimental effects of increased ultraviolet radiation but also to global warming. The Senate committee was told by Robert Watson of NASA that "Global warming is inevitable – it is only a question of magnitude and time,"[28] and that CFCs, along with such other factors as carbon dioxide emissions and the destruction of the rain forests, were responsible. Two of the major U.S. environmental organizations concerned with the issue, the Natural Resources Defense Council (NRDC) and the Environmental Defense Fund, now called for action much stronger than a simple freeze on production, advocating instead a complete elimination of CFCs over a ten-year period.

During that summer, staff at Environment Canada began to develop a proposal for a way around the U.S.-EC deadlock. The Canadian officials proposed adoption of a number of guiding principles, including recognition of the global nature of the problem and the need to establish a "Global Emission Limit." Moreover, they suggested the use of both population and national GNP to allocate reductions among nations, recognizing that those nations that to date had received no benefits from either production or use of CFCs were entitled to receive "some equitable share of the benefits which accrue from CFCs (notably their use as refrigerants)."[29] This approach was adopted at a UNEP workshop in September, which led to resumption of formal negotiations, on December 1, 1986, for the first time since the signing of the Vienna Convention in March, 1985.

In the fall of 1986 American CFC producers, including DuPont, responsible for 25 per cent of the world's total production of CFCs, indicated for the first time a willingness to limit production and endorsed the UNEP negotiations. Four reasons have been given for this change of position on the part of the American industry. (1) There were increasing worries about the possibility of American regulation, resulting from a lawsuit against the EPA undertaken by the NRDC; just as the industry in 1977 had preferred federal regulation to a jumble of state requirements, it now preferred regulation under terms of an international agreement, which would also place restrictions on its foreign competitors, than unilateral American action. (2) Scientific evidence was accumulating to prove that ozone depletion was caused by CFC emissions, and this evidence was coupled with the scientists' new concern over the CFC contribution to the greenhouse effect. (3) DuPont had moved management of the issue from its freon division to its head office, where growing concern for the effect on the company's public image, in light of the fact that CFC production accounted for only 2 per cent of total DuPont revenues, was leading to a willingness to act. (4) Interest had grown in developing alternatives to CFCs, stimulated by fear that the Japanese might be moving ahead in this area.[30]

At the December, 1986, negotiations in Vienna, the United States representatives put forth a proposal, basically the same position as that taken by the NRDC, for an immediate freeze followed by a 95 per cent reduction over ten years. The Europeans and Japanese replied that they were only willing to consider a freeze and talks were broken off. At further negotiations in January both sides gave slightly – the U.S. suggested a reduction over ten to fourteen years and the Europeans agreed to a 20 per cent reduction. At the third round, in April, the U.S. put forth the proposal eventually adopted at Montreal in September – a freeze in 1990, followed by a 20 per cent cut in 1992 and a second round of cuts to produce a further 30 per cent reduction at an unspecified date. No decision was made in April but worldwide environmentalist lobbying throughout the summer of 1987, including the release of 1,000 helium-filled balloons on Parliament Hill in Ottawa to symbolize the ascent of CFC molecules, moved the nations closer to action. The European position was also affected that summer by the fact that Britain, due to the rotation of offices, had moved out of the presidency of the EEC and three supporters of action, Germany, the Netherlands, and Belgium, held the key positions.

Thus when the representatives of forty-three nations convened in Montreal, on September 14, 1987, the stage was set for an agreement. A last minute roadblock was the American demand for a "level playing field," in the form of an agreement that the Montreal Protocol would not come into effect until 90 per cent of the producing and consuming nations had agreed. This was strongly resisted by Canada and other nations, pointing out that such a stipulation would give a country like Japan a veto power over the agreement. After a full day of talks on September 14, followed by late evening discussions convened by UNEP head Mostafa Tolba, agreement was reached the next day – a 1990 freeze, a 20 per cent cut by 1994, and a further 30 per cent by 1999.

As data continued to accumulate, the world scientific community concluded, only months after signing of the 1987 Protocol, that a 50 per cent reduction was not enough to save the ozone layer. On January 1, 1989, the Montreal Protocol, having been ratified by the requisite number of nations, came into force, but international negotiations continued through 1989 and 1990. In July, 1990, the international community agreed to end all CFC production by the year 2000 and to establish a fund to help countries like China and India with the cost of developing alternative technologies.

The 1987 Montreal Protocol did not solve the problem – but it did establish, for the first time, that nations could negotiate an agreement to reduce international pollution.

Both acid rain and CFCs represent success stories: they resulted in programs, based in a firm foundation of legally binding regulations, that will significantly reduce total annual quantities of each pollutant. Why has success been achieved in these two areas and not in others?

The first answer has to be the relative simplicity of regulating single substances that are emitted, or produced, by a relatively limited number of sources. Reduction objectives, in each case a 50 per cent cut, were established in each case. In the case of acid rain the figure was somewhat arbitrary and with CFCs it was immediately seen as completely inadequate, but this does not detract from the political importance of a clear-cut objective. In both cases a forum existed for the negotiations that were essential to success – CCME for the federal-provincial discussions and UNEP for the negotiations leading up to the Montreal Protocol. In each case the scientific evidence supporting the need for a reduction continued to accumulate during the course of the political battle and was used, naturally enough, to further the arguments of the environmental lobby. Finally, the lobby, for both issues, was able to make its case to the public in graphic and compelling terms – using the power of the symbols of a dying lake and a hole in the sky.

PART V

Where Do We Go from Here?

Before we can decide where we go from here we need to be sure we have a clear understanding of where we are now. We now stand hesitating at the edge of the lake, braving ourselves to dive in, but still reluctant, unable to take the plunge.

The preceding pages have demonstrated that while the individuals and organizations lobbying governments for action on pollution have gained considerable public support over the last two decades and have been successful in changing political rhetoric – bringing us, at least, to the edge of the lake – they have still not secured meaningful political power. This is demonstrated, among other things, by the following:

• Despite the endless green rhetoric and posturing – on election platforms, in "green consumer" marketing campaigns, and in earnest consultations over what we really *mean* when we call for "sustainable development" – the fact remains that each year Canadians generate and discharge to their environment many millions of tonnes of polluting substances. Canada is more polluted this year than it was last year and will be even more polluted one year hence.

• The financial and human resources devoted by governments to setting and enforcing pollution standards are a minuscule fraction of total annual spending and staffing.

• Even the major Canadian success story, the Canadian acid rain program, gives reason for pause: the first regulatory action to reduce annual sulphur dioxide loadings from the Inco plant was taken in 1970; the standards of the Canadian program, implemented in 1985, were predicated on a comparable 50 per cent cut in emissions from U.S. sources, something which, under the Bush administration Clean Air Act amendments, will not be achieved until the year 2000. Thus the "success story" will have taken thirty years, and at the end of that time the success will still only be partial – acid rain pollution will not have been stopped, it will simply have been reduced to the "acceptable" average loading of twenty kilograms per hectare.

- If our "success" tells us something, our undoubted failure – industrial hazardous waste – tells us even more. While regulatory standards have been imposed on virtually every hazardous waste generator in the country, the fact remains, leaving aside the issue of illegal dumping, that some 8 million tonnes is legally discharged to our environment each year. We have not yet been able to put in place treatment and disposal capacity for more than a fraction of the total produced each year. Everyone agrees that the real answer is not to produce the wastes in the first place, but there has not been a single regulatory action taken by any jurisdiction in Canada to require reduction, re-use, or recycling of hazardous wastes.

Why has the anti-pollution lobby been unable, despite all the noise and fury surrounding the issue, to achieve its basic goal of significantly reducing annual quantities discharged to the environment? Three possible reasons are worth discussion.

1. *The inherent limitations of the human health argument.* Certainly this argument vaulted pollution, particularly in the context of toxic chemicals and drinking water, back into the limelight in the early 1980s, but there are limits to its effectiveness as a motivator of political change and it would seem those limits have now been reached.

2. *Failure to address successfully the cost and the allocation of cost argument.* The Canadian acid rain program, in which federal-provincial negotiations led to an agreement on sharing of cost, in terms of both the relative portion of total load reduction each province would provide and the direct financial assistance from government to the polluting industry, is one of the few examples, as is the 1987 CFC agreement, of a successful resolution of this issue. In almost all other cases, such as the pulp and paper industry, the issue of cost and cost-sharing, particularly in terms of job impacts, still impedes regulatory action.

3. *Failure to resist the co-opting tactics of endless consultation.* Discussion, negotiation, and compromise are as essential to success in pollution politics as in any other political issue. However, over the past twenty years they have been used very successfully by those who favour the status quo as a means of deferring action, with the present discussion of "integration of

environmental and economic decision-making" being only the most recent instance.

Possible actions that might be taken in each of these three areas, then, form the basis for the following discussion. Attention is first paid to the set of values, referred to as an "environmental ethic," that, as we have seen, has begun to emerge but must be strengthened if it is to supplement human health concerns and provide a firm basis for political action.

The ideology of environmentalism has not yet been fully developed, in Canada or elsewhere. This must be done to provide a coherent analysis to carry into the political debate, particularly in terms of economic analysis; to strengthen the nascent connections between environmentalism and other progressive social movements; and, most importantly, to remove the greatest stumbling block to environmental protection – the issue of allocation of cost and the argument that the environment can only be saved at the expense of jobs.

The third subject of discussion is the political strategy that environmentalists should pursue during the coming decade. Should they concentrate on bringing about changes in public and private-sector decision-making procedures – such things as strengthening the role of environment ministers within cabinet, for instance? Or should they concentrate instead on an "end-of-the-pipe" strategy – forcing changes in the standards that govern pollution quantities emitted from a particular source, while leaving the agencies involved to make whatever changes in decision-making procedures are needed to meet those new requirements? Or yet instead should they divide their forces and attempt to pursue both objectives simultaneously?

Finally, the closing section briefly discusses the role Canada might play in helping to protect the global environment. Increased Canadian attention to international environmental protection is essential for at least two reasons. The threat to the global environment posed by the harsh realities of population growth and poverty in the less industrialized nations is far more severe than is that posed to the Canadian environment by Canadian activities. Canadians may consume more energy and produce more waste, on a per capita basis, than almost any other nation, but because there are so few of us we do not represent the major threat. Because pollution crosses borders, this global threat is as real in Canada as anywhere else and out of simple self-interest, if nothing else, we should act to save the global environment at the same time that we attempt to protect our own. But we also cannot solve our own problems in isolation. Taking the kind of actions required in this country, without corresponding action by our major trading partners and competitors, will impose a politically unacceptable price, one that will prevent meaningful action.

CHAPTER 17

Values, Ideology, Strategy

Values

Since 1962, when Rachel Carson wrote about children dying at play, those working to rally public support in the fight against pollution have emphasized, more than anything else, the threat it poses for human health. The two major exceptions have been the acid rain campaign, which was centred on the symbol of dying lakes, not people, and the efforts to publicize the plight of the Beluga whales in the St. Lawrence, unable to live in the polluted water emptying out of the Great Lakes and whose carcasses, washed up on the shores of the river, are said to be contaminated with toxic chemicals at concentration levels high enough that they are technically classified as hazardous waste. For the most part, however, the human health threat – children whose mental development is affected by high lead levels; increased skin cancers caused by stratospheric ozone layer depletion; the unknown threat of cancer in the water we drink or food we eat – drives the issue. Obviously this is a powerful argument the anti-pollution lobby must continue to make, as clearly and as forcefully as possible. However, it is also an inherently limited argument, particularly since it is presented in the reform environmentalism mode of rational self-interest with no reference to either spiritual or moral values. The human health argument is unlikely, by itself, to provide the political support and motivation needed to transform Canada into a non-polluting society.

The first limitation is inherent in the logic of cost-benefit analysis and risk assessment, the two mainstays of the reform environmentalist approach to pollution reduction. These approaches accept the fact that human health is inevitably an issue freighted with varying degrees of anxiety and emotion, but as much as possible they attempt to function on the basis of rational analysis alone. Both approaches also start with the assumption that some level of pollution is acceptable (otherwise there would be no need to either weigh costs and benefits or assess relative degrees of risk) and then aim to provide means for deciding what that acceptable level should be. These approaches, to date at least, have had little effect other than to provide a rationale for doing very little to reduce existing levels of pollution. This is in part because of the lack of good data in such areas as long-term health effects associated with chronic low-dosage exposures, but it is also because they rule out inclusion of values or mores as valid criteria for decision-making.

The next limitation comes from the fact that if human well-being is the only criteria for environmental decision-making, at a certain point it makes more sense to adapt to environmental degradation than to continue working to prevent it. In the closing stages of negotiation of the Montreal Protocol on CFC emissions, the Reagan administration presented an alternative to pollution reduction. Based on adaptation instead of environmental protection, the July, 1987, Personal Protection Plan (equipping all Americans with umbrellas, hats, and sunglasses) was a far cheaper and more quickly implemented protection against skin-cancer effects than reducing CFC production.[1] Although that particular proposal was quickly laughed out of the ballpark, the logic is irrefutable – if all we are concerned about is human health then it only makes sense to concentrate on that one problem and to leave the rest of the natural world to fend for itself.

Another example of willingness to consider adaptation instead of environmental protection is provided by two very similar news articles, one American and one Canadian. The cover story of *Maclean's* for September 5, 1988, was titled "Our Threatened Planet," while a few months later *Time* magazine (January 2, 1989) nominated earth as "Planet of the Year" and provided a cover story reviewing the various global problems such as atmospheric change, population growth, waste disposal, oil spills, and destruction of forests and arable land. Both magazines illustrated the emerging environmental ethic by including the now familiar but still emotionally powerful image of earth seen from space – the east coast of Africa, the Red Sea, Madagascar, the blue of the Indian Ocean contrasting with the swirling white of the clouds and the snows of Antarctica.

Both articles concluded, however, with discussions of the need to adapt to environmental change – as *Time* put it, "If the nations of the world take immediate action, the destruction of the global environment can be slowed substantially. But some irreversible damage is inevitable. . . . Sooner or later the earth's human inhabitants, so used to adapting the environment to suit their needs, will be forced to adapt themselves to the environment's demands."[2] Methods discussed ranged from Chinese efforts to plant a "Green Wall" to slow desertification, to U.S. Environmental Protection Agency (EPA) cost estimates of $111 billion for sea walls to protect coastal America from rising sea levels. The most bizarre was Biosphere II, a 5-million-cubic-foot capsule constructed in Arizona as an experiment in the creation of man-made environments, where eight men and women will spend two years sharing a self-contained environment with 3,800 other species, "from ladybugs and shrimp to fowl and deer."[3]

The articles conclude that adaptation may not, in the face of environmental change on a scale now posited and in the absence of meaningful action, ensure survival and that "simple prudence" suggests a reliance on prevention over adaptation. However, the message is clear – as the environment becomes a major political issue, mainstream thought does not automatically turn to ending pollution and preserving wilderness. It also, for very understandable reasons, turns to evaluating what environmental damage should be considered inevitable, and therefore adapted to, and what should be fought against.

Environmentalists who argue solely on the basis of anthropocentric concern are in danger of having their own arguments turned against them. Because it is often cheaper and because we are not particularly concerned for the well-being of any species other than our own, except insofar as it meets human needs, surely it makes more sense to adapt to the damage we have wrought than to pay the price of environmental protection. After all, we can always meet our human-centred needs for wilderness by creating museum replications of the natural world – such as the University of Wisconsin Greene Prairie project, a painstaking transplanting of the grasses and other vegetation found in the virgin North American West before the arrival of the settler's plough.[4]

Two other limitations to the human health argument should be mentioned. First, there is considerable evidence – provided by such things as the number of people who continue to smoke cigarettes or live in earthquake-prone cities like San Francisco – that people will accept a considerable degree of risk in preference to changing their behaviour. As discussed in Chapter 4, the health threats associated with environmental contamination pose a special case, because of such things as their involuntary nature and invisibility, leading to less willingness to accept risk from these causes than others. That may change, however, particularly when the price to be paid for ending pollution becomes more obvious. The day may come, if health is the only argument used, when Canadians are as willing to accept illness caused by pollution, as a trade-off for the benefits that living in a chemical society confers, as they are to accept traffic fatalities in exchange for the mobility provided by the automobile.

Finally, as suggested earlier, an argument for political action based on rational self-interest can never achieve the same force as one based on a moral absolute. Roderick Nash compares the modern environmental movement to the nineteenth-century crusade of the abolitionists against slavery. A sound argument can be made, based on cost-benefit analysis, to the effect that from the perspective of both the slave owner and the larger society, to say nothing of the slave, a wage labour system is preferable to slavery. Under a wage system workers are better motivated, do better work, and can be laid off when not needed. But slavery was not abolished in the British Empire or the United States because of such appeals to rational self-interest. It ended because preachers thundered from the pulpit that slavery was a sin in the eyes of God and that abolition of the institution was a moral imperative. In the same way we will only stop polluting when we are convinced it is morally wrong and that it must be stopped regardless of the price.

What, then, are the values that need to be inculcated or strengthened to reinforce the existing human-centred arguments against pollution? Chapter 2 provided a listing of values and assumptions of modern environmentalism. The concepts of a value (an ethical norm) and assumption (an unquestioned perception of reality) were grouped together because they tend to flow one into the other. Values change, it is suggested, largely in response to changes in perspective. The empirical knowledge that we live in a world of finite resources reinforces the environmentalist value of frugality and abhorrence of waste. The list provided there ranges from the spiritual harmony that unites humanity with the other elements of the universe all the way through to a conviction that small, decentralized institutions are preferable to large concentrations of power.

For purposes of this discussion, however, the essential values of environmentalism can be summarized as, first, the belief that the natural world has inherent value in and of itself, and second, the belief that we humans are part of that world and not separate from it.

The concept of inherent value has provided the basis for two schools of thought. The concept of "animal rights" is the conviction that other species, particularly mammals, are imbued with some degree of ethical rights. The concept of a "land ethic" is concerned not with the individual animal but with the ecosystem and embraces both sentient beings and other elements, such as rocks and stars. Today animal protectionists and environmentalists occupy two very separate political camps. These differences, however, are less important, in terms of the political strength of environmentalism, than is the fact that both base political action not on utilitarianism but in a moral concern for the non-human world. What is needed is not the abandonment of either approach, or the expenditure of time and energy in conflicts between these camps or others, such as shallow and deep ecology, but instead a strengthening of the element that unites them – the shared belief in the inherent value of nature.

In a similar manner, awareness of the connections between humanity and the natural world today takes many forms. Barry Lopez, who plays the same role today as did Charles G.D. Roberts at the turn of the century, describes in *Arctic Dreams: Imagination and Desire in a Northern Landscape* his experiences in the light and landscape of the Canadian Arctic:

> This is an old business, walking slowly over the land with an appreciation of its immediacy to the senses and in anticipation of what lies hidden in it. . . . I remember the press of light against my face . . . I had never known how benign sunlight could be. How forgiving. How run through with compassion in a land that bore so eloquently the evidence of centuries of winter.[5]

Lopez immersed in the northern light feels the same connection with the natural world as did Jeffers in "Oh, Lovely Rock," seeing through and into the fire-lit rock-face across the gorge of Ventana Creek. Petra Kelly of the German Greens, writing the forward to *Healing the Wounds: The Promise of Ecofeminism*, talks about the need to "see wholly, to see 'outsidely', to hear and transcend the cleavage between humanity and nature."[6] The ritual of a "Council of All Beings," practised by some deep ecologists, is performed by members holding or wearing the emblem of that part of the natural world they have chosen to represent – a plant, feather, rock, and so on – and then giving voice, on behalf of that entity, to the pain felt by the natural world as it is destroyed by human activity.[7] Ecofeminism and deep ecology share a belief in the need to practise environmental politics on the personal as well as the societal level, based in one's connections to nature.

Neil Evernden, author of the philosophy text *The Natural Alien: Humankind and Environment*, has provided an academic study of the way our values and perspectives have led to a perceived separation of the human and natural worlds. Like the adherents of deep ecology, Evernden argues that reform environmentalism is doomed to failure precisely because it accepts the majority perspective that nature exists in order to meet human needs: "The basic attitude toward the non-human has not even been challenged in the rush to embrace utilitarian conservation. By basing all arguments on enlightened self-interest the environmentalists have ensured their own failure whenever self-interest can be perceived as lying elsewhere."[8] Evernden documents how Western philosophy and science have led to the objectification of the natural world as something completely distinct and separate from the human, something to be exploited and used, but not to be identified with. His central argument is that this perspective of "environment" as something outside ourselves must change before real progress can be made in protecting it.

The task can be easily stated – we need to inculcate greater respect for the inherent value of the natural world, of which our own species is an integral part. Finding ways to accomplish this is more difficult. The only solution Evernden can offer, after a book-length explication of the problem, is that the environmentalist shed the "shell" of the label "environmentalist," presumably as a first step in moving away from objectification of "environment" as something outside the human.[9] As a prescription for how we might get from where we are to where we want to be, such a suggestion is of limited value.

Peter Timmerman, in an essay on environmental ethics, suggests that "any new relationship [between the human and the natural worlds] can be developed only in the context of a new mythology, or new 'cosmic story', which would marry the insights of contemporary science to the rapidly emerging global awareness." This would be done through "an unprecedented collaboration between artists, poets, writers, theologians, and scientists."[10] Certainly the scientist will play a role since, as is suggested in Chapter 4 above, the changes in scientific understanding of physical reality have stimulated changes in the values governing our relationship with the natural world. But science, of course, is a two-edged sword since it is the separation between the observer and the observed, the basis of empiricism which, as Evernden suggests, is a large part of the problem. Even as science moves in the other direction, for instance by suggesting that such separation is not possible, it also continues to give us knowledge that increases our ability to manipulate the natural environment in ever more powerful ways. With one hand science tells us we are born of star-fire and with the other it allows us to engage in speculation of how we might reshape the environments of Venus or Mars to make them more accessible for human exploitation.

More than the scientist or the philosopher, it is the artist who will allow us to redefine ourselves and our relationship to the natural world. The stories we tell and the things of beauty we create, in a never-ending process, both express and simultaneously redefine the values and perspectives of ours or any other society. This is done by addressing the conflict that is central to the artistic experience. The artists of each generation struggle anew to come to terms with the conflict – the love and hate – within each of us. As we move to a new environmental ethic, the expression and, in some cases, the resolution of inherent conflicts through the artistic voice will shape new values.

Establishment of a new environmental ethic will certainly engender conflict. Each of the five billion humans who presently inhabit the globe has a desire to exploit available resources in order to provide a life of dignity and security, and for many there is an equally strong desire to bring children into the world. This is precisely the same desire felt by each of the billions and billions of members of the other species with which we share the planet. It is difficult to consider that desire, in either its human or non-human form, as anything other than natural and just, but it repeatedly comes into conflict, because of the enormous powers humanity now wields, with an ethic of maintenance of the natural integrity of ecosystems. The "rights" that animal protectionists would accord to fur-bearing animals clash, claims the Fur Council of Canada, with the "right" of the consumer to decide what kind of coat to buy. The government of China wishes to provide each of its households with a freon-driven refrigerator, a laudable and humane objective which directly competes with our desire to prevent further depletion of the stratospheric ozone layer. And so on.

For us to come to terms with such conflicts they must be explored in the arts. In the final pages of *A Whale for the Killing*, Farley Mowat admits in a candid fashion his failure, during the days he struggled to save a stranded whale from the sport-killing of his Newfoundland neighbours, on two counts. He did not save the whale, nor did he save his relationship with people for whom he felt admiration and respect. He could not resolve the conflict between his regard for the natural world and the damage his actions did to Newfoundlanders' self-esteem. The Ojibway protagonist of M.T. Kelly's *A Dream Like Mine* is able to resolve the conflict he is caught in – driven to desperation by the pulp mill pollution that threatens the life of his people, he captures and tortures the plant manager – only by suicide.

Conflict is found not only between traditional values and those of the new environmental ethic that seeks to replace or redefine them but also between various of the values that ethic embodies. Greenpeace is devoting many millions of dollars to a campaign intended to make tuna-fishing less harmful to dolphins. Why does it not campaign to eliminate tuna-fishing on the grounds that it is harmful to tuna? Are dolphins, which are mammals, inherently of greater moral worth, and therefore deserving of Greenpeace's time and energy, than tuna, which are fish? Are fish imbued with greater inherent value than micro-organisms? In a world of finite resources where, of necessity, some degree of lifeboat ethics is practised, how do we decide, once we move away from the criterion of usefulness to humanity, which parts of the natural world we will protect and which we will abandon?

As the environmental ethic becomes more firmly established, these questions will become of more than philosophical interest. They may never be answered in any precise or final fashion, but they must be grappled with. Ultimately they will be addressed by courts and legislatures, but it is the work of the philosophers, the scientists, and above all the artists that will provide the moral context for their decisions.

Ideology

Developing an ideology of environmentalism is as important a task as strengthening and developing environmental values since it is needed to provide a coherent context and grounding for political action. Paehlke is correct when he argues that environmentalism is a nascent ideology with elements both in common and in conflict with each of the prevailing ideologies. What needs to be done is to make a coherent whole of environmentalism by both clarifying its relationship to the dominant ideologies and developing its own internally consistent analysis. The splitting of ideological hairs is the trademark of the powerless – political groupings of the extreme left or right who speak only to one another and have the luxury of endless ideological debate because they are so completely excluded from the central political dialogue. But environmentalism has done so little in this area that it is a long way from falling into that particular trap.

A political ideology contains three elements. The first is a set of values, unquestioned assumptions about what is good and what is bad. The second is an explanation of social or physical reality, a "world view" that has internal coherence and logic, based on accepted values. Since development of an ideology is a polemical and not a scientific exercise, the world view inevitably leads back to and strengthens the initial assumptions upon which it is based. Facts are chosen to fit the theory and not the other way around. The third element is a political strategy intended to implement the values and objectives of the ideology.

Certainly the most pervasive Western ideology of this millennium has been Christianity. It offered values, an understanding of the workings of the world, and a strategy for using that understanding to achieve those values. Marxism, in the twentieth century, proved to be a powerfully persuasive ideology with values, world view, and political strategy counter to the ideology of industrial capitalism. The ideologies of perhaps greatest political sway in Canada today are liberalism, socialism, and conservatism. Each has its initial value – for liberalism, individual liberty; for socialism, a greater equalizing of wealth and power; and for conservatism, maintenance of a hierarchical, but communal, society based on accepted disparities of wealth and power. Each offers explanations of reality that are based on and buttress its respective values. Thus socialists and conservatives take different sides in the "nature versus nurture" debate, because the two views of reality represented there – a malleable and improvable human nature, influenced primarily by social environment, versus a human nature largely conditioned by genetic heredity – have profound implications for the possibility and desirability of social change. Liberals, socialists, and conservatives follow a variety of strategies in their efforts to win a majority of their fellow Canadians over to their point of view.

An ideology of environmentalism must contain the same three elements. The first, environmental values, is discussed above and the third, political strategy, is the subject of the next section. What is discussed here is the environmentalist world view which is, above all, a recognition of the finite nature of the planet's resources – the limits to growth – and the implications that has for the prevailing conviction that continual economic expansion is both desirable and possible.

The Canadian environmental movement has done little to articulate either a general or specifically Canadian environmental ideology. Such an effort is overdue. Undertaking the task would bring about a number of benefits. It would inevitably draw attention away from the nuts and bolts of particular environmental battles, to the underlying issues that must be resolved before significant progress can be made. It would force the Canadian environmental movement to address the major criticisms which, as it becomes more powerful, will increasingly be directed against it – for instance, the charge that it knows nothing of economic realities and therefore can never be allowed to get its hands anywhere near the levers of true power. Development of an explicit ideology would allow the environmental movement, in conjunction with others, to think its way through not only the criticisms but also the very real issues and problems that confront environmentalism. How *do we*, within the constraints of political reality, both stop pollution of a river and treat a one-industry town with the fairness and social justice it deserves? How *do we* both protect the global environment and at the same time alleviate the all too real suffering and anguish that are the lot of the majority of our fellow citizens on the globe? In summary, what can environmentalism suggest as a means of alleviating the pain of the dislocations and costs that would follow from implementation of its central thesis – that economic expansion must be slowed or stopped?

Finally, development of an ideology would provide the vehicle for the further essential task of identifying the links and common ground that environmentalism shares with other sectors, movements, and interests. Without that common ground and the tactical battle alliances which are then forged upon it, environmentalism can never expand its political power-base sufficiently to achieve meaningful change.

As discussed earlier, those concerned with environmental protection before the 1960s saw their concerns as apolitical and largely accepted the prevailing ideology of capitalism, suggesting only that, from enlightened self-interest, governments pay more attention to such things as clean drinking water, safe sewage disposal, and resource conservation. The 1960s saw environmentalism expand, for the first time, to include a questioning of prevailing assumptions concerning consumerism and government and corporate decision-making, for example, but the focus remained limited to the specifics of resource depletion or pollution. Environmentalists during that decade did not develop either a comprehensive critique or an alternative social vision.

The "conserver society" concept was a step in that direction but such a work as the 1978 *Canada as a Conserver Society* report, excellent as it is, offers only a series of institutional, regulatory, and fiscal measures which, the report implies, could be grafted relatively easily on to the existing economic and political structure. Implicit in the report is the assumption that there is no need even to examine, let alone alter, the basic distribution of wealth and power within Canadian society.

Following very much in that vein is the 1987 Brundtland Commission report, the conclusions and recommendations of which, given their far-reaching nature, are necessarily based on a fundamentally radical critique of both socialist and capitalist economies. But that critique remains implicit and is never brought to the fore. Supporters of Brundtland might argue that the critique has to remain implicit to allow the report to gain the widespread acceptance it has. Opponents might argue that this acceptance is in fact counter-productive and that the proclaimed need for extensive study and discussion of "sustainable development" has become, in Canada at least, another excuse for inaction.

Both the "conserver society" and "sustainable development" are direct descendants of the utilitarian school of resource conservation that became prominent in the time of Teddy Roosevelt and Sir Wilfrid Laurier. As such, they offer no ideological guidance.

Environmentalism first began to develop an explicit ideology, offering a real alternative to the established ideologies, with the development of party platforms by the European green parties. Environmentalism for the Greens was inevitably linked by the logic of their social analysis to such issues as feminism, peace, consumerism, and the distribution of wealth and power. The value of the Green platforms was not the depth or sophistication of their analysis so much as the fact that these connections for the first time were made explicit and advanced for discussion in the arena of electoral politics. In addition, a number of writers, primarily European, have engaged in a dialogue surrounding the question of what the new environmentalism means for traditional left political analysis.[11]

In America the leading effort to develop an environmental ideology has been the work of Murray Bookchin, who has developed the concept of "social ecology" which has been described in these terms:

> Social ecology, developed primarily in New England and New York by Murray Bookchin and his colleagues at the Institute for Social Ecology, emphasizes the embeddedness of human consciousness in nature, a radical ecological critique of hierarchy and domination in society, and the historical unity of ecological and social concerns. . . . Social ecology prefigured many of these developments, [the rise of green parties] its proponents having argued since the mid-1960's that the view of nature as a force to be dominated and controlled was a

result of the rise of social hierarchies, especially in warrior societies. Domination, argues Murray Bookchin, is not intrinsic in nature; neither has it ever been an appropriate response to the needs of human survival. Rather, the patterns of the natural world call upon us to embrace the values of co-operation, complementarity and unity-in-diversity, both in our relations with the rest of nature and within the human community.[12]

Building on these foundations, an ideology of environmentalism that addresses the implications of limiting growth must wrestle with two issues – population growth and economic growth, the latter defined as ever-increasing productivity and ensuing resource consumption. The central issue posed by exponential population increase is the extent to which it alone should be seen as the root cause of all environmental evils and the means by which the problem can be addressed without an unacceptable infringement of individual liberties. The issue has received considerable attention since the Second World War and is not the subject of further discussion here, although this is not meant to suggest it is not an essential component of any ideology of environmentalism – in particular it should be noted that the emerging view that birth-rates can best be lowered through the greater empowerment of women provides yet another avenue for alliances between feminism and environmentalism.

The environmentalist maintains that perhaps in Canada, and most certainly on a global basis, consumption of natural resources, defined to include raw materials, arable land, and (marrying pollution and conservation concerns) clean air and water, has come close to or has already exceeded the carrying capacity of the ecosystem. The only possible answer, it is argued, is to reduce consumption both by reducing per capita consumption and by reducing the total population the planet must support.

The Brundtland panacea of "sustainable development," on the other hand, suggests that we must *increase* resource consumption because there is no other way to address the very real problem of Third World poverty, but that we must become more efficient and less wasteful in order that this accelerated rate of consumption can be maintained indefinitely. The difficulties of the Brundtland position become apparent simply by so stating it. Not surprisingly, a large portion of the environmental community rejects the Brundtland thesis. One analysis points to the fact that Brundtland calls for a fivefold increase in energy and a five to tenfold increase in industrial activity in the developing world to allow those nations to achieve the living standards of the developed nations. Increased efficiency would allow the developed nations to maintain present living standards with no increase or even some decrease in energy and resource consumption but the result is still a net increase in consumption. "The Brundtland argument does add up to expecting the global environment to support a great deal *more* wealth at a time when it seems evident that we are already overstraining our planet's capacity to withstand human impositions. Environmentalists may reasonably respond that the Commission's solution fails to meet its own test. Such growth cannot be sustained. What is needed instead is action to *reduce* human impacts on the biosphere."[13] Furthermore, the Brundtland argument assumes that human happiness is dependent on North American standards of consumerism, an assumption that deserves to be challenged.

The argument for reduced consumption was stated by David Suzuki in his *Toronto Star* column of November 11, 1989, the thesis of which is presented by the title "Time to cut back on everything so we have a chance of survival: There are too many people demanding too much of our planet." As well as recommending increased aid and birth control information for the developing world, Suzuki recommended that Canada "Set an example by deliberately and speedily cutting back on our unnecessary and excessive consumption and pollution because if we don't, every poor nation will legitimately aim to reach the same levels of affluence."[14] Although he did not say so, presumably Suzuki would recommend that pollution be reduced by the relatively straightforward means of environmental regulation. What would have been most useful, however, would have been suggestions for precisely how Canada should go about "speedily cutting back" on consumption.

Four interconnected elements must be considered together in any attempt to address Dr. Suzuki's recommendation:

• production of goods and services, which is responsible for resource consumption and pollution;
• consumer demand, which decides the level of that production;
• paid labour, since the number of jobs available depends on a combination of production levels and efficiency of production;
• distribution of wealth, which lies at the heart of any discussion of employment.

At present Canada, like most other industrialized countries, is locked into a cycle of ever-increasing economic expansion, and therefore environmental degradation, by these four elements. Political realities have effectively ruled out any change in the existing distribution of wealth from rich to poor. (In fact, over the last decade distribution has begun to change in the other direction – the rich are slightly better off, relative to the rest of society, than they were ten years ago.) This means that governments can only improve the position of those on the lower rungs of the economic ladder by absolute increases in wealth, shared according to the existing distribution pattern. The poor will get more only if *everybody* gets more. This can only be achieved through an expanding economy.

Furthermore, we continue to rely on paid labour as the primary means of sharing the wealth we produce. We provide a minimal level of financial assistance to those who do not work, but it is given grudgingly, with no acceptance of the principle that those who receive it are entitled to it and indeed might be said to be performing a socially useful service by fractionally lessening competition for that scarce commodity: jobs. We are willing to pay farmers to refrain from producing a particular crop but we are not willing to pay people to refrain from entering the job market. Full employment is our goal.

The only way we can achieve an expanding economy and full employment is through the ever-increasing consumption of resources, which in turn requires continually increasing consumer demand, in the absence of population growth, for more and more goods and services. *Canada as a Conserver Society* illustrates how governments have deliberately adopted policies of stimulating demand to achieve full employment.

> ... we find ourselves, in the so-called *consumer* society with what has been termed the *institutionalization of high demand*. ... Many features of our consumer society have grown from solutions sought to the great depression of the thirties. The solution to depression and unemployment was discovered in the stimulation and maintenance of demand.[15]

The paper went on to discuss post-war policies to encourage investment in capital goods and government spending in such areas as defence to stimulate economic growth. "The conditions for maintaining the growth of demand involved a generally rising level of incomes and an inflationary component." The other element of increasing demand is increased borrowing, both by governments and consumers. All of this has led, the report argued, to acceptance of a norm in which standards of living are expected to rise continually. "It is easy to see how people have come to aspire to first one automobile, then two, and perhaps three, along with continually growing incomes that will allow more of everything else too."[16]

The environmentalist response to the problem of resource consumption stimulated by consumer demand is to look for ways to reduce that demand. There are three ways of doing this:

- strengthening the values of simplicity and frugality and moving away from the pursuit of happiness primarily through greater and greater accumulation of consumer goods;
- increasing the efficiency and durability of goods so they consume less energy during their operating life and need to be replaced less often;
- increasing the price of environmentally damaging goods in order to reduce demand.

As discussed, an ideology of environmentalism must rest on a firm foundation of values. The next line of attack, efficiency and durability, is attractive since it seems to let us have our cake (increased consumption) and eat it too (reduced environmental impact). The area in which this has been most successful is energy consumption: reduced demand during the latter part of the 1970s and early 1980s, resulting from increased energy efficiency prompted by the OPEC oil price increases of 1973, allowed reduced consumption without affecting economic growth. The same argument can be applied to pollution and waste – increased efficiency of manufacturing and other operations can significantly reduce both, which leads to the Brundtland prescription.

But increased efficiency can solve only part of the problem. The real answer, the environmentalist argues, is to reduce demand by incorporating the full environmental costs of production into goods and services, by taxation, regulation, or both. A possible starting point for such a policy is pollution regulation and waste disposal pricing. If we no longer allow pollutants to be discharged to the environment but instead impose regulations requiring that they be contained, treated, and disposed of as hazardous waste (an expensive process) we both provide an incentive not to produce them in the first place and increase the price of the manufactured product. By then imposing a hefty surcharge on solid and hazardous waste disposal we do even more to achieve our goal of limiting demand.

But this immediately raises issues of equity and distribution of wealth. It is not fair to use price to reduce demand, without some compensating measures, because the poor will be deprived of goods and services in a way that the rich will not. For that reason proposals for surtaxes on gasoline or large cars to reduce demand often include some form of credits or transfer payments for the less well off.

Reduced demand and consumption also lead us back to employment, the third element in the equation. If consumption is reduced, it seems reasonable to expect that employment will also be reduced. The argument is made that a non-polluting, conserver society would be more labour-intensive. But even if this is the case, jobs will be lost in some areas and created in others, which will result in unemployment for those unable to make the adjustment.

Paid labour continues to be considered the only legitimate source of income for the mass of society. Significant redistribution of existing wealth is ruled out and full employment is our unquestioned, overriding social and economic goal. Our greatest fear is depression or recession. Thus environmentalism runs up against a major political challenge and as we have seen, time and time again a particular political struggle is lost because the issue is framed in either/or terms – jobs versus environment. This despite the fact that over the past twenty years almost no jobs have been lost because of environmental regulation.[17]

If the problems of consumption and pollution are to be addressed and if we accept the notion that some jobs will have to be lost either on a net basis or in a particular sector, there are two possible responses. The first is simply to increase the financial support given to the unemployed – in direct payments, through unemployment insurance or social assistance programs, or by indirect assistance in the form of retraining programs and other means. This is the easiest and politically most attractive option because it does not call into question the goal of full employment.

The second answer is to re-examine the role of paid labour in our society. Perhaps we should move away from the goal of full employment. Perhaps we should pay people *not* to work. Or pay them for tasks that are socially useful but at present receive little or no compensation. The rationale for doing so is that, first, full employment is a goal we are unable to achieve in any event. Only in some parts of the country are we able to approach "full employment," defined as being in the neighbourhood of 3 to 5 per cent unemployment. Secondly, pursuit of this impossible goal is what has kept us in the position of accepting a large measure of environmental damage.

For the most part, environmentalists in Canada have not undertaken any such examination, accepting the goal of full employment and arguing that environmental protection will create, not reduce, the total number of jobs. This was the general thrust of the Ontario Environmental Network Conference on Jobs and the Economy, of November, 1986. The OEN, in its background paper for the conference, did, however, raise the possibility that a re-examination of the role of work might be forced upon us by mechanization. The paper quoted reports predicting that up to half the labour force might be unemployed due to advancing technology: "The phenomenon of widespread technological unemployment is likely to open up the entire question of the nature and purposes of work – subjects to which both trade unionists and environmentalists can make a positive contribution."[18] Some ten years earlier, *Canada as a Conserver Society* had raised the issue in the context of environmental policy:

There is a growing realization that many people in the production processes are becoming redundant. What should be the response of the system? Conventional wisdom would say that we must create more investment to create more jobs. But is this the best way to deal with the situation? With capitalization and automation, we already have the capacity to provide more than our basic goods and services with the present workers. There is nothing in economic theory that says all people must be employed for wages, and certainly, as the domestic sector of our economy demonstrates, it is not necessary to be a direct participant in the wage-and-market sector to be a useful and productive member of society.[19]

Robert Paehlke argues along similar lines:

[we] need to introduce into our language a clear distinction between *work* and *wage labour*. *Work* can be defined as productive activities one might do even if they did not provide income. . . . Bearing in mind the distinction between work and wage labour, one wonders at a society, polity and economy whose central goal is the creation of jobs. . . . The need for a gradual but significant separation of income and wage labour seems inescapable.[20]

Paehlke goes on to suggest that we begin this process by doing more to reduce the number of hours each of us works, on average, per week. But does this mean our incomes would be reduced by the same proportion? He argues they need not because it would be possible to finance reduced work time through increased productivity – we would produce the same amount of materials or services in less time and receive the same pay. "Work time reductions would be paid for by applying the savings associated with productivity improvements to something other than higher wages and profits."[21]

There are two problems with this argument. The first is that increased productivity, and therefore resource consumption and pollution, is exactly the problem we are trying to solve. The second is that, in any case, productivity increases alone will not lead us far enough in our search to reduce reliance on wage labour, or jobs, as the central element of our society.

If we are to make the transition from wage labour to work, as defined by Paehlke, we must not only reduce work hours but also pay more for "productive activities" – writing poems, raising children, absorbing the beauty of the evening sky – which now receive only minimal compensation. That leads directly to the fourth element in the equation, distribution of wealth, which has to be addressed as an integral part of an environmental ideology.

These connected issues – the role of work and the distribution of wealth – will inevitably lie at the centre of an environmental ideology. Doing so in an explicit and direct manner would provide environmentalism with a number of advantages, most notably placing the movement squarely in the progressive camp and thus allowing it to establish the political alliances it must make. Such an analysis would provide benefit to the left as well as to environmentalism. Since the rise of the new conservatism in the 1970s, those who argue for a redistribution of wealth have been on the defensive. But the environmental analysis, set forth most clearly in terms of global action and the need for a new transfer of wealth from North to South as part of global environmental protection, provides an entirely new and compelling rationale for their argument. This is particularly so because it can be framed in the language of Brundtland and sustainable development to which, whatever their real intent might be, government and corporate leaders have fully subscribed.

The logic of environmentalism departs from traditional socialist analysis insofar as it calls into question, in a way socialism never has, the role of wage labour. However, it also suggests that environmental protection can only be achieved if it is accompanied by a redistribution of wealth, thus leading directly back to the traditional, central concern of socialism. Development of an ideology will not only strengthen alliances with other social movements but will also place environmentalism clearly in the camp of a thus revitalized and resurgent left-wing movement fighting for greater equity and fairness *both* among humans and between humanity and the natural world.

Strategy

A clear distinction must be made between long-term objectives, which are the stuff of strategic planning, and the choice of day-to-day tactics in a particular political battle – whether to litigate as well as lobby, the search for short-term allies, the means of gaining media exposure, and so on. Although fascinating, the latter is not the subject of discussion here.

While working to put in place values and an ideological analysis, the environmental lobby is also presented with two basic strategic options – to work for pollution reduction by means of end-of-pipe standards or by changes in decision-making procedures. An end-of-pipe strategy means imposing and enforcing pollution loading-reduction standards at the point of pollution discharge, be it a smokestack, sewer discharge pipe, the clay liner of a landfill, or the exhaust pipe of a motor vehicle, with no attempt made to dictate the way the polluter will meet those standards. In the case of products, the analogy is a simple ban on the use of substances in their manufacture that will impose environmental damage either during the use of the product or when it is disposed of as a waste.

Changing the process means reaching up the corporate or governmental decision-making process, by requiring increased public access through such things as environmental assessment hearings or increased access to information, changing external pricing factors or introducing other variables, such as giving the environment minister or corporate environmental affairs officer more powers, in the hope that such changes will lead to better decisions.

This decision on strategy for achieving desired change is faced in all sectors of society by all of the players, regardless of the issue. Western Canada feels it is not getting a fair shake from Confederation and must then decide whether to press directly for substantive objectives, be they transportation rates, oil tax revenues, or whatever, or to reach back up the decision-making process, for instance by pressing for an elected, regionally representative Senate. The latter is an indirect, but possibly more effective strategy. The fights over substance must be waged over and over again, but presumably the fight over decision-making process, if it is won, must be fought only once.

In practice those pressing for change usually follow both strategies – western Canada continues to press for both an elected Senate *and* increased agricultural subsidies. Although not the product of any conscious strategy, this has been the approach followed by those fighting for environmental protection in Canada and other countries over the past two decades. While pressing for stronger standards and better enforcement, the environmental movement has always paid attention to process changes, such as increased "environmental rights."

Continuing to work on both fronts, however, may not be the best possible strategy for environmentalists in the critical years ahead. For one thing, pursuing two objectives simultaneously means that much less time and energy can be devoted to either. During the two decades since initial passage of environmental legislation and creation of ministries of the environment, the pursuance of both process and substantive objectives has not been successful. The environmental lobby has been able neither to achieve decision-making procedures that ensure environmental protection, nor, other than in a few instances, to secure the passage and enforcement of standards that reduce annual pollution loadings. While this lack of political success has resulted in part from failure to develop values and ideology fully, it must also be attributed to a division of scarce resources between two different strategies.

As we have seen, two major process battles were fought during the 1970s and 1980s: environmental assessment and adoption of some form of an environmental bill of rights. Legislation requiring environmental assessment has now been adopted by most jurisdictions, but the great majority of the decisions on the amount of pollution allowed to enter the environment are still made through licensing approvals, which do not require or even allow public involvement. The concept of an environmental bill of rights, presumably because of fears for the implications it might have in other areas of judicial and government proceedings, has not come anywhere close to adoption by any government.

During the 1980s, attention to process issues was focused as much as anything on enforcement, and in that area some progress has been made. The concept of separating abatement and enforcement functions, pioneered by Ontario in 1985, increased spending on enforcement, and the development by Environment Canada of an explicit compliance and enforcement policy to accompany the Canadian Environmental Protection Act were all steps in the right direction. Even here, however, there is much more to be done. On other process issues, such as access to the standard-setting and licensing functions, government spending on environment, and relative power given to environment ministers at the cabinet table, progress has been virtually nil.

This failure suggests two things. First, the environmental lobby should concentrate on using law to reduce pollution at the point it enters the environment. Second, while not completely ignoring process change, objectives of this strategy should be limited and clearly focused. Finally, environmentalists must be very aware of the fact that a strategy of process change now presents the very real danger of playing directly into the hand of those interests who are resistant to environmental change and who see in the rhetoric of sustainable development a perfect opportunity to engage in yet more discussion, study, and delay.

Sustainable Development

The Brundtland Commission identified a major institutional problem when it pointed to the fact that in almost all nations "Those [government agencies] responsible for managing natural resources and protecting the environment are institutionally separated from those responsible for managing the economy. . . . The mandates of ministries of industry include production targets, while the accompanying pollution is left to ministries of environment."[22]

As noted in Part II, the Canadian Task Force on Environment and Economy took "the integration of environment and economy" as its major objective. Since 1987 governments have looked at decision-making processes and ways they can be changed to better integrate environmental and economic decision-making. This is illustrated in the discussion document released by the federal government in the spring of 1990, after Lucien Bouchard's *Green Plan* failed to gain cabinet approval. The document echoes Brundtland by stating that "Environmental considerations must be formally recognized as essential decision-making criteria within government and private sector organizations." The document then enumerates the steps taken toward this end:

> The Government of Canada has introduced a number of reforms in its policy-making process to achieve a better integration of environmental and economic considerations. For example, it recently created a new Cabinet Committee on the Environment and it established a National Round Table on the Environment and the Economy.
>
> The Government will table this spring legislation to strengthen application of the federal Environmental Assessment and Review

Process (EARP). In accordance with this new law, the Government will not approve, without a rigorous environmental assessment, initiatives that could have an impact on the environment.[23]

The round tables themselves are concentrating on process changes. The National Round Table, for instance, has established sub-committees in such areas as foreign policy, education, and decision-making processes in the private and public sectors. These sub-committees will search for changes in policies and procedures that can lead toward sustainable development.[24] The Ontario Round Table, in July, 1990, enunciated six principles, including "full cost accounting," "informed decision-making," and "quality of development over quantity." These principles are intended to guide the work of sectoral task forces that will look for changes in procedures and practices in such areas as transportation, mining, energy, and agriculture.

A number of the provincial round tables are developing "sustainable development strategies," which presumably are not dissimilar to the "conservation strategies" that all of the provinces have been developing since 1980 under the aegis of the UNEP World Conservation Strategy. To date, only P.E.I. and the Yukon have completed this task.[25] If after ten years nine of the provinces have not yet even developed a statement of objectives and principles, with no legislative teeth or administrative means for implementation, one has to wonder about the value of a process change strategy.

End-of-the-Pipe Strategy

By far the most promising avenue for success lies in a strategy of fighting for loading-reduction standards imposed on specific polluting sources, coupled with vastly strengthened enforcement mechanisms. Such a strategy is attractive because it does not represent a radical departure from existing government practice and commitments. Governments have accepted the principle of percentage reductions, such as the 50 per cent acid rain reduction, the 100 per cent CFC reduction, and the 25 and 50 per cent solid waste reduction objectives. Governments do not have to be convinced to consider a new approach. Furthermore, this strategy has at least one major domestic success under its belt, the Canadian acid rain program, and one international, the CFC phase-out initiated by the Montreal Protocol. These can be pointed to as models for future action.

An end-of-the-pipe strategy, unlike process change, inherently leads to the establishment of clear, quantifiable objectives, which in turn become rallying cries and means of mobilizing action. Political support for pollution reduction already exists and more can be mustered. The same cannot be said for less acceptable measures, such as a "carbon tax," or less easily understood measures to change public and private decision-making procedures. Such clear objectives allow measurement of progress toward their achievement, thus making possible the essential watchdog role of the environmental movement of holding governments accountable for their promises.

Many disagree with such an approach. Barry Commoner makes a distinction between pollution "control," defined as end-of-the-pipe standards that eliminate some but not all pollution discharged to the environment, and pollution "prevention," which is a complete ban on the manufacture, use, or sale of a particular substance. Reviewing the success of the "control" system of pollution regulation in the United States since 1975, Commoner concludes that reduction in air pollution emissions has been "at best modest," that water pollution regulation has "failed to improve water quality in most rivers," and that, taken as a whole, the "effort to restore the quality of the environment has failed."[26] What does he suggest?

Commoner points to the success in those cases in which a "prevention" strategy, a ban on a substance, has been used – the elimination of lead from most gasoline, the ban on DDT, the elimination of strontium 90 from milk by the above-ground nuclear test ban. But he does not stop there. Commoner goes on to argue that environmental lobbying must focus on the underlying issues, such as "the present reliance on nonrenewable energy sources . . . the present chemically based system of agriculture . . . heavy dependence on cars and trucks."[27] Ultimately, he argues, the environment cannot be protected until the economic decision-making powers of private-sector corporations are significantly changed: "What is called for is the extension of democracy into the arena in which production decisions are made. In the United States, this means the corporate board room. . . ."[28]

Commoner's focus on underlying issues is similar to the "conservation strategy" approach, set forth in the 1978 Science Council report, the World Conservation Strategy effort, and more recently in the sectoral studies initiated by the provincial and national Round Tables on Environment and Economy. Instead of a piecemeal, fragmented approach that concentrates on particular polluting sources or substances, Commoner and many others believe we have to step back, look at how decision-making in such areas as transportation, energy, and urban planning is causing environmental degradation, and then concentrate on improving the methods or procedures by which those decisions are made.

This appears to be both a logical and more sophisticated approach. Unfortunately, it simply cannot be done. Commoner is whistling in the wind when he calls for "extension of democracy into . . . the corporate boardroom." "Democracy" necessarily means representative democracy, which means government heavily influencing or controlling private-sector decision-making. It will never happen in the U.S. or Canada, even if Jesse Jackson becomes President or Audrey McLaughlin becomes Prime Minister. Nor yet should it. If the unfolding of recent events in the European

Communist bloc nations has demonstrated anything it is the impossibility of managing an economy through central planning. National economies are simply not capable of functioning on the basis of administrative decision-making alone, with no reference to market forces.

The sectoral approaches of conservation or sustainable development strategies, however, suggest nothing more than centralized planning. The only difference is that in the Soviet bloc nations the central planners had the power to implement their plans by administrative fiat. The Science Council and round tables can only recommend their plans. If such an approach failed in an authoritarian police state it is difficult to see how it can work in a democracy. Experience has shown that we must rely on the marketplace, albeit a regulated one, allowing public and private agencies to establish whatever decision-making procedures they feel are best suited to achieve their ends as they function within a context of unequivocal and strictly enforced legal requirements to reduce or eliminate pollution.

Commoner is right when he says that pollution regulation has not yet achieved its objectives, but he is wrong when he concludes that the system should for that reason be abandoned. As discussed at some length above, the system has not yet worked for two very simple reasons – the standards set have been too lenient and, once set, they have not been enforced.

The other argument made against an end-of-the-pipe strategy is that it simply changes the way pollution enters the environment, without reducing quantities. What is the sense, it is argued, in capturing air pollutants before they go out the stack, or liquid wastes before they are discharged into the sewer, containing them and trucking them to a landfill from whence they leach out and contaminate groundwater? Again, the answer is not to abandon the existing system but instead to use it more fully. The answer to the problem is to impose and actually enforce stricter standards at the receiving landfill. This in turn will motivate the polluter to change operating procedures so as to generate less of such pollutants in the first place.

This does not mean, however, that changes in process should be completely ignored. In particular there is need for increased public access to decision-making and increased government accountability to the public.

The essence of environmental regulation, as we have seen, has always been closed-door negotiations in which industry held the balance of power. Opening the doors and providing increased public access takes two forms – access to information and the right to participate in decision-making procedures.

Access to government information primarily takes the form of increased access to the large number of studies and reports used as the basis for government decision-making but never made public. An example is the Sinclair report on federal regulation of the pulp and paper industry, which was only published by Environment Canada after it had been leaked to the

Vancouver Sun. Presumably, many other similar studies have been under-taken by the federal and provincial governments but never made public. While such works are in the initial drafting stages there may be some justification for restricting public access, but once completed and as they are being used in the policy development process, they should be public.

Access to information held by business corporations raises the difficult issue of the legitimate right of a business to keep secret information about its operations that might benefit its competitors. This claim of confidenti-ality for "proprietary information" is regularly advanced by industry. The difficulty lies in determining when the claim is valid and when it is being used to conceal information the public needs if it is to monitor progress toward environmental improvement. The concept of "community right to know" in the United States has been incorporated into legislation, adopted as an amendment to the Resources Conservation and Recovery Act in 1986. U.S. industries are now required to provide basic information on the types and quantities of pollution emitted to the environment each year. In Can-ada, similar steps have been taken only in the area of occupational health. Pressure for community-right-to-know legislation is likely to come from the environmental movement as the political benefits it has provided in the United States become apparent.

Public access in the form of participation in the decision-making process can come about in two ways. The first is through what is known as "consul-tation," a process whereby government seeks the views of all parties, not just the regulated industry, prior to introducing new policies or regulatory requirements. The most traditional form of consultation is the publication of a government White Paper, which sets out a proposed course of action and invites public comment. In recent years, consultation has become more complex, particularly in the environmental area. Instead of simply inviting public comment, full consultation involves a form of bargaining or negoti-ation that may go on over a period of weeks or months and may conclude with a very specific set of agreed-upon actions that government will take. The best example of the successful application of such a process is the development, in 1986 and 1987, of amendments to the Environmental Contaminants Act by a committee representing federal and provincial gov-ernments, the chemical industry, and environmental public-interest organi-zations. Such a process can only work, however, when the scope of the discussion is very narrow, such as amendments to one piece of legislation, the general thrust of which has already been set forth by government, and when the players, or "stakeholders," can be clearly identified.

The second type of participation is provided when the public or public-interest organizations are provided an opportunity to litigate a particular aspect of environmental decision-making before the courts or administra-tive tribunals. Although common in the U.S., court actions are rare in

Canada. Administrative litigation, on the other hand, is becoming more common as environmental assessment procedures are more widely applied. The success of such a process, as discussed earlier, depends on the extent to which it can be precisely defined and the availability of at least some funding for the citizen intervenors. Thus the environmental movement is pressing for both increased access to the courts, through the more liberal standing provisions set forth in environmental bills of rights, and increased intervenor funding.

Accountability is obtained through requirements for regular reporting. The regulated industry reports to the environment department on its success or failure in meeting environmental requirements; government, in turn, reports to the public on its progress in meeting the stated objectives of its environmental policies. Neither industry nor government reporting was common when the regulatory system was being put in place during the 1960s and 1970s, but it has become more so since. The best example is the requirement for annual reporting on progress that was agreed to by Canada and the United States during renegotiation of the Great Lakes Water Quality Agreement in 1987.

A number of environmental organizations have recommended that such reporting be augmented not only by increased government reporting but also by creation of an independent agency to scrutinize government action and issue annual public reports. The closest analogy is the annual reporting of the Auditor-General on government fiscal performance. In the same fashion, an environmental auditor could report on progress in meeting environmental goals.

The environmental movement in Canada should pursue a strategy of progressively more stringent waste and pollution reduction requirements, ultimately leading to complete elimination of harmful pollution discharges, set in law and rigorously enforced. Such a strategy should include procedural changes that lead to increased access and accountability but must ignore the siren calls to spend the next decade participating in the development of "sustainable development strategies."

Canada and the Global Environment

The efforts to give environmentalism in Canada the political strength it needs cannot be taken in isolation. Because Canada is a part of the global environment and is thereby threatened by pollution and resource consumption that originates outside our borders, and because action that imposes a significantly higher price in Canada than is borne in other countries will be politically impossible over the long term, we must work simultaneously for the protection of both our global and domestic environments. This section reviews the major difficulties to be faced in working toward international environmental protection in a world of sovereign states that is now experiencing change on a scale not seen since the end of World War Two. Various challenges and opportunities could exist if Canada were to adopt a foreign policy that replaced collective security intended to guard against Soviet aggression with global efforts to fight the threat of environmental degradation.

The Changing International Order

Two major factors, discussed in Chapter 3, make international environmental protection a completely different challenge from action within one country. The first is the absence of any international authority with powers greater than those of the nation-state. The institutions of international law and international agreements are only as strong as the desire, based on enlightened self-interest, of the nations of the world to make them work. The flagrant breach of international law that occurred in 1984 when the United States mined harbours in Nicaragua demonstrates what slender reeds we have to rely on. The second factor is the impossibility of asking the underdeveloped nations to accept the price of protecting their own or the global environment in a way that none of the northern nations did during their industrialization over the past century. Giving them the assistance they need will require the voluntary transfer of wealth from one set of nations to another that is quite literally unprecedented in the history of the world.

Since the Stockholm Conference of 1972, at least some progress has been made. Scientific understanding of the global environment has progressed rapidly and mechanisms for sharing that information have been strengthened. International lobby organizations with sufficient power to influence international events have been established. The UNEP continues to function, albeit with a scarcely adequate total budget of $30 million a year, and such initiatives as the World Conservation Strategy and the Brundtland Commission have done an excellent job of delineating the global challenge. International agreements, most notably the Montreal Protocol, have been confirmed and are being implemented and others, such as a global convention on atmospheric change, are in the works. The UN Conference on Environment and Development, to be held in Brazil in June of 1992, may well be as significant an event as the Stockholm Conference twenty years earlier.

There is no escaping the fact, however, that these efforts seem almost insignificant in the face of the problems of desertification, global atmospheric change, and cumulative global production of toxic wastes. The global financial resources devoted to meeting such challenges, furthermore, are a minuscule fraction of that which goes to the annual manufacture of armaments. The annual UNEP budget, for instance, would cover only a few minutes worth of expenditure in the Persian Gulf war.

The task of strengthening our collective ability to protect the global environment is made more challenging by the rapidly changing and, therefore, unpredictable nature of the international order. The relative stability of the post-war world, with the U.S., the primary economic and military power, facing with its allies the Soviet bloc, has disappeared. Predominant economic power has shifted from the U.S. to Europe and Japan and eastern Asia. Whether a comparable movement of military dominance will follow remains to be seen – the notion of the two vanquished nations of the Second World War, Japan and a unified Germany, as having *both* economic and military dominance may set off too many alarm bells, within their own countries as much as others, for that to be allowed to happen.

That we live in a new world, however, cannot be denied. Regional groupings of states, of which the most developed manifestation is the European Economic Community, are becoming more significant. At the same time, pressures for decentralization within nations, a phenomenon with which Canada has always been familiar, seem to be stronger than ever. It seems very possible that during the next few decades we will come to live in a world made up of many more nations than now exist, all of which will be tied by closer bonds – various categories of "sovereignty-association" – than those at present.

It may be that in such a new context Canada can pursue both its traditional foreign policy objectives and the new challenges that lie ahead by adopting a foreign policy that has as its central objective the protection of the global environment.

A Foreign Policy for the Environment

From the time of the first European settlement, Canadian foreign policy has taken as its primary objective the defence of the country against military invasion. Until late in the nineteenth century the primary military threat was deemed to come from the United States. In this century the threat has been first Germany and then, since 1945, the Soviet Union. In 1987 the Canadian government issued a White Paper on Defence, setting out plans for spending on the armed forces over the coming decades on the assumption that action in concert with Canada's NATO allies to repel Soviet aggression would continue to be the primary foreign policy objective for some time to come. The White Paper, of course, was quickly overtaken by events, and now both NATO and the Warsaw alliance are in the process of transforming themselves from military to political organizations. The Brundtland report also appeared in 1987. The discrepancy between those two documents – the White Paper, positing a global threat from

Communist subversion and aggression, and the Brundtland report, arguing that the globe was threatened by the manufacture of arms, not their use, and that the overriding threat was the twinned dangers of environmental degradation and poverty – prompted the Canadian Institute for International Peace and Security to undertake a review of threats to Canadian security and the manner in which they can best be countered.

The changed perception of what constitutes threats to Canadian security, which was the starting point for the CIIPS study, was expressed in the following manner:

> Two major influences have produced these changed perceptions:
> * first, the rapid easing of the East-West tensions that have dominated international relations since the end of the Second World War.
> * second, the growing understanding that our Earth's resources are finite, and human beings are plundering them at a rate and in a manner that cannot be continued without irrevocable damage to the processes on which all life depends.
>
> Together these two influences have led people everywhere to rethink their very notion of what constitutes security. Security has always been a fundamental concern of human groups, and in the years since the Second World War we have poured immense resources into defending ourselves against perceived threats to our military security. In the last few years, however, people have begun to realize that long-term changes to the basic elements on which all life depends may prove to be as threatening to human security – or even more threatening – than the nuclear war and military aggression against which we have been so assiduously defending ourselves.[29]

The CIIPS study suggested four areas in which Canadian domestic and foreign policy had to be adapted to meet the changed circumstances of the 1990s:

* development of a sustainable economy, requiring "difficult – one might almost say, revolutionary – decisions about energy use";
* increased acceptance of foreign immigration to Canada and the changes this would impose on Canadian society;
* explicit action to achieve environmental protection at home and globally, through development of a "foreign policy for the environment";
* strengthening of international institutions through increased Canadian financial support and participation.

Increased Canadian spending on the global environment presumably would take two forms. The first would be an increase in the financial assistance given to the less-developed nations. This would take the form of a stronger effort, in conjunction with others, to alleviate those nations of the debt load that now puts them in an annual net loss position of more than $40 billion, because debt repayments to the industrialized nations are greater than the total of government foreign aid and private capital flows.[30] The next step would be an increase in annual foreign aid payments. Canada has never achieved either the goal of the 1970s, to increase official development assistance until it represented 1 per cent of GNP, or the later Mulroney government goal of 0.6 per cent. In the fiscal year 1989-90 the total was 0.43 per cent. Finally, Canada would need to spend in support of institutions, such as UNEP, that allow for collective action. Such spending would include both increased annual payments to such bodies and increased Canadian participation.

A foreign policy for the environment would require not only changes in annual expenditures but also institutional changes to allow Environment Canada and other agencies with environmental responsibilities a greater voice in development and implementation of foreign policy. It would be likely to require changes, as well, in the role of other institutions, such as the armed forces, that play a role in implementing foreign policy. There is no reason to assume that such changes in institutions and decision-making procedures should be the primary means of achieving foreign policy objectives, however. As is the case in domestic policy, substantive cuts in annual pollution emissions must remain the primary objective. But unlike the domestic arena, where the institutional means for achieving such cuts already exist, substantive and procedural reforms will have to be pursued in tandem.

Adopting such a foreign policy for the environment would entail major costs and difficulties. It would also bring benefits. An environment-motivated foreign policy would be a means of directly addressing the major security threat now facing the nation and would lead to new alliances and communications, particularly with other mid-powers such as the Scandinavian countries and some of the Commonwealth nations, which are beginning to take similar action. This, in turn, would be another means of meeting the long-standing Canadian objective of finding a way to balance the overwhelming presence of the United States in both our domestic and international deliberations.

In any case, an environmental thrust to foreign policy is bound to happen. Whether Canada explicitly moves to place environment at the head of its list of international priorities or not, it will eventually assume that position as the effects of global pollution and resource consumption come to be more and more directly felt within this country.

Contemplation of the problems posed by environmental degradation, particularly on a global scale, can lead to profound pessimism. However, for the majority of the global citizens who came of age or were born after the invention of the nuclear bomb in 1945, such pessimism is the norm rather than the exception. This stems from the simple fact that science and technology have given us immense benefits and at the same time have brought with them frightening costs and dangers.

But the challenge of environmental protection need by no means be a source of despair. Inculcation of the values of environmentalism – a search for harmony with the world around us, fairness in our dealings with other species and with other members of our own – will bring its own benefits. Meeting this new challenge, like others that have gone before, will assist us in the further development of our moral understanding of ourselves and our place in the universe – a process that has been under way for many thousands of years and that will continue as long as we, one species among many, continue to inhabit this planet.

GLOSSARY

Discussion of pollution regulation is hampered by confusion over the precise meaning of terms. Often the same term will be used by different people to mean different things – for instance, the word "standard" is used to refer both to the environmental quality objective that pollution regulation is intended to achieve, such as uncontaminated drinking water, and the legally binding limit on emissions from a particular source. To avoid confusion, the following short glossary provides definitions of terms used.

Pollution

- *pollution* – a contaminant deposited in or discharged to air, land, or water.
- *pollution prevention* – reducing the quantity of pollution discharged to the environment; this can be done by capturing it and then treating it as a waste (e.g., scrubbing sulphur dioxide out of acid rain-producing emissions and then disposing of it in some manner) or by changing the production process to generate less pollution in the first place (e.g., switching to a low-sulphur coal).
- *pollution clean-up* – "remediation," the treatment and disposal of existing pollution, such as asbestos in a school or contaminated soil on the site of a former factory.
- *tonne* – 1,000 kilograms or 2,200 pounds. In some places in the text reference is made to "tons" of pollution – these are references from the 1970s when the Imperial measurement system was still used by environmental agencies. A ton is 2,000 pounds.

Waste

- *waste* – pollution that is contained and, in some cases, treated to reduce toxicity before being deposited in its final resting place; as used here, the terms *municipal waste* and *solid waste* refer to household garbage and commercial and industrial non-hazardous waste, and *hazardous waste* refers to industrial and other wastes, such as biomedical or radioactive materials, which are governed by special regulatory requirements.
- *waste reduction* – action taken to reduce the quantity of waste initially generated; for instance, putting less packaging on a product before it is sold or improving the efficiency of a pulp mill so that more of the tree is used to make pulp instead of being discharged to the river as waste.
- *waste re-use* – using a product, such as a pop bottle, again instead of throwing it away.
- *waste recycling* – using waste, such as a discarded pop bottle or newspaper, as a raw material to make a new product.
- *waste recovery* – capturing something of value from the waste instead of disposing of it, for instance, by composting the biodegradable portions of household waste.

The Regulatory Process

- *data* – as used here, the term encompasses the availability, quality, and credibility of the information upon which pollution regulation is based, including both sources and effects of the various toxic substances under consideration, and the economic and other implications of regulatory activity.
- *loading* – the quantity of pollution emitted to a particular environment each year.
- *objective* – a desired state of environmental quality, usually expressed in a government policy that is not in itself legally enforceable; examples include the Ontario government objective of removing soil in urban areas that contains lead concentrations of more than 500 parts per million and the Canadian and provincial objective of limiting acid rain loadings to 20 kilograms per hectare per year; sometimes referred to as an "ambient standard."
- *standard* – a legally enforceable limit on the concentration or total quantity of pollution that can be emitted from a given source; the legal force comes from either incorporating the standard in a regulation, in which case it is generally applicable, or making it a condition of a licence, in which case it applies only to that particular polluting source.
- *approval* – the process by which a potentially polluting operation, such as a sewage treatment plant or petrochemical plant, is authorized by the regulatory agency to begin operations; a distinction is made between *licensing approvals*, a process carried out by administrative officials with no public input, and *environmental assessment*, which provides for some form of public comment.

- *environmental assessment* – one component of the approvals process; an *environmental impact assessment* is a report that attempts to predict the effects a particular project, such as a new highway or pulp mill, will have on the surrounding environment, and generally includes not only the physical environment but also the social, cultural, economic, and other aspects of the human environment; *environmental assessment* is used here to refer to an approvals process that requires that an environmental impact assessment be prepared and then considered not only by the regulatory agency but also by interested members of the public, often through a hearing before a quasi-judicial administrative board such as the Ontario Environmental Assessment Board.
- *abatement* – action taken by the regulatory agency to reduce pollution from an existing source; the term often refers to negotiation of non-enforceable pollution reduction measures.
- *order* – a legally enforceable requirement to reduce or stop pollution from a given source.
- *enforcement* – action taken by a regulatory agency to ensure requirements are obeyed; the means used vary from disseminating information about such requirements, discussion and negotiation, through to investigation and prosecution of infraction of environmental regulations; the objective is to ensure compliance with environmental law – the term *compliance strategy* is sometimes used to refer to a regulatory approach in which prosecution is rarely undertaken, relying instead on negotiation, in distinction from *enforcement strategy*, which is based on prosecution.

NOTES

Introduction

1. It is impossible to give a precise estimate of the total quantity of pollution entering the Canadian environment each year, both because of a shortage of data and because of the varying ways in which terms such as "pollution" and "toxic substances" can be used. It can be said with some certainty, however, that annual quantities of pollution are in the millions of tonnes rather than either the thousands or billions. The Ontario Waste Management Corporation stated in June, 1990, that "Ontario business generates over four million tonnes of liquid industrial and hazardous wastes every year." See "Hazardous Waste Reduction: What's Stopping Us?" *OWMC Courier*, June, 1990. By 1994, when the Ontario acid rain program has come fully into effect, annual emissions of sulphur dioxide in that province will be 885,000 tonnes. The Ontario government estimated in 1989 that "more than six million tonnes of gases and particles pour into our atmosphere every year from Ontario sources." See Environment Ontario, "Working together for a better environment" (1989); These Ontario sources likely represent about half the national quantities. See Environment Canada, *State of the Environment Report for Canada* (May, 1986), Table 8.18.

2. "The human species came into being at the time of greatest biological diversity in the history of the earth. Today as human populations expand and alter the natural environment, they are reducing biological diversity to its lowest level since the end of the Mesozoic era, 65 million years ago. The ultimate consequences of this biological collision are beyond calculation and certain to be harmful." Edward O. Wilson, "Threats to Biodiversity," *Scientific American*, 261, 3 (September, 1989), p. 108.

3. The extent of the threat to human health posed by various forms of pollution remains a highly controversial and politically sensitive subject, but there is agreement that the threat is real. For one example, the health effects associated

with smog, see Margaret Mellon *et al., The Regulation of Toxic and Oxidant Air Pollution in North America* (Toronto, 1986), pp. 74-76. A 1990 study of the Great Lakes ecosystem, done by the Conservation Foundation and Institute for Research on Public Policy, reached this conclusion: "The weight of present evidence suggests that human health probably is affected by exposure to the persistent chemicals found in the [Great Lakes] ecosystem." *Great Lakes: Great Legacy?* (Waldorf, Maryland, 1990), p. 183. In extreme cases, such as the Eastern European nations, health effects are obvious. In Canada the problem is much more subtle.

4. For an account of the scientific controversies surrounding global warming predictions, see Robert M. White, "The Great Climate Debate," *Scientific American*, 263, 1 (July, 1990), pp. 36-43. See also Stephen H. Schneider, *Global Warming* (San Francisco, 1989).

5. Nathan Keyfitz, "The Growing Human Population," *Scientific American*, 261, 3 (September, 1989), p. 119. See also Susan A. McDaniel, "People Pressure," in Constance Mungall and Digby J. McLaren, eds., *Planet Under Stress* (Toronto: The Royal Society of Canada, 1990), pp. 225-38.

6. Boyce Richardson, *Time to Change* (Toronto: The Canadian Institute for Peace and Security, 1990), p. 23.

I Pollution Politics in the 1990s

1. Andrew Nikiforuk and Ed Struzik, "The Great Forest Sell-Off," *Globe and Mail Report on Business Magazine*, November, 1989.

2. See Jeffrey Simpson, "The environmental card," *Globe and Mail*, September 8, 1988, p. A6.

3. "Last November's federal election was the first one in which the environment was the major issue among voters." "Greening the Provinces," *Maclean's*, June 26, 1989, p. 44.

4. "Trade deal brings ecology concerns," *Winnipeg Free Press*, September 29, 1988, p. 7. "Environmentalists lash free trade," *London Free Press*, September 23, 1988. See Canadian Environmental Law Association, Friends of the Earth, Movement pour L'Agriculture Biologique, *Selling Canada's Environment Short: The Environmental Case Against the Trade Deal* (no date).

5. "The greening of Sinclair Stevens," *Globe and Mail*, April 7, 1990, p. D2.

6. "Business, environmentalists becoming unlikely bedfellows," *Toronto Star*, March 25, 1990, p. 1. "Development the planet can tolerate," editorial, *Globe and Mail*, March 19, 1990.

7. "Assess impact of Alberta dam on environment, Ottawa ordered," *Globe and Mail*, March 14, 1990, p. 1.

8. "Provinces seek final say on megaprojects," *Globe and Mail*, May 11, 1990.

9. "Power to burn," *Maclean's*, May 21, 1990, p. 51.

10. *Ibid.*

Chapter 1

1. "Ranked 10th a decade ago, environmental issues, particularly those that impact on human health, now place [in opinion polls] in the top two": "Canadians demand environmental leadership," *Eco/Log Week*, 16, 16 (April 22, 1988). Michael Adams of Environics has said: "the environment now ranks higher in what we pollsters call top-of-mind concern than any quality of life issue in the 50 year history of polling": "The Impact of Social Change on Canada's Environmental Agenda," an address to the Inaugural Meeting of the

National Round Table on the Environment and the Economy, June 14, 1989. See also Michael Valpy, "Great Lakes pollution as a political issue," *Globe and Mail*, October 16, 1989, reporting on a Decima Poll commissioned by Pollution Probe, which reported on polling done August 26 to September 3, 1989, of residents living within twenty kilometres of Lake Ontario. The Decima Report, "Report to Pollution Probe/Lake Ontario Organizing Network on American and Canadian Attitudes Toward the Environmental Problems in and around Lake Ontario," stated (p. 1) that "To Lake Ontario's residents, the most important problem in their area is the environment. This is consistent with recent results of national studies by Decima which show that environmental concerns have overtaken economic issues as the most important problem."

2. The most recent information available, for the year 1985, provides the following total national air pollution loadings (tonnes per year) from motor vehicle exhaust:

particulate matter	43,256
sulphur dioxide	18,622
nitrogen oxides	392,077
carbon monoxide	4,015,545
hydrocarbons	523,039
volatile organic compounds	470,735

Figures refer only to cars and not other transportation vehicles. Data supplied by the Ontario Ministry of the Environment, Air Resources Branch, June 1, 1990.

3. The estimate of 1.7 kilograms per capita per day is provided in "Reduction and Reuse: The First 2rs of Waste Management," Environment Canada Fact Sheet, 1990.

4. "Vancouver Declaration on Survival in the 21st Century," Symposium on Science and Culture for the 21st Century: Agenda for Survival, UNESCO, September 10-15, 1989.

5. Robert C. Paehlke, *Environmentalism and the Future of Progressive Politics* (New Haven: Yale University Press, 1989), p. 103.

6. "Report on Reducing Greenhouse Gas Emissions," Federal/Provincial/ Territorial Task Force on Energy and the Environment, August, 1989, pp. 97, 99.

7. "America is still demanding a full tank," *New York Times*, August 12, 1990, p. E3.

8. Kai Millyard, "Demolishing the Fire Hall," report by Friends of the Earth, November 7, 1988. The 81 per cent budget reduction figure is provided in a letter to the Prime Minister, November 7, 1988, appended to the report.

9. "An Energy Glut in the Ground Imperils Ecological Hopes," *New York Times*, October 15, 1989.

10. "Greenprint for Canada: A Federal Agenda for the Environment," Greenprint for Canada Committee, Ottawa, June, 1989, pp. 23, 26.

11. Of particular concern is the fact that little is done to reduce the toxicity of hazardous industrial wastes before they are disposed of by discharge to water or landfills. In January, 1990, the Ontario Round Table on Environment and Economy stated that "almost 80 per cent" of the 4 million tonnes of hazardous waste produced in Ontario annually "ends up in the environment untreated." "Ontario advisory panel to recommend defence strategy for the environment," *Globe and Mail*, January 8, 1990. That statement was contained in an early draft of the Round Table *Challenge Paper*. When the paper was released in July, 1990, immediately prior to the Ontario election, the statement read:

"Ontario generates somewhere between 3 and 4 million tonnes of hazardous waste each year. A large but uncertain percentage of this waste ends up in the environment without receiving adequate treatment." *Challenge Paper*, 1990, p. 26.

12. Doug Macdonald and Peter Pickfield, *From Pollution Prevention to Waste Reduction: Toward a Comprehensive Hazardous Waste Strategy for Ontario*, Canadian Institute for Environmental Law and Policy, March 14, 1989, Table 2-2, provides an estimate of annual generation of 3,338,000 tonnes in Ontario, of which 2,256,000 are discharged to water or sewers and 439,000 deposited on land, with the remainder disposed of by other means.

13. Mr. David Lacelle, Environment Canada, Inland Waters Directorate, to Ms. Dina Appleton, June 19, 1990. Note that "urban" here means a municipality with a population larger than 1,000.

14. Macdonald and Pickfield, *From Pollution Prevention to Waste Reduction*.

15. Canadian Council of Resource and Environment Ministers, *The PCB Story*, (Toronto, 1986), pp. 6-8.

16. The hazardous waste figure is based on a doubling of estimated Ontario quantities, as discussed above. Ontario is estimated to produce between 10 and 14 million tonnes of solid waste each year, of which approximately half is generated by industrial and commercial sources. Thus manufacturing industries might produce 4 million tonnes in that province each year and twice that amount on a national basis. See Ontario Ministry of the Environment, *Towards a Sustainable Waste Management System* (1990), p. 4; Pollution Probe, *Five Years of Failure: A Documentation of the Failure of the Ontario Government to Reduce Solid and Hazardous Waste Quantities* (1990), p. 6. The 1985 data on air emissions, referred to in note 2 above, give these estimates for industrial air pollution loadings (tonnes per year):

particulate matter	910,000
sulphur dioxide	2,572,912
nitrogen oxides	88,931
carbon monoxide	774,849
hydrocarbons	577,931
volatile organic compounds	258,283

17. This three-to-one ratio is based on two sources: Economic Council of Canada, *Reforming Regulation*, (1981), p. 88. Environment Canada, Environmental Protection Service, "Report on the Economic Profile of the Hazardous Waste Management Service Subsector in Canada" (unpublished, August 1988), pp. 4-21.

18. Environment Canada, *State of Environment Report for Canada* (Ottawa, May, 1986), Table 8.14, p. 172.

19. Agriculture Canada, *An Economics Assessment of the Benefits of the 2.4-D in Canada* (Ottawa, September, 1988), p. viii.

20. *Great Lakes: Great Legacy?*, p. 39.

Chapter 2

1. Paehlke, *Environmentalism*, p. 36.

2. Barry Commoner, *Making Peace with the Planet*, (New York: Random House, 1990), p. 179.

3. See Bill Devall and George Sessions, *Deep Ecology* (Salt Lake City: Gibbs M. Smith, 1985); Brian Tokar, "Exploring the New Ecologies: Social Ecology, Deep Ecology and the Future of Green Political Thought," *Alternatives*, 15, 4 (Nov./Dec., 1988), pp. 31-43; Rick Boychuk, "eco-terrorism," *This Magazine*,

24, 1 (June, 1990), pp. 14-17.
4. Devall and Sessions, *Deep Ecology*, p. 67.
5. *Ibid.*
6. Boychuk, "eco-terrorism," p. 14.
7. Dave Foreman, founder of Earth First!, quoted in Tokar, "Exploring the New Ecologies," p. 40.
8. The divisions between deep ecology and other branches of the environmental movement are discussed by Tokar, "Exploring the New Ecologies."
9. David McRobert, "Green Politics in Canada," *Probe Post*, 8, 2 (Autumn, 1985), p. 12.
10. Brian Tokar, *The Green Alternative* (San Pedro, Calif.: R. & E. Miles, 1987), p. 46.
11. "Green and Pleasant Land," *This Magazine*, 23 (Jan.-Feb., 1990), p. 6.
12. *Ibid.*
13. McRobert, "Green Politics"; Helga Hoffman and David Orton, "Canadian Greens: On the Political Margins," *Canadian Dimension*, 23, (November-December, 1989), p. 21.
14. "Supping with the innocent," *Toronto Sun*, September 2, 1988; Thirty-fourth General Election Report of the Chief Electoral Officer, 1988.
15. Information on provincial votes supplied by staff of the chief electoral officers of the various provinces, personal communication with Paula Vopni, August, 1990.
16. Staff, Chief Electoral Officer, personal communication, November 15, 1990.
17. Personal communication, Chris Lea, Ontario Green Party, to Paula Vopni, August, 1990.
18. A summary of policies presented in The Ontario Greens, "Ratified Policy," August, 1988.
19. See Hoffman and Orton, "Canadian Greens."
20. See McRobert, "Green Politics," p. 15.
21. There are no published studies on sources of financing for environmental organizations and the portions here are estimates based on the author's experience and on review of a number of environmental organizations' financial statements. The Pollution Probe statement of revenues and expenses for 1988-89 shows total revenues of $1,601,302, divided as follows:

individuals	$1,071,317
foundations	121,443
government	209,418
corporations	121,647
sales	77,477

22. Personal communication, John Wilson, Environment Canada, August 29, 1990.
23. "Advocacy groups battle to survive," *Globe and Mail*, July 17, 1990, p. A8; David Simpson, Consumers' Association, personal communication with Paula Vopni, August 25, 1990.
24. Anne Rowan, Greenpeace, personal communication to Paula Vopni, July, 1990.
25. The *Directory of Canadian Public Interest Groups*, published by Pat Delbridge and Associates, for December, 1988, provides information on annual budget ranges for a number of organizations. It should be noted that some deal with both pollution and resource conservation issues:
    Budgets between $100,000 and $500,000
    Canadian Coalition on Acid Rain, Toronto

Canadian Environmental Law Association, Toronto
Canadian Institute for Environmental Law and Policy, Toronto
Friends of the Earth, Ottawa
Greenpeace, Vancouver
Greenpeace, Toronto
National Survival Institute, Ottawa
The Harmony Foundation, Ottawa
Conservation Council of New Brunswick, Fredericton
Association Québécoise de Luite Contre Les Pluies Acides, Québec
Conservation Council of Ontario, Toronto
Canadian Environmental Defence Fund, Toronto
Great Lakes United
Environmental Law Centre, Edmonton
West Coast Environmental Law Association, Vancouver
West Coast Environmental Law Research Foundation, Vancouver

26. This information is considered confidential by the Canadian Chemical Producers' Association and the Canadian Pulp and Paper Association. Personal communication, Dave Goffin, CCPA, and Pierre Marchand, CPPA, to Paula Vopni, July, 1990. The Canadian Manufacturers' Association is unable to segregate spending in this area from other activities. Personal communication from John Dillon, CMA, to Paula Vopni, July, 1990.
27. Andrew Thompson, ed., *Environmental Regulation in Canada* (Vancouver: University of British Columbia, 1980).
28. See Economic Council of Canada, *Managing the Legacy: Proceedings of a Colloquium on the Environment* (Ottawa, 1985).
29. G. Bruce Doern, ed., *The Environmental Imperative: Market Approaches to the Greening of Canada* (Ottawa: C.D. Howe Institute, 1990); Walter E. Block, ed., *Economics and the Environment: A Reconciliation* (Vancouver: The Fraser Institute, 1990).
30. Notes for remarks by the Honourable Tom McMillan, Minister of the Environment, to the Canadian Chemical Producers' Association, November 19, 1986.
31. "Environmental attacks not fair, Noranda exec tells conference," *Globe and Mail*, March 21, 1990, p. B1; "Noranda chief takes aim at so-called 'environmental terrorists,'" *ibid.*, November 22, 1989, p. B2.
32. Terence Corcoran, "Mob bays for polluters' blood – and Ontario's ready to oblige," *Globe and Mail*, March 1, 1990, p. B2.

Chapter 3

1. Rebecca Aird, "Animal Rights and Environmentalism," *Probe Post*, 9, 2 (August, 1986), p. 22. In 1985, because of protests from Canadian natives, Greenpeace U.K. abandoned its European campaign against buying fur.
2. W. Christian and C. Campbell, *Political Parties and Ideologies in Canada* (Toronto: McGraw-Hill Ryerson, 1983), p. 30.
3. Kenneth M. Gibbons, "Environmental Politics in Manitoba: Institutions, Issues, and Interests in the 1980's," *Alternatives*, 13, 1 (December, 1985), p. 27.
4. Harry Poch, *Corporate and Municipal Environmental Law* (Toronto: Carswell, 1989), p. 11. "The references in CEPA to 'the environment on which human life depends,' are attempts to create the legal and constitutional framework for federal action in this area." Margaret Smith, *Toxic Substances: Federal-Provincial Control*, Library of Parliament Research Branch, November 1, 1988, revised, May 29, 1989, p. 4.

5. Poch, *Environmental Law*.
6. Alastair R. Lucas, "Natural Resource and Environmental Management: A Jurisdictional Primer," in Donna Tingley, ed., *Environmental Protection and the Canadian Constitution* (Edmonton: Environmental Law Centre, 1987).
7. "Environmental Regulation Course, February 20-22, 19980, Toronto," Executive Enterprises Inc., background papers prepared by McCarthy and McCarthy, p. 1-3.
8. Rod McLeod "The Provincial Perspective," in Tingley, ed., *Environmental Protection and the Canadian Constitution*, p. 13.
9. "Environmental Regulation Course," p. 1-2.
10. Douglas A. Smith, "Defining the Agenda for Environmental Protection," in Katherine Graham, ed., *How Ottawa Spends, 1990-91: Tracking the Second Agenda* (Ottawa: Carleton University Press, 1990), Table 5.3, p. 119.
11. Alastair R. Lucas, "Harmonization of Federal and Provincial Environmental Policies: The Changing Legal and Policy Framework," in Owen J. Saunders, ed., *Managing Natural Resources in a Federal State* (Calgary: Canadian Institute of Resources Law, 1986), p. 34.
12. "Exemption from PCB storage rule is sought by all provinces but PEI," *Globe and Mail*, October 14, 1988, p. A12.
13. Interview with G.A. Henderson, Executive Director, CCME, August 15, 1989; Lucas, "Harmonization," p. 48.
14. Canadian Council of Ministers of the Environment, Annual Report, 1988-89; Henderson interview.
15. See Stephen Garrod, Margaret Mellon, Leslie Ritts, Marcia Valiante, *The Regulation of Toxic and Oxidant Air Pollution in North America* (Toronto: CCH, 1986), pp. 170-77.
16. "Rae among 16 arrested at Temagami protest," *Globe and Mail*, September 19, 1989; Larry Kuehn, "Living and prospering without growth," *New Dimensions* (September-October, 1989), pp. 14-19; "B.C. NDP averts public rift over logging issue," *Globe and Mail*, March 12, 1990, p. A4.
17. Interview with Dr. Robert Slater, Assistant Deputy Minister, Environment Canada, February 1, 1990.
18. Wayne Roberts, "Undermining the Minister," *Now Magazine*, April 26-May 2, 1990, pp. 8-10.
19. Paehlke, *Environmentalism*, p. 57.
20. David Scheffer, Carnegie Endowment for International Peace, quoted in Roger Rosenblatt, "Give Law a Chance," *New York Times Book Review*, August 16, 1990, p. 16.
21. Canadian Institute of International Affairs, *Behind the Headlines* (Ottawa, 1989), p. 1.

Chapter 4

1. See, for example, "Is excellent ever good enough?" editorial, *Globe and Mail*, May 2, 1990: "Is Canada in danger of becoming a nation of environmental hypochondriacs? . . . The toxicologist who reports an infinitesimal risk is often drowned out by the clamor for no risk whatever. . . . the U.S. Environmental Protection Agency said recently that the release of dioxin from pulp-and-paper mills posed a generally small risk. . . . It would seem a better bet than flying a CF-18, crossing a street or sharing a restaurant with smokers."
2. See Lester W. Milbrath, *Environmentalists: Vanguard for a New Society* (New York: State University of New York, 1984), for a report on questionnaire-based

studies that indicate a majority of American environmentalists consider themselves to be left of centre.

3. This is argued by Jonathon Porritt, *Seeing Green: The politics of ecology explained* (Oxford: Basil Blackwell, 1984).
4. Paehlke, *Environmentalism*, p. 177.
5. *Ibid.*, p. 190. The figure is the same as that presented by Paehlke.
6. See *Preserving Both Jobs and the Environment*, background paper and six issue papers for the conference held November 21-23, 1986, McMaster University, by the Ontario Environment Network.
7. Roderick Nash, *The Rights of Nature: A History of Environmental Ethics* (Madison: University of Wisconsin Press, 1989), pp. 3-12.
8. Aird, "Animal Rights and Environmentalism," p. 22.
9. Interview with Liz White and Tita Zierer, Animal Alliance of Canada, December 7, 1990.
10. Sonya Dakars, *Animal Rights Campaigns: Their Impact in Canada*, Library of Parliament Research Branch, January 18, 1988, revised May 26, 1989, p. 11.
11. "Animal Protection through Education and Advocacy," brochure published by the Animal Alliance of Canada.
12. Personal communication, Mr. Del Haylock, the Fur Council of Canada, December 4, 1990. See Alan Herscovici, *Furs – An Environmental Ethic* (1988), booklet distributed by the Fur Institute of Canada.
13. "3 whales captured despite protesters," *Globe and Mail*, August 13, 1990, p. A4.
14. Mark Safaft, "Animal Liberation and Environmental Ethics: Bad Marriage, Quick Divorce," *Osgoode Hall Law Journal*, 22 (1984), p. 297.
15. Quoted in Nash, *The Rights of Nature*, p. 128.
16. *Crimes Against the Environment*, Working Paper 44, Law Reform Commission of Canada, 1985, p. 14.
17. From *The Selected Poetry of Robinson Jeffers* by Robinson Jeffers. Copyright 1938 and renewed 1966 by Donnan Jeffers and Garth Jeffers. Reprinted by permission of Random House, Inc.

II The Evolution of Pollution Politics in Canada
Chapter 5

1. R. Brian Woodrow, "Resources and Environmental Policy-making at the National Level: The Search for Focus," in O.P. Dwivedi, ed., *Resources and the Environment: Policy Perspectives for Canada* (Toronto: McClelland and Stewart, 1980), p. 29.
2. Janet Foster, *Working for Wildlife* (Toronto: University of Toronto Press, 1978), pp. 16, 23.
3. Jamie Swift, *Cut and Run: The Assault on Canada's Forests* (Toronto: Between the Lines, 1983), pp. 54-55.
4. F.J. Thorpe, "Historical Perspective on the 'Resources for Tomorrow' Conference," *Background Papers and Proceedings* (Ottawa: Department of Northern Affairs and Natural Resources), p. 6.
5. *Ibid.*, p. 10.
6. *Ibid.*, p. 1.
7. Foster, *Working for Wildlife*, p. 3, argues that in the latter part of the nineteenth and first quarter of the twentieth centuries there was no strong public constituency for wildlife conservation. The issue was influenced primarily by "the determination, understanding, and foresight of a small group of remark-

ably dedicated civil servants who were able to turn their own goals of wildlife preservation into a declared government policy."

8. Roderick Nash, *Wilderness and the American Mind* (New Haven: Yale University Press, 1967).
9. George Woodcock, *The Century that Made Us: Canada 1814-1914* (Toronto: Oxford University Press, 1989), p. 203.
10. *Ibid.*, p. 258.
11. "Stefansson created more interest in the Arctic among Canadians than any other individual of his time." Richard J. Diubaldo, *Stefansson and the Canadian Arctic* (Montreal: McGill-Queen's University Press, 1978), p. 3.
12. Woodcock, *The Century that Made Us*, p. 210.
13. Paehlke, *Environmentalism*, p. 29.
14. *Ibid.*
15. Nash, *The Rights of Nature*, p. 56.
16. *Ibid.*, p. 57.
17. *Ibid.*, p. 64.
18. *Ibid.*, pp. 69, 71.

Chapter 6

1. Samuel P. Hays, *Beauty, Health and Permanence: Environmental Politics in the United States, 1955-1985* (Cambridge: Cambridge University Press, 1987). Clarence Davies, *The Politics of Pollution* (New York: Pegasus, 1970), p. 22, also argues that environmental awareness was related to increased affluence and leisure time after the war.
2. Hays, *Beauty, Health and Permanence*, p. 3.
3. *Ibid.*, p. 174.
4. *Ibid.*
5. Rachel Carson, *Silent Spring* (Boston: Houghton Mifflin, 1962), pp. 1-3. The work was serialized in three issues of *The New Yorker*, beginning June 16, 1962. Reprinted with permission of Houghton Mifflin Inc.
6. "Biology: Pesticides: The Price for Progress," *Time*, September 28, 1962, p. 66.
7. *Ibid.*, pp. 66, 69.
8. Davies, *The Politics of Pollution*, p. 47.
9. Department of Environment, *Canada and the Human Environment* (Ottawa, 1972), p. 61.
10. R. Brian Woodrow and Don Munton, "Phosphates, eutrophication and the Great Lakes: A case study into science and policy-making," paper prepared for a workshop on "Science, Values and Environmental Policy," Elora Mill Inn, Ontario, November, 1984, p. 7.
11. "The polluted waters of the Great Lakes: A 'horrifying picture,'" *Toronto Star*, August 19, 1972.
12. Don Munton, "Great Lakes Water Quality: A Study in Environmental Politics and Diplomacy," in Dwivedi, ed., *Resources and the Environment*, p. 153.
13. Quoted in Woodrow and Munton, "Phosphates," p. 2.
14. *Ibid.*, p. 17.
15. *Ibid.*, pp. 20, 32. Some state and local governments did regulate phosphate limits.
16. *Ibid.*, p. 20.
17. *Ibid.*, pp. 21-22; personal communication, Professor Don Munton, August 16, 1990.
18. *Great Lakes: Great Legacy?*, p. 95.
19. "Invitation List by Affiliation," Background Papers and Proceedings, Pollu-

tion and Our Environment, sponsored by the Canadian Council of Resource Ministers, 1966.

20. *The Rape of the Environment: A Statement on Environmental Pollution and Destruction in Canada*, prepared by M.J. Dunbar, Canadian Society of Zoologists, McGill University, September, 1969, p. 1.
21. *Ibid.*, pp. 2-3
22. *Ibid.*, p. 38.
23. Davies, *The Politics of Pollution*, p. 85.
24. *Submission by S.P.E.C. to the Coasting Trade Inquiry*, Canadian Transport Commission, January 12, 1970; brochure titled SPEC, undated.
25. Interview with Don Chant, October 25, 1989.
26. *CELRF: A New Anti-Pollution Device that Works*, undated brochure. The reference is to the Canadian Environmental Law Research Foundation, the original name given to the research and environmental law advisory office. The latter was named Canadian Environmental Law Association in the early 1970s, while CELRF became the Canadian Institute for Environmental Law and Policy in 1989.
27. Quoted in Michael Brown and John May, *The Greenpeace Story* (Scarborough, Ont.: Prentice-Hall, 1989), p. 13.
28. All of the above based on *ibid.*

Chapter 7

1. "Haves, have-nots could clash at Stockholm," *The Financial Post*, May 27, 1972.
2. D.A. Chant, "No empty ritual, conference went beyond its limited goals," *International Perspectives* (September-October, 1972), p. 11.
3. Environment Canada, *Conference on the Human Environment* (1972), p. 7.
4. Chant, "No empty ritual," pp. 11-12.
5. Environment Canada, *Conference on the Human Environment*; Environment Canada, *Canada and the Human Environment* (1972).
6. Environment Canada, *Conference on the Human Environment*, p. 10.
7. Donella H. Meadows *et al.*, *The Limits to Growth: A Report for the Club of Rome's Project on the Predicament of Mankind* (New York: Signet, 1972), p. ix.
8. The quotation is from the commentary on the report and the discussion it elicited, prepared by the Club of Rome. Meadows *et al.*, *Limits to Growth*, p. 199.
9. *Ibid.*, p. 21.
10. Paehlke, *Environmentalism*, p. 53.
11. Interview with Don Chant, October 25, 1989.
12. Paehlke, *Environmentalism*, p. 50, states that "the details of the simulation, and even its technical soundness, have been roundly refuted."
13. David Brooks, *Zero Energy Growth for Canada* (Toronto: McClelland and Stewart, 1981).
14. *Canada as a Conserver Society: Resource Uncertainties and the Need for New Technologies*, Science Council of Canada Report No. 27, September, 1977.
15. Fikret Berkes, "The Mercury Problem: An Examination of the Scientific Basis for Policy-making," in Dwivedi, ed., *Resources and the Environment*, p. 270.
16. Ross Howard, *Poisons in Public: Case Studies of Environmental Pollution in Canada* (Toronto: James Lorimer and Company, 1980), p. 32.
17. *Ibid.*, p. 20.

18. *Ibid.*, p. 26.
19. Mathew Fisher, "Indians eating contaminated fish," *Globe and Mail*, November 5, 1990.
20. Robert Page, *Northern Development: The Canadian Dilemma* (Toronto: McClelland and Stewart, 1986), ch. 2.
21. *Ibid.*, p. 89.
22. Professor Robert Gibson, personal communication, May 28, 1990.
23. Woodrow, "Resources and Environmental Policy-making," p. 25.
24. "Court decision to allow spraying called ruinous for losers," *Globe and Mail*, September 17, 1983, p. 13; "The high cost of community action," *Maclean's*, September 26, 1983.
25. Interview with Alex Manson, Environment Canada, February 2, 1990; the same point was made by Elizabeth May, interview, February 1, 1990.
26. "Don't drink the water," *Maclean's*, June 22, 1981.
27. Pollution Probe, *Toxics on Tap: A Report on the Quality of Drinking Water in Toronto* (Toronto, 1982).
28. F.J. Horgan, Commissioner of Works, Report to the Metropolitan Toronto Council Works Committee, November 4, 1981.
29. Monica Campbell, *Drinking Water: Make it Safe!* (Toronto: Pollution Probe, 1983), Summary, p. 1.
30. Frank Horgan, on "Toronto Drinking Water: Is It Safe?" radio program CJRT-FM, October 7, 1984.

Chapter 8

1. "The Great Forest Sell-Off," *Globe and Mail Report on Business Magazine*, November, 1989, p. 64.
2. "Kowalski calls environmental group 'anarchists,'" *Edmonton Journal*, September 11, 1987.
3. "An agreement for a reform minority parliament," document signed by David Peterson, Leader, Ontario Liberal Party, and Bob Rae, Leader, Ontario New Democratic Party, Toronto, May 28, 1985.
4. Michael Keating, "Where There's Smoke: Polluters Beware: Cleaning Up the Environment is an Ontario Priority," *Globe and Mail*, August 9, 1986.
5. For a discussion of the impact of the Kenora spill on the 1985 election, see Rosemary Speirs, *Out of the Blue: The Fall of the Tory Dynasty in Ontario* (Toronto: Macmillan, 1986), p. 120.
6. "Environment: All parties promising a clean-up," *Toronto Star*, September 4, 1987.
7. "Conservation in Conservative Times," an address by Tom Beck to the National Audubon Society, Lake George, New York, June 20, 1985.
8. Blais-Grenier was never able to overcome the mistrust caused by the spending cuts she had to defend when she first took office. Widely viewed as unsympathetic to environmental protection, she quickly became a liability to the Mulroney government. A European junket, ostensibly on government business, which played in the media as an extended shopping spree, ended Blais-Grenier's brief tenure in the Environment portfolio.
9. Lucas, "Harmonization of Federal and Provincial Environmental Policies," p. 35.
10. "The promised land," *Toronto Star*, November 9, 1988.
11. "The narrow scope," editorial, *Ottawa Citizen*, December 3, 1989.
12. François Bregha, "Needed: An environmental action plan," *The Financial Post*, May 2, 1990.

13. An example is the question posed on page 10: "Should the government emphasize compliance (i.e., advising firms on how to meet requirements) or enforcement (i.e., inspecting and initiating legal actions as required)?" *A Framework for Discussion on the Environment: The Green Plan* (Ottawa, 1990). But this was the central issue discussed during the 1987 Environment Canada consultation process to develop an enforcement policy for CEPA. The answer to the question – a judicious mixture of both – is provided in the Environment Canada document *Canadian Environmental Protection Act: Enforcement and Compliance Policy* (Ottawa, May, 1988).
14. *Green Plan*, p. 1.
15. Ross Howard, "$3-billion Green Plan unveiled by Ottawa, but details scarce," *Globe and Mail*, December 12, 1990, p. A1; Martin Mittelstaedt, "Groups sought tree, 'given seedling,'" *ibid.*, p. A6.
16. *Our Common Future*, Report of the World Commission on Environment and Development (Oxford: Oxford University Press, 1987), p. 6.
17. *Ibid.*, p. xi.
18. *Ibid.*
19. *Ibid.*, p. xii.
20. *Ibid.*
21. *Ibid.*, pp. 9, 8
22. See Report of the Canadian Chamber of Commerce Task Force on the Environment, *A Healthy Environment for a Healthy Economy: A New Agenda for Business*, August, 1989.
23. *Report of the National Task Force on Environment and Economy*, submitted to the Canadian Council of Resource and Environment Ministers, September 24, 1987.
24. *Sustainable Development: Issues from Two Canadian Conferences*, Marion G. Wrobel, Research Branch, Library of Parliament, November 29, 1988, pp. 1, 4.
25. "Conservatives grope through 'grey zone' over environment," *Globe and Mail*, June 19, 1989. The Mulroney government did proceed to carry out a perfunctory "environmental assessment" of the Via decision, although no public hearing was held. Greenpeace, the federal NDP, and others took court action to prevent Via cuts on the grounds that the federal environmental assessment cabinet guidelines had not been complied with, but they were unsuccessful.
26. Ontario Round Table, *Challenge Paper*, p. 9.
27. *A Report to Canadians June 1989-1990*, National Round Table on the Environment and Economy, pp. 11-12.
28. "B.C. bankrolls environment fund, cuts school taxes in new budget," *Globe and Mail*, April 20, 1990.
29. "Greening the Provinces," *Maclean's*, June 26, 1989.
30. Smith, "Defining the Agenda," p. 117.

III Regulating Pollution

1. Environmental Protection Act, Section 5(1), Regulation 308 General – Air Pollution, Schedule 1, Item 1, from David Estrin, *Environmental Law* (Toronto: Carswell, 1984).
2. These figures are given in Roberts, "Undermining the Minister."

Chapter 9

1. Dr. Albert Berry, "Environmental Pollution and its Control in Canada: A Historical Perspective," background papers to the 1966 CCRM Conference, Pollution and Our Environment, pp. 5-6.
2. Davies, *The Politics of Pollution*, pp. 39,50.
3. Hays, *Beauty, Health and Permanence*, p. 53.
4. "Revisions to Legislation," in Air Pollution General Regulation Workshop background papers, Ontario Ministry of the Environment, November, 1985, p. 111-1.
5. *Ibid.*
6. "Flashback through the years," *Water and Pollution Control,* July/August, 1983, p. 31.
7. The Ontario Water Resources Commission Act gave it the power to establish regulations "prescribing standards of quality . . . for industrial waste," with a maximum fine level set at $1,000. Philip Anisman, "Water Pollution Control in Ontario," *Ottawa Law Review*, 5 (1972), p. 383.
8. Berry, "Environmental Pollution," p. 7.
9. "The Commission has published 'Guidelines and Criteria for Water Quality Management in Ontario.'" Anisman, "Water Pollution Control," p. 393. The new Ministry of the Environment published a document with the same title in 1972. David Estrin and John Swaigen, eds., *Environment on Trial*, revised edition (Toronto: CELRF, 1978), p. 8.
10. Professor P.H. Bouthillier, *A History of Stream Pollution Assessment and Control – North Saskatchewan River 1950's to 1980's*, Alberta Environment, September, 1984. Draft water quality criteria May 29, 1967, following p. 14.
11. Ontario Ministry of the Environment, *Status of Industrial Water Pollution Control in Ontario as of Dec. 31, 1971*, p. 3.
12. *Ibid.*, p. 5.
13. "A recent amendment to the [Ontario Water Resources Commission] Act gave the Commission power to create standards for water quality management by order as well as by regulation." Anisman, "Water Pollution Control," p. 392. The figure of thirty-two orders is provided in *MOE Status . . . as of Dec. 31, 1971*, Table VIII, p. 21. When Ontario acted on mercury pollution, it was through the OWRC: "when mercury was detected in fish in the St. Clair River in 1970, the Commission issued orders to six chlor-alkali plants and mercury losses were 'virtually eliminated.'" Anisman, "Water Pollution Control," p. 408.
14. Ontario Water Resources Commission, *The Story of Water*, undated, p. 4.
15. "It would appear, therefore, that quasi-criminal prosecutions are initiated by the Commission only as a last resort." Anisman, "Water Pollution Control," p. 399.
16. *MOE Status*, p. 21.
17. An Environment Canada brochure from the time stated that the department "originated with the former Department of Fisheries and Forestry": *Environment Canada: Its organization and objectives*, 1971.
18. Alain F. Desfossés, *Environmental Quality Strategic Review: A Follow-on Report of the Task Force on Program Review* (Ottawa: Supply and Services, 1986), pp. 28-29.
19. *Ibid.*
20. Department of the Environment, Alberta, *Annual Report*, 1971, p. 1.
21. See Environment Canada, *The Environment Needs You*, 1972.
22. Garrod, Mellon, Ritts, Valiante, *Toxic and Oxidant Air Pollution*, p. 91.

23. Desfossés, *Environmental Quality Strategic Review*, p. 33.
24. *Ibid.*
25. Paul Muldoon, "The Fight for an Environmental Bill of Rights," *Alternatives*, 15, 2 (1988), p. 33; Paul Muldoon and Toby Vigod, "Bill of Rights Sidelined," CELA Newsletter, *Intervenor*, 14, 4 (July/August, 1989).
26. Ontario Hazardous Waste Management Forum, August 30-September 1, 1987, Background Papers, CELRF, p. 12-2.
27. "Environment Ontario Prosecutions Increase Nearly Five-Fold Since 1985," MOE news release, August 18, 1990.

Chapter 10

1. CCME, *Interim Guidelines for PAH Contamination at Abandoned Coal Tar Sites,* November, 1989, p. 6.
2. Jane M. Weninger and Donald M. Gorber, "Decommissioning and Site Clean-up: A Look at the Ataratiri Project," paper delivered at The Clean-up of Toxic Real Estate, Industrial Plants and Natural Resource Sites conference, January 29-30, 1990.
3. "High costs and pollution cast shadow on Ataratiri," *Toronto Star*, April 14, 1990.
4. *Eco/Log Week*, 18, 2 (1990).
5. "Cleaning of Toxic Dumps is Still Lagging, Study Says," *New York Times,* September 10, 1989, reporting on release of a report by the Rand Corporation.
6. Letter from Richard L. Dalon, CCME, to Doug Macdonald, May 23, 1990.
7. CCME press release, October 19, 1989.
8. *Ibid.*
9. Barbara Wallace and Kathy Cooper, *The Citizen's Guide to Lead* (Toronto: NC Press, 1986), p. 74; C.C. Lax, "The Toronto Lead-Smelter Controversy," in *Ecology versus Politics in Canada* (Toronto: University of Toronto Press, 1979), p. 69, says the level was 3,000 ppm. Independent studies done at the time recommended a standard of 1,000 ppm, which, if adopted, would have significantly increased the cost of the 1976 clean-up.
10. Lax, "The Toronto Lead-Smelter Controversy," p. 70.
11. MOE Fact Sheet "Lead in Soil," Summer, 1989.
12. Personal communication, Russ Boyd, MOE, May 18, 1990.
13. *Ibid.*
14. *Overview Economic Assessment of Remedial Action Plans for the Great Lakes Areas of Concern*, Appendices, MOE, April, 1990, RAP Site: Hamilton Harbour, no pagination.
15. "The cost of managing contaminated sediments depends on the type of remedial action to be taken (from monitoring to removal) and the type of process used to treat the sediments. For example, treatment of contaminated sediments can cost from U.S. \$30 to U.S. \$1,800 per cubic yard, depending on the process required." *Great Lakes: Great Legacy?*, p. 204; see also Northeast-Midwest Institute, *Cleaning Up Great Lakes Areas of Concern: How Much will it Cost*, August, 1989: "incineration [of contaminated sediments] is highest at \$1,500 to \$1,800 per cubic yard" (p. 17).
16. Lax, "The Toronto Lead-Smelter Controversy," p. 70; Boyd, personal communication, May 18, 1990.
17. Environment Canada, Waste Management Division, *Discussion Paper: Waste Disposal Sites Program*, October 30, 1987, p. 1.
18. Interview with Tom Foote, Environment Canada, February 1, 1990.
19. *Discussion Paper*, p. 3.

20. Ulo Sibul, "Waste Site Investigation and Remediation," 35th Ontario Waste Management Conference Proceedings, June, 1988.
21. *Great Lakes: Great Legacy?*, p. 205.
22. Northeast-Midwest Institute, *Cleaning Up Great Lakes*, Table 5, p. 18.
23. The Honourable James Bradley, speech to the Entomological Society of Ontario, 123rd Annual Meeting, St. Catherines, November 1, 1986.
24. CCME press release, October 19, 1989.
25. CCME, *Interim Guidelines for PAH Contamination.*
26. *Guidelines for the decommissioning and cleanup of sites in Ontario*, MOE, February, 1989.
27. *Eco/Log Week*, 17, 4 (April 14, 1989).
28. Interview with Ulo Sibul, MOE, May 18, 1990.
29. "Goose Bay PCB Destruction Project Completed," National Defence News Release, August 7, 1990.
30. "Wealth-from-waste dream now a nightmare for town," *Globe and Mail*, July 9, 1988; MOE Fact Sheet, November, 1989, "The Smithville PCB Cleanup," says total cost expected to exceed $20 million; *Globe and Mail*, quoted above, gave figure of $48 million; Sibul, interview, May 22, 1990, said it will be close to $50 million. Also "Smithville PCB-Destruction Operation Approved by Environment Ministry," MOE news release, July 11, 1990.
31. "PCB pollution underestimated, NDP says," *Globe and Mail*, November 9, 1989.
32. Environment Canada and Nova Scotia Department of the Environment, *Sydney Tar Ponds Clean-Up*; "Striking at Sydney's Waste," *Globe and Mail Report on Business Magazine*, January 3, 1989; personal communication, Gary Campbell, Nova Scotia Department of Trade and Technology, November 15, 1990.
33. Quoted in *Great Lakes: Great Legacy?*, p. 205.

Chapter 11

1. Interview with the Honourable Jim Bradley, February 7, 1990.
2. *Great Lakes: Great Legacy?*, p. 223.
3. National Air Quality Objectives for Ozone and Nitrogen Dioxide, referenced in Garrod, Mellon, Ritts, Valiante, *Toxic and Oxidant Air Pollution*, p. 113.
4. Norman Bonsor, Neil McCubbin, and John B. Sprague, *Kraft Mill Effluents in Ontario*, Environment Ontario, 1989, pp. 1-15, 1-3.
5. This description is based primarily on that provided in M.A.H. Franson, R.T. Franson, and A.R. Lucas, *Environmental Standards: A Comparative Study of Canadian Standards, Standard Setting Processes and Enforcement*, Environmental Council of Alberta, 1982, ch. 2.
6. Garrod, Mellon, Ritts, Valiante, *Toxic and Oxidant Air Pollution*, pp. 123-24.
7. Franson, Franson, and Lucas, *Environmental Standards*, p. 23.
8. *Ibid.*, p. 7.
9. Air Pollution, 1985 Workshop, p. 11-5.
10. Franson, Franson, and Lucas, *Environmental Standards*, p. 67.
11. Garrod, Mellon, Ritts, Valiante, *Toxic and Oxidant Air Pollution*, p. 96.
12. "Standards established in 1987 and 1988 under the Motor Vehicle Safety Act will effectively lower air pollution from on-road vehicles over the next decade. But without new measures, Canadian emissions levels of NOx and VOCs are currently forecast to increase by 24 per cent and seven per cent, respectively, between 1985 and 2005, as transportation and industrial demands for gasoline and diesel increase": Benoit Bouchard, in "Federal Government to Tighten

Emission Controls for all Internal Combustion Engines," Environment Canada News Release, April 20, 1989.
13. Franson, Franson, and Lucas, *Environmental Standards*, p. 65.
14. *Ibid.*, p. 90.
15. See Ministry of National Health and Welfare, *Guidelines for Canadian Drinking Water Quality* (Ottawa, 1987).
16. Bradley interview, February 7, 1990.
17. Franson, Franson, and Lucas, *Environmental Standards*, pp. 100, 99.
18. Thompson, ed., *Environmental Regulation in Canada*, p. 33.
19. *Ibid.*, pp. 35-36.
20. *Ibid.*

Chapter 12

1. Harry Poch, *Corporate and Municipal Environmental Law* (Toronto: Carswell, 1989), p. 146.
2. *Public Consultation on Certificates of Approval: An Evaluation*, Synergistic Consulting Limited report to the MOE, undated, p. 14.
3. Robert B. Gibson and Beth Savan, *Environmental Assessment in Ontario* (Toronto: CELRF, 1986), p. 157.
4. *An Action Plan for Environmental Law Enforcement in Alberta*, prepared by the Review Panel on Environmental Law Enforcement, undated, p. 21.
5. *Ibid.*
6. "Environmental Regulation Course," McCarthy and McCarthy background papers, p. 14-3.
7. L. Graham Smith, "Evaluating Canadian Impact Assessment Provisions," paper presented at the annual meeting of the International Association for Impact Assessment, Montreal, June 24-28, 1989.
8. "Federal court rejects bid to halt cuts in Via service," *Globe and Mail*, July 5, 1990, p. A8.
9. Environment Canada news release, October 20, 1988.
10. See parliamentary discussion of the new Act in *Hansard*, June 26, 1990, pp. 13093-109.
11. Michael Jeffery, *Environmental Approvals in Canada: Practice and Procedure* (Toronto: Butterworths, 1989), p. 4.4.
12. *Ibid.*, p. 4.6.
13. *Ibid.*, p. 4.8.
14. *Ibid.*, pp. 4.23-4.24.
15. "Big polluters not prosecuted, Fisheries memo indicates," *Globe and Mail*, December 5, 1989.
16. "Fishier and fishier," editorial, *Vancouver Sun*, December 6, 1989.
17. The Honourable Jim Bradley, "Notes for Remarks to the Canadian Manufacturers' Association Environmental Quality Committee," March 28, 1988.
18. The Honourable Tom McMillan, "Notes for an address to the Fourth Environmental Government Affairs Seminar," October 29, 1986.
19. Canadian Environmental Advisory Council, *Enforcement Practices of Environment Canada*, January, 1987, p. 5.
20. Duncan Chappell, *From Sawdust to Toxic Blobs: A Consideration of Sanctioning Strategies to Combat Pollution in Canada* (Ottawa: Supply and Services, 1989), p. 12.
21. John Elliot, *The Sociology of Natural Resources* (Toronto: Butterworths, 1981), p. 136.
22. As discussed in Chapter 15, the major example of this is compliance with pulp

mill effluent regulatory requirements, which has been almost completely on a negotiated basis. See Thompson's discussion of this example in *Environmental Regulation in Canada*, p. 35.

23. John Lilley and Brian Free, Environment Council of Alberta, *Improving Enforcement of the Clean Air Act and the Clean Water Act*, September 15, 1987, p. 9.
24. "Mandate revision prescribed," *Edmonton Journal*, August 10, 1987.
25. *Turning the Tide: A New Policy for Canada's Pacific Fisheries*, Commission on Pacific Fisheries Policy Final Report, September, 1982, pp. 213, 205.
26. A. Ackerman and B. Clapp, *Fraser River Task Force Report*, July 30, 1980.
27. Peat Marwick and Partners, *Economic Incentive Policy Instruments to Implement Pollution Control Objectives in Ontario*, report to MOE, July, 1983, p. II-11.
28. CEAC, *Enforcement Practices*, p. 1.
29. New Brunswick Conservation Council, *A Critique of the Draft Enforcement and Compliance Policy for the Canadian Environmental Protection Act*, September, 1987, p. 3.
30. *Ibid.*, pp. 10, 11.
31. See H.R. Eddy, *Sanctions, Compliance Policy and Administrative Law* (Ottawa: Law Reform Commission of Canada, 1981).
32. John Swaigen and Gail Bunt argue, however, that "the average fine handed down by the courts is commensurate with the gravity of the typical offence that comes before the court": *Sentencing in Environmental Cases* (Ottawa: Law Reform Commission of Canada, 1985), p. 71.
33. The Honourable Harry Parrott, "Statement to the Legislature Re: Special Environmental Police Force," October 16, 1980.
34. Alex Douglas, director of the MOE Enforcement Branch, had spent thirty-two years with the Toronto and Metropolitan Toronto Police before joining the ministry. Ed Keough, also of the Branch, was a twenty-nine-year RCMP veteran when he was appointed. "Investigators Protect Environment from Man," *Ottawa Citizen*, February 23, 1987.
35. Interview with Paul Complin, formerly MOE Air Resources Branch, September, 1989.
36. Alberta Law Centre, *Enforcement of Environmental Law in Alberta*, August, 1983, p. 4.
37. "Alberta Environment Enforcement Action," Alberta Environment News Release, November 9, 1989.
38. Eco/Log, *Hazardous Waste Management Handbook Fourth Edition* (Toronto: Corpus Information Services, 1986), p. 127.
39. *Ibid.*, p. 197.
40. Environment Canada Fact Sheet, "Recycling in Canada," February, 1990, gives the figure of 300,000 tonnes recycled since the Exchange started in 1978.

Chapter 13

1. *Improved Program Delivery: Environment*, A Study Team Report to the Task Force on Program Review, July 10, 1985 (Ottawa: Supply and Services, 1986).
2. *Great Lakes, Great Legacy?*, Figure 1, pp. XXX-XXXI.
3. "Efficient Investments in Wastewater Treatment Plants," Congressional Budget Office, 1985, quoted in Ralph Luken, U.S. EPA draft report, "A Review of the United States Experience with Market-based Incentives," delivered at a workshop in Jelenia, Gora, Poland, September 26-29, 1989.
4. *Ibid.*, p. 2.

5. Walter Block, "Environmental Problems, Private Property Rights Solutions," in Walter Block, ed., *Economics and the Environment: A Reconciliation* (Vancouver: The Fraser Institute, 1990).
6. *Ibid.*, pp. 292, 293.
7. *Ibid.*, p. 293.
8. *Ibid.*, p. 307.
9. Roy Aitken "Industry's Response," in Mungall and McLaren, eds., *Planet Under Stress*, pp. 283, 284.
10. G. Bruce Doern, "Getting it Green: Environmental Policy in the 1990's," in Doern, ed., *The Environmental Imperative: Market Approaches to the Greening of Canada* (Ottawa: C.D. Howe Institute, 1990).
11. Environment Canada, *A Framework for Discussion on the Environment*, 1990, p. 10.
12. Government of Canada, *Canada's Green Plan*, p. 157.
13. *Great Lakes: Great Legacy?*, p. xxiii.

IV From the Green Garbage Bag to the Stratosphere
Chapter 14

1. Martin Anderson, *Christian Science Monitor*, January 4, 1989, quoted in Block, ed., Preface to *Economics and the Environment*.
2. Toby Vigod, "Halton Region Landfill Approved," *Intervenor*, Newsletter of the Canadian Environmental Law Association, 14, 2 (March/April, 1989), p. 3. Lucien F. Cattrysse kindly provided a draft of that portion of the M.A. thesis he is preparing that reviews the Halton decision.
3. *Towards a Sustainable Waste Management System*, Ontario MOE, Discussion Paper, 1990, p. 4.
4. Report of the Chief Administrative Officer to Council of the Regional Municipality of Ottawa-Carleton, January 10, 1990.
5. "Six years wasted: Sorry tale of garbage foulup," *Ottawa Citizen*, editorial, January 31, 1990.
6. *The Waste Management Planning and Approvals Process*, Report prepared by the Association of Municipalities of Ontario, March, 1989, pp. 5, 7.
7. Pollution Probe: *Five Years of Failure: A documentation of the failure of the Ontario Government to reduce solid and hazardous waste quantities* (Toronto, 1990), p. i.
8. *Towards a Sustainable Waste Management System*, pp. 4, 5.
9. *Ibid.*, p. 20.
10. Pollution Probe Newsletter, 11, 6 (October, 1970), p. 10.
11. Hays, *Beauty, Health and Permanence*, p. 81.
12. See Pollution Probe, *Five Years of Failure*, p. 19, n.46. The regulations were never in fact implemented. The MOE relied instead on a "gentleman's agreement" with the soft drink industry that it would reach the 75 per cent goal. Pollution Probe unsuccessfully attempted to take court action in 1978 to force the government to implement the regulations.
13. Dave Sparling, Waste Reduction Branch, MOE, in Strategies for Waste Reduction, a forum at the University of Waterloo, June 10, 1988, Waterloo Public Interest Research Group.
14. The Honourable Keith C. Norton, "A Blueprint for Waste Management: The Challenge for Ontario in the 1980's," Remarks to the 30th Ontario Industrial Waste Conference, June 13, 1983.
15. *Ibid.*, p. 12.

16. See Recycling Council of Ontario, *A History of the Battle*, December, 1985.
17. Richard Gilbert, "Why recycling pop bottles is a third-rate idea," *Toronto Star*, March 17, 1989.
18. Pollution Probe, *Five Years of Failure*, p. 23.
19. See *Towards a Sustainable Waste Management System*, p. 26, which shows an increase in MOE waste management spending from $0.8 million in fiscal year 1984-85 to $54.2 million in 1990-91. Note that this includes all forms of waste management, including landfill approvals and hazardous as well as municipal solid waste.
20. *Globe and Mail*, October 5, 1989.
21. "Ontario blue box recycling plan falling victim to its own success," *Globe and Mail*, January 3, 1990.
22. Pollution Probe, *Five Years of Failure*, p. 29.
23. While the 1983 *Blueprint for Waste Management* referred to reduction, re-use, recycling, and recovery, the 1990 discussion paper, *Towards a Sustainable Waste Management System*, refers only to the first three. Presumably "recovery" had been dropped because the Ministry of Environment was no longer promoting solid waste incineration, but no explanation was given.
24. "Workers bitter at activists as incinerator shuts down," *Globe and Mail*, July, 1988.
25. See Robert Sheppard, "Metro Toronto, adjoining regions seek common trash solution," *Globe and Mail*, February 4, 1989; David Lewis Stein, "Who will profit from the trash crisis?" *Toronto Star*, March 30, 1989; David Israelson, "Great Pyramid of trash Rises in N.Y.," *Toronto Star*, May 13, 1990; Royson James, "Metro blamed in trash crisis," *Toronto Star*, August 20, 1990; Wayne Roberts, "Blue Box Throwaway," *Now Magazine*, August 23-29, 1990; Pollution Probe, *Five Years of Failure*.
26. "A Campaign Setback," *Maclean's*, September 4, 1989.
27. "In the chemical soup," editorial, *Globe and Mail*, August 8, 1989.
28. "Chemical inferno," *Globe and Mail*, September 7, 1988.
29. "Exemption from PCB storage rule is sought by all provinces but PEI," *Globe and Mail*, October 14, 1988.
30. "Dangerous cargo," *Maclean's*, August 28, 1989.
31. *Ibid.*
32. "Quebec failings exposed at toxic waste forum," *Globe and Mail*, December 14, 1989.
33. J.McQuaid-Cook and K.J. Simpson, ASWMC, "Siting a Fully Integrated Waste Management Facility in Alberta," *Journal of the Air Pollution Control Association* (September, 1986); William H. Glenn and Deborah Orchard, eds., *Hazardous Waste Management Handbook: Fourth Edition* (Don Mills, Ont.: Corpus, 1986), pp. 32-38.
34. Glenn and Orchard, eds., *Handbook*; Hazardous Waste Management Coalition, *Media Update*, January 11, 1985.
35. "BC waste treatment facility sought," *Eco/Log Week*, 16, 28, (July 15, 1988).
36. "New strategy to manage hazardous wastes," B.C. Ministry of the Environment news release, December 5, 1989.
37. "Hazardous waste corporation to be established," B.C. Ministry of the Environment news release, May 25, 1990; personal communication, Jim Knock, B.C. Hazardous Waste Management Corporation, to Paula Vopni, August 16, 1990.
38. Manitoba Hazardous Waste Management Corporation, *The Development of a Hazardous Waste Management System in Manitoba*, August, 1988, p. 10.

Chapter 15

1. Canadian Pulp and Paper Association, *From Watershed to Watermark* (Montreal, 1987); see also William F. Sinclair, *Controlling Pollution from Canadian Pulp and Paper Manufacturers: A Federal Perspective*, Environment Canada, July, 1988, p. 69.
2. Sinclair, *Controlling Pollution*, p. 104.
3. *Ibid.*, p. 163.
4. *Environment Update* (Environment Canada), 9, 1 (Summer, 1989).
5. James W. Parlour, "The Politics of Water Pollution Control: A Case Study of the Canadian Fisheries Act Amendments and the Pulp and Paper Effluent Regulations, 1970," *Journal of Environmental Management*, 13 (1981), p. 128.
6. *Ibid.*, pp. 128-33.
7. *Ibid.*, p. 139.
8. *Ibid.*, p. 141.
9. *Ibid.*, pp. 141-42.
10. Sinclair, *Controlling Pollution*, p. 341.
11. *Ibid.*, p. 177.
12. *Status Report on Abatement of Water Pollution from the Canadian Pulp and Paper Industry (1982)*, Environment Canada, 1984.
13. Parlour, "Politics of Water Pollution Control," p. 138.
14. Sinclair, *Controlling Pollution*, p. 183.
15. Abitibi-Price, *Annual Report*, 1976, quoted in K.E.A. de Silva, *Pulp and Paper Modernization Grants Program – An Assessment* (Ottawa: Economic Council of Canada, May, 1988), p. 35, n. 49.
16. De Silva, *Pulp and Paper Modernization Grants Program*. De Silva concluded that the grants were not needed since the industry could have generated capital funding without government assistance, and that the program did not achieve its objective of improving the international competitive position of the Canadian industry. See summary of conclusions, p. 150.
17. Carol van Strum and Paul Merrell, *No Margin of Safety: A Preliminary Report on Dioxin Pollution and the Need for Emergency Action in the Pulp and Paper Industry*, Greenpeace USA, Inc. 1987, pp. II-1, II-2.
18. Jamie Swift, "Pulp Friction: The growing controversy over kraft-mill pollution," *Harrowsmith*, January/February, 1990, p. 37.
19. van Strum and Merrell, *No Margin of Safety*, p. IV-4.
20. "Pulp, paper mills linked to dioxin contamination," *Globe and Mail*, October 14, 1987.
21. "EPA links dioxin to paper mills," *Christian Science Monitor*, September 1, 1987.
22. *Globe and Mail*, October 14, 1987.
23. "Pulp and paper industry sets out its environmental principles," *Globe and Mail*, June 23, 1989.
24. Ontario, Report of the Expert Committee on Kraft Mill Toxicity, April, 1988, p. 1-19.
25. *Ibid.*, p. 6-106.
26. *Ibid.*, p. 9-68.
27. *Ibid.*, p. 1-17.
28. *Ibid.*, p. 12-227.
29. "Preliminary Results of Fish and Sediment Sampling Program for Dioxins and Furans Announced," news release from Fisheries and Oceans, Environment Canada, Health and Welfare Canada, May 16, 1988.

30. West Coast Environmental Law Association, *Important Notices - Pulp Mill Pollution* June 28, 1988.
31. Sinclair, *Controlling Pollution*, pp. 298, 302.
32. *Ibid.*, p. 245.
33. *Ibid.*, p. 351.
34. *Ibid.*, p. 506.
35. *A Blind Eye: Federal Regulation of the Pulp and Paper Industry in Canada*, Greenpeace, Spring, 1989.
36. "Pulp, pollution and politics," *Alberta Report*, November 13, 1989, p. 49.
37. "The Great Forest Sell-Off," *Globe and Mail Report on Business Magazine*, p. 63.
38. Canada-Alberta News release, "Major diversification initiative with new $500 million pulp mill approved for Peace River area," February 8, 1988.
39. "Alberta's pulp mill plans raise a stink," *Toronto Star*, December 2, 1989.
40. "Pulp, pollution and politics," *Alberta Report* November 13, 1989, p. 49.
41. *Ibid.*
42. *Ibid.*, p. 52.
43. "The Great Forest Sell-Off," p. 63.
44. Christopher Donville and Kimberley Noble, "Alberta pulp project review puts a scare into investors," *Globe and Mail Report on Business Magazine*, March 6, 1990.
45. "Pulp and paper mill effluent," Environment Canada news release, March 15, 1989.
46. "The Pulp and Paper Industry of Canada Issues an Environmental Statement," CPPA press release, June 22, 1989.
47. "Regulatory reforms for pulp and paper industry outlined," Environment Canada news release, January 3, 1990.
48. Interview with Vic Shantora, Environment Canada, February 1, 1990.
49. "New rules for mill clean-up forecast to cost $5-billion," *Globe and Mail*, April 18, 1990.
50. Environment Canada, "Cleaning Up Pollution in the Pulp and Paper Industry: An Overview of the Federal Regulatory Strategy," information sheet for public consultation session, May 5, 1990.

Chapter 16

1. Bruce W. Hodgins and Jamie Benidickson, *The Temagami Experience* (Toronto: University of Toronto Press, 1989), p. 77.
2. "Revisions to Legislation," Air Pollution General Regulation Workshop background papers, MOE, 1985, p. III-1.
3. Ross Howard and Michael Perley, *Acid Rain: The North American Forecast* (Toronto: House of Anansi Press, 1980), p. 51.
4. Jurgen Schmandt and Hilliard Roderick, eds., *Acid Rain and Friendly Neighbors: The Policy Dispute between Canada and the United States* (Durham: Duke University Press, 1985), p. 159. It is suggested that Harvey's 1971 article had little impact and it was not until the 1976 series by Ross Howard was published in the *Toronto Star* that the issue started to gain visibility.
5. Michael S. Mahon, "Balancing the interests: an essay on the Canadian-American acid rain debate," in John E. Carroll, ed., *International Environmental Diplomacy* (Cambridge: Cambridge University Press, 1988), p. 155.
6. Howard and Perley, *Acid Rain*, p. 137.
7. *Ibid.*, p. 173.
8. *Ibid.*, p. 182.

9. Interview with Mark Rudolph, January 11, 1990.
10. *Ibid.*
11. Schmandt and Roderick, eds., *Acid Rain and Friendly Neighbors,* p. 64.
12. Interview with Alex Manson, Environment Canada, February 2, 1990.
13. Interview with Robert Slater, Environment Canada, February 2, 1990.
14. *Acid Rain Milestones,* Environment Canada Fact Sheet, March, 1984.
15. Rudolph interview.
16. Slater and Rudolph interviews.
17. Slater and Rudolph interviews.
18. Slater and Rudolph interviews.
19. Sharon L. Roan, *Ozone Crisis* (New York: John Wiley & Sons, 1989), p. 33.
20. *Healing the Sky,* report by Friends of the Earth, Ottawa, 1989.
21. Philip Shabecoff, "As Ozone is Depleted, Much of Life Could Go with It," *New York Times,* April 17, 1988, p. E28.
22. Richard Elliot Benedick, "Ozone Diplomacy," *Issues in Science and Technology* (Fall, 1989), p. 45.
23. *Ibid.*
24. Roan, *Ozone Crisis,* p. 102.
25. Interview with Victor Buxton, Environment Canada, February 3, 1990.
26. Benedick, "Ozone Diplomacy," p. 40.
27. Roan, *Ozone Crisis,* p. 142.
28. *Ibid.,* p. 148.
29. G.V. Buxton, A. Chisholm, J. Carbonneau, Environment Canada, "A Canadian Contribution to the Consideration of Strategies for Protecting the Ozone Layer," August 15, 1986.
30. Roan, *Ozone Crisis,* p. 231.

Chapter 17

1. Roan, *Ozone Crisis,* p. 201.
2. "Preparing for the worst," *Time,* January 2, 1989, p. 62.
3. "A new world for the future," *Maclean's,* September 5, 1988, p. 50.
4. See Frederick Turner, "A Field Guide to the Synthetic Landscape," *Harper's* (April, 1988), pp. 49-55.
5. Barry Lopez, *Arctic Dreams: Imagination and Desire in a Northern Landscape* (New York: Charles Scribner's Sons, 1986), pp. 254, xx.
6. Judith Plant, ed., *Healing the Wounds: The Promise of Ecofeminism* (Toronto: Between The Lines, 1989), p. 10.
7. John Seed *et al.,* eds., *Thinking Like a Mountain: Towards a Council of All Beings* (Philadelphia: New Society Publishers, 1988).
8. Neil Evernden, *The Natural Alien: Humankind and Environment* (Toronto: University of Toronto Press, 1985), p. 10.
9. *Ibid.,* p. 144.
10. Peter Timmerman, "Grounds for Concern: Environmental Ethics in the Face of Global Change," in Mungall and McLaren, eds., *Planet Under Stress,* p. 218.
11. See Robyn Eckersley, "Green Politics: A Practice in Search of a Theory?" *Alternatives,* 15, 4 (November-December, 1988), pp. 52-61.
12. Brian Tokar, "Exploring the New Ecologies," *ibid.,* p. 31.
13. Robert B. Gibson, "Should environmentalists pursue 'sustainable development'?" paper presented at Global Change and Sustainable Development: the 19th annual conference of the Canadian Nature Federation, May 18, 1990; see also Brewster Kneen, "The contradiction of 'sustainable development,'"

Canadian Dimension, 23, 1 (January/February, 1989), pp. 12-15.

14. David Suzuki, "Time to cut back on everything so we have a chance of survival: There are too many people demanding too much of our planet," *Toronto Star*, November 11, 1989.

15. Science Council of Canada Report No. 27, *Canada as a Conserver Society: Resource Uncertainties and the Need for New Technologies* (Ottawa: Supply and Services, 1977), p. 62.

16. *Ibid.*, p. 63.

17. See the discussion in Richard Swift, "Preserving Both Jobs and the Environment," Ontario Environment Network Background Discussion Paper, Conference on Jobs and the Environment, November 21-23, 1986.

18. *Ibid.*, p. 13.

19. *Canada as a Conserver Society*, p. 26.

20. Paehlke, *Environmentalism and the Future of Progressive Politics*, p. 257.

21. *Ibid.*

22. Brundtland Commission, *Our Common Future*, pp. 9, 10.

23. Minister of the Environment, *A Framework for Discussion on the Environment* (Ottawa: Supply and Services, 1990), p. 11.

24. National Round Table on Environment and Economy, *A Report to Canadians, 1989-1990*, June, 1990, pp. 11-12.

25. "New Conservation Strategy for Yukon," *Almanac*, newsletter of the Canadian Nature Federation, 4, 4 (July, 1990), no pagination; for a review of status of provincial conservation strategies, see *ACS Update*, Alberta Conservation Strategy, Environment Council of Alberta, June, 1990.

26. Barry Commoner, *Making Peace with the Planet* (New York: Random House, 1990), pp. 24, 26.

27. *Ibid.*, p. 175.

28. Barry Commoner, "Ending the War against Earth," *The Nation*, 250, 17 (April 30, 1990), p. 594. The same argument is made in Commoner's "A Reporter at Large: The Environment," *The New Yorker*, June 15, 1987, pp. 46-71.

29. Boyce Richardson, *Time to Change* (Ottawa: The Canadian Institute for International Peace and Security, 1990), pp. 14, 15.

30. David Runnalls, "The Grand Bargain," *Peace and Security*, 4, 3, p. 7.

ACKNOWLEDGEMENTS

Financial assistance from the Explorations Programme of the Canada Council is gratefully acknowledged.

I owe a particular debt of thanks to those who first taught me the little I know of environmental law and policy – my former colleagues, staff and volunteers, at the Canadian Environmental Law Research Foundation and Canadian Environmental Law Association.

I would like to thank my former colleagues at Tricil, who gave me the opportunity to see environmental protection from the perspective of a regulated industry, staff of the Ontario Ministry of the Environment who over the years have answered my questions with unfailing courtesy, and, above all, the many environmentalists throughout Canada with whom I have worked during the past decade.

Many people helped with the preparation of this book. Particular thanks are due my friend Peter Farncombe, who ploughed through an early, turgid manuscript draft. A number of people, whose names appear in the notes, kindly submitted to interviews. Others who commented on drafts or otherwise provided assistance were Dina Appleton, Tom Beck, Bob Bossin, Charles Caccia, Paul Complin, Roger Cotton, Bob Gibson, Jeanne Jabanoski, Phil Jessup, Rod Northey, Glen Okranitz, Robert Paehlke, Peter Pickfield, Bob Redhead, Kirk Roberts, Mark Rudolph, John Swaigen, Doug Thompson, Donna Tingley, and Paula Vopni. I would also like to thank my editors, Michael Harrison and Richard Tallman.

My family – my wife Marilyn and our daughter Astra – lived with this project for three years. Three people in the same house with an embryonic book, particularly when one of them is undergoing the tribulations of adolescence, occasionally generate a little heat. But where there's heat there's love.

INDEX

Abbey, Edward, 37
Acid rain, 18, 20, 22, 48, 111, 115, 120,
  143, 161, 167, 195, 199, 241, 242,
  243, 244, 245, 246, 247, 248, 249,
  250, 251, 259, 260
Action Seminar on Acid Precipitation,
  247
Air pollution, 87, 119, 131, 135, 141,
  143, 166, 167, 194
Air Pollution Control Association, 126
Aitken, Roy, 126, 198
Alberta, 17, 23, 101, 128, 137, 142, 144,
  151, 173, 174, 219, 240; pulp mills,
  15, 17, 115, 236, 237, 238; Department of Environment, 141, 181, 186,
  187, 220, 238
Alberta Clean Air Act, 173, 174, 181,
  183
Alberta Clean Water Act, 173, 174,
  181, 184
Alberta Energy Resource Conservation
  Act, 177
Alberta Environmental Law Centre,
  36, 44, 46, 186

Alberta Environmental Protection and
  Enhancement Legislation, 128
Alberta-Pacific Forest Industries, 237,
  238
Alberta Special Waste Management
  Corporation, 221
Alcan, 210, 211
Algonquin Wildlands League, 85
Andrews, Bill, 240
Animal Alliance of Canada, 74
Animal Defence League, 74
Animal Fund, 73
Animal Liberation Front, 74
Animal Protection Institute, 73
Animal protection movement, 14, 63,
  73, 74, 75, 265, 268
Association of Municipalities of
  Ontario, 205
Audubon Society, 32

Bacon, Lise, 217
Baker, Kenneth, 39
Berger, Thomas, 107
Berger-Inquiry, 56, 107, 108, 109, 177

318